Cinematic Hauntings

edited by
Gary J. and Susan Svehla

Midnight Marquee Press, Inc.
Baltimore, Maryland, USA

Copyright © 2011 Gary J. Svehla and Susan Svehla
Interior layout and cover design by Susan Svehla

Without limiting the rights under copyright reserved above, no part of this publication may be reproduced, stored in or introduced into a retrieval system, or transmitted, in any form, or by any means (electronic, mechanical, photocopying, recording or otherwise), without the prior written permission of the copyright owner or the publishers of the book.

ISBN 978-1-936168-11-8
Library of Congress Catalog Card Number 2011924053
Manufactured in the United States of America
First Revised Printing Feb. 2011

When we are young
We read and believe
The most fantastic things.
When we grow older and wiser
We learn with perhaps a little regret
That these things can never be.
We are quite, quite wrong!
--Noel Coward, *Blithe Spirit*

Dedication
For lovers of films that go bump in the night...

Table of Contents

- 6 — PREFACE
- GHOSTLY GUIDANCE: A Lisiting of Appealing Apparitions
- 49 — D.W. GRIFFITH'S AVENGING CONSCIENCE
- 53 — BLITHE SPIRIT
- 57 — CARNIVAL OF SOULS
- 64 — THE CHANGELING
- 69 — CURSE OF THE DEMON
- 79 — THE HAUNTING
- 93 — HIGH PLAINS DRIFTER
- 102 — THE INNOCENTS
- 111 — LADY IN WHITE
- 121 — THE LEGEND OF HELL HOUSE
- 130 — NOMADS
- 138 — PORTRAIT OF JENNIE
- 145 — SCROOGE
- 150 — THE UNINVITED

PREFACE

The history of ghost cinema, as well as the haunting literature upon which the films are often based, is a noble tradition. Ghost films go back as far as the era of the Silents. This Midnight Marquee Press volume presents respected film writers' personal analyses of their favorite ghost films. Not necessarily the best of the genre, but always films of merit. The Mt. Everest of ghost films—the acclaimed classics—*The Uninvited, The Innocents, The Haunting*—are of course included. But also many neglected cinema specters are covered: *Carnival of Souls, Lady in White, Portrait of Jennie, High Plains Drifter*, etc. Most of these films are known by the average film buff, but several titles included may not be recognized (but are equally of merit and should be sought out).

Often Ghost films have been overlooked by film historians and critics alike. This revised collection of *Cinematic Hauntings* hopes to remedy the situation.—GJS

In revising *Cinematic Hauntings* we have tightened up the chapters and added a listing of films we recommend fans of phantasms check out. MidMar books are not meant to be all inclusive, and let's face it, with the ease of filmmaking, there are literally thousands of DVDs being released every year and it is impossible to keep up with them. Also, we find that as we age our tolerance for crappy movies is wearing out. It is also much more difficult to make it through a good movie—let alone a bad one—without falling asleep. Where was I?—we're also getting forgetful. Oh yes, all inclusive—well we're not. But we do include a wide range of ghosts, from silly to scary, beautiful to horrifying and good to bad (and that goes for the movies too!)—SS

GHOSTLY GUIDANCE
A Lisiting of Appealing Apparitions

by Barry Atkinson, Gray J. Svehla, Susan Svehla

SPIRITUAL ROMANCE

There have been many love stories between mortals and supernatural beings, and ghosts are right up there with vampires and angels and demons. But usually the romance is bittersweet. This is not a reference book with a complete listing of ghost films, but we do want to comment upon some of our favorites.

A GUY NAMED JOE
1943, Director Victor Fleming

A Guy Named Joe stars Spencer Tracy as hotshot pilot Pete Sandidge who crashes his plane after one too many foolish risks. He goes to heaven and finds out from The Boss that pilots killed in action return to Earth to guide new flyers. His girlfriend Dorinda (Irene Dunne) can't get over his death, but she has caught the eye of new flyboy, Ted Randall (Van Johnson). And he is determined to romance Dorinda. Pete isn't that happy about his girl falling for with this new flyer, but eventually he sees the wisdom of allowing her to live her life and helps Ted romance her so they can live happily ever after, thus enabling Pete to also move on.

Brilliant screenwriter Dalton Trumbo provides typical witty rat-a-tat-tat dialogue for the madly in love, but constantly bickering Pete and Dorinda. There is a fine line between angels and ghosts, but we'll lean on the side of ghosts for Joe.

Film critic Roger Ebert in his Dec. 22, 1989 review of the remake, *Always* wrote: "Sometimes there are movies that strike you in a certain way, that haunt your memory and provide some of the terms with which you view your own life. For Steven Spielberg and Richard Dreyfuss, *A Guy Named Joe* must have been a movie like that. Released in 1944, it starred Spencer Tracy as a pilot who dies in combat and is assigned by heaven to return to earth to inspire the younger pilot Van Johnson who will take his place. The kicker is that Tracy also has to stand by helplessly and watch while Johnson falls in love with Tracy's girlfriend Irene Dunne. Dreyfuss says he has seen *A Guy Named Joe* at least 35 times.

"Spielberg watched it again and again on the late show when he was a kid, and it was one of the films that inspired him to become a movie director. When Spielberg and Dreyfuss were making *Jaws* in 1974, they quoted individual shots from the movie to each other—and finally, in 1989, they got to make it themselves."—SS

ALWAYS
1989, Director Steven Spielberg

Spielberg remade *A Guy Named Joe* but rather than WWII bomber pilots, we have daredevil firefighter pilots. Holly Hunter, while super talented, is no Irene Dunne and Richard Dreyfuss and Brad Johnson could not replace Tracy and Johnson. But as with any Spielberg project, it's beautifully filmed and worth a look.

Film critic Roger Ebert in his Dec. 22, 1989 review of the film noted, "the remake…takes place now instead of then and the pilots are fighting forest fires instead of enemy planes, but the basic ideas are all still in place. They do not, unfortunately, add up to much; this is Spielberg's weakest film since *1941*. Dreyfuss stars as a guy named Pete, who fights fires in the Pacific Northwest and spends his off-duty hours romancing a cute forest service air traffic controller (Holly Hunter). Pete is a guy who likes to take chances, and there are cliffhanging scenes

"Go on, sweetheart, live your life!"

early in the movie where he runs out of gas and glides to a landing and when he nearly crashes into a blazing forest fire. His best pal is a pilot named Al (John Goodman), who also likes to take chances and crashes into some burning trees one day, setting his plane on fire. Pete the daredevil goes into a dive and puts out the fire on Goodman's plane by dumping chemicals all over it, but then Pete's plane crashes and he wakes up in a heavenly forest grove presided over by an angel (Audrey Hepburn).

"My reaction to *Always* resembled the critic James Agee's merciless review of the 1944 film, which he admired less than Spielberg and Dreyfuss. 'Joe's affability in the afterlife is enough to discredit the very idea that death in combat amounts to anything more than getting a freshly pressed uniform,' he wrote,

adding that Tracy 'is so unconcerned as he watches Van Johnson palpitate after Irene Dunne that he hardly bothers to take the gum out of his mouth.' One of the problems with *Always* is that the cause itself seems less urgent. It's one thing to sacrifice your life for a buddy in combat and quite another to run unnecessary risks while fighting forest fires. Another problem seems to stem from Spielberg's love of spectacular special effects. The airplanes in this movie—World War II surplus bombers, modified to dump chemicals on fires—seem to crash and bludgeon their way through acres of blazing treetops. You'd think a collision with just one of these trees would cause a plane to crash, but the firefighters in *Always* mow through the woods like airborne Lawnboys. The effects are so spectacular they're not believable. All the movie's risks seem to be the same—laughable."

Ouch. But while my objection to the film are not so eloquent and thought out, I just found it dull and never quite believed in the romance of Hunter and Dreyfuss.—SS

BEYOND TOMORROW
1940, Director A. Edward Sutherland

"Bah Humbug" could have just as easily been uttered by crusty old George Melton in this RKO Christmas fantasy. Charles Dickens was surely the inspiration for scripters Mildred Cram and Adele Comandini, who wrote this light comedy in which three old gentlemen take a young man and woman under their wings and, when the three are tragically killed, come back as ghosts to try to help the estranged lovers.

The beginning of the film stresses there is nothing sadder than being alone on Christmas Eve. George Melton (Harry Carey, Sr.) and Chad Chadwick (C. Aubrey Smith) keep their employees late this Christmas Eve, frantically working on an important engineering project. In bustles partner Michael O'Brien (Charles Winninger), a sparkling elf-like character with more than a touch of the blarney about him. Michael distributes Christmas presents to the staff and dismisses the eager-to-get-home workers. George exclaims, "Christmas. Nothing but a merchant's holiday." The men expect dinner guests, but they cancel at the last minute. George feels they have canceled because they didn't want to associate with him. In his younger days George lost his wife and children over a loose woman. The experience has made him angry and bitter even though his two best friends have stood beside him. Chad also has no family; he lost his only son to the war and his wife is long dead. Michael never married and he too is alone.

The three form an extended family with their beloved Russian servants Madame Tanya (Maria Ouspenskaya) and Josef (Alex Melesh).

At first we expect to find the old men as mean and tight as Scrooge, but this is not the case, they are merely eccentric, using their work to shield them from their loneliness.

As the three celebrate Christmas Eve, they toss three wallets containing $10 out into the snow. They hope the wallets with bring them a welcome Christmas guest. The first wallet is found by a rich couple that gives it to their chauffeur. Two wallets are returned, one by a down-on-his-luck young cowboy, James Houston (Richard Carlson), and the other by a young woman, Jean Lawrence (Jean Parker). Jean and Jim notice each other immediately and they and the gentlemen spend a charming holiday eve together.

The group becomes great friends, and of course James and Jean fall I love. The old men are killed in a plane crash while on a business trip. Jean and Jim were going to tell them of their engagement when they returned from their trip. But the old gent are not gone, they are there looking after their young friends. Jim gets a break singing on radio and becomes a star and of course is stolen away from Jean by a slinky seductress Helen Vinson (Arlene Terry). The ghosts try their hardest to set things right, but one by one they go into the light. Chad joins his dear son, George is called to a dark oblivion, and soon Michael is alone; he is called but cannot go, feeling responsible for the troubles of Jim and Jean. Michael watches in horror as Jim is gunned down by Helen's ex-husband and lays dying on the operating room table. Michael appeals to God to save Jim and his faith and goodness are rewarded, for Jim is spared and Jean forgives him. Michael walks toward the light as the credits roll.

The film was not critically well received and does become slow going after the initial Christmas scenes. *Variety*'s Walt noted, "Picture carries initial handicap of no strength for marquee dressing, and its overall content won't help to either get customers in or to provide entertainment during its unfolding. It's one of those pictures that turn up so often to present the question 'Whatisit.'" The only critical praise offered the film was for cinematographer Lester White and producer Lee Garmes for their special effect photography of the spirit scenes.

Although the film has flaws, it is still a sweet movie and as you watch it, for a little while it pushes away the cynicism of today.—SS

CASPER
1995, Director Brad Silberling

The popular Harvey comic book/cartoon hit the big screen with an impressive cast including Bill Pullman, Christina Ricci, Eric Idle and Cathy Moriarty. The film was a family-friendly blockbuster, raking in over 100 million. The Tinseltown rumor mill is currently buzzing about a new Casper film starring Steve Guttenberg and film with a big budget and in 3D (that is if 3-D is still around by the time of filming).

Pullman stars as a widower Dr. James Harvey who is trying to raise his teenage daughter Kat (Christina Ricci, whose last movie role was Wednesday in *Addams Family Values*, 1993)

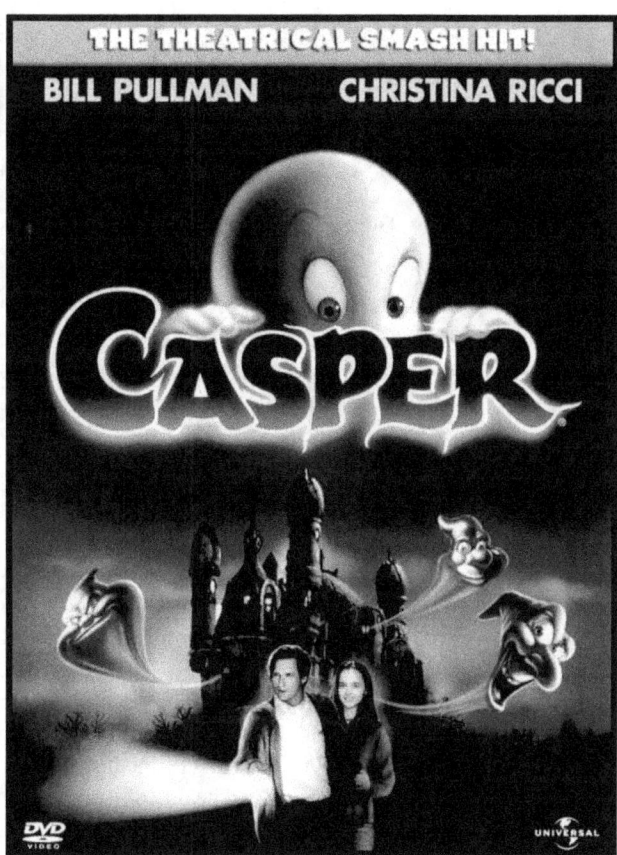

as they struggle to get over the death of their wife and mother. Dr. Harvey is hired to drive away the ghosts from a gloomy old house in Maine and help the greedy owner Carrigan (Cathy Moriarty) find a hidden treasure. In-jokes run rampant as once upon a time *Saturday Night Live* performers Father Guido Sarducci and Dan Aykroyd (star of the *Ghostbuster* films) try to get rid of the pesky spirits. Cameo appearances also include Rodney Dangerfield, Clint Eastwood and Mel Gibson.

Kat and Casper meet and become best friends. Unfortunately, Casper's nasty uncles, Stinkie, Stretch and Fatso, want to drive away the fleshies. The ghosts are not too frightening for pre-teens and Casper is just too cute for words (hey, it's a kids movie!), but there are some scary moments and when Casper talks about his life and death, it's quite sad. Kat helps Casper remember his past and his grief-stricken father who invented a machine to help him become human. Of course the critics hated it, but they don't really pay for movie tickets, do they?

While this is standard kiddy fare, when Kat's mother appears in the finale, it really hit me that the reason we need to believe in ghosts and heaven is to help us ease the grief of losing our loved ones, the fact we will be reunited with them. —SS

CAROUSEL
1956, Director Henry King

Carousel is another film that asks, ghost or angel, but I don't think Billy Bigelow (Gordon MacRae) was angel material, so we'll go with ghost.

Rogers and Hammerstein debuted *Carousel* on Broadway at the Majestic Theater on April 19, 1945 to rave reviews. The

film was released in 1956 and starred Gordon MacRae as Billy and Shirley Jones as his abused wife. R&H began adding a dark undercurrent to Broadway musicals right from the beginning with their first collaboration, Oklahoma! In 1943, they also began incorporating the songs into the plot of the film. Their next project was directed by film legend Rouben Mamoulian (*Dr. Jekyll and Mr. Hyde*, 1931). The stars of the film version of *Oklahoma!* returned for *Carousel* and beautifully performed the brilliant songs by R&H including "If I Loved You," "June is Bustin' Out All Over" (entire cast) and the powerful "You'll Never Walk Alone," sung by Shirley Jones and Claramae Turner, which still makes me cry whenever I hear it.

Carnival barker and ladies man Billy Bigelow is charmed by innocent Julie Jordan (Shirley Jones) and the two fall in love. Unfortunately they both lose their jobs and go to the seashore to stay with Julie's cousin Nettie (Claramae Turner). Billy is frustrated and unable to find a job and takes it out on Julie, striking her (off screen). Billy's old carnival boss Mrs. Mulin (Audrey Christie) offers her boy toy his job back but only if he'll leave Julie behind. Before he can make up his mind, Julie tells him she is going to have a baby. Billy, rather than being angry is happy but gets himself involved with baddie Jigger (Cameron Mitchell) who talks him into a robbery. Things go wrong and Jigger runs away leaving Billy to run from the police. He falls on his own knife and dies in Julie's arms.

It's now 15 years later and Billy is allowed to return to Earth to help his daughter Louisa (Susan Luckey), who is an outsider because locals will forget her father's mistake. He goes to Earth and meets his daughter, but when he tries to give her a star as a gift, she becomes afraid and he slaps her hand. Billy doesn't seem to have learned to control that temper. The Broadway play lets the audience know that Billy can only get into heaven by helping his daughter, unlike the film, which has Billy just wanting to help his child.

Billy realizes his mistakes and shows up at the graduation of Louisa and both Julie and Louisa feel his love and support, while leads to the song "You'll Never Walk Alone." Tears flow (including mine) and Julie and Louisa can both now move on to a better life. Multiple sources tell us that Frank Sinatra had been cast as Billy but walked when he found he'd have to do each scene twice for the CinemaScope version and the regular 35 version. Sinatra later recorded several of the songs of various albums.—SS

CORPSE BRIDE
2005, Director Tim Burton

A young couple, Victor (Johnny Depp) and Victoria (Emily Watson), is forced into a marriage of convenience (convenient for their parents that is) in this animated film in which two lost souls find true love. Victor, the shy bridegroom cannot find the courage to say his wedding vows and goes to the local church

Scraps happily greets his master Victor and his Corpse Bride Emily in *Corpse Bride*.

cemetery to practice. He recites the vows and places the ring on an old twig sticking out of the ground. But it's not a twig; it's the bony (and we do mean bony) finger of Emily (Helena Bonham Carter) the Corpse Bride, who was murdered the night before her wedding. It seems the Land of the Dead considers this a legal marriage and soon a jolly old wedding reception is being held with singing skeletons and all sorts of ghostly goodies. Victor had actually fallen in love with Victoria but also feels for the sad Emily. But the broken-hearted Victoria has now been set up by her money-grubbing parent with evil Barkis Bittern (Richard Grant), who plans to marry her and then do away with her. Victor must help Emily, and the shy Emily throws off the bonds of her overbearing family and bravely sets out to save Victor.

Victor and Barkis dual with sword and fork to save Victoria. I suppose the most amazing thing about the Corpse Bride is that Burton managed to make all this work out for a happy ending. Horror old-timers Christopher Lee and Michael Gough provide voices and Danny Elfman again turns in a beautiful score. The film was done stop-motion and has a nice tribute to Ray Harryhausen.—SS

CURSE OF THE CAT PEOPLE
1942, Director Robert Wise

Curse of the Cat People is not really a sequel to *Cat People*, although many of the same characters and actors do reappear. But while the original film focused upon the sexual tension of dysfunctional adult love relationships, this sequel instead focuses upon the daughter of Oliver Read and wife Alice (portrayed by Kent Smith and Jane Randolph once again) and how the child's overly vivid imagination reminds Daddy Ollie of his first wife Irena and the tragedy caused by Irena's fantastic imaginings. The dysfunctional relationship here is between father and daughter and the father's failure to allow daughter Amy to simply be an imaginative, solitary little girl. Contrasting this dominant parent/child relationship is the parallel relationship between a senile old woman Mrs. Ferrin (Julia Dean), a former actress who traveled all over the world, and her estrangement from daughter Barbara (Elizabeth Russell in her finest hour) as her adult daughter who she rudely rejects and ignores—claiming her real daughter Barbara died at age six (exactly the same age as Amy, the daughter of Ollie and Alice who comes to befriend the aging actress). At the very end of the movie, this light fantasy (as Amy befriends the spirit of Irena who comes to the little girl's imaginative salvation) turns momentarily dark and horrific as Barbara, jealous of the attention her mother gives to young Amy, attempts to strangle the utterly innocent young child. Unable to harm a young child who insists on calling her "friend," Barbara walks off screen never to be seen again (her mother Mrs. Ferrin has just collapsed and died on the stairwell only seconds before). At the movie's conclusion, Amy claims to see the departing spirit of her friend Irena, and for the first time, Ollie, accepting his daughter's imaginative personality, also claims he too sees Irena. Now Ollie is able to let go of the past and comes to accept Amy for who she really is, a bright, sensitive child with a vivid imagination (and not the hell spawn of former wife Irena). The tone of this Lewton production is unlike all the others, but its moments of horror play a secondary role to the intense and well-drawn characterizations.—GJS

GHOST
1990, Director Jerry Zucker

Derived from the afterlife ghost fantasies of the 1930s and 1940s, embellished with the emotional appeal emphasizing relationships à la *Field of Dreams*, *Ghost* is a powerhouse fantasy film that involves the audience's feelings and carries us along for almost two hours.

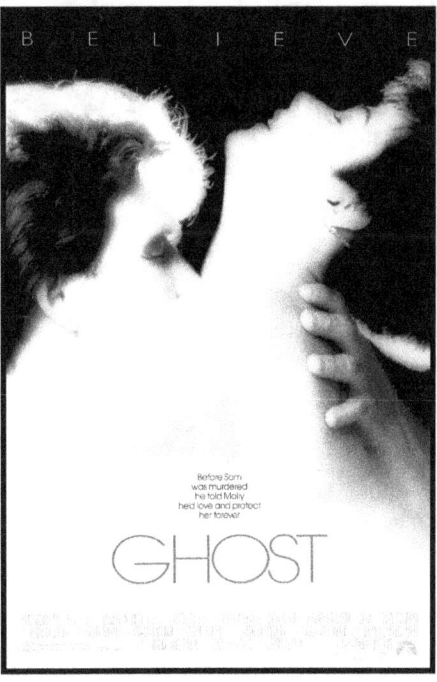

The romantic relationship established between Patrick Swayze and Demi Moore becomes the core of the entire productions, the central chemistry on which the film depends. The added plus of a marvelous, wacky supporting performance by Whoopi Goldberg (for which she won an Academy Award), only makes the production that much more special. The wonderful special effects, never overwhelming the film, only allow the magic of the ghost fantasy to be more fully realized in the techno-90s.

Director Jerry Zucker, part of the team who brought us the comedic gems

Airplane and *The Naked Gun*, here tugs at the heartstrings instead of belching forth the belly laughs and the results are worthy of the romcom cult status the film has attained.

The interplay of music (the recurring use of "Unchained Melody" has never sounded more powerful nor romantic), special effects, acting and script all come together to deliver a marvelously affecting, involving movie. One of the strongest films of 1990.—GJS

Marg Helgenberger and Alan Rosenberg in *Giving Up the Ghost*

GIVING UP THE GHOST
1998, TV Movie, Director Claudia Weill

This Lifetime movie starred Marg Helgenberger as Anna, an attorney who has lost her husband Jake (Helgenberger's real-life husband at that time, Alan Rosenberg). Jake comes back as a ghost and tries to talk her into committing suicide so they can be together. Hmmm, that doesn't sound like he has her best interests at heart. But this is a comedy, really it is, so this suicide stuff gets pushed aside as the duo work to solve a murder. Anna gets over Jake with the help of hunky PI Kevin (Brian Kerwin). The film appeared on Lifetime Sept. 7, 1998. John Martin, TV reviewer for the Doylestown, PA *Intelligencer* said, "Once in a great while a TV movie comes along that has an intelligent premise, sticks with it and leaves viewers fully satisfied. *Giving Up the Ghost (LIF at 9)* is not one of those movies."—SS

THE GHOST AND MRS. MUIR
1947, Director Joseph L. Mankiewicz

The Ghost and Mrs. Muir is one of the all-time great romances, a love that cannot be consummated. Gene Tierney is the beautiful widow Lucy Muir who escapes her overbearing in-laws when she rents a suspiciously cheap seaside cottage. The lovely cottage comes with everything including stunning scenery, furniture and oh yes, the ghost of crusty sea captain Daniel Gregg (Rex Harrison). The Captain tries to scare away the widow, her daughter and the maid, but Lucy, after surviving bossy in-laws for years can easily handle the Captain. The lonely souls, one living and the other dead form a bond that turns to love. The Captain takes pleasure in shocking the proper Mrs. Muir, who really isn't that shocked, but pretends to be for the sake of the Captain. When Mrs. Muir's money run out, the Captain dictates his randy life story to Mrs. Muir who, after a tiring series of meetings with condescending male publishers, manages to get it published.

But a ghost can't give you a hug when you need comforted or a kiss when you heart aches for him and the Captain sees that Lucy needs a real man, not a ghost. Meanwhile Mrs. Muir falls under the spell of suave children's author Miles Fairley (George Sanders). The Captain decides to disappear from Lucy's life and while she is sleeping tells her he has been a dream. Unfortunately, Fairley is a scoundrel and a married one at that. Mrs. Muir swears off men and returns to her cottage, but it is now much emptier because the Captain's presence is no longer felt. The Captain has finally laid his demons to rest that kept him haunting Gull Cottage. He is leaving for the good of Lucy, knowing she needs to live her life with the living. But Lucy feels an emptiness in her heart, although she doesn't know why. She raises her daughter and lives out her life at the cottage. We see time passing and when the elderly Lucy passes quietly away, the young and beautiful widow and the Captain are reunited in a better place. Bernard Herrmann provides the stunning score to this romantic fantasy.—SS

HIGH SPIRITS
1988, Director Neil Jordan

Neil Jordan, (*The Crying Game*) golden boy of critics and independent film snobs, shook up his fan base up with *High Spirits*, a film almost universally despised. But for some reason, every time it's on TV, I watch it. I love Peter O'Toole as the drunken castle owner, Peter Plunkett, who is so broke he has his staff impersonate ghosts so they can attract tourists. And say what you want to about Steve Guttenberg, but I find him always personable and enjoyable to watch. He doesn't tax me and sometimes I just want to watch something nice and easy that requires no deep thought or jarring emotions. The wonderful Beverly D'Angelo is funny as the shrewish wife who can't stand her milquetoast husband (Guttenberg).

O'Toole has allowed the family castle to fall into disrepair and is desperate for cash. Even turning it into a hotel hasn't helped, so he and his willing staff go to extremes to haunt the house. But their attempt doesn't impress the guests. But O'Toole doesn't realize that place is really haunted and the ghosts are not happy they might be losing their home. D'Angelo as Sharon Crawford is there to check out the hotel for her rich daddy, dragging along husband Jack. Living with Sharon would drive anyone to drink and Jack ties one on and in his drunken stupor stops the ghostly murder of Mary Plunkett Brogan (Daryl Hannah), who was murdered on her wedding night by her brutish husband Martin (Liam Neeson) because she wouldn't sleep with him because he squished—yeah, I have no idea, but it doesn't really matter. Anyway, Mary is forced to relive, or is that redie her murder every night until one night Jack sees them and steps in front of Martin's knife, breaking the cycle. Mary and Jack fall in love and Jack finds there is a way they can be together, if you know what I mean. Meanwhile the other ghosts decide to show the American tourists some real haunting and set about terrorizing Peter Gallagher as a priest can't resist the temptations of Jennifer Tilly and Martin Feeero, a ghost hunter and his family along with several other visitors. Martin falls for the feisty Sharon who seems to have found a real man—even though he's dead. Don't worry, everything eventually works out after some really creepy ghost sequences.

Spanish one-sheet for *High Spirits*

Reviewers call it "a piece of crap," "flat and sitcomy," and a "ghastly ghost story." But who listens to reviewers anyway? It's a silly romp that has a few chuckles in it and some great scenery and talented actors. I can think of a worse way to spend a Saturday afternoon.—SS

KISS ME GOODBYE
1982, Director Robert Mulligan

Kiss Me Goodbye tells the story of bereaved widow Kay (Sally Field), who is engaged to marry again, but while she loves the slightly uptight academic Rupert (Jeff Bridges) she cannot put her feeling for her late husband Jolly (James Caan) to rest.

Kay moved out of her house three years ago when Jolly fell down the stairs and was killed. However, she and Rupert decide to return to the house for their wedding.

Jolly pops back into Kay's life, but this time the suave choreographer is a ghost that only Kay can see. Of course this is used as a basis for many "Kay's going crazy" bits as she seems to be arguing with thin air. Rupert believes humoring Kay will help her move on, so he pretends to see Jolly. He also hires an inept exorcist to help get rid of the annoying ghost. Bridges manages to endear himself to the audience as they pull for him to marry the confused Kay. The finale engages in a bit of slapstick when Rupert believes Jolly's spirit is in a dog. The movie is neither terrible nor groundbreaking, but if you like the three leads, it will make you smile and offer a pleasant diversion for the 101-minute running time. Sally Field was nominated for a Golden Globe for her performance.—SS

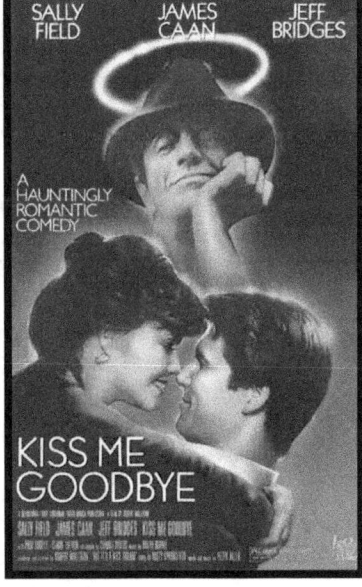

THE TIME OF THEIR LIVES
1946, Director Charles Barton

Abbott and Costello, trying to branch out from the buddy format, their partnership on the verge of splitting up, take a stab at a ghostly comedy in *The Time of Their Lives*. The two are rarely on the screen at the same time.

In 1780 Tom Danbury (Jess Bareker) is hosting a ball for his wife-to-be Melody. Meanwhile Melody's maid Nora (Anne Gillis) is in love with tinker Horatio Prim (Lou Costello), who is trying to raise money to pay Nora's way out of indentured service. Unable to raise enough money, he has gotten a letter from George Washington, which will impress Melody (Marjorie Reynolds), who will then allow them to marry. Nora is so happy she rushes to tell Melody, but hides when she hears Tom approaching. Tom is helping

Benedict Arnold betray the revolutionaries. Melody also hears the plan. Nora is discovered, as is Horatio's letter and she handed over to Tom's accomplices while Tom hides the letter in a clock. Meanwhile, the butler Cuthbert Greenway (Bud Abbott) is jealous of Horatio and locks him in a trunk. Melody runs to the barn and opens the trunk, and she and Horatio ride off to warn General Washington. However, they are arrested on the grounds of

the house and shot as traitors. Their bodies are thrown into a well. Their killer Major Putnam not only executes the without a trail, he also curses them, and the two must stay in the house until their innocence is proven.

Now, in the present, well the 1946 present, the new owner of the manor house, Sheldon Gage (John Shelton) bring his fiancée Lynne Baggett and Mildred (Binne Barnes) to check out the restored house. Cuthbert's descendent, Ralph Greenway (Bud Abbott) also visits and explains the legend. Horatio thinks Greenway is the cad who locked him in the trunk and he and Melody decide to haunt the joint. Director Barton has lots of fun playing with invisibility gags and the ghosts trying to understand modern appliances.

Eventually the clumsy haunting convinces the humans that the legend is true. The present maid Emily (Gale Sondergaard) provides spooky support, and Tom speaks through her when a séance is held. Tom, who has seen the error of his ways, reveals the location of the letter, it is finally found and Horatio and Melody can move on and hook up with their loves.—SS

WONDER MAN
1945, Director Bruce Humberstone

What's better than one Danny Kaye? Two Danny Kayes, as he plays twins in this lighthearted romp. Kaye stars as Buster Dingle, a suave entertainer whose stage name is Buzzy Bellew. Buster witnesses a gangland murder and is rubbed out by the crooks. His ghost convinces his brainy twin Edwin Dingle, help him reveal the murderer. So Buzzy possesses Edwin and the stodgy old Edwin gets a new education when he sings at the nightclub and makes whoopee with Buster's girl, dancer Vera-Ellen. Edwin also has an admirer, lovely librarian Ellen (Virginia Mayo). Unfortunately, Buster doesn't always show up when Edwin needs him, forcing Edwin to perform and fight the bad guys on his own.

Danny Kaye is allowed free rein to indulge in his manic silliness including a number as a Russian singer with allergies as he sneezes his way through "Otchi Chornya," and his opera number sung in Pig Latin. Wonder Man won the Academy Award that year for special effects.—SS

SEX GHOST FILMS

The concept of ravishment by sex-crazed ghosts has become an esoterically popular sub-genre of movies in recent years, particularly with the licentious

cinema of Asian hard-core horror hybrids. Hong Kong's *Erotic Ghost Story* (1982), *House of Intimate Ghosts* (1985), and *Man of a Nasty Spirit* (1993) are just three of the films among scores of these fulsome curiosities; Japan has entered the market with titles like *Entrails of a Virgin* (1987). Anglos have seized upon the idea as well, most often in full-blown pornography, e.g. *Deep Ghost*, *Hungry Eyed Woman*, and *Dream Lover*, the last with an underage Traci Lords. For the mainstream, England played it straight in—*And Now The Screaming Starts!* (1973) and disconcertingly for laughs in *Bloodbath at the House of Death* (1985), as has America in the softcore *Ghosts Can't Do It* (1990).—DHS

Spanish one-sheet for *Wonder Man*

RACE GHOST FILMS

African-American filmmakers turned out many titles in the 1930s and 1940s, which are an undiscovered treasure trove of goodies for the film buff in need of a new fix for their obsession. The all-black films are known as race movies and were shown at inner city segregated theaters. While trying to research them, I could not even find listings in newspapers of the time, although there are now many one-sheet movie posters and lobby cards finally coming to light. Many of the films were dramas and mysteries but of course many were comedies. And what's funnier than the supernatural, just ask the Ghostbusters? The two main sources of these silly scares are Pigmeat Markham and Mantan Moreland. Of course comedians and ghosts go hand in hand and our two heroes met their fair share of spirits. Moreland, Eddie Anderson and Willie Best provided able support in numerous big-budget horror films including *King of the Zombies* (1941), *Cabin in the Sky* (1943), *Revenge of the Zombies* (1943), *The Ghost Breakers*, *Topper Returns* and *Zombies on Broadway*. In addition Moreland helped Charlie Chan solve many mysteries in the 1940s as Birmingham Brown. Markham may best be known to Baby Boomers as the Judge on *Laugh-In,* which used his most famous sketch "Here Come De Judge" as a running gag after Sammy Davis, Jr. introduced it to TV audiences. In 1940 Markham produced, directed and acted in *Mr. Smith Goes Ghost* and once again took on the spirits in 1946's *Fight That Ghost*, which was directed by the prolific Sam Newfield (*Dead Men Walk*, 1943, *The Monster Maker*, 1944). I could find no info on *Mr. Smith Goes Ghost* other than it was a short directed by Heckle and Pigmeat Markham and included Laurence Criner and Monte Hawley. Radio station WFMU's *Beware of the Blog* offers this comment on the film, "By the late nineteen thirties, a series of fly-by-night companies started filming B-movies with all-black casts. The pictures went on roadshow tours, visiting areas with large African-American populations. Markham ventured to Hollywood to participate in some films for the low-rent Talzman studio. 'I made two comedy shorts,' said Markham. 'In fact, I

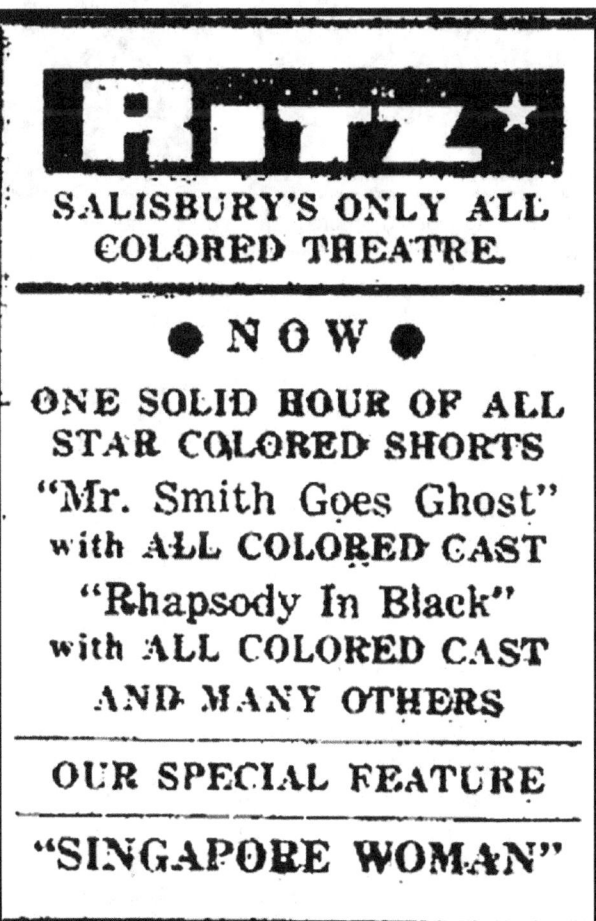

wrote 'em and worked in 'em both. I got one thousand dollars ... My two featurettes were the same sort of thing I'd been doing on the stage—I just worked 'em over for the camera. One was called *Mr. Smith Goes Ghost* ... the other movie was *One Big Mistake* ... We made ours cheap—and they made money.' Beyond the initial novelty factor, they are also unwatchable."

Most of the comedy movies with ghosts allowed their leads to experience a good scare and then the ghosts were proven to be evildoers out to find a treasure, frighten a pretty girl, or steal a will. However there were a few exceptions.

FIGHT THAT GHOST
1946, Director Sam Newfield

The only info I could find on the plot was from Michael H. Price's Forgotten Horrors 3, "Pigmeat "Alamo" Markham and Shorty (John "Rastus" Murray) have run their tailoring shop into ruin, and suicide seems the only way out. A telegram arrives with hopeful news: The pals stand to inherit $5,000 and a house—on condition that they spend a night in their dead benefactor's room. Locked inside the darkened bedchamber, they are startled by the appearance of disembodied hands holding a candle. Voices, seemingly from nowhere, assail them, and a face in a framed portrait suddenly grows a beard. Or so it might seem. But no—the haunting is the work of a crooked mob that has been using the place as a hideout and hopes to scare the heirs into leaving. Pigmeat and Shorty turn the tables on the hoods. And now that's all settled, a new barrage of eerie noises causes the pals to light a shuck out of the premises."—SS

LUCKY GHOST
1942 Directed by William Beaudine (credited as William X. Crowley)

Again, it's almost impossible to find material discussing these films. The American Film Institute catalog does describe *Lucky Ghost*. Layabouts Washington Delaware Jones (Mantan Moreland) and Jefferson (F.E. Miller) are tossed out of town by a local judge and the duo set off for greener pastures. They discuss getting real jobs, their hunger pains leading them to decide becoming Food tasters. The duo get some practice for their chosen profession by stealing chickens. But their luck quickly changes when they meet a wealthy man and his friend whose chauffeur-driven car has broken down. They talk the duo into a crap game and win all their money, the car and even the services of the chauffeur, who proceeds to take them to Dr. Brutus Blake's Sanitarium and Country Club, a crooked gambling joint.

Blake (Maceo B. Sheffield) thinks the pair are rip for the picking, but his deceased relatives, who have left the family manse to him are unhappy he has turned it into a den of sin and set about haunting Blake. Meanwhile, the crooked Blake has managed to lose the family homestead to Washington and Jefferson! The ghosts manage to frighten off the pair who hand over their money to a piano-playing skeleton. —SS

WESTERN SPIRITS

Although many B Westerns have Ghost in their titles, few actually had spirits in them, well at least otherworldly spirits, including films such as *Three Live Ghosts* (1929), *The Galloping Ghost* (1931), the Buck Jones serial *Gordon of Ghost City* (1934), *Ghost Patrol* (1936), *The Ghost Rider* (1935 and 1943), and *His Brother's Ghost* (1945). One notable exception was *High Plains Drifter*, which is discussed in another chapter.

SERIOUS SPECTRES AND GOOFY GHOSTS

13 GHOSTS

William Castle tried to scare the pants off his audiences in the late 1950s with the haunted house antics of *House on Haunted Hill* and the biological horror within of *The Tingler*. However, in 1960, Castle opted for the quaint, childhood ghost-oriented *13 Ghosts*, making child actor Charles Herbert the leading character and thus making his impressions of the world more innocent and childlike (father Donald Woods' character is very hesitant and stiff, conveying the more heroic self-image children have of themselves and their un-cool impressions of parents). Instead of shocking us out of our seats, Castle, working again from a script by collaborator Robb White, wants to entertain us with the circus antics of the actual ghosts; fiend Martin Milner's fake ghost becomes the only ominous member of the pack.

The Ghost-Viewer is perhaps Castle's most entertaining gimmick, creating the illusion of 3-D glasses that really aren't three-dimensional at all. Instead, when the special effect ghosts appear, the 35mm print is printed using blue tint, which almost makes the ghosts disappear when viewed from the blue tint bottom section of the viewer. However, when the ghosts are observed through the top red filter of the viewer, the ghosts are clearly seen. The widescreen print is absolutely gorgeous, and the viewer has the option of watching the print in Illusion-O (with the tinted sequences) or the viewer can watch the second side and see a regular black and white print that clearly shows the spirits all the way through. Very clever of Columbia Tri-Star! Several trailers are included, but most interesting is the documentary *The Making of Illusion-O* including promos from Castle himself as well as reflections from Bob Burns, Donald Glut, Fred Olen Ray and others. As presented here, *13 Ghosts* is a very special DVD release. —GJS

1408
2007; Director: Mikael Hafstrom

Adapted from Stephen King's short story, *1408*'s plot is not exactly original but nevertheless intriguing. Take one room in a big hotel that has a history of 56 deaths and that no one can bear to stay in for more than one hour. Add to that a best-selling author on haunted sites throughout America, a cynic who *doesn't* believe in the supernatural. Put the two together and what have you got? Well, you should have all the ingredients in place for a first-class spooky thriller. Unfortunately, this glossy, flashy picture fails to deliver the goods and, for its climax, goes all out for destructive hokum that ruins any atmosphere the movie *may* have had. John Cusack is the word-weary psychic investigator, mourning the loss of his recently deceased daughter and leaving his wife in the process. In his mail he receives a mysterious postcard from the Dolphin Hotel in New York which simply states "Don't Enter 1408". His interest aroused, he visits the hotel and after pestering manager Samuel L. Jackson to let him spend the night there (Jackson is firmly set against the idea), and reading a book on the gruesome deaths that have happened in that one room only, he is reluctantly given the key and lets himself in. The room, despite its reputation, seems to be perfectly normal—well-furnished, sprucely turned-out, tasteful lighting and a fridge full of goodies. But after a few minutes, odd things begin to happen. His radio comes on, with one hour being counted backwards (the amount of time people have spent there), the thermostat registers a stifling 80 degrees, two chocolates appear out of nowhere on his pillow, the TV bursts into life with images of his wife and daughter, a ghostly shape crosses the room and throws itself out of the window and in one of the movie's more alarming moments, Cusack waves frantically to a man in the building opposite to grab his attention, only to realize with horror that the person is a mirror-image of himself, albeit in another room. Sweating with fear, Cusack tries to get out but breaks the key in the lock—he is now imprisoned. Up to this point, there has been a certain amount of suspense to maintain the interest, but Mikael Hafstrom then seems to abandon the "haunted room" concept and throws in so many weird occurrences that you reach the point where you begin to lose track of just what is going on, including a lengthy sequence in which the audience is lead to believe that Cusack has imagined it all as a result of a surfing accident, only for him to wake up in a wrecked, fire and water damaged room. The frenzied climax sees Cusack confronted by the spirit of his dead daughter and torching the dreaded hotel room to purge it of its visitations once and for all, perishing in the inferno. There is no doubt that this could have been a whole lot better than it turned out—for example, the moment when Cusack attempts to inch along the outside ledge of the building to gain access into the next room, only to discover that the window has been bricked up, is fairly nerve-wracking. However, Cusack's half-jokey performance didn't seem to sit too well with this kind of material (Jackson was just as guilty in his encounter with Cusack)—ghost stories need gravitas to chill the blood (MGM's 1963 *The Haunting* is the benchmark for this type of fare); *1408* didn't possess any. It was therefore a major disappointment to fans of the genre as they probably pondered what *might* have been, instead of what was. One day, perhaps, modern-day producers/directors will get it right—after all, Alejandro Amenabar admirably achieved all the right results in *The Others*, so it *can* be done.—BA

THE AMITYVILLE HORROR
1979, Director Stuart Rosenberg
2005, Director Andrew Douglas

Amityville Horror, released in 1979 was based on a best-selling novel by Jay Anson, which told the tale of a supposedly real haunted house. James Brolin and Margot Kidder are the husband, who along with their kids move into the house even though the real-estate agent has told them about the son who killed his parents and brothers and sisters while they slept saying the house made him do it. In the book they lasted 28 days before leaving everything behind and moving to the West Coast. The family has their priest exorcise the ghost, but he goes blind and gets sick. Stairs fall, gunk runs down the walls, doors fly off the hinges, a pig looks in the window, a ghost marching band parades through the house, dad sharpens ax and looks menacing. Critics seem to agree the film pretty much stinks and it has been pretty much proven the book was a hoax. The film was successful, but only because it was a "true story." Perhaps he was a relative of the guy who said his kid was in a runaway balloon. The score by Lalo Schifrin was nominated for an Academy Award. Peter Travers in his *Rolling Stone* review of the remake in 2005 said the first film "was a hit despite being boring, stupid and excruciatingly overacted.... The remake isn't much better."—SS

BEETLEJUICE
1988, Director Tim Burton

Three years after his first directorial feature Pee-Wee's Big Adventure (1985), Tim Burton hit box-office gold with his ghostly comedy *Beetlejuice*. Very happily married, Barbara and Adam Maitland (Geena David and Alec Baldwin) live in a charming small town where they know all their neighbors and goodwill reigns. They have restored a charming house and plan to settle down to a life full of love and happiness. But things go horribly wrong when they die in an accident. But they don't know they're dead until they try to leave their house—the front door leads to a Dune-like world with giant sandworms. Just as they are getting used to the whole being ghost thing, their house is sold to a pretentious family from New York, Charles (Jeffrey Jones) and Delia (Catherine O'Hara) and their mini-Goth daughter Lydia (Winona Ryder), who set about removing the charm and turning the house into an architectural artsy horror.

The Maitlands try to scare away the interlopers but they are just too nice and just don't have it in them to be mean. They flee to the attic and lock themselves in, hoping the Deetz's don't find them. They turn to their trusty Handbook for the Dead and they visit the afterlife looking for some help. Unfortunately the afterlife office is manned by suicide victims who are about as helpful as the DMV. Lydia finds the handbook and eventually meets the Maitlands and tries to help them get their house back. As nothing seems to be working, they say the name Beetlejuice (Michael Keaton) three times and the obnoxious ghost appears. He scares the Maitlands and they tell him they don't need his services, but Beetlejuice isn't that easy to get rid of.

There are numerous hilarious scenes in Beetlejuice but my favorite is at a dinner party when he makes the guests dance and sing "The Banana Boat Song," or as you probably know it by the lyrics "Day-o, daylight come and me want to go home." The horror gags are plentiful and the silliness gruesome enough to satisfy even the diehard horror fans.—SS

BLACKWOODS
Tanus Films 2002; Director: Uwe Boll

This is one of those convoluted movies where every so often your partner will turn and say "Is he really dead or dreaming all of this?" and a short while later, you'll turn to your partner and say exactly the same thing. It's all very well producing cut-price mystery thrillers if you have a fairly satisfactory conclusion—*Blackwoods* doesn't, leaving far too many loose ends untied. A young guy (Patrick Muldoon) is driving with his girlfriend (Keegan Connor Tracy) to meet her family who live in remote woodlands—accompanied by blaring rock music, the action is interspersed with short flashbacks, shot in bluish monochrome, showing the same man involved in a car crash in which a young women was killed. After a hectic bout of lovemaking in a seedy hotel, the girl promptly disappears, a man wielding an ax tries to murder Muldoon who is then arrested by the local police officer and warned that he should pay for damage to the room, as the ax-man has *also* vanished without trace. Telephoning a friend to drive out to his aid, Muldoon eventually discovers his missing girlfriend, holed up in her dilapidated woodland house with her crazy old father in charge of his group of deranged sons. Held captive, Muldoon is put on mock trial, found guilty of murdering the girl in the accident (who *might* be another daughter of the family) and given two minutes to escape into the woods before the rednecks start yelling "We're comin' to git yer!" In between all this are those puzzling flashbacks—why did a waitress give Muldoon and Tracy such a funny look when they stopped at a roadside eatery for refreshments and videoed each other? When the porno-loving geek in charge of the motel looks at the footage in the camcorder which Muldoon has left behind in his room, the girl isn't in the eatery. Is she a ghost? How come Muldoon has spent three years in a psychiatric hospital nursing his guilt over the accident. The sheriff interviews the waitress who states that only Muldoon came in for a bite to eat but ordered meals for two, and the sheriff also mentions that the family in the woods (since relocated elsewhere) only had *one* daughter. Was the guilt-ridden Muldoon carrying out this charade with his invisible companion to erase the painful memories of the past? The final 10 minutes becomes even more confusing as Muldoon, after being stabbed in the leg by his girlfriend (who may or may not be a ghost) wipes out two of the rednecks *and* his friend before re-enacting the whole sequence—*he* stabs himself and runs through the woods with nobody in pursuit. The sheriff arrives on the scene, spots Muldoon and chases him across a highway where he disappears like a puff of smoke. Perhaps the clue to all this rigmarole lies in the final voice-over statements made by the sheriff as Muldoon wanders like a lost soul through the woods—"You can't escape your past, no matter how you try" and "Things have a way of coming back; some folks might call it a haunting". Cop-out endings like this only serve to aggravate and point to a lack of belief in the subject from the producers—it's no wonder that this picture went straight out on DVD after a very short theatrical release. —BA

THE CANTERVILLE GHOST
1944, Director Jules Dassin

In 1887 a new young writer had his first story published in *The Court and Society Review* magazine. The writer was Oscar Wilde and the story was *The Canterville Ghost*.

An American family purchases Canterville Chase, even though they have been warned it is haunted. The husband laughs off the ghost and they move in. The family, a husband and wife, Mr. and Mrs. Otis, an older son named Washington, a 15-year-old daughter Virginia and two twin boys. The day of their arrival, Mrs. Otis sees a stain on the floor of the library. The housekeeper tells them, "It is the blood of Lady Eleanore de Canterville, who was murdered by her own husband, Sir Simon de Canterville, in 1575. Sir Simon survived her nine years, and disappeared suddenly under very mysterious circumstances. His body has never been discovered, but his guilty spirits still haunts the Chase." A returning bloodstain convinces the family of the existence of the ghost.

One night Mr. Otis hears clanking chains. "My dear sir," said Mr. Otis, "I really must insist on your oiling those chains, and have brought you for that purpose a small bottle of the Tammany Rising Sun Lubricator. It is said to be completely efficacious upon one application, and there are several testimonials to that effect on the wrapper from some of our most eminent native divines. I shall leave it here for you by the bedroom candles, and will be happy to supply you with more, should you require it." Poor old Sir Simon was then frightened by two young terrors that threw pillows at him. He fled to his secret room, highly insulted and considered all the suicides and terror his past hauntings had caused. He vowed revenge. But the sensible Americans and the rambunctious twins were too much for him and he gave up, not even bothering to keep up the bloodstain, which he had been painting with Virginia's paints. Finally Virginia finds the depressed and ill ghost who tell her he only wants to sleep.

"Then the ghost spoke again, and his voice sounded like the sighing of the wind. 'Have you ever read the old prophecy on the library window?' 'Oh, often,' cried the little girl, looking up; 'I know it quite well. It is painted in curious black letters, and is difficult to read. There are only six lines:

When a golden girl can win
Prayer from out the lips of sin,
When the barren almond bears,
And a little child gives away its tears,
Then shall all the house be still
And peace come to Canterville.

But I don't know what they mean.' 'They mean,' he said, sadly, 'that you must weep with me for my sins, because I have no tears, and pray with me for my soul, because I have no faith, and then, if you have always been sweet, and good, and gentle, the angel of death will have mercy on me. You will see fearful shapes in darkness, and wicked voices will whisper in your ear, but they will not harm you, for against the purity of a little child the powers of Hell cannot prevail.'" (from *The Canterville Ghost*)

Virginia bravely goes with Sir Simon and disappears through the wall. Her family finds her missing and frantically search the countryside and house, but can find no trace of her. At midnight a crash sounds and thunder booms and unearthly music plays as Virginia, with a little casket in her hand, Virginia steps onto the stair landing.

"'Papa,' said Virginia, quietly, 'I have been with the Ghost. He is dead, and you must come and see him. He had been very wicked, but he was really sorry for all that he had done, and he gave me this box of beautiful jewels before he died.' The whole family gazed at her in mute amazement, but she was quite grave and serious; and, turning round, she led them through the opening in the wainscoting down a narrow secret corridor, Washington following with a lighted candle, which he had caught up from the table. Finally, they came to a great oak door, studded with rusty nails. When Virginia touched it, it swung back on its heavy hinges, and they found themselves in a little low room, with a vaulted ceiling, and one tiny grated window. Imbedded in the wall was a huge iron ring, and chained to it was a gaunt skeleton, that was stretched out at full length on the stone floor, and seemed to be trying to grasp with its long fleshless fingers an old-fashioned trencher and ewer, that were placed just out of its reach. The jug had evidently been once filled with water, as it was covered inside with green mould. There was nothing on the trencher but a pile of dust. Virginia knelt down beside the skeleton, and, folding her little hands together, began to pray silently, while the rest of the party looked on in wonder at the terrible tragedy whose secret was now disclosed to them. 'Hallo!' suddenly exclaimed one of the twins, who had been looking out of the window to try and discover in what wing of the house the room was situated. 'Hallo! the old withered almond-tree has blossomed. I can see the flowers quite plainly in the moonlight.' 'God has forgiven him,' said Virginia, gravely, as she rose to her feet, and a beautiful light seemed to illumine her face. 'What an angel you are!' cried the young Duke, and he put his arm round her neck, and kissed her.'" (from *The Canterville Ghost*)

It's surprising a remake of this isn't in the works, because a CGI-happy Hollywood would have a field day with Virginia's trip to the other side and the spectacularly gory appearances of Sir Simon.

Like Dickens' *A Christmas Carol*, the story has seen numerous film versions but the first is probably the best, although the plot has been changed considerably. Sir Simon of Canterville, challenged to a duel sometime in the 1600s runs away and hides in the family castle. His father insists no son of his would be a coward and to prove Simon isn't there has the alcove where he is hiding bricked up. Simon pleads with him to save him but his father not only murders him, he curses him to walk the halls of the castle until a decent performs an act of bravery. The film has been updated to WWII, and the Canterville who must perform an act of bravery is an American solider, Cuffy Williams (Robert Young), who is related to the Cantervilles. The Americans are staying on the grounds of the Canterville castle while it's owner the precocious Lady Jessica de Canterville (an utterly charming Margaret O'Brien) lives with her aunt nearby. Cuffy introduces Lady Jessica to Sir Simon who explains that all the Cantervilles have been cowards and that's why he is still haunting the castle. Lady Jessica notices Cuffy bears the Canterville birthmark and sets about convincing him to perform an act of bravery. Which eventually he does but only after Lady Jessica forces him into it. Today, she would have been the Canterville who saved the day, but as it was the 1940s, it is Cuffy who sets Sir Simon free.

Most of the other versions have been TV movies including the latest where Patrick Stewart played Sir Simon, but it has also been adapted as a play and even a ballet.—SS

CASTLE OF BLOOD
1964, Director Antonio Margheriti
[aka Danse Macabre]

Castle of Blood, reedited and released in America in 1964 to the drive-in circuit, is here restored (using four different audio and video sources) as an uncensored International version, restoring a few erotically charged sequences of nudity and interrupted sexuality. Still, this Euro-horror mood piece, directed by Antonio Margheriti (who usually directed under the Americanized name of Anthony Dawson), is not a classic along the lines of Mario Bava or Dario Argento's best. Working under a very low budget, Margheriti does a marvelous job of controlling the photography and the atmosphere, most of it generated by slow-panning shots, well-dressed castle sets and lots of ambient sound effects with spooky musical score. Audiences could cut the mood in *Castle of Blood* with a knife, but unfortunately, the plot and characterization suffer.

The plot involves American author Edgar Allan Poe visiting London, insisting all his tales of horror are based in fact. In a bar Poe encounters a British journalist and his friend Sir Thomas Blackwood, who happens to own a haunted castle. They wager Poe cannot spend the night alone in the castle, and Poe, in need of money, accepts the bet.

Interestingly enough, the supposedly abandoned castle is filled to the gills with spirits of the dead, but to Poe, these ghosts appear to be regular people in need of help and release. As the plot unravels characters Poe meets in the castle returns to ghostly life one night each year on the anniversary of their interconnected deaths, literal crimes of passion, of lust and deceit. Barbara Steele, who portrays her typical tormented, sensual stereotyped role, falls in love with Poe, and while he wishes to take her away from the castle, in truth, she cannot ever leave the scene of the crime. By movie's end Poe is dead, and his spirit is then released to enjoy the ghostly company of Barbara Steele forever, a knockoff of *Wuthering Heights* for the Eurotrash set. By morning, when the journalist and Blackwood travel by coach to pick up Poe, they in fact find the author standing next to the steel gate, but upon closer examination, they discover the poor bastard is dead, impaled in an upright position, only inches away from surviving the most horrific night of his life. And this ironic undertone is one of the film's chief joys, reinforcing the darker underbelly the film tries desperately to project.

But for fans of Euro-horror, characterization and mood come secondary to cinematography and mood, and as stated earlier, *Castle of Blood* superbly demonstrates this dream reality that links the world of the living and the dead and the inability, sometimes, to distinguish between the two. The film does chill the blood with its ghostly plot, which causes all the victims of the household to relive their tragic final night for eternity, never to escape their collected sins. American horror lovers may be bored, but Euro-horror fanatics might find *Castle of Blood* to be their cup of tea.

Extras on the DVD include a fine-grain letterboxed 35mm print (either dubbed in American or in French with English subtitles), restored to its original running time, insightful liner notes by Tim Lucas, still and poster gallery, American version title credits and trailers. The film lingered in my thoughts weeks after I saw it, and this alone is significant praise indeed.—GJS

DARK WATER
2005, Director Walter Salles

From *Ringu*'s director (Hideo Nakata), based on another story by *Ringu*'s Soji Suzuki, comes *Dark Water* (2002), another terrifying vision of ghosts and sacrifice. Once again American producers dipped from the Japanese well when the American version starring Jennifer Connolly was released last year.

And once again the original production demonstrates why Japan lies at the cutting edge of horror films this decade. To be honest, *Dark Water* is less successful than *Ju-On* and *Ringu*, yet it is vastly superior to most contemporary horror chillers. The film's strength is its murky, moody photography, its blistering editing, its emphasis on acting and characterization and its slow building sense of dread and horror.

Recently separated mother Yoshimi (Hitomi Kuroki), fighting an intense custody battle over her six-year-old daughter Ikuko (Rio Kanno), is forced to move with her child into a very old apartment building which is gloomy and in terrible need of maintenance, with water drips and puddles everywhere. The manager who shows the apartment glances upward to grimace at the increasing wet spot on the ceiling and hopes Yoshimi does not see it.

Her ruthless husband tries to show that Yoshimi cannot properly care for the child, when she takes on a new job as editor in a very undesirable office where she often has to work late, leaving the daughter to stand outside her school. The father becomes upset when he arrives to pick up the child from school who is alone, waiting on the parking lot and vulnerable from any sexual predator.

Soon both mother and child have visions of a water-soaked child, about the same age as Ikuko, who seems to be living in the apartment immediately above their own (and must be the source of all the water drippings). The child and its water-soaked squeaking shoes appear when Ikuko plays hide-and-seek at school and the child's little red bag is abandoned on the rooftop of the apartment.

Yoshimi discovers that years ago the child fell into a water filtration tank on the apartment's roof and drowned (shades of *Ringu* I know), thus the motivation for all the horrific water imagery. Ikuko runs bath water one night after tufts of hair come out of the faucet while she gets a glass of water. The bath water is dark and murky and bubbles. As the water overflows Ikuko tries in vain to shut off the valves but the water keeps surging. Soon the arms of the ghost child emerge from the water and grasp Ikuko and try to pull her in. Yoshimi arrives home and finds her child wet and unconscious on the floor. Yoshimi cradles the broken child and carries her to the elevator hitting the up button. Immediately the elevator fills with dripping, leaky water and the electrical wiring shorts out stopping the elevator at the next floor up. While stuck, Yoshimi watches as Ikuko emerges from an open apartment dazed and wet. But who is the child the mother cradles in her arms? In an abrupt shock, a decaying and faceless child lunges toward its mother figure and clutches her as Ikuko approaches the elevator and watches mother and child, still in the elevator, start to move upward. Ikuko faces the door and waits for the elevator to open, which it does, spilling out tons of water upon her, knocking her down. But no people are inside. Her mother and the ghost child are gone, and Ikuko lies wet and abandoned. The wide-eyed puzzlement on the child's face and Yoshimi's haunted resolve to protect her daughter linger long.

A coda occurs 10 years later that reunites 16-year-old Ikuko and her mother in a tender but haunting finale… with the presence of the ghost child always lingering in the background, unseen by Ikuko.

The problem with *Dark Water* is the simple fact that too much of the movie is devoted to parental divorce, angst and the problems every single mother faces alone. The film takes too long to generate its supernatural elements and introduce the ghost. *Dark Water* just cannot make up its mind if it wants to be dysfunctional drama or a horror movie, but once the horror elements are introduced, they become emotionally stronger because of the family elements. *Dark Water* is no *Ringu* or *Ju-On*, but it is an imaginative and terrifying exercise in ghosts and horror. The DVD is available with an American 5.1 surround sound and a Japanese version with English dubbing. A theatrical trailer is included. —GJS

THE DEVIL'S BACKBONE
2001, Director Guillermo del Toro

"What is a ghost? An emotion, a terrible moment condemned to repeat itself over and over? Something dead which appears at times alive? A sentiment suspended in time?" the narrator of *The Devil's Backbone* asks.

Variety in it's review describes the plot as, "a tale of life in wartime; the other, a pretty standard ghost yarn."

Pre-teen orphan Carlos (Fernando Tielve) begins to see ghosts and hearing stories about a boy called Santi who disappeared from the orphanage when a bomb fell. The children know the spirit as "the one who sighs." Santi warns Carlos that many are going to die, which seems possible, since an un-

exploded bomb in the orphanage courtyard. But this is no warm and fuzzy ghost tale. Things turn sickeningly brutal. *Washington Post* critic Stephen Hunter notes, "This dark Spanish ghost story, by turns chilly, tough and nauseatingly violent, has no particular interest in coddling an audience. It doesn't give a damn about you people or your delicate sensibilities. It's built around the violent murder of a child, and that boy's consequent reemergence to the plain of the actual as ghostly protoplasm, hell bent on retrieving some sense of justice."

While Carlos and the orphans are dealing with the ghostly Santi, the adults are involved in a bizarre sexual tangle and plot to steal gold. In the end, the murderer of Santi gets his just desserts.

Roger Ebert says in the *Chicago Sun Times*, "Ghosts are more interesting when they have their reasons. They should have unfinished affairs of the heart or soul. Too many movies use them simply for shock value, as if they exist to take cues from the screenplay. *The Devil's Backbone*, a mournful and beautiful new ghost story by Guillermo del Toro, understands that most ghosts are sad, and are attempting not to frighten us but to urgently communicate something that must be known so that they can rest." — SS

DON'T LOOK NOW
1973, Director Nicholas Roeg

Nicholas Roeg took a Daphne du Maurier story and turned it into one of the strangest films of the 1970s.

Laura and John Baxter (Julie Christie and Donald Sutherland), living in Venice while John restores a church, are unable to get over the drowning death of their young daughter. The Baxters are haunted by images of their daughter walking to streets of Venice in a red coat.

Two strange old Englishwomen tell them that they have spoken with the little girl. But John insists she is gone and that is all there is to it. They also warn John that he is in danger. Some critics consider this one of the best horror films ever made, as do many fans. Others say, "What!?"

It seems the daughter's ghost is trying to warn John that he is in danger, and that John is psychic but won't accept that. And then you have the killer dwarf. To me, it's just very confusing.

Film critic Edward Guthmann of the San Francisco Chronicle said, "Until Nicolas Roeg made *Don't Look Now*, Venice was always used in films to symbolize romance, passion and sensuous dreams. But when Roeg went there in the dead of winter to make his now classic Gothic thriller, the city's canals and ancient buildings were shrouded in fog and sinister mystery. The result, released in 1973 and now showing at the Castro in a new 35mm print, is a haunting, beautiful labyrinth that gets inside your bones and stays there."

David Wood of the BBC says, "Adapted from a short story by Daphne du Maurier, Roeg's film is a characteristically elliptical and genuinely unsettling affair, heightened by a palpable sense of atmosphere and ominous portent in which nothing is what it seems.

"Effective enough as a chiller in its own right, with Roeg of course it all goes so much deeper, acting as a labyrinthine but none the less moving and perceptive mediation on loss, love, and the indefinable nature of time itself. As if piecing together an intricate puzzle, key motifs constantly recur: the color red, shattered glass, water, until their ultimate meaning is finally revealed to horrifying effect.

"With Sutherland and Christie in fine form it all adds up to one of Roeg's finest films and an undeniably key work in British cinema."

The film was nominated for seven BAFTA Awards, but only won one for Cinematography. — SS

THE EYE
2002; Directors: Oxide Pang and Danny Pang

The Asian fantasy genre has produced some real eye-opening horror movies over the past few years—the *Ring* movies, *The Grudge*, *The Host*, among others. *The Eye* is one of the better of the bunch, even though it sags two-thirds of the way in before reaching its gruesome finale. The premise that someone given a cornea transplant and then starts seeing "other things" is nothing new in the world of horror cinema but this thriller serves up a fair quota of shocks along the way. A blind violinist (Angelica Lee) is given a transplant and, from the outset, sees black shadowy shapes seemingly escorting the ghostly figures of the dead as they pass away. One scene after another jolts the

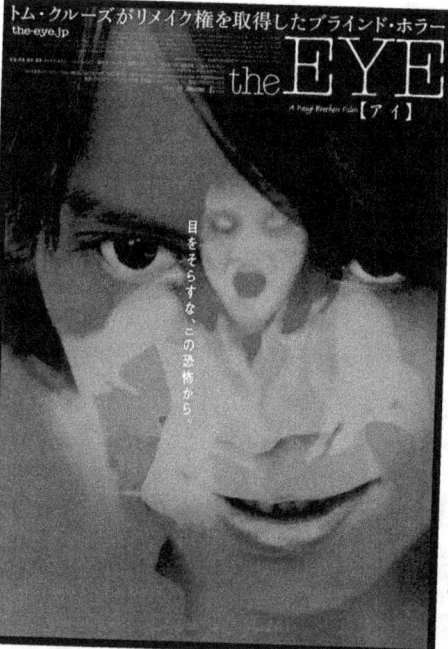

audience in the first hour—the moaning, bleached-out spirit of a freshly deceased woman lunging at Lee in a hospital corridor; another apparition shrieking and rushing at her as she takes lessons in calligraphy; the faded outline of a mother and baby licking meat from a delicatessen with long mauve tongues; a small boy running straight through her, the victim of a road accident; and the spine-chilling moment in which Lee finds herself trapped in a lift with a floating, deformed corpse. Pleading with her young physiotherapist for help, as she is now experiencing nightmares, seeing a different bedroom to the one she sleeps in and even gazing at another face in a mirror, they journey to Bangkok to find out all there is to know about the original donor. After the splendidly creepy first hour, the pace slows (and interest in what's going on can begin to wane with it) as the pair discover that the donor was a young girl who others believed to be "evil" and a "witch", foreseeing death and disasters before they happened—hounded by the villagers after she foretold of a fatal fire, she hung herself in her room. After staying in the dead girl's room to put her soul to rest, the pace picks up in readiness for the horrendous climax. Lee and her partner become caught up in a massive traffic jam caused by an overturned tanker. As the girl sees the black phantom shapes descend on the scene, she tries to warn people (as did her donor) of the oncoming carnage, but too late—the tanker explodes and car passengers in their scores are incinerated, Lee and the therapist surviving but the violinist blinded by flying embers. In the final shot, a blind Lee is consoled by the fact that although she was given the gift of sight for such a short space of time, she experienced so much that being blind again does not necessarily worry her, a somewhat pessimistic note on which to end another satisfactory outing in Asian horror.—BA

THE FATAL WITNESS
1945, Director Lesley Selander

An extraordinarily popular radio series, CBS' *Suspense*, yielded the source of this twist-ending hair-raiser. *The Fatal Witness* not only generates a lingering chill beyond its ghostly ruse to expose a murderer; the film also provides Evelyn Ankers with a more satisfying star vehicle than even Universal Pictures' horror-movie unit had ever allowed her as a leading lady in the likes of *The Mad Ghoul*, *The Ghost of Frankenstein*, *Captive Wild Woman*, *Son of Dracula* and—but you get the drift.

Miss Ankers is Priscilla Ames, ward of a wealthy and cantankerous Londoner, Lady Ferguson (Barbara Everest). Lady Ferguson accuses her playboy nephew, John Bedford (George Leigh), of theft. John leaves in a huff and makes a point of getting himself jailed for drunken misbehavior.

Lady Ferguson is found slain. John, the likeliest suspect, falls back on his disgraceful alibi. But John proves also to have a paid accomplice in a jailer, Scoggins (Barry Bernard), who had secretly released John for an hour on the night of the murder.

Inspector Trent (Richard Fraser), who is falling in love with Priscilla, becomes ever more determined to nail John. Scoggins turns up strangled after demanding more money from John. Knowing John's superstitious nature, Trent stages a dinner party where an actress will appear as Lady Ferguson; he instructs the other guests to pretend not to see the impostor. John, certain he has encountered a ghost, betrays himself as the killer.

Then comes the belated message so crucial to any such shaggy-dog yarn, explaining that the actress could not appear as planned. Trent and Priscilla realize that the apparition they saw must have been the

25

Stuart (Jim Fyfe) and Cyrus (Chi McBride) help Frank (Michael J. Fox, center) scare clients in *The Frighteners*.

genuine article. The climax is more a punch line than a resolution—but it works, with all the elemental gooseflesh urgency of a campfire spook-story. Only a grump would resist the urge to cringe.

Miss Ankers (1918-1985), of Chilean birth and British ancestry, had established herself as a screen actress in England several years before she arrived in Hollywood. The contrived English setting of *The Fatal Witness* brings out a more reserved style than Miss Ankers had lavished on her many Hollywood films up to now. For one thing, the little Republic production does not require her to react to any overtly monstrous characters—and, indeed, calls upon her to do more *acting* than *re*acting. Richard Fraser is quite good as the romantically inclined Scotland Yard man, and George Leigh is properly loathsome as a cunning, however impulsive, killer.

The story would reassert itself in 1959—under its original radio-play title, "Banquo's Chair," alluding to a ghostly intrusion in Shakespeare's *Macbeth*—as an episode of Alfred Hitchcock's network teleseries.—MHP (from *Forgotten Horrors 3*)

THE FRIGHTENERS
1996, Director Peter Jackson

The Frighteners, like *Beetlejuice*, was directed by one of horror's wunderkinds—Peter Jackson. It is also a haunted house movie, but like *Beetlejuice*, there is nothing cliché about this ghostfest.

Frank Bannister (Michael J. Fox) is so traumatized by the death of his wife that he can now see and talk to ghosts. He uses this ability to scam unsuspecting clients after sending in some ghosts to frighten them, he shows up and gets rid of the ghosts. While Bannister hangs around funerals to drum up business, he begins to notice many murder victims have ghostly numbers carved into their foreheads. He tracks down a serial killer from the other side who is doing all the killing, but there is a surprise, the innocent woman Patricia (Dee Wallace) being kept prisoner by her mother is really the partner of the ghost and comes after Frank and his new love, who are trying to send the killer back to the other side. While billed a comedy, I had a hard time watching this, it was just too scary for me, but my scare threshold is really low. Critics weren't impressed citing too many special effects and not enough story. Roger Ebert said, "But all of that incredible effort has resulted in a film that looks more like a demo reel than a movie—like the kind of audition tape a special-effects expert would put together, hoping to impress a producer enough to give him a real job." And the San Francisco Chronicle said, "smothers whatever merits it may have had in a rush of bells, whistles, bombast and smoke."

Today, it looks restrained compared to most of the crap being released to theaters.—SS

THE GHOST BREAKERS
1940, Director George Marshall

Unbelievable that Bob Hope, still holding on to that thread of life, was already in his prime in 1940 (62 years ago!) when he starred in *The Ghost Breakers*, one of the funniest films of his career (but come on Universal... when will you release *Cat and the Canary*, an even superior blending of humor and horror). All the ingredients for first-rate entertainment are here: First, we have Bob Hope, playing radio celebrity Lawrence Lawrence, who mistakenly assumes his gun accidentally went off and killed Anthony Quinn;

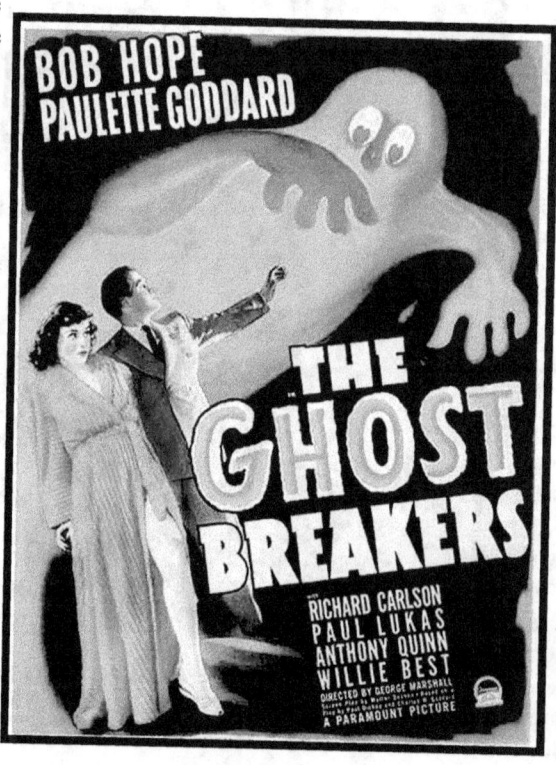

secondly, we have a marvelous supporting cast featuring Paulette Goddard as the sexy heroine, Willie Best as second-banana comic relief and Anthony Quinn, Richard Carlson and Paul Lukas as the red-herrings/villains; thirdly, we have expert art direction and wonderful makeup molding Noble Johnson into one of the most gruesome zombies in filmdom; and finally we have a script with clever dialogue and lots of plot twists expertly blending yuks and chills. True, once in a while the excellent direction by George Marshall does become lethargic for a moment or two before refocusing and returning to its fast track, but this is a minor quibble.

The print used by Universal is overall a beautiful one, full-frame; however, it is a tad on the soft and grainy side in segments and does not quite compare to some quality black and white DVDs of movies made during the same time period. However, the extras are in themselves worth the price of admission. We have several wartime shorts and documentaries featuring Bob Hope entertaining the troops overseas or doing USO work for the troops here in the states. Prominent Hollywood starlets make cameo appearances, including Judy Garland, but unfortunately, all the musical numbers have been omitted (probably due to a rights/licensing fee). These shorts are simply incredibly and a solo DVD release of all of them would be a delight! Also included is a trailer, production notes, filmographies of the cast and crew (limited) and a superb photo/poster gallery. —GJS

THE GHOST GOES WEST
1935, Director Rene Clair

As the winds of war were brewing in Europe, René Clair crafted the overly cute *The Ghost Goes West* (1935) from a screenplay by Robert E. Sherwood. In it, an enormously wealthy American (Eugene Pallette, who specialized in such roles) buys himself Glourie, an ancient Scottish castle and ships it to Florida brick by brick, inadvertently bringing along with it the spirit of Murdoch Glourie (the elegant Robert Donat, who also plays the ghost's 20th century cousin, Donald). Despite the film's somewhat ham-fisted approach, it proved enormously popular and paved the way for several future ghost comedies.

Variety in their review of the film remarks, "The first film in the English language directed by Rene Clair, ace French director, it shows that Clair still has full rein on his sense of humor and one of the screen's best from an artistic and intelligent standpoint.

"Story is a bit different from his past (French) efforts. It has to do with an American who picks up a Scottish manse, which has only one fault: it is ancient, it is famous, it has back-ground, it has color—but it also has a ghost. Nevertheless, the American buys the castle and imports it to America stone by stone, ghost and all. In Florida he sets it up again, his daughter, by way of romance, falling for the penniless heir of the castle and ghost.

"Robert Sherwood, in working up the story with Clair from a London Punch piece [by Eric Keown], has injected a number of hilarious sequences, and some splendid dialog. Robert Donat as the young heir and doubling as the ghost, Jean Parker as the girl, and Eugene Pallette as the father drain every possible bit of good out of their roles."—DF

THE GHOST GOES WILD
1947, Director George Blair

The only description of this film was from *Forgotten Horrors 4* by Michael H. Price:

"Painter Monty Crandall (James Ellison) incurs the wrath of a snooty widow, Susan Beecher (Ruth Donnelly), when his unflattering likeness of her sees print. It helps matters none at all that Monty's fiancée, Phyllis Beecher (Anne Gwynne), is Susan's niece. Dogged by the threat of a lawsuit, Monty retreats to his farmhouse in Connecticut, a historic site called Haunted Hill... The very name of Monty's home bespeaks an old superstition, and in fact Monty has purchased the place because it is reputed to harbor the ghost of Benedict Arnold.

"A séance staged by Monty and Phyllis is interrupted by the arrival of Irene Winters (Stephanie Bachelor), a wayward wife who considers Phyllis her rival for Monty's affections. Irene's husband, Bill Winters (Grant Withers), barges in—brandishing a gun. Monty, who is innocent of any such canoodlery, retreats outside, only to become lost in a thunderstorm. He stays missing for days. A premature report of Monty's death prompts his boss,

So Eric and Monty masquerade as ghosts to throw a scare into Susan—who seems convinced of a haunting at first but soon wises up and escalates her grudge campaign. Things are looking bad for Monty until Timothy throws his voice into the courtroom, revealing old embarrassments that cause Susan to drop her lawsuit. Bill is likewise moved to stop threatening Monty, who is last seen locked in an embrace with Phyllis."—MHP

GHOST OF DRAGSTRIP HOLLOW
1959, Director William Hole

Ghost of Dragstrip Hollow was released in 1959 and closed out the decade that featured crisp black-and-white B productions and bargain basement monsters created in part by Paul Blaisdell, ending the *I Was a Teenage*—barrage of movies and ending the fascination on J.D. and drag racing teens. In fact, while the *She Creature* makes a spooky return, even dancing and partying at the movie's conclusion, even better is the on-film appearance of Paul Blaisdell who takes off his monster head and whines at the camera in a clever comic bit stating how the insensitive studio heads rejected him for *Horrors of the Black Museum* (inaugurating the new era of color and widescreen AIP horrors) after he terrified audiences for close to a decade. Only American Inter-national would include such a dose of reality in an otherwise teenage fantasy.

Following the moneymaking formula, *Ghost of Dragstrip Hollow* features teens that belong to a drag racing club who are into engines and racing, who are typically good kids, but kids misunderstood by their parents. Even a few girls with bullet bras and tight-fitting jeans belong to the group, including leading teen Lois (Jody Fair), and everyone in the club is distressed that they will be losing their garage/clubhouse in a few weeks. An adult reporter working on a story

Max Atterbury (Jonathan Hale), to propose a séance at Haunted Hill. Monty has sneaked back home and is taking a snooze beneath a sheet in this same room.

"The participants in the séance scram in terror after they hear Monty yawn and see the stirring of his bed sheet. Monty's butler, Eric (that delightful scene-stealer, Edward Everett Horton), recovers his wits sufficiently to suggest that Monty remain hidden until the troubles with Susan Beecher and Bill Winters can be sorted out. Among all the ghost-gawkers on parade here, only Eric succeeds—without half trying—at summoning a wraith. This spook would be one Timothy Beecher (Lloyd Corrigan), Susan's late husband. Timothy declares his intention to get back at his wife for the humiliations she had visited upon him in life; he also seems to know some information that could prove damaging to Bill Winters. Timothy seems incapable of materializing except at short range.

becomes their sympathetic ally, proving not all adults are jerks, like their parents always seem to be (in a cute, loving way). Even though the reporter considers himself a square, his intelligence comes to the rescue of the teens more than once. Soon an eccentric old lady Mrs. Abernathy (Dorothy Neumann), who stays at the home of Lois and her parents for two weeks, allows the kids to use her old house as their base of operations, if they can get rid of the ghosts and the She Creature. But worldly Lois, when sitting on her daddy's knees, is told she is on the verge of womanhood, she gloats and beams, "Haven't you noticed, I've arrived!" When daddy asks if she had *that* talk with her mother, she responds, yes, and she brags of all the things she taught her mom. But basically she is a good, intelligent kid who feels more comfy with hot rods than hot romances, even though instead of having a catfight with her catty rival, she challenges the vixen to a drag race that always ends with her father grounding her and she having to pay the fine for violating the rules of the club. This movie establishes the fact that even teens have rules and standards.

Abernathy's pet parrot's over-dubbed voice shenanigans provide some of the silliest laughter of the film ("Polly want a cracker?"… "What the hell would I want with a cracker??!!"). Mrs. Abernathy with her eccentric nature and sense of wild fun again demonstrates that old, old adults can be just as wild and crazy as the younger teens. Of course the haunted house is played more for laughs than chills, and during the spook ball, when the house band plays "Mustang," the kids all dressed in their finest Halloween customs dancing in wild abandon, the movie resembles *American Bandstand* more than AIP horror. Finally the house ghost, resembling Jonathan Haze, glumly leaves the house, "driven out by the rock and roll jam," as the kids dance away ending with the end title "The Endest Man," as the band's vocalist yells "charge."—GJS

GHOST IN THE INVISIBLE BIKINI
1966, Director Don Weis

Ghost in the Invisible Bikini, although produced just seven years after *The Ghost of Dragstrip Hollow*, is actually one generation ahead of the image of 1950s teens. Now *Horrors of the Black Museum* has led to all of AIP's movies being filmed in garish color and widescreen, but this time, with a larger B budget, featuring fading stars Boris Karloff (as the Corpse Hiram Stokely), Basil Rathbone (Mr. Ripper) and silent film star Francis X. Bushman as the butler, with TV star Jesse White along for the ride as Ripper's flunky. The story, sillier than silly, features Susan Hart (the main squeeze of AIP president Jim Nicholson) as the now dead but former circus star "girl in the invisible bikini" who appears to movie audiences (she is invisible to the onscreen cast) in blue tint with the top and bottom of her bikini totally transparent. She is the helper of recently dead Stokely who must commit one good deed in order to go to heaven and regain his youth (so he can entertain the Ghost).

So we have the team of villains, masterminded by evil Ripper, whose sexy daughter Sinistra (Quinn O'Hara), a teen built like a brick shithouse whose prominent glasses make her geeky yet sexy, seduces and tries to murder youthful heirs to the hidden household treasure (pushing them off rocky bluffs; however, without her glasses, she actually tumbles stone statues instead). Added to the mix we have Eric Von Zipper (Harvey Lembeck) and his motorcycle gang The Rats who join the hijinks trying to find the hidden treasure, and we have the lovable teens headed by Tommy Kirk and Deborah Wally reacting to the festivities in the (once again) haunted house. We see adults are not to be trusted and that the kids are the true heroes with the right morals and courage. Sinistra, evil daughter of Mr. Ripper, is the major exception, but with that name she must not have many friends.

Like an update of *Ghost of Dragstrip Hollow*, we have a counterpart to Mrs. Aberthany, here Patsy Kelly as the elderly and slightly eccentric Myrtle Forbush. Instead of drag racers we have motorcyclists, and under the control of their "boss" Von Zipper, the slapstick gets thick and gooey. Yet Harvey Lembeck's persona becomes one of the strong points of the entire AIP Beach Party series, of which this movie is an extension. Instead of some faceless house band from *Ghost of Dragstrip Hollow*, we have the immortal Bobby Fuller Four who perform solo and with Nancy Sinatra and others. However, we are not treated to their biggest hit, "I Fought the Law."

And poor Boris, he is forced to rise from a coffin and make intelligent conversation with the over-mugging Susan Hart, who does look mighty cute in her teensy bikini. Both Tommy Kirk and Deborah Wally's parents owned carnivals and were swindled by Stokely, and now as his good deed he aims to leave his inheritance to the two young heirs and Mrs. Forbush (his mistress) to make amends for his evil past. However shady lawyer Mr. Ripper has his own sights on the fortune. In fact, once Sinistra whacks the golden statue of Cupid who fires his arrows, the treasure is released from a chandelier above. While everyone fights over the money, Mr. Ripper comes armed with a rifle and demands all the cash, but the Ghost literally blows him up, and in the only truly hilarious sequence in the ridiculous movie, a little cartoon of an angel Rathbone, plucking his little harp, rises toward heaven. And poor, poor Boris, who was

promised as part of his reward that he would regain his youth so he could get together with the sexy Ghost, discovers that he is restored to his youth—his childhood youth, and that he once again will ascend to heaven alone.

The movie ends with a defeated Von Zipper asking "why me, why me again" as the rock and roll credits come up on screen and the entire cast dances the night away, happy as larks, the music and dancing reminding us more than a little of the similar conclusion to *Ghost of Dragstrip Hollow*.

Amazingly, both films offer similar takes of comic horror romps geared toward a teen audience, but each film is formulated to appeal to a slightly different teen audience. Focus on the world of teens and their problems, throw in some aging adults as villains, but also offer some eccentric adults and one or two oldsters who become friends of the teens and their causes. Present the young adults as mild rebels but make them also responsible and willing to make amends for their errors. Offer lots of rock music and scantily clad couples wiggling and squirming to the music. Add a little spooky haunted house action, but drape the horror in large dabs of slapstick and emphasize the fun.

Both teen romps (*Ghost of Dragstrip Hollow* and *Ghost in the Invisible Bikini*) are basically mediocre/bad movies that can be redeemed merely by their infectious sense of harmless fun. Both films succeed as mindless drive-in theater fodder. Incredibly the stark black and white fine grain 35mm print used for *Ghost of Dragstrip Hollow* is exceptional, as is the bold soundtrack.

Even better is the deeply saturated Pathé color widescreen print used for *Ghost in the Invisible Bikini* that is exceptionally sharp. Both films are not worthy of their terrific presentation here (even *Ghost* is enhanced for 16:9 monitors). Neither film is the best AIP offered during either decade, but with a stunning presentation here, both films deserve one more viewing to remind us of lost innocence. —GJS

GHOST STORY
1981, Director John Irvin

Ghost Story, based on a best-selling novel by Peter Straub, created quite a stir the year it was released because the cast of elderly victims of a haunting included Fred Astaire, Melvyn Douglas, Douglas Fairbanks, Jr. and John Houseman. Once again the film has been drastically changed from the source material.

Four old men get together to tell each other ghost stories, but the stories become all too real when one man's twin sons meet a mysterious woman who is responsible for the death of one of the boys. Of course the four are responsible for the death of the woman, who is taking her ghostly revenge. Today that story has been done to death, but in 1981, it was relatively new.

Roger Ebert in his review states, "At least, [Peter Straub] knows how to make a good story, if not how to tell it, and that is one way in which the book and the movie of GHOST STORY differ. The movie is told with style. It goes without saying that style is the most important single element in every ghost story,

since without it even the most ominous events disintegrate into silliness. And GHOST STORY, perhaps aware that if characters talk too much they disperse the tension, adopts a very economical story-telling approach. Dialogue comes in short, straightforward sentences. Background is provided without being allowed to distract from the main event. The characters are established with quick, subtle strokes. This is a good movie."

Unfortunately, Ghost Story is almost two films, one dull and talky and one filled with scares, but the two never seem to mesh, and there is not enough of those great old actors, too much time spent in the past and not enough with these old Hollywood legends.—SS

GHOSTBUSTERS
1984, Director Ivan Reitman

Humor is very personal and what makes on person laugh may leave another person bored. As I watched *Ghostbusters* break 100 million dollars in sales, I was amazed. I like Bill Murray and find him and the others of his ilk funny, but *Ghostbusters* to me was not very funny. The story was slow in developing and I found myself becoming a little bored near the middle. I enjoyed Sigourney Weaver's performance parodying the demon possession movies initiated by *The Exorcist*, and during these scenes, I found the humor effective. I loved the (at the time) state-of-the-art special visual effects supervised by Richard Edlund, formerly of Industrial Light and Magic. And I enjoyed the goofy glob-spirit that slimed Bill Murray. The film's final 20 minutes were for me the high point of the production simply because this final segment featured the pinnacle of special effects technology and paid a tribute to the great stop-motion animators with the giant marshmallow man. I kept thinking how incredibly great this entire sequence would be if it were properly utilized in a decent horror movie, not as the icing on the cake of a mediocre comedy. *Ghostbusters* becomes the most extreme sample of special effects technology creating the substance of the movies, but why can't the public see beyond this transparent magic of and light show and see that the viewer has been slimed?—GJS

GILDERSLEEVE'S GHOST
1944, Director Gordon Douglas

Comedian Harold Peary started working on radio in 1925, but didn't get his big break until 1935 when he created the character Throckmorton Gildersleeve on *The Fibber McGee and Mollie Show*. This character earned Peary his own radio show, *The Great Gildersleeve*, in 1941. The Gildersleeve character became the basis for four movies, including *Gildersleeve's Ghost*. *Variety* details the plot as a "minor league affair" that has Throckmorton is running for police commissioner and his two ghostly ancestors decide to make him a hero so he will win. Their scheme involves having Throckmorton visit a spooky old manor house to discover the mad scientist experimenting there. They throw in all the horror movie clichés including secret panels, a thunderstorm, a gorilla, a guy dressed in a gorilla suit (of the obvious mistaken identity) and an invisible girl. *Variety* concludes that one must really be a fan of Peary to enjoy this spoof.—SS

THE GRUDGE
2004, Director Takashi Shimizu

Sam Raimi's Ghost House Pictures had the best intentions for remaking the Japanese *Ju-On* as *The Grudge,* an American language remake, using the same Japanese director Takashi Shimizu and his major crewmembers to rethink the movie for American audiences. *The Grudge* was even filmed in Japan with a mostly Japanese cast.

Fans can purchase *Ju-On* on DVD and chose to either see an English subtitled version or a sensitively dubbed version, but Raimi understands the bias that many horror movie fans here in the States hold toward foreign-produced movies. One thing is sure, people here have been exposed to *The Grudge* in ways they would never have been exposed to *Ju-On*, and this is a good thing.

I was very critical as I watched *The Grudge*, seeing vanilla Sarah Michelle Gellar and lover Jason Behr make Asian horror palpable for America, but her performance connected as the movie unrolled. For the most part, I was disappointed that the American version seemed to be almost a virtual remake of the Japanese original, until the final third of the movie. In that segment, American screenwriter Stephen Susco, working with Shimizu, improved upon the plot of the original and explained the motive, the extramarital affair, that led to the murders and the haunting of the house. For keeping the best of the Japanese original, and for improving the story's final act, *The Grudge* deserves to be judged on its own. I do believe the dark ectoplasmic ghost with haunting eyes is better in the American remake simply because the funds and improved special effects were available; however, some aspects work far better in the original. For instance, the subplot with the group of schoolgirls who visit their friend who lives isolated in her bedroom has been dropped in favor of creating the American Bill Pullman character. Also, the ghostly little boy is far more insidious and haunting in the original, and when the camera pans over to view him staring from atop the stairs in the original, audiences jump; here in the American remake, we hardly bat an eyelid. The Japanese policeman in the Japanese original is more sympathetic and more richly drawn than his Asian counterpart in the American remake. The unsettling, almost comatose mother in the Japanese original is much more unworldly and creepy than Grace Zabriski, in the remake. Overall, the original Japanese horror sequences seem to have the edge over the U.S. counterparts (the frightened ghost who balloons up under the covers, her terrifying face emerging from the edge of the covers, terrifies the viewer more effectively in the original than in the remake). However, Geller's American-in-Japan character that seems to have a difficult time adjusting to an alien culture adds an air of malaise that was missing in the all-Asian-cast original. Ultimately, both films have been created by the same vision and directorial eye, and while over half of both films are nearly identical, the differences are significant. Both films shine in their ability to terrify in new inventive visual ways.

The Grudge contains a five-part documentary involving on-the-set production details and interviews with the cast and crew. A documentary on fear is also interesting. An audio commentary is included.

One thing is certain, Americans should look to Asia (not only Japan but Korea as well) to find the best in horror cinema today, and while Americans still focus on nonstop action and special makeup effects, Asia has returned to the more difficult arena of atmospheric chills that resonate by getting under the skin. Hopefully America will learn to do this on its own and not feel compelled to remake every superior Asian horror movie imported to our shores. That will get old fast.—BA

THE ILLUSIONIST
2006; Director: Neil Berger

In the frenetic, CGI effects-driven climate of 21st-century filmmaking, Neil Berger's elegiac essay concerning an illusionist scheming to win back his lost love harked back to the good old-fashioned story-telling values of the 40s and 50s—this is a film to make you think a bit, to revel in the beautiful sepia tones that saturate the screen and to appreciate the commendable period atmosphere, not to mention the intelligent script and exceptional acting. Told mostly in flashback, we learn of a young boy, a budding magician, involved in a frowned-upon relationship with Sophie who is from upper-class breeding stock as opposed to his peasant roots. This early part of the picture is presented in a series of fades and dissolves, similar to old photographs whose edges are blurred, a cunning ploy to present a long-forgotten time and place. Split up by her family, the boy (Edward Norton) reappears 15 years later in Vienna as Eisenheim the Illusionist, the year 1900, packing the theater with his tricks and illusions. Berger, having set out his stall, then focuses on the four main characters—Eisenheim, the girl (Jessica Biel) who is now a Duchess, the Crown Prince Leopold (Rufus Sewell) and a police inspector (Paul Giamatti). Giamatti, an amateur magician, admires Norton's skills as a master magician and is obsessed by the illusions, but the cold-hearted, haughty Sewell refuses to believe in it all, denouncing the illusionist as a fraud. Things turn nasty when Biel, betrothed to the loathsome Prince, is brought on stage during a performance—Norton and the woman recognize each other and rekindle their romance,

despite the inspector (who has a secret liking for the illusionist) warning him off. To make matters worse, Norton, at a private performance for the Prince, gently mocks the heir to the throne when executing a trick with the Prince's sword (it becomes firmly wedged in the floor like Excalibur and nobody can remove it)—fuming, Sewell orders Giamatti to close Eisenheim down, seeing him as a threat to his integrity. But after the two lovers have spent the night together, Norton puts into plan his greatest illusion yet, to steal his beloved Sophie from the arms of the sadistic Prince and disappear without trace. If you're concentrating hard enough, you can see all this coming a mile off but still enjoy the moves and intrigues of the sting in the tail as Eisenheim reinvents himself as a magician who can bring back the spirits of the dead. Established once again in the eyes of his adoring public, Sophie's sudden demise is cleverly faked by Norton in order for him to conjure up her spirit, which then implicates the Prince as the person responsible for her death. In the end, Sewell shoots himself dead as the imperial guard storm his castle to arrest him for murder, and a puzzled Giamatti follows who he thinks is Norton in disguise to a railway station—as the train pulls away, it suddenly dawns on him that he, the Crown Prince, in fact everybody, has been subjected to a colossal con-trick, the various clues all slipping into place as he grins, mentally applauding the illusionist for his sheer audacity in pulling it off. The final, and quite moving, shot is of Eisenheim walking across a sunlit meadow towards Sophie, the two lovers reunited at last. To complement the exemplary production work, Philip Glass' semi-classical score is a delight, a satisfactory piece of film music for a change in a movie that is just a bit more bewitching than most and a fulfilling experience for lovers of solidly crafted cinema. —BA

JU-ON
2002, Director Takashi Shimizu

Just as the decades of the 1960s and 1970s creatively sparked by Italian horror cinema, the horror of the Millennium seems to belong to Asia (Japan and Korea), who are producing cutting-edge horror cinema. Americans might be talking about *The Grudge* (*Ju-On* was the original Japanese version) and *The Ring*, but the original Asian movies must be commended.

What makes Japanese horror movies so exciting is the fact that these movies return to what I've always labeled atmospheric horror, the type of shock sequence that punctuates a slow-building terror sequence based upon cinematography, editing and general creepiness, abetted by characters about whom we care. We can go back to the Val Lewton productions and his infamous "walks" and "buses" to get that atmospheric jolt, or more recently, Mario Bava's "A Drop of Water" sequence from *Black Sabbath* comes closest to becoming the thermometer for such eerily mounted chills. And in this modern era of special effects chills and splatter-heavy shock sequences, it is wonderful to be returning to an era where chills are no longer cheap and audiences are forced to look at the screen through clenched fingers over the eyes (as one of the leads in *Ju-On* does in the climax).

The structure of *Ju-On*, each separate sequence focusing on one character who is a victim of the ghostly haunted house, allows the house and its history of a wife and six-year-old child brutally murdered by an irate husband to remain front and center. Interestingly, as more and more characters are introduced, some overlap in the lives of others, and by the movie's end we see the bond between many of these characters that was not apparent while each individual sequence was presented. Thus, the piece-meal structure of the narrative is innovative and clever, but the use of sound, cinematography and acting congeal to produce one of the most exciting horror movies of the decade. And youthful director/writer Takashi Shimizu has a firm control of both interest and shock.

Like the little girl who dies in the well in *Ringu* and crawls outside the television screen, the ghost of *Ju-On* played by Takako Fuji is creepily haunting. She is shown crawling upward under bed covers toward her victim; she is shown bent and hovering over her victim who lies in bed; she comes upward between a victim whose hands cover her eyes; and most hauntingly, she crawls on her belly, snakelike, squirming, as though her backbone were broken, across the floor and down a staircase. And her easily identified calling card is her clicking, gurgling sound that announces her proximity to unaware victims. Her also dead son, portrayed by Ryota Koyama, is

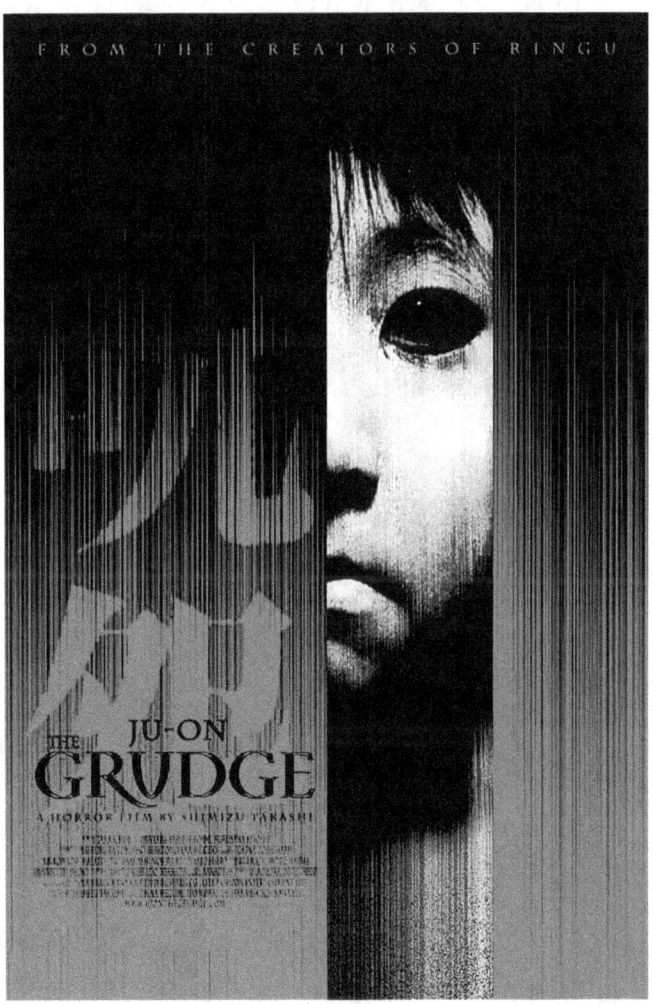

also strikingly haunting. Whether he, stone face, peers from behind the staircase grilling, dashes across the room behind adults or suddenly appears hunched in a closet or standing by the edge of a bed, his pancake makeup, dark eyes and icy stare proclaim that he is not among the living. His mother, strangely enough, sometimes appears as brown ectomorphic fog with darkly hidden eyes that is able to eerily envelop victims.

While *Ju-On* is more an exercise in short segmented horror where visuals and mood mean more than plot, ultimately, all the pieces of the puzzle do strangely come together at the end (the only exception is the appearance of the cat-ghost). Even when the narrative dangles momentarily, the haunting visuals and youthful actors simply reacting to mesmerizing horror is sublime. *Ju-On* becomes a creepy, unsettling and visual tour-de-force of horror, where acting, visuals and sound merge to create perhaps one of the most unsettling horror films of the decade. Movies such as *Ringu*, *Ju-On* and *The Eye* are creating the new lexicon of horror cinema, and isn't it about time something saved the limp horror film genre.—GJS

KWAIDAN
1964, Director Masaki Kobayashi

The Japanese have always been way ahead of Hollywood in their love of a good ghost story. Kwaidan is more an arthouse film than a horror lover's scarefest. The New York Times says, "STRANGE, ululating ghostly voices and spectral, rattling sounds that raise an image of dry bones clattering in a cosmic void are the major effects that stir the senses in the telling of three super-natural tales in the Japanese color picture, "Kwaidan," which came to the Fine Arts yesterday. Couple these sound effects and voices with some remarkable pictorial images and the consequence is a horror picture with an extraordinarily delicate and sensuous quality." Most critics can't even decide if it is three or four stories, which doesn't bode well for the attention-deficient viewer of today. Just so you know how horror-oriented it is, it was nominated for the Best Foreign Language Film Academy Award in 1966 and won the Cannes Jury Special Prize. So that pretty much guarantees that it is serious arthouse material.—SS

THAT LADY IN ERMINE
1948, Director Ernst Lubitsch

Betty Grable stars as Angelina, the ruler of a small European principality whose country has been invaded by Hungarians led by handsome Colonel Teglas (Douglas Fairbanks, Jr.) on her wedding day. She has just married a Baron, Mario (Cesar Romero), who flees when they attack. Angelina finds herself attracted to the Colonel, but remains true to her cowardly husband. Meanwhile the Colonel is fascinated with a portrait of an ancestor of Angelina, Francesca (also Grable), who looks exactly like Angelina. He hears to story of how Francesca, under siege for invaders went to the tent of the Duke (also Fairbanks) wearing nothing but an Ermine coat. When she leaves the Duke is found with a knife in his back.

The ghost of Francesca steps out of her portrait and causes Teglas to have a strange dream where instead of stabbing him, Angelina stops time so they can be together. Eventually Angelina does come to him after her husband has left her and they agree to marry.

The story has been the basis for a stage musical in 1922 and then filmed in 1927 and 1930. But in 1948 they had to change to story to conform to the Hayes Code, so the adultery was cut out and the Baron left Angelina not the other way around.

Director Ernst Lubitsch died 8 days into filming. Pic was completed by Otto Preminger, who, according to *Variety* insisted only Lubitsch be credited. The film uses Technicolor to stunning advantage. Like most Fox musicals, the songs do not come up to the standards of MGM, but Variety called "This is the Moment" a "standout."—SS

LADY IN THE WATER
2006; Director: M. Night Shyamalan

One hour into Shyamalan's so-called "bedtime story for adults", one is tempted to call it a day and shout from the nearest rooftop—"What the hell is *this* all about?" But no, persevere with the remaining 50 minutes and *then* decide that what you've sat through is either a thought-provoking allegorical fantasy tale on man's follies or a pretentious load of old twaddle. The jury is still out on Shyamalan's directorial style and his output—*The Sixth Sense* was unusually eerie, if a little plodding, but *Signs* and *The Village* bore all of the director's now familiar traits; a deadly slow pace, much philosophizing, one or two shocks, ultimately followed by the obligatory trick ending. Without doubt, *Lady in the Water* is his worst movie to date, even having a cartoon-like pre-credit sequence, which more or less informs the audience of the meaning behind the muddled events due to unfold on the big screen. And what muddled events they turn out to be. Paul Giamatti is the superintendent of a Philadelphia apartment block who we first see exterminating a bug in someone's kitchen, a protracted scene that goes on for over five minutes and bears no relation to the rest of the film—a portent of things to come. Someone, or something, is unlawfully using the apartments' pool of a night and the stammering Giamatti is determined to find out who or what. It turns out to be a wan-looking young girl from "The Blue World" (Bryce Dallas Howard) who has entered our realm to help mankind, or various members of mankind, sort out their woes and hang-ups. Legend has it that these waif-like people retreated back into the vast oceans eons ago while the rest of us took to the land and became warlike. Now one of the nymphs has appeared with various cryptic messages but she herself is in danger from this other world—a ferocious wolf-like carnivore with green fur prowls the edges of the block, waiting to kill her, and she can only return to where she came from if a select group from the apartments meets her requirements; a guardian, an interpreter, a healer and seven maidens. When all the satisfactory ingredients are in place, a giant eagle will descend and safely whisk her away. "Totally absurd nonsense" runs through the mind as the bemused Giamatti (did he, as an actor, honestly understand *any* of this?) finds out who the girl's guardian is (Surprise! Surprise! Turns out to be him!), who can interpret her whispered meanings (you can't hear a word the nymph says, so inaudible is the dialogue), who the healer is to get rid of those horrible scratches on her bone-white legs and who the seven maidens are in a block full of feisty, distinctly non-virginal women. From one incredulous piece of incoherent gobbledygook to the next, the picture staggers towards its merciful climax. During a poolside party, as the seven

shop-worn maidens clasp hands and touch Giamatti who in turn is cuddling Howard, a group of woody tree monsters leap down and drag the carnivore away and then, with a clap of thunder, a gigantic eagle swoops from the heavens and carries Howard off to a better world than ours. Giamatti, eternally grief-stricken over the loss of his family in an accident, no longer feels any grief—but if that was all the girl was sent to Philadelphia for, big deal! It is all woeful beyond belief, not even entertaining or meaningful, simply mind-numbing in its sheer pomposity, and boring to boot. If you're going to make another "bedtime story" Mr. Shyamalan, take a good look at Guillermo del Toro's *Pan's Labyrinth* to see how fantasy *should* be done without hoodwinking an audience into thinking that what they are watching is something clever and worthwhile—*Lady in the Water* is neither of these, period. —BA

LOST HIGHWAY
1997, Director David Lynch

To me David Lynch's *Blue Velvet* is a masterpiece of the 1980s, taking eccentric cinema to new, artistic highs. Lynch's follow-up, *Wild at Heart*, was also an exuberant ride but ultimately not as satisfying. While I loved *Twin Peaks* and consider it one of television's finest hours (the censorship inherent in the TV medium forcing Lynch to express kinky sex, violence and mysticism in more subtle ways), I hated *Twin Peaks: Fire Walk With Me* (the theatrical prequel that negated all the subtlety that the TV series managed so well) for it dared alter the tone of the original series and lost touch with the clear narrative story-telling which made the television series so intense and satisfying.

Lost Highway, even though it shares *Fire Walk With Me*'s distorted narrative, is a step back in the right direction.

Lost Highway is two movies in one, the film's first 55 minutes being the most satisfying. There jazz saxophonist Fred and wife Renee (Bill Pullman and Patricia Arquette) become trapped in a Hitchcockian tale of intense fear as Renee discovers videocassettes carefully placed on their front door steps. The first tape simply shows the outside of their home. However, the second tape, instead of fading to static, continues onward and shows the sleeping forms of Fred and Renee in their bedroom at home. At this point the police are called. Ultimately, the final tape depicts Renee's bloody murder at the hands of Fred, who watches the tape not knowing of his actions as his wife lies lifeless in the bedroom only a few feet away. Fred is arrested, tried, and sent to death row, all in about two minutes' worth of screen time.

Then something very Lynchian occurs: The prison guards look in on Fred one morning and find Fred has become someone else, a 24-year-old named Pete (who has a nasty bump on his forehead and no memory of the past events).

Patricia Arquette and Balthazar Getty in *Lost Highway*

Pete, released from prison, returns to his job as auto mechanic extraordinaire, where he is the preferred mechanic of mob boss Robert Loggia. Interestingly enough, Loggia's mistress is Patricia Arquette, now sporting femme fatale blond hair, who shows immediate physical interest in Pete. Before long Pete and Arquette are having wild sex and speak of how they will be dead meat if Loggia finds out about them. Arquette, in the best noir fashion, sets up an elaborate plan to have Pete rob one of her rich friends while she is bedding the sucker upstairs. Of course the plan goes wrong, the man is murdered and then robbed, and the duo head out to the desert to meet their "fence" at a deserted old shack in the middle of nowhere.

In subtle Lynch fashion, both stories are slowly connected. Fred, before he disappeared in prison, suffered from intense headaches, which now affect Pete. The murdered man hosted a party at the beginning of the film that Fred attended and at that party met caricature Lynchian pasty-faced fiend Robert Blake (who tells Fred straight-faced that he's at Fred's home now and gives Fred a cell phone to check out his claim). Near the end of the film, in the murdered man's apartment, we see a photo showing the auburn Arquette posing with the blond-haired current version. And guess who the "fence" turns out to be: none other than Loggia's porno-making moviemaker Robert Blake. However, after Pete enjoys intense lovemaking in the desert just killing time waiting for Blake's arrival, Pete suddenly transforms again into Fred, and now working with Blake, kills Loggia as the totally nude form of Arquette disappears into the shack never to be seen again. The film ends with the dazed Fred returning to his home and, from outside, speaking a simple message into his apartment's intercom, the same message heard by Fred from within the apartment at the film's beginning. Thus, just like Robert Blake, both men can be in two different places at the same time. Kinda' like dream reality.

Did you follow all this?

Don't even try!

Simply put, the narrative is so disjointed that it is impossible to logically follow or properly explain. As Lynch stated in interviews, the movie was based upon a dream Lynch had, and the entire movie is told via this dream reality with characters being in two places at the same time, characters transforming from one personality to another, and back again. It would take a dream analyst to explain this narrative mess, not a movie critic.

However, David Lynch the director is at the top of his form, crafting eerie walks down dark, deserted corridors and displaying ungodly videotapes via electronic static and distortion. Noises become an important part of his mood mix, with the amplified sounds of breathing during sex juxtaposed to sudden telephone rings, straining our ears to hear whispery dialogue contrasted to loud saxophone wailing at a nightclub. Just like a musician, David Lynch understands the dramatic effect of the dynamic range of sounds, contrasting melancholy quiet to intense noise. The musical soundtrack equally segues from the lush, mood music of Lynch regular Angelo Badalamenti to the grating modern sounds interwoven by Trent Reznor that create a most fitting menagerie of noise.

But the bottom line is this: In spite of the disjointed narrative, Lynch has woven a mesmerizing tale, which enthralls the viewer. The visuals, the editing, the sound, the performances, the mood all work to involve the viewer and cause us to feel and care. We might not always understand (and the film's final 15-minute ending is generally unsatisfying), but we cannot take our eyes from the screen.

David Lynch, besides being a screenwriter/director, is also a painter. And this movie projects the impressionistic, cubist, abstract quality of his cinematic artistic vision. No simple Norman Rockwell plot here, for in the world of *Lost Highway* the abstract vision prevails, and while that vision is not always successful, even a David Lynch failure is better than most mainstream movie successes.

Get on the highway and ride! —GJS

THE ORPHANAGE
2008; Director: J.A. Bayona

After the stunning *Pan's Labyrinth*, surely destined to become a future classic, Guillermo del Toro's next foray into the world of fantasy (he was executive producer) is something of a disappointment. Combining elements of a fairy tale (*Peter Pan* is the motif here), a detective mystery and a haunted house thriller, the overall effect is of a sumptuously photographed ghost story with periods of *longueur* that in the end fails to connect or chill the marrow. Belen Rueda plays Laura who returns to an orphanage 30 years after she spent her childhood there. Together with her doctor husband and seven-year-old son Simon, they hope to reopen the vast building and care for other misfortunate children suffering from disabilities. Not longer after they move in, Simon starts to play with imaginary friends, spotting one in a cave on a nearby beach near which stands a derelict lighthouse. Then an old woman turns up from nowhere, claiming to be a social worker—Simon is adopted and is HIV positive, and she wants to help the couple look after him. Sending her packing (although she is mysteriously found rummaging around in an outhouse), Rueda throws a party to welcome a few disabled children (who strangely are never featured again in the film; an oversight surely), has a row with Simon and is shut in her bathroom by a strange little figure wearing a sack mask. When she is let out, her son has disappeared. Bayona partially succeeds in building up the required ghostly atmosphere and the orphanage, a colossal Gothic-like structure, lends itself to supernatural disturbances, but there are far too many lingering shots of dark empty corridors and Rueda's alarmed features, not to mention numerous doors slamming of their own accord, which has all been done before. Six months after his disappearance, with the police baffled, Rueda, countermanding her husband's orders, brings in a team of psychic researchers and one of the mediums "sees" five children, all sick and in imminent fear of death—but no Simon. The clues as to what is behind all the strange noises and Simon's disappearance come thick and fast—Rueda discovers a bricked-up alcove in the outhouse containing the cremated remains of five children, including skulls, leg irons and hearing aids and the old lady-cum-social worker, run over and killed in a horrific accident, used to be a nurse at the orphanage around the same time Rueda was a resident. She gave birth to a hideously deformed infant (Tomas) who had to wear a mask and was tormented to death by the other children; in revenge, she poisoned them all. Is this the same Tomas that locked Rueda in the bathroom? Her husband is desperate to leave the place and she agrees to join him in two days—after he drives off, Rueda performs a makeover, creating the rooms as they were in the 1970s in an attempt to summon up the little phantoms which she succeeds in doing. The tragic truth finally emerges—months ago, she inadvertently locked Simon in a cupboard behind which was an ancient flight of stairs leading to Tomas' dingy hideaway, a room that her son had been exploring. He fell through the rotted banisters and died, joining the other six spirits. Distraught at her loss, Rueda overdoses on tablets and, a spirit herself, is last seen with her son and the six children, reading them a bedtime story about The Lost Children (from *Peter Pan*) as the decaying lighthouse beams its rays over them. The twee ending diminishes any climatic impact and you are left with the distinct feeling that *The Orphanage* could have been a lot more frightening than it turned out, regardless of the acting, set design and expert direction—beautifully presented, yes, but scary, as all ghost stories should be? No.—BA

THE OTHERS
2001, Director: Alejandro Amenabar

Can there have been a more perfectly realized ghost story made in recent years than *The Others*? With minimal effects, this tale of a woman and her two children terrorized by "intruders" in their cheerless old mansion managed to raise the hackles,

chill the blood, tingle the spine, yet end on a truly heart-rending note. It is 1945, the location Jersey in the Channel Islands. Nicole Kidman and her young son and daughter, Nicholas and Anne, are holed up in their fog-bound mansion, awaiting the arrival of servants, the last lot having fled the building under strange circumstances. Three turn up—an elderly housekeeper, her mute assistant and an old gardener, and Kidman hires them but lays down strict ground rules. Every door must be locked behind them when coming and going and the curtains remain shut—both children are allergic to light, and exposure to the sun could prove fatal. So far, so good. But Amenabar gradually and cunningly (with minimal music and the deathly silence of the dimly lit surroundings) cranks up the goose-bumps: The servants are not quite what they appear to be; Anne, the daughter, talks of a boy, Victor, and draws pictures of a family which, she states, are in the house; scuttling noises and voices are heard; and curtains that have been drawn are found open. Disbelieving at first, Kidman is then *forced* to believe that maybe ghosts are disturbing her children—hearing music being played, she enters the music room, closes the lid of the piano, exits the room and tests the door, only for it to be violently slammed in her face by an unseen force. The part where the two children are in bed and suddenly (out of focus) the open curtains are swiftly drawn is just one of the many clammy sequences that this movie has to offer, as is the moment when Kidman walks into a darkened room to watch her daughter playing with a marionette, walks over to her and sees an old crone's face behind the girl's veil. Then Kidman's husband mysteriously returns from the war, has a brief reunion with her and the children, and vanishes as quickly as he arrived. With tension mounting, Kidman finds several macabre photographs taken of the dead, including her three servants, building to a powerful climax. The children discover three headstones at night—it's the servants' graves, all having died from tuberculosis in 1891; they have returned to the mansion to warn Kidman that the "intruders" are in the building, waiting to talk to her and to reveal all. As Kidman climbs the stairs and enters a lighted room, she stumbles across a séance taking place and the shocking truth is uncovered—mother, son and daughter are all ghosts. Kidman suffocated Nicholas and Anne and, in remorse, shot herself dead; the "ghosts" they have encountered are, in fact, a family wishing to purchase the mansion but who have decided not to go ahead with the sale. As the family drive off the next morning, Kidman, her children and the three servants are left to roam the mansion as Earth-bound spirits, their cries of "This is our house" echoing through the empty corridors and rooms. A haunting score written by the director himself, exemplary acting by all concerned (especially Fionnula Flanagan as the knowing housekeeper—and the two children are fine as well), it is Kidman's powerhouse performance as the tortured mother that galvanizes the screen. However, it is also the picture's overwhelming sense of loss and guilt that remains in the memory—the loss of Kidman's husband, a wandering spirit, never to return, and the devastating loss of her children at her own hands; this is what packs the final punch. A highly accomplished supernatural thriller that will surely rate as a classic in years to come. —BA

OUTWARD BOUND
1930, Director Robert Milton

A misty cloud still surrounds *Outward Bound* (1930), a film that seemingly defies the bounds of genre placement. A mere footnote in film history, *Outward Bound* has long deserved a reevaluation. It is at once a ghost tale, a religious statement, a morality play, a love story, and a moody drama. Though perhaps an early, dated talkie at times, elements of its plot, cinematography, and performances remain rich.

The tale itself begins with what appears to be a young married couple agreeing to do "it." "It," however, is relatively unexplained. Their regret about leaving their dog Laddie behind clearly shows a plan to leave. In reality, the couple—Henry and Ann—plan to leave life itself.

Soon, however, they are aboard a small ocean liner at harbor. A steward named Scrubby shows them to a dining area. Shortly thereafter, other passengers arrive. One, Tom Prior, jubilantly expresses to the steward that they will become close friends during the voyage; he intends to stay near the bar and his beloved scotch. Then, the wealthy Mrs. Cliveden-Banks ("with a hyphen") boards the ship and quickly recognizes Prior. Soon, a kindly but timid priest enters the lounge; an old charwoman, Mrs. Midget, also introduces herself. While Cliveden-Banks believes the woman beneath her, Prior kindly—albeit drunkenly—asks the steward to look after her. Finally, the rich Mr. Lingley ("of Lingley Limited") joins the group as the last of the voyagers.

Though some do not wish to admit it at first, none can remember what his or her destination actually is. Each recalls that he or she is to "meet someone," but only Cliveden-Banks remembers who that someone is. She matter of factly states that she is on her way to meet her husband, though Prior knows that he is dead. Both Henry and Ann hope quietly that they will not be separated; Henry vaguely recalls committing a horrible sin, though he knows their mutual love is strong and pure.

Despite his intake of alcohol, Tom soon sobers to the cold fact that all the passengers are dead. Regardless of the tangible vessel and their apparently physical bodies, each is deceased. The vessel has no captain or crew; the boat has no lights. It is a ship of ghosts headed for an unknown port. Scrubby—the only crewmember—confirms his fears.

Slowly, the passengers come to realize their fate. The group mutually votes to send the Reverend Duke on deck to investigate. He is met by fog and darkness; ethereal rays coming from the cabin windows are the only light to be seen. More than anything else, the Reverend meets the truth. The passengers really are dead.

At first, he conceals this from the women on board. Eventually, however, they too understand their reality.

Of all, the arrogant Lingley is perhaps the least accepting of their lot and most ready to believe he can escape. At one point, he attempts to convince himself it's only a dream. Prior also has a momentary breakdown, feeling the guilty weight of what he imagines to be his own worthlessness. The Reverend also releases frustrations; in life, he had lost a highly valued job. Together, the men form an interesting triangulation of the material, the sensual, and the spiritual.

As each comes to grips with their mutual position, the somber ship moves forward. It is slow, but eventually reaches its destination. Scrubby informs the crew that the "Examiner" will see them soon. The Examiner, he explains, is the "wind and the sky and the earth. He'll know all your evil thoughts." More than that, the Examiner will decide their individual fates in the underworld. Though his appearance is topped with a floppy hat and his voice carries a humorous drawl, the Examiner quickly metes out harsh judgment.

The Reverend Duke will have a job near a parish; in fact, he begins his apprenticeship immediately with the Examiner himself. Mrs. Cliveden-Banks, in life a harlot who trapped her husband, will be returned to him. As her punishment, she will spend eternity with the man she despises; everyone in the underworld—except Mr. Cliveden-Banks himself—will know of her scheming ways. Lingley, who cheated others to obtain his fortune, will also suffer, as he "made others suffer." As a result, he Examiner reminds Scrubby to "just see that he goes the right way."

By contrast, the kindly Mrs. Midget, who was so caring and thoughtful in life, receives a beautiful home by the sea. Her request, however, is that Mr. Prior be allowed to live with her so she can take care of him. Tom, however, has to prove his own unselfishness by sincerely refusing the offer and citing his perceived unworthiness. With that, the Examiner happily agrees to Midget's request. Moreover, he promises never to tell Tom that she—in fact—is his estranged mother. At long last, Midget will be reunited with her son.

Reverend Duke then requests that the Examiner see Henry and Ann, but their names do not appear on his list. The two committed suicide by leaving on the gas in their little flat. Because of that great sin, the couple are "Half-Ways" that cannot be judged. They—like Scrubby before them—will stay on the boat forever and endlessly travel the seas. Henry, however, begins to hear the bark of their dog Laddie. The loyal pet breaks through the window of their home. The police arrive and the loving couple return to the land of the living.—GR

THE PHANTOM SPEAKS
1945, Director John English

In a purely political development at Universal Pictures, the intended Karloff-Lugosi starrer *Black Friday* (1940) had found itself transmogrified into a vehicle-by-default for Stanley Ridges, a distinguished character man from Southampton, England. Ridges inherited a split-personality role intended for Boris Karloff when Karloff assumed the renegade-surgeon part that had been written for Bela Lugosi. Lugosi faced demotion to a backup gangster position,

which he nevertheless rendered commanding by sheer force of will and a strategic publicity ploy.

The conflicted scholar-turned-killer portrayal worked well enough for Ridges that he replayed it on a supernatural note for Republic's *The Phantom Speaks*. Either performance is a gem,

until Bogardus balks at helping with any research and asserts his will over the professor. Renwick becomes Bogardus, in effect, stalking the various objects of the badman's resentment and leaving evidence that suggests a return from the grave. He is about to attack a child (Doreen McCann) who had testified against Bogardus when Renwick's intellect reasserts itself. Bogardus prevents Renwick from committing suicide, then finally overplays his hand by sending Renwick against the district attorney (Jonathan Hale) and a newspaperman (Richard Arlen) who has come too near the truth. Overpowered by these intended victims, Renwick faces up to a death sentence. His final words echo Bogardus' death-march declaration—an oath that he has not finished his rampage.

Ridges' work here and in *Black Friday* would remain unmatched until 1996, when a then-unknown Edward Norton would achieve similarly gripping results as an altar boy accused of murder in *Primal Fear*. Director John English senses vitally that neither top-billed Richard Arlen nor token leading lady Lynne Roberts holds the key to *The Phantom Speaks*, allowing Ridges the dominant presence throughout and closing on a note even grimmer than the manifold tragedies that climax *Black Friday*.

Ridges, too, raises the stakes: Where his character in *Black Friday* is an innocent transformed through the illicitly benevolent intentions of Karloff's character, Ridges makes the professor of *The Phantom Speaks* more of a self-serving manipulator who brings down misfortune upon himself. Tom Powers holds forth admirably as the snarling phantom, and his tense confrontations with Ridges convey a quietly nightmarish quality that render mere shock value quite beside the point.—MHP (from *Forgotten Horrors 3*)

RINGU
1998, Director Hideo Nakata

Japanese cinema has held my interest as of late, recently discovering both this little gem from 1998 and *Audition*, two of the most riveting horror thrillers released during the last decade.

Of course, most people know the American remake called *The Ring* that took audiences by storm during the last year. The American *The Ring*, directed by Gore Verbinski (who also directed the comedic shenanigans of *Mouse Trap* a few years ago), steals quite blatantly from the Japanese original, perhaps even upping the ante by including a wonderful horse suicide sequence aboard a ship (the digital death sequence, where the horse literally jumps to its death by going overboard, is haunting), which the Japanese version lacked. But every icon from the Japanese original (the two teens who joyfully open the film, one of them dying a horrible death only minutes later; the horrifying sequence down in the well; the bone-chilling image of the dead child who crawls slowly out of the TV set to enter our real world) is aped almost letter perfect in the U.S. remake.

though of course *Black Friday* is the superior piece in terms of production values and star appeal. *The Phantom Speaks* takes the cake for atmosphere, however. A brooding malevolence underpins the Republic production, which benefits as well from surly Tom Powers' impersonation of a brute whose vengeful ghost takes possession of Ridges at the right moments. Right for the picture, that is.

Harvey Bogardus (Powers) is the truer villain of the piece, a remorseless killer whose capture in connection with a playground slaying attracts the attention of Dr. Paul Renwick (Ridges), a psychic researcher. Renwick, who maintains that the so-called soul is a stream of energy beyond the grasp of death, has staked out Bogardus' Death Row cell in the belief that Bogardus' defiant nature can provide the proof this theory requires.

Following the execution, Renwick concentrates upon summoning the spirit of Bogardus. His experiment seems a success

And here the DreamWorks release of *Ringu* is cause for celebration, as the letterboxed print including a remixed 5.1 Dolby Digital Surround soundtrack, subtitled, presents the Japanese original as it should be seen and heard. What makes *Ringu* so special is its reliance on the modern urban legend mythos (people who view the haunting videotape have one week to make a copy of the tape and show that copy to another person, or die) and its attention to classic ghost cinema. In the Japanese original the demon child Sadako (in a creepy performance by Rie Inou), possessing both ESP and telekinetic powers (of the *Carrie* variety), is savagely murdered (but not quite) and thrown down a well, where the child actually dies seven days later, a horrible death due to starvation and exposure to the elements.

The videotape, a strange creation from beyond the grave, is Sadako's revenge by inflicting a one-week death sentence on anyone who views the video (and after finishing watching the video, the phone always rings to signal the death sentence countdown is starting).

Talented director Hideo Nakata does a masterful job of creating both the sudden shock (the phone rings suddenly and loudly, the camera twists around and we see the contorted frightened-to-death face of the latest victim, an arm emerges from the muddy waters at the bottom of the well, etc.) and the atmospheric chill (the teenager at the film's beginning slowly walks to the kitchen and there, after several false starts, suddenly meets an abrupt ending; the sequence at the film's end where the TV suddenly turns itself on and the haunted video plays, in spastic video-cuts, leading to the living-dead zombie-like appearance of Sadako, who slowly emerges from the TV set and stalks her final victim, etc.). Simply stated, *Ringu*, like the American *The Ring* that followed, creeps us out from the playful but deadly initial sequence to the downbeat ending that follows the seemingly successful defeating of the ghostly curse. *Ringu* may not have the psychological depth to ever be considered a classic horror movie, but it does manage to chill the blood and make us think, one week later, as our time is running out, that perhaps maybe, just maybe, the curse might actually be real. Startling and upsetting as any effective horror movie is expected to be, *Ringu* deserves to be seen for being the original that it most definitely is.—GJS

THE RING TWO
1999, Director Hideo Nakata

Director Hideo Nakata created *Ringu* and *Ringu 2*. Then the American version of *The Ring* followed, directed by Gore Verbinski. For the sequel, *The Ring Two*, the production ran into trouble and the Japanese originator Hideo Nakata replaced the original director.

The bottom line is that *The Ring Two* is not as successful as the original, but it still becomes a horror film of merit. Thank heavens the Japanese influx of horror to American shores upped the scare quotient. The Japanese depend less on gore and special effects and more on directorial manipulation that creeps out audiences and truly gets under our skin.

Within 15 minutes the movie does away with its videotape urban legend premise left over from the original film (a male teen has an hour remaining before he is destroyed by the watching-the-video curse, but he tries to snare an innocent female to watch the video to doom her and save his life). From this point onward Naomi Watts as mother Rachel works overtime to save her son Aidan (David Dorfman) from being possessed by evil Samara (Kelly Stables). Although dead, Samara just wants to find a mother who loves her. And by possessing her son, Aidan, Samara can be part of a loving family.

Audiences can criticize the lack of a developed plot, but the movie comprises sequences showing subtle ways in which Aidan comes under the influence of Samara (calling his mother Rachel, not mommy). Once again the movie is filled with water imagery and the exploding bathtub with water running toward the ceiling becomes a major sequence, with shell-shocked Aidan being pulled beneath the dark bath waters as Samara emerges.

Unfortunately, the climax involves

Rachel being transported via a fancy special effects sequence to the well where Samara died, becoming a tad overblown, with Rachel's escape trying to climb up the well's walls being pursued by creepily flexible Samara, who moves in a terrifyingly herky-jerky fashion (in this sequence Samara is played by a contortionist). The scene's only false moment is when Rachel escapes and seals the well shut, cursing out Samara in a rather insensitive and heartless manner. This sequence might be a crowd pleaser, but it's emotionally hollow.

The film's publicity cheats by playing up the participation of Sissy Spacek, who portrays a demented mother confined to an institution who rants and raves all so seriously. Her performance amounts to a quick cameo that does not warrant such attention and billing.

The Ring Two still has snatches of the original videotape and Samara creeping about both in and out of her tomb-like television set. However, the film's best sequence seems almost out of context, but it works beautifully. In a startling montage of horror, Kelly and Aidan are driving in their vehicle in a wooded area when a deer suddenly runs in front of the car and is hit. Soon innocent-looking deer gather by the roadside, at first one, then several, and pretty soon many deer totally surround the vehicle. Aidan quietly commands they drive away, but mother Kelly is transfixed by this weird display of nature. But shockingly two deer butt the doors of the car from both sides, ramming their heads hard into the car's frame. Glass shatters and the doors buckle, and the surround sound makes the head butts sound like atomic explosions. After this initial attack, broken glass everywhere, Kelly does rev up her car and speeds away, killing all deer who stand in her path. Such an odd and quirky sequence becomes the most memorable sequence of horror. It rivals the horse sequence from the first American *The Ring*.

Besides a pristine unrated print with fabulous sound, *The Ring Two* features a short film, *Rings,* that connects *The Ring* with *The Ring Two* (although the short is not directed by Hideo Nakata, it stars the actors from the beginning sequence of *The Ring Two*) and features deleted scenes and two documentaries, one of which is a fascinating analysis of the visual symbols used in the film. *The Ring Two*, while a solid sequel, once again demonstrates how directors can use atmospheric chills to generate goose bumps that get under the skin and continually creep you out. —GJS

THE SHINING
1980, Director Stanley Kubrick

For Stanley Kubrick, the horror film became an almost expected step into a rich genre that has so often fallen short of its possibilities. With his bent on sheer perfection, the director could painstakingly raise the horror film to a new and epic level, much as he had with science fiction in *2001: A Space Odyssey* (1968). *The Shining* would thus become an amalgam of talented actors, cinematographers, and crewmembers under the direction of one man attempting to make the best horror film in cinema history.

The Shining relates the tale of Jack and Wendy Torrance, and their young son Danny. After losing his teaching position and attempting to "dry out" from alcohol, Jack receives a job as winter caretaker of the Overlook Hotel. During the harsh snow season, the hotel closes and—in his new role—Jack is hired to look after the premises.

After a month, however, ghosts seem to walk the hallways, drawing Jack slowly into their circle. In the meantime, his son—who possesses a psychic power to see elements of past, present, and future ("the shining")—becomes more and more aware of the dangers present at the Overlook. Jack's mental descent into the hotel drives him to attempt killing Wendy and Danny with an ax. With the help of an off-duty hotel cook who also "shines," the wife and son manage to escape. At different times, both Danny and Wendy witness the Overlook's various ghosts and horrors,

Jack murders the cook before the two escape; however, he becomes lost in the hedge maze outside the hotel. By the next morning, he is dead. Frozen. A camera pans to a 1921 photograph that pictures Nicholson at a Roaring Twenties Overlook party. The film ends.

Stephen King recalled Kubrick's incessant search for the proper story. Supposedly, the director would buy stacks and stacks of horror novels, read the first few pages of each, then—out of dislike or disinterest—hurl the books across his office at the wall. His secretary remained outside Kubrick's domain, hearing the slow, methodical beat of rejected texts hitting the wall. One day the rhythm ended; Kubrick had found *The Shining* (Doubleday, 1977).

According to American Film (June 1980), Stephen King himself had already penned a screenplay of the novel for Warner Bros. Kubrick decided against even reading it, however, hoping to imbue the movie with his own thoughts and opinions. To write the script, the director teamed with Diane Johnson, a novelist and university professor. It is highly possible he drew on her talents not only to help adapt the tale for the screen, but also to fine tune the dialogue to a contemporary and Americanized style.—GR

THE SIXTH SENSE
1999, Director M. Night Shyamalan

After most people had written the entire decade off, 1999 came on like gangbusters with *The Blair Witch Project* and a slew of ghost movies (most disappointing being the remake of *The Haunting*), including *The Sixth Sense*. Derivative of trippy, surreal visual feasts such as *Don't Look Now* and the more recent *The Color of Night* (where Bruce Willis played a psychiatrist whose life is shattered when one of his patients commits suicide during the movie's first few minutes), *The Sixth Sense* is a gimmick movie not in the sense of those blatant William Castle showmanship tricks of over 30 years ago, but a gimmick in the sense that viewers will need to view the movie a second time to see how the gimmick manages to distract the viewer from the truth. Let's face it, people who are dead and do not know they are can be traced back further than 1960s films such as *Carnival of Souls*, but that film with its meandering pacing and strong sense of visuals is a direct influence here. While *The Sixth Sense* propels shocking images at the viewer, these images make the audience feel uneasy and perhaps even queasy rather than shocking them. The movie features a few jumps here and there, but the emphasis is always more cerebral and intellectual. Director/screenwriter M. Night Shyamalan is completely in charge here, and his tinker toy of a movie always plays upon its audience, counting on them missing the obvious. But the acting of the cast, primarily a low-volume and pensive Bruce Willis, along with wunderchild Haley Joel Osment (as Cole Sear, the young child who sees dead people, but dead people who do not know they are dead), is stunning. Osment is more than cute, he is introspective, fearful but keenly aware that he has been blessed/cursed with a strange power that makes him different from the rest of the world. Unlike most children who are concerned with trivia, Osment will calmly turn to Willis and tell him a dead woman, just moments ago killed in a car collision, is standing right outside the window of their car, bloodied, motorcycle helmet failing to save her life.

Once the cinematic secret is discovered, it is interesting to rewatch the movie and see how Bruce Willis only speaks to the child and never is addressed by anyone else, not even his depressed wife who is seeing other men (Willis feels behind his back). Retracing the movie, scene by scene, new insights become apparent upon repeated viewings.

Jack Torrance (Jack Nicholson) becomes part of the Overlook Hotel in *The Shining*.

Cole Sear (Haley Joel Osment) is terrified by the ghosts who want him to help them in *The Sixth Sense*.

However, for me, something keeps this movie from evolving into the four-star movie that many critics claim it is. Perhaps it is the lethargic pacing that slows up the first half of the movie (after the stunning first sequence where practically naked Donnie Wahlberg appears in Willis' bathroom and ultimately blows out his brains with his gun after first shooting Willis in the gut), and while the mystery intensifies, the movie is basically Willis (Malcolm Crowe) working with child patient Cole Sear to help him come to accept the fact that these dead people will not harm him, but that the young child has to find a way to help them. As Osment begins to understand his mission and purpose in life, he knows that his mission involves helping Willis as well.

43

The Sixth Sense is a wonderfully clever movie, but it is also a one trick pony whose gimmick overplays the importance of plot and character study. While the acting is totally involving and the plot mesmerizing, *The Sixth Sense*, to me, becomes another solid psychological horror film, not a classic of the genre that viewers are starved to see. —GJS

SPIRITED AWAY
2010, Director Hayao Miyazaki

I have come late to the world of Japanese anime and haven't seen most of the classics of the animation genre, but when *Spirited Away* won the Academy Award for Best Animated Feature (winning over *Ice Age* and *Lilo and Stitch*), I became curious about this film that has garnered such positive press.

I subscribe to that arena of film criticism that holds that movies sometimes are great simply because they create a universe that has never been shown before and thus, by creating that totally original cinematic universe, such films deserve our attention. *Spirited Away*, written and directed by Hayao Miyazaki, would quite simply have been considered a "head" film back in the 1960s, its psychedelic visuals detailing two parallel worlds, one the world of human beings, the other a world of gods, spirits and imagination. The visual innovation inherent in *Spirited Away* makes it definitely one of the finest examples of animation in this generation. Where I have problems with the anime genre is in its lack of logic, relying mostly upon dream imagery and subconscious logic that tends to annoy me. Dream reality is fine for some, but I like my plot to tidy-up all loose ends by the film's conclusion. However, in the world of Japanese animation I have to accept the fact that I am experiencing something akin to the American world of David Lynch and accept the fantasy, at face value, for all that it offers.

I love the bridge between the mundane world where lead character and girl child Chihiro first appears as a spoiled brat, with little heroic qualities. In the car drive Chihiro appears very Westernized and her parents seem very Occidental in appearance (especially Dad's beer gut that hangs well over his belt). However, once the parents have been transformed into pigs and Chihiro crosses the threshold tunnel into this parallel world, she suddenly seems more Asian and becomes more wide-eyed anime looking.

In this *Alice in Wonderland* world, Chihiro soon becomes Sen and meets the evil (yet, at the same time, not quite evil) Yubaba, whose matronly presence is haunting with her high-stacked gray hair, her large nose with pimple and her intense eyes and glasses. The various gods and spirits who frequent the bathhouse where Sen is required to work are always fascinating, with attention to rich detail (mostly involving the grime left in the tub by the stink demon). By movie's end, Sen has had encounters with a grotesque giant infant, a worm-like dragon, twin witch sisters, transparent no-face spirits and assorted nether-world creatures of the imagination. When Chihiro returns to the real world and is reunited with her parents, she has matured, becoming more self-sufficient and adult. Where her parents caution her concerning her adjustment to a new home (the family is moving to the suburbs) and new school, stating the change will be challenging, Chihiro confidently proclaims it's no big deal, and after all her adventures, she really means it.

The DVD double-disc set contains an absolutely gorgeous Dolby Surround 5.1 soundtrack (in dubbed English or original Japanese, with subtitles) and contains a second disc of fantastic extras including behind-the-scenes production documentaries and featurettes, as well as original Japanese trailers. It might take the unacquainted American eye a little time to adjust to the rich supernatural world created by Hayao Miyazaki, but it is a world definitely worth visiting and attempting to understand.—GJS

STIR OF ECHOES
1999, Director David Koepp

Like The Sixth Sense, Stir of Echoes involves people being about to see and communicate with the dead. Kevin Bacon stars as an everyday guy who works for the phone company and sees dead people. His young son also has that ability, but with the easy acceptance of youth, he's not afraid and makes his dad understand it's not a bad or scary thing. Bacon's character must try to find out what the ghost wants him to do, which seems to be dig up his backyard. Film didn't get much notice, being considered just a copycat of *The Sixth Sense*—SS

SUPERNATURAL
1933, Director: Victor Halperin

Assuredly uneven, *Supernatural* remains an interesting treatment of the (for that time) novel issue of bodily possession by supernatural forces. Although constructed rather primitively by modern standards (given the state-of-the-art special effects technology currently available), it is definitely undeserving of obscurity.

A well-structured montage of newspaper headlines, courtroom vignettes, and flashbacks introduce us to Ruth Rogen (the splendid Vivienne Osborne), who is going to fry shortly—Ruth Rogen 4th Woman to Pay via Electric Chair"—for having strangled her three lovers. Rogen is not only not contrite, she's raring to pick up where she left off, given half a chance and a reprieve from the governor,

While RR is on death row, Dr. Carl Houston (the venerable H.B. Warner) cuts a deal with the warden for Rogen's electrocuted body. Rogen agrees to Houston experimenting with her remains, as she has a definite target for any post-mortem hostilities she may be able to inflict. She has, it seems, been betrayed to the police by Paul Bavian (Allan Dinehart), a spiritualist who makes Iago look like a piker in the opportunism field. "Ruth Rogen Swears Vengeance as Execution Draws Near," a later headline shouts, lest anyone miss the point due to subtleties.

Meanwhile, Roma Courtney (Carole Lombard) is morning the loss of her brother. Roma mopes about her his room, caressing his personal effects, listening wistfully to a recording of his voice, but oblivious to his double-exposed presence, which both establishes the discorporate John as a watchful sentry, and points out to the dolts that this afterlife stuff is *for real*.

Moments later, a letter from Bavian arrives, wherein he suggests that Roma attend a séance so that John's troubled spirit can communicate its disturbing secret. While Hammond phones Bavian and sputters about money, fraud, and the like, Grant Wilson (Randolph Scott) tries to convince his sweetheart that this is not the path to take. Despite everyone's good intentions, however, Roma decides that she's off to see the mystic.

Eight o'clock sharp, the following evening finds Roma, Grant, Hammond, and Dr. Houston seated round what must have originally been an overhead light-fixture from a train station, as the haughty Bavian prattles about the type of spirit manifestation they will most likely witness (automatic writing being the odds-on favorite). Draping a rigged handkerchief over the "crystal," the medium starts to play atmospheric music at the Steinway. The heat from the light reveals secret writing (which, of course, reiterates the Hammond accusation), while Bavian whips a pocket lantern from the voluminous folds of his jacket and projects an image of the late J. Courtney for the edification of the uneasy group.

All heck breaks loose, and while Roma faints again, the understandably miffed Hammond grabs Bavian by the lapels and is rewarded for his efforts with a good shot from the poison ring. The much-maligned financial manager staggers off to expire while the attention of the others is focused on the supine Roma.

Unseen by the cast, Ruth Rogen's spirit (which has been hanging around, apparently waiting for another crack) enters the heiress's body, and it is a very *different Roma* who opens her (more heavily made-up) eyes; the menacing sneer which plays on her lips rivals the best Mae Busch ever gave to Laurel and Hardy.

Later, aboard a yacht, Roma/Ruth and Bavian closet themselves in the master stateroom, where she locks the door (hiding the key), and he proceeds to pour himself a stiff one. After a few cuts between Grant (hurtling through the foam in a small launch) and Bavian (guzzling the complimentary champagne), Roma/Ruth gets those hands around the Judas's neck, confesses that she is, indeed, she, and gloats that "I'm going to kill you before I leave this body you love so much."

But help has arrived; Grant has tied up the launch in the interim and manages to break down the stateroom door in time to save Bavian, who hightails it onto the deck. Grant grabs Roma, who continues to laugh menacingly even as the spirit of the electrocuted strangler leaves her body and moves in on the hysterical medium. Bavian rather unconvincingly gets the launch's ropes caught about his neck and neatly hangs himself.

Grant moves Roma to a chaise lounge where, in close-up, the harsh edge to her face softens and most of her eye make-up disappears. Moments before the final clench, John Courtney's spirit returns to play travel agent, as it manipulates magazine pages and suggests Bermuda for the coming honeymoon.—JS

With the basic tenet of the film holding that the existence of life after death is a given, spiritual activity positively gallops throughout. In addition to Ruth Rogen's various meanderings, John Courtney's rather banal manifestations are evident everywhere. Between providing the *deus ex machina* tip to Grant to hie himself to the pier and the stupefying trivial holiday recommendation at the close, Courtney's intrusions into the affairs of the flesh make one wonder whether even the most innocuous of everyday occurrences is not due to some form of ethereal meddling.—JS

TOPPER
1937, Director Norman Z. McLeod

The king light fantasy was Thorne Smith, whose novel *I Married a Witch* (1942) was adapted by Clair into one of the all-time great horror comedies with the main roles frolicsomely played by Fredric March, Veronica Lake (at both her funniest and sexiest), and Cecil Kellaway. However, Smith's most significant contribution to the ghost subgenre was his creation of *Topper*.

Norman Z. McLeod directed Jack Jevne's adaptation of Thorne's novel in 1937 and provided us with a screen perennial. Producer Hal Roach purchased the rights to the late Thorne Smith's book after the success of *The Ghost Goes West*, wisely perceiving its screwball potential and starred that ultimate screen incarnation of smooth suavity, glamour, and fun: Cary Grant, for a $50,000 fee. Grant co-stars with Constance Bennett as George and Marion Kerby, a fun-loving, high-rolling couple who are killed after driving drunkenly and recklessly in their roadster. They are prevented from entering heaven until they accomplish one good deed and decide to select their staid banker, Cosmo Topper (Roland Young, who made a career playing such milquetoasts, in a part originally intended for W.C. Fields).

However, as only Topper can see and hear the ghosts, their antics tend to drive him frantic rather than provide him with the *joie de vivre* that they possess so fully and he so desperately needs. But, in time, exposure to their hedonistic ways causes old Cosmo to lighten up and enjoy life.

The film was an enormous success, garnering two Academy Award nominations (one for Roland Young as Best Supporting Actor, and the other for Best Sound), leading to two film sequels, *Topper Takes a Trip* (1939) and *Topper Returns* (1941), both with Roland Young reprising his befuddled banker bit. There have been at least three television presentations, the best known being the fifties' television series starring Leo G. Carroll as Cosmo Topper.—DF

TOPPER RETURNS
1941, Director Roy Del Ruth

Topper Returns belongs to the breed of wonderful old dark house comedic thrillers that flourished during the 1940s. In other words, it appeals to fans of comedy, horror and mystery and thus guarantees an ever-increasing circle of box-office. The Topper series ended with *Topper Returns*, and fortunately, the series went out with a bang. Roland Young again deadpans and presents his low-key interpretation of Topper, but this time two beautiful women, Joan Blondell and Carole Landis, go along for the ride, and Topper's wife, Billie Burke, ain't bad either. On the spooky front we have the always eye-shifting George Zucco as the family doctor, the most blatantly *red* of all the red herrings. On the comic front we have Eddie "Rochester"

Anderson as Topper's household servant who earns some of the best laughs by falling down secret passages into the murky river below the ghostly mansion and having to confront a frisky seal. In other words, in this 1941 Roy Del Ruth-directed crowd-pleaser, the audience chuckles aloud, jumps out of its seat and constantly guesses whodunit! It's a superior B production with a marvelously decorated haunted mansion photographed to imbue every frame with shadows and fog.

Basically, the plot involves the reunion of a 21-year-old Carole Landis (if she survives one more day, that is!) with her long-lost father; Landis inherits everything on her 21st birthday. Of course, within the first few minutes of the movie, a mysterious black-cloaked fiend shoots out the tire of her cab, forcing the car to stop inches away from the edge of the road; and after switching bedrooms in the mansion with friend Joan Blondell, Blondell is mistakenly murdered before sunrise (of course in the Topper universe, she immediately returns to transparent existence to help Topper catch her murderer by the last reel). Soon the entire household seems to be in cahoots, and poor Carole Landis and Roland Young (Topper) have to solve the mystery with only the help of Eddie Anderson, who is not much help at all.

Topper Returns moves along at a brisk clip featuring energetic performances, genuinely spooky cinematography and a creaky plot that keeps us guessing (even though everyone knows that when the house servant is ready to tell the police the identity of the murderer with all assembled in the living room, that when the lights go out, so will her life). What adds to the enjoyment of the movie is a pristine, absolutely unspeckled, minimal grain, dense black-and-white print with superb soundtrack. For 1941 and Hal Roach, the print is miraculous. The only extra is a theatrical trailer, but the print offered here by Hal Roach and Image is worth the price of admission. For 89 minutes of fluff and solid entertainment, *Topper Returns* cannot be beat!—GJS

TOPPER TAKES A TRIP
1938, Director Norman Z. McLeod

In the first *Topper* sequel, *Topper Takes a Trip*, Constance Bennett returned in an adaptation of Smith's own sequel, taking a trip to Europe to help Cosmo patch things up with his equally addled wife Clara, (played throughout the film series by Billie Burke, best known as the Good Witch from *The Wizard of Oz*). However, the gags weren't as fresh and the comedy doesn't recover from the lack of Grant's amiable presence.—DF

THE WOMAN IN BLACK
1989; Director: Herbert Wise

Writer Nigel Kneale's adaptation of Susan Hill's ghost story has now achieved something of a cult status because of its unavailability. Broadcast on Britain's Channel 4 in 1989 and repeated in 1994, this involving tale of supernatural retribution has never been seen since; the only chance of catching it is on pirate DVD. Kneale's scripts always carried the promise of the strange and the unsettling (witness the legendary *Quatermass* serials) and he doesn't disappoint here. In London, 1925, a young solicitor (Adrian Rawlins), married with two children, is sent by his boss to the market town of Crythin Gifford to minister the estate of the recently deceased Alice Drablow—he's to attend her funeral, sort through her papers, and place her residence (Eel Marsh House, located on a causeway cut off at high tide) up for sale. But there is a disquieting undercurrent of fear associated with the business. Rawlins' boss is just that little bit *too* anxious to send his young charge out to the back of beyond and in the train on his way there, the solicitor shares a carriage with landowner Bernard Hepton who visibly blanches at the name of Drablow. At the funeral service, with only Rawlins and a local solicitor present, Rawlins turns to see a woman, attired entirely in black Victorian dress, standing stock-still by the pews (an unnerving, indistinct shot) who then vanishes. On leaving the church, the same woman appears like an unmoving statue among the ornate headstones, the older solicitor agitated and trembling. Unbeknown to Rawlins, Crythin Gifford is cursed and when the solicitor saves a gypsy girl from being crushed to death by logs falling from a truck, he has unwittingly brought that curse on himself, condemning his family in the process. Rawlins is puzzled—why does Eel Marsh House induce such terror in the locals? Why are there numerous graves of young children aged between three and seven? Taken out to the Drablow's grim old abode in a trap, Rawlins surveys the graveyard at the rear of the house. He starts to go back in, rubs his neck with the odd feeling that someone is looking at him, swivels round and the woman in the black dress is standing there, staring malevolently, gradually moving closer and closer as he bolts indoors. As if that wasn't bad enough, he hears a horse trotting up along the misty causeway, followed by a crash, screams and a child crying "Mummy! Mummy!"—and then nothing materializes. Events escalate when Rawlins decides, against Hepton's advice, to spend the night in Eel Marsh House. With Hepton's dog Spider as company, those disturbing noises are heard on the causeway again, a child's voice emanates from an empty room and Rawlins, frightened out of his wits and babbling, is rescued by Hepton. Back in the village, it transpires that Drablow's sister, Janet Goss (played by Pauline Moran), gave birth to an illegitimate son—unable to care for the infant, Drablow herself adopted the boy but her sister, full of hate, kidnapped her son; crossing the causeway in fog, the horse and trap sank into the marshes, Moran and the boy perishing. Drablow's evil sister now haunts the town, taking out revenge by orchestrating the deaths of children at random and because Rawlins saved the little gypsy girl, the spirit has channeled its malignant attentions on him. In an icy scene guaranteed to raise the hackles, Rawlins, asleep in the inn, wakes to find a tin soldier in his hand and a child's voice whispering "It's for you." Suddenly, a shadow passes across his bed and the revengeful apparition floats in through the window, shrieking at Rawlins who collapses in a dead faint. After a spell of recovery, the solicitor returns to London, setting fire to a box full of Drablow's papers when they turn up in his office (the house mysteriously burned to the ground when Rawlins was convalescing). The solicitor is sent home, preparing us for the inevitable tragedy—rowing peacefully on a lake with his family, Rawlins, to his horror, sees the Woman in Black standing in the middle of the lake. Petrified, he freezes and then his wife screams—a tree collapses on their boat, crushing all within it and sinking the craft and its occupants beneath the freezing waters; Drablow's sister has had her revenge. Containing an eerie score by Rachel Portman which adds measurably to the spooky atmosphere, this is 102 minutes of expertly crafted ghostly shocks, a spine-chiller of the first order that you need to view with the light on, and preferably in the company of another! —BA

Hammer is now back in the moviemaking biz and working on a new version of The Woman in Black for 2011 release. The film stars Daniel Radcliffe (Harry Potter if you live in a cave). The film is directed by James Watkins and the screenplay (based on the Susan Hill novel) is by Jane Goldman (*Kick Ass*).

Writers contributing to this section:

BA—Barry Atkinson
DF—Dennis Fischer
MHP—Michael H. Price
GR—Gary Rhodes
DHS—David H. Smith
JS—John Sositer
GJS—Gary J. Svehla
SS—Susan Svehla

Daniel Radcliffe as Arthur Kipps in Hammer's *The Woman in Black*.

D.W. GRIFFITH'S AVENGING CONSCIENCE

by Arthur Lennig

Edgar Allan Poe was no stranger to the early days of the movies. In 1909, D.W. Griffith, often considered to be the father of the American cinema, made a one-reel biography called *Edgar Allan Poe,* consisting of six shots. In it, Poe cares for his ailing wife, writes "The Raven," goes to a publisher who refuses the manuscript, then to another who accepts it, and returns with the good news to his wife, only to find out that she has died. Griffith would return to Poe five years later, just prior to directing his landmark film, *The Birth of a Nation* (1915), and make one of the cinema's first forays into the horror genre. Originally called *The Murderer's Conscience* and shot from April 15 through the beginning of June 1914, it was released that August as *The Avenging Conscience; or "Thou Shalt Not Kill."* In it, Griffith would try to capture the nightmare quality of Poe's fiction.

The Avenging Conscience starts with the death of a young mother whose baby is adopted by her one-eyed brother (Spottiswoode Aitken). During the boy's youth, the two have a strong, loving relationship. Years later, the young man (Henry B. Walthall) and his uncle are shown in an office at home, where they work at separate desks. (What the young man is doing at this desk is not clear; he may be working on his uncle's books, but at the end of the film we discover that he is also an author. The nephew is not named, but I shall refer to him as Henry.) The uncle through the years, says a title, has lavished both "time and money" on the lad and glances over at him with a look of possession, crosscut with a cat studying a bird in a cage that hangs directly over the seated Henry.

After these symbolic images, Griffith shows Henry reading "The Tell-Tale Heart," a photograph of Poe, lines from the poem "Annabel Lee" and images of his girlfriend (Blanche Sweet), whom he chooses to call "Annabel." He also receives a letter from her inviting him to a garden party. Griffith subtly suggests that Annabel represents sexual attraction by showing her not in a living room but in her bedroom, with the bed clearly visible behind her. The old man is jealous of his nephew's love for the girl and wants him to part with her and concentrate solely on work. "I have sacrificed everything for you," says the uncle naggingly, "and you owe me in return a few years of gratitude." The two men quarrel. When Annabel pays a visit, the uncle angrily tells her, "You are after my boy like a common woman."

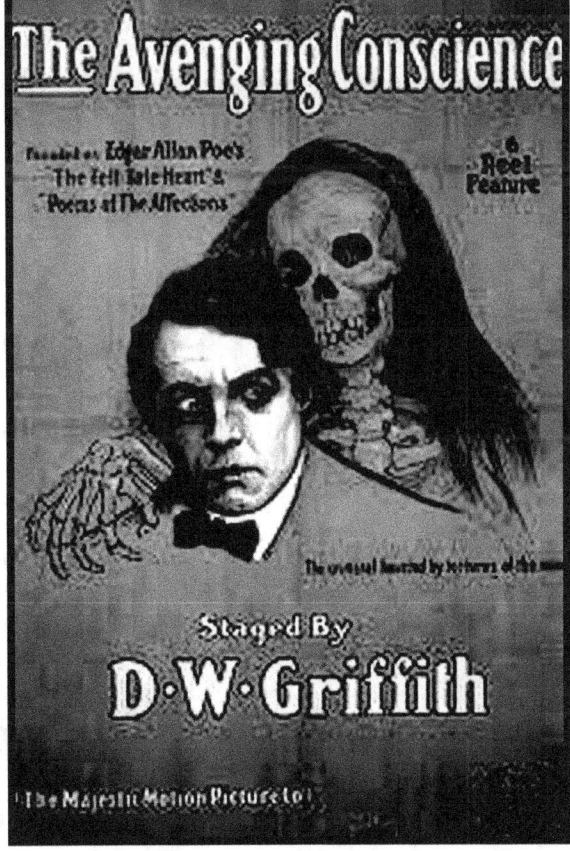

After this ugly confrontation, Henry meets the girl and the two stroll out in the country by a lake. Although he loves her, he reluctantly decides to follow his uncle's command to sever his relationship. Meanwhile, the embittered uncle goes to a public park filled with lush vegetation where he views a young married couple with their child, a scene reminding him that a family unit, implying love and fruition, is the usual course of humanity. At the same time, Annabel, in her bedroom, sadly puts away Henry's photograph. The uncle, torn between demanding his nephew's full attention and allowing them to have happiness, returns to his house where he prays to God "to guide him right."

Henry, frustrated and angry, sits alone on a park bench. This shot is followed by the title: "THE BIRTH OF THE EVIL THOUGHT; Nature's one long system of murder—the spider, the fly and the ants…"

The young man watches as a spider kills a fly, followed by another shot of hundreds of

49

ants devouring a bug. Reacting to this episode, the critic for the *Dramatic Mirror* would later complain, "Really this has nothing at all to do with the problem confronting the young man, but it lends events a pseudo-scientific aspect and therefore makes them appear more serious." (*Dramatic Mirror*, August 12, 1914.) To the contrary, these shots do pertain to the theme in a suggestive way: They demonstrate the principle of nature in which one creature kills another for its own survival, suggesting that the stronger or more clever will win out and that murder is a principle of life. On this basis, the old and decrepit uncle, by standing in the way of passion and potential procreation, deserves to die.

After the title, "Realization that his uncle on whom he is dependent, stands between him and happiness," Henry returns to his room and falls asleep on the couch while the unhappy Annabel goes to bed and cries. Now, Henry's "fevered brain" devises a plan to kill his uncle. When the old man leaves on a business venture, Henry contrives that no one should see his uncle return in order to avoid any suspicion that he had anything to do with the disappearance.

Henry takes out a gun, aims it at his dozing uncle, but then puts it away. Here, Griffith cuts to a howling dog and ominous clouds, after which the young man retrieves the gun, walks towards the uncle and places it at the man's head. But he hears people outside and, afraid that they might hear the shot, puts away the gun and picks up a cane, as if to club him, and then changes his mind. The old man awakes and Henry demands money so that he can go away with Annabel. When the uncle refuses, the young man—a title links him to the spider and the uncle to the fly—chokes him to death, while an Italian (George Siegmann), in a tight close-up, peers in through a window. Moments later, the Italian knocks on the door, reveals that he saw the murder and blackmails the boy. This plot complication, however, goes nowhere and would better have been omitted.

The nephew bricks the dead man's body behind the wall of the fireplace, but he cannot bury his conscience. Shortly after, when Annabel, unable to endure her rejection, visits her boyfriend, the figure of the uncle appears to Henry in a double exposure. Particularly effective is a shot of the murdered man, with outstretched hands, emerging from the fireplace. The tormented nephew is also haunted by visions of Christ and of a stone tablet stating "Thou shalt not kill." Such Biblical images, with which Griffith was fascinated, later reappear in *Intolerance* (1916) and *Dream Street* (1921).

When a suspicious detective (Ralph Lewis) comes to Henry's house to question him, he leaves his men outside to watch the house in case there is an escape attempt. During this interrogation, the young man's conscience again plagues him. Griffith, in an impressive montage of close-ups, intercuts Henry's face with the detective's hand incessantly rapping a pencil on the desk, "Like the beating of the dead man's heart," says a title. The director, of course, couldn't record the sound of a heartbeat but he does capture Poe's intent visually. Griffith also shows brief images of a swinging clock pendulum, closer shots of the hand, the detective's tapping foot, a hooting owl, Henry's hands nervously folding and unfolding and then extreme close-ups of the faces of the questioning detective and guilt-ridden Henry. Griffith also renders Henry's torment by dollying the camera in on him as a garbed skeleton besets him. Finally, the specter of the uncle again enters, and Henry, imagining that he is once more strangling the man, confesses his deed. He grabs the detective's neck for a second and then flees.

Pursued by the police, the young man hides in a building and then attempts suicide, after which the heartbroken Annabel jumps off a cliff.

This is in essence the story, although there are some wholly unnecessary plot complications that clutter the narrative. Namely, at the garden fête there is a brief, irrelevant subplot in which a grocer boy (Bobby Harron) woos a maid (Mae Marsh)—proletarian roles that would be fully developed by the same actors later that year in *The Mother and the Law*. More serious and awkward is the plotting towards the end of the film: Henry hires the blackmailing Italian and his henchmen for protection (against what?) and devises, in another building, a secret trapdoor through which he might escape. One policeman who has accompanied the detective finds the trapdoor immediately and nails it shut. When Henry escapes after his confession, he holds off the police with a rifle and, when he cannot open the trapdoor,

Henry (Henry B. Walthall) does away with his uncle (Spottiswoode Aitken).

he hangs himself. (He is cut down before he dies.) Perhaps Griffith wanted to add some action and suspense to his film, but the inclusion of the Italian's henchmen and the detective's aides merely muddies the story.

After Henry is prevented from hanging himself and the girl commits suicide, the young man wakes up from the couch where he had fallen asleep and is surprised to see his uncle still alive. He pokes the man's chest to feel whether he is really there and then embraces him. "Oh, such a dream," he says. Meanwhile, Annabel arises from her bed, "Her mind cleared of resentment," and hurries over to see her beloved. Instead of the old man throwing her out, he has been purged of his selfish possessiveness through prayer and therefore welcomes her and agrees to their marriage.

The next scene, prefaced by the title, "The Aftermath," shows the happy couple by the lake. Henry reads from his "successful" book: "In your voice I hear Pan playing in the woods and all the world gives heed." Griffith then shifts to a symbolic scene where, in a nature setting, we see Pan (playing his pipes) causing a mountain lion, a leopard and rabbits to gambol about in innocent joy, accompanied by elves. These allegorical moments, of which Griffith was inordinately fond, have not worn well over the years and were even criticized in their day. *Motography*, although full of praise for the film, thought that it would "benefit" with "less of the allegorical, to which perhaps one hundred feet of the film's finish is given over" (*Motography*, August 1914, p. 270). Griffith was so proud of his film that he did not conclude it with the usual "The End" but for the first and only time with "Finis."

Obviously, Poe inspired most of this film's content. The young man is taken in by his uncle (just as Poe himself was taken in by a guardian), the girl is called Annabel (a reference to "Annabel Lee"), the uncle has one eye (from "The Tell-Tale Heart") and he is entombed in the wall (as in "The Black Cat" and "The Cask of Amontillado").

The Avenging Conscience is an ambitious cinematic undertaking, one that falters by not establishing in early scenes a closer, warmer relationship between the nephew and his uncle and by not making the scenes between Annabel and the young man more romantic. The emotional engagement that Griffith often achieves in his work does not occur here. We do not share the young man's dilemma as much as we should, nor, in fact, do we much care what happens to any of the principals. Here the director reveals he is less interested in developing character than in conveying cinematically the aspects of a tormented conscience.

Although *The Avenging Conscience* touches on the dark night of the soul that the Germans later would evoke in their

The tormented Henry is haunted by Christ figures.

post-war films, it does not anticipate their stylized settings or ominous lighting. Shot on sets lit by the sun, Griffith's picture lacks the shadows necessary to create a pervasive sense of evil. If he is not so metaphysical, he is a gifted dramatist who here captures through editing, rather than through pictorial composition or chiaroscuro, the essence of Poe and shows that he could approach the nightmare world, if not quite be comfortable in it. Griffith was drawn more to love and sunshine and happiness than to the darker side of humanity, but this film—one of his few in which the central figure is not a woman—shows that he was capable of more than what some critics have called his Victorian effusions. Particularly subtle was the use of the caged bird and the watchful cat, the kind of symbolism that Erich von Stroheim would later employ more fully in *Greed* (1924).

During production, Griffith heard of a garden fête to be held in Pasadena and asked permission to film it (*Moving Picture World*, July 11, 1914, p. 243). He also used the lushness of the gardens of the public park and the leaves draping down close to the camera to suggest the fertility and beauty of nature and to underscore the sexual attraction between the grocer boy and the maid and also that between Henry and Annabel. Although Griffith in his outdoor work would sometimes frame a long shot with a tree, he almost never placed anything in the foreground through which we saw his players. This film is an exception. Here he also uses settings in a suggestive, even symbolic manner. The scene where the young man takes one final aching look at Annabel after they break up is placed in a formal garden with strictly sheared hedges, suggesting how his life is now constrained; in contrast, Annabel is shown among branches moving in the wind, hinting of her turmoil and desire.

The re-creation of the mood of Poe's stories also prompted the use of double exposures and other special effects. Although

Griffith's photographer Billy Bitzer is praised as a great craftsman, his handling of trick work is often faulty when compared to the accomplishments of other cameramen of the time. There are flaws in the double exposures not only in *The Avenging Conscience*, but also at the end of *The Birth of a Nation* (the honeymoon) and portions of the allegorical conclusion of *Intolerance*. (Some of the shots in *The Avenging Conscience*, among them the superimposed clouds, were shot by Bitzer's assistant, Karl Brown, but Bitzer was still responsible for the overall concept.) Aside from such limited technical flaws, *The Avenging Conscience*, because of its immense amount of cutting and crosscutting, is by far the best of Griffith's first four features.

Although *The Avenging Conscience* has its awkward moments, it certainly was the most advanced motion picture made to that time and shows Griffith wholly in command of his medium. In its brilliant and unprecedented use of the camera to convey psychological states by means of close-ups and editing, the film is far beyond the theatrical style, then current, of long takes photographed from a distance. The reviewer for *The Los Angeles Herald*, who had felt that *The Escape* (1914) was Griffith's greatest achievement, altered his view after seeing *The Avenging Conscience,* calling it "by all odds the greater of the two, both photographically and histrionically" (Guy Price, *Los Angeles Herald,* no specific date, 1914).

Shortly after *The Avenging Conscience* was completed, a reporter spotted Griffith walking out of the Mutual offices and asked him about his profession. At first, he sympathized with the reporter for having to write about motion pictures, opining "the crime of anyone obliged to look at them daily must have been something awful," declaring that for him it is punishment enough to look at his own productions. Here, Griffith, who had hoped to be a great playwright, seems almost embarrassed about his films and his occupation in general. He complained that up to the present "we haven't had the time or the brains or the money" that the movies deserve (Unidentified clipping in trade press, c. June 1914). He even criticized *The Avenging Conscience* "by off-handedly declaring it 'crude and full of mistakes.'" But perhaps this was false modesty, for he also revealed pride in the film, saying, "People can't realize it, but it took me three months to make *The Avenging Conscience* in order to get into it all of the things that go to the making of life" (Ibid). Even with all the effort expended, he was keenly aware of his current film's limitations. He knew he could do better and was already beginning on *The Birth of a Nation,* his long dreamed of supreme work for which, finally, he hoped at last to have both the time and the money. The horror genre would have to fend for itself without the further aid of D.W. Griffith.

[Note: This is an excerpt from Arthur Lennig's forthcoming book on D.W. Griffith]

BLITHE SPIRIT

by Dennis Fischer

While ghosts and spooks have often been the subjects of horror, these genial spirits have also frequently been the source for jests and japery. While post-war periods are often a rich field for horrific fare as the public tries to exorcise the experiences with which they were inundated, typically shattering experiences for most cultures leading to a deep revulsion of the offshoots of war, pre-war periods are often marked by general escapism, whimsical attempts at depicting stories where the protagonists leave the confines of this world to find a happier place.

Of course, the success of *Topper* opened up a floodgate of afterlife comedies. While the postwar disillusionment created the style known as film noir (literally "black film"—so-called because of its emphasis on darkness, scenes set mostly at night, in deep shadows, or on rain-drenched streets), the wartime escapism created a short-lived vogue for film blanc. Film blanc drenched the screen with sweetness and light, an overall whiteness, often depicting a beautiful cloud-covered afterlife.

Examples of such films include *The Ghost Breakers* (1940), *Here Comes Mr. Jordan* (1941), *The Remarkable Andrew* (1942), *A Guy Named Joe* (1943), *It Happened Tomorrow* (1944), *The Horn Blows at Midnight* (1945), *Stairway to Heaven* (a.k.a. *A Matter of Life and Death*), *The Bishop's Wife* (1947) and, of course, *Blithe Spirit* (1946), the funniest and wittiest of them all.

David Lean has remained one of the glories of British cinema and certainly deserves to be acclaimed as one of England's greatest directors. He was a Quaker by upbringing and was not allowed to go to the cinema as a boy. However, after attempting a career in accountancy, he joined the film industry and rose from tea boy to clapper/loader, to assistant editor, then assistant director, to editor of Movietonews.

Lean was first given the chance to direct on *In Which We Serve*, where he shared directorial credit with acclaimed playwright Noel Coward, who starred in, wrote, produced, and scored the film as well. Lean followed the film with *This Happy Breed*, an adaptation of the Coward play scripted by Lean himself.

Lean continued his association with Coward for two more films, both classics: *Blithe Spirit* and *Brief Encounter*. Coward considered his satire on spiritualism "an improbable farce," and was quite willing to let Lean have a go at it. *Blithe Spirit* is David Lean's best comedy, and the best supernatural farce ever committed to film, so its relative obscurity among horror film fans remains a bit puzzling. The script by Noel Coward is brimful of sparkling wit, the cast, which includes Rex Harrison, Kay Hammond, Constance Cummings and Margaret Rutherford (Miss Marple of the movies), is superb, and Lean proves himself adept at both farcical humor and supernatural flourishes.

Coward himself provides a charming poetic preface, reading:

When we are young
We read and believe
The most fantastic things.
When we grow older and wiser
We learn with perhaps a little regret
That these things can never be,

Which is subverted by Coward's own voice intoning, "We are quite, quite wrong," which delightfully sets the tone for what follows.

Following Lean's production of *This Happy Breed*, it was Coward who suggested that he next tackle *Blithe Spirit*, despite the fact that Lean professed to know nothing about comedy. The play had premiered at London's Piccadilly Theatre on July 2, 1941, with Cecil Parker playing Charles Condornine, supported by Fay Compton as Ruth, Kay Hammond as Elvira, and Margaret Rutherford as Madame Arcati. (Clifton Webb starred in a Broadway production that opened later that same year.)

Despite his producer's credit, Coward was off entertaining WWII troops during most of the production. According to Stephen Silverman's book *David Lean*, when Lean took Coward to a preview of the film, Coward told him, "My dear, you have fucked up the best thing I ever wrote." Later Lean was to have his revenge after Coward assayed the role of Charles Condomine for a 1956 television production. When Coward asked him what he thought of it, Lean smartly replied, "You have fucked up the best thing you ever wrote."

While Lean was noted more as a serious person than a humorous one (Harrison accused him of having no sense of humor at all), he was respectful enough of Coward's work to not muck about with it. Watching the film today certainly doesn't bear out Coward's low opinion of it, as it is largely faithful to his original play (though it prunes some excess verbiage, only the ending is altered somewhat), and the performers delightfully embody the characters and make Coward's lines sparkle.

Coward actually manages to achieve a level of wit worthy of Oscar Wilde. The protagonist, Charles Condomine (Rex Harrison), is an archetypal English aristocrat-snob who can turn a phrase ("It's discouraging to think how many people are shocked by honesty and how few by deceit," he says saucily). As a character, he is funny but also extremely insensitive and egotistical.

Harrison himself proved to be rather imperious during production, refusing to take direction if it meant that he would have to be photographed from his "wrong side." (Harrison preferred his left profile.) He also refused to shout lines to his dead wife because he feared it would lose him audience sympathy, apparently little realizing that the character's appeal lies in his good natured, self-serving heartlessness.

Charles and Ruth make for an endearing couple, particularly with their dialogue exchanges, some of the best outside of the famous *Thin Man* series. For example, here are the Condomines on why they lost their last maid:

Charles: What do you suppose induced Agnes to leave us? (Agnes, the former maid, was pregnant).
Ruth: The reason was becoming increasingly obvious..
Charles: Mm. We must keep Edith (the new maid) in the house more.

The major complication in their lives is that Charles starts being haunted by the spirit of his first wife, Elvira. According to Charles, Elvira passed away because "She was convalescing from pneumonia and one evening began to laugh helplessly at one of the BBC musical programmes and died of a heart attack." After spending seven years wandering the astral plane, she can think of nothing better to do than plague her former husband with complaints about the garden. "You've absolutely ruined the border by the sundial; it looks like a mixed salad. All those nasturtiums are so vulgar."

Ruth perceives her husband Charles as "hag-ridden," that is, dominated by women, beginning with his mother. Charles returns that if she is going to make an inventory of his sex life, she is leaving out several episodes, and offers to consult his diary and provide her with a complete list.

Rutherford steals every scene in which she appears as the misshapen, mixed up medium. Madame Arcati is characterized as a bicycling enthusiast and haphazard medium of dubious gifts. I thought I was going to have a puncture, so I went back to fetch my pump—and then, of course, I didn't," she says, to which Charles offers the far from consoling though goodnatured retort, "Perhaps you will on the way home." Her abilities are offered up as entertainment for Dr. and Mrs. Bradman, but she makes the mistake while conducting her séance of selecting Irving Berlin's "Always" for the gramophone, which happened to be a favorite of Elvira's. The muddleheaded maid, Edith, just happens to be a natural medium, which is enough to allow Elvira's mischievous spirit into their lives.

Elvira is visible only to Charles and has a vivid gray-green appearance, with an extremely red, pouty mouth and a snooty,

self-centered derisive demeanor. She is delightfully played with an absence of artificial charm by Kay Hammond, whose career was tragically cut short by illness. Her subsequent film appearances were few and unremarkable. She imbues Elvira with a very sensual, vivacious personality in contrast to the more restrained, brittle and no-nonsense character of Charles' current spouse, Ruth, who seems less passionate but more Charles' intellectual equal.

One of the most impressive shots in the movie has the camera tracking past Charles and Elvira on a couch, through French windows which open themselves, and into a mirror in which the couple is reflected, but the camera isn't. There's also a nice special effect when Ruth runs right through the transparent Elvira on the stairs, mussing Elvira's hair in the process. The film won an Academy Award for its special effects, even though most of them were achieved with wire work and careful editing. Still, the scene where Elvira proves she's real to Ruth, mostly by menacing her with various objects, remains a delight as the confrontation increases the conflict between the two women until Ruth runs out screaming in capitulation.

The outstanding and vividly colored cinematography was done by Ronald Neame, who shot such films as *The Prime of Miss Jean Brodie*, *Scrooge*, *The Poseidon Adventure*, *The Odessa File*, *Meteor* and *Hopscotch*.

Given his background, it is not surprising that one of the hallmarks of Lean's work is his editing. For example, he adds a comic touch to Arcati's apprehension about dinner, saying, "Oh, no red meat, I hope. I make it a rule never to eat red meat before I work," then cutting immediately to an extremely bloody slice of roast being carved and served for dinner. Or going from Arcati's "It upsets my vibrations" to a teakettle boiling and blowing steam. Or he conveys the sense of an endless argument as Charles and Ruth discuss the "reality" of Elvira in the dining room, the hall, the supper table, concluding with coffee on the terrace.

Lean also shows he knows when not to cut, as when Elvira has sabotaged Charles' car and Ruth winds up driving it instead. Charles, who is familiar enough with his ex to know that Elvira is up to something, interrogates her with Lean concentrating his camera on her and her agitated exclamations as she realizes what's gone awry which increases the comic tension in the scene.

Following Ruth's death in the "accident, Charles realizes clearly that Elvira is no prize, and she feels the same way about him. "The silliest thing I ever did in my whole life was to fall in love with you," she tells him, to which Charles, ever the stuffed shirt, responds, "That remark comes perilously close to impertinence."

The film makes a brief reference to the afterlife as an interminable bureaucracy—Elvira says something about "having to fill in all those forms, wait about in drafty passages for hours", an idea that later became central in Tim Burton's exquisite *Beetlejuice*. However, Coward doesn't provide too many clues about life beyond, except when Elvira wryly comments on Madame Arcati's attempts to send her back with the observation, "Merlin does this sort of thing at parties and bores us all stiff with it."

The spectral appearances simply lead to everyone getting disenchanted with each other. Elvira tells Charles about his insensitivity towards her and how she tried to have fun behind his back—"Why shouldn't I have fun; I died young, didn't I?" she rationalizes. She calls Charles on his petty jealousies, his fussings and fumings, saying she laughed at him "steadily from the altar to the grave." However, Arcati's attempt to send her back simply summons up the spirit of a rather put out Ruth.

Lean sends up a few horror film clichés, such as building up the shadow of Arcati on the wall at the initial séance and providing howling winds and a rainstorm at the second one. He also builds suspense around the revelation of a mysterious, sleepwalking figure in the scene where Arcati demonstrates that it is Edith—and *not* Charles—who wished for the appearances of Elvira and Ruth, causing them to materialize. Ruth warns, "If we're not very careful, she'll materialize a hockey team."

While the film benefits from Rex Harrison's impeccable timing and helped introduce him to U.S. audiences, the film clearly belongs to Dame Margaret Rutherford's delightfully dotty medium. She even has a talking parrot that chants, "Poltergeists, pretty poltergeists." Rutherford later appeared in the early mermaid comedy, *Miranda* and appeared as the Duchess of Fenwick in Richard Lester's science fiction comedy, *Mouse on the Moon*, and made four appearances as the inquisitive Miss Marple in Agatha Christie mystery films made in the '60s.

The film ends with the disappearance of Ruth and Elvira and the planned departure of Charles, who decides that Ruth was right about him being hag-ridden and is now determined to enjoy his freedom at last. That his suitcases magically appear by his side when he talks of going on a long trip seems to indicate that the now invisible spirits are equally anxious to be rid of him. However, the female ghosts sit peacefully by the roadside where Ruth's accident took place, and sure enough, Charles zooms by in his motorcar, skids and soon the pair are making room for a surprised third party—the now ghostly green Charles who will apparently share the company of his ex-wives throughout eternity.

Lean became a specialist in epics, making two masterpieces, *Bridge on the River Kwai* and *Lawrence of Arabia*, and two decorative but lumbering leviathans, *Dr. Zhivago* and *Ryan's Daughter*.

His plans for a remake of *Mutiny on the Bounty* became sidelined by producer Dino de Laurentiis into Roger Donaldson's *The Bounty* (1984), while the same year he crafted a canny adaptation of E.M. Forster's *A Passage to India*. Producer Steven Spielberg offered Lean an opportunity to direct an episode of *Amazing Stories*, but Lean turned it down unless, he said jokingly, he could have a six month shooting schedule and a multi-million-dollar budget. Lean passed away in 1991 before he could get his planned adaptation of Conrad's *Nostromo* off the ground.

Lean's collaboration with Coward was an extremely felicitous one, and never more delightful than on *Blithe Spirit*. Rather than spurning the film's theatrical origins, it delights in them and delights the viewer as well. Anyone looking for shivers would be severely disappointed, but those out for a witty, rollicking, supernaturally good comedy with a generous portion of ghostly guffaws would find it hard to beat. This merry movie proves very blithe in deed!

CREDITS: Director: David Lean; Producer: Noel Coward; Screenplay: Noel Coward from his Play; Adaptation: David Lean, Ronald Neame, and Anthony Havelock-Allan; Director of Photography: Ronald Neame; Music: Richard Addinsell; Special Effects: Tom Howard; Distributed by General Film Distributors (U.K.) and United Artists (U.S.); Released April 5, 1945 (U.K.) and September 1945 (U.S.); 96 minutes, 1945

Lean's last Coward collaboration, *Brief Encounter* (1945), is surprisingly slight, but it works. Celia Johnson stars as an unglamorous, married, middle- aged, middle class housewife who meets an equally married, middle-aged, middle class doctor (Trevor Howard) at a train station, when he removes a cinder from her eye. They start meeting in secret on successive Thursdays and contemplate having an affair, but they decide they can't bear the betrayal implicitly involved and end up going their separate ways. The film fared poorly at the box office but achieved great critical acclaim, with Johnson being nominated for an Academy Award and winning the New York Critics' Best Actress Award.

CAST: Rex Harrison...Charles Condomine, Constance Cummings...Ruth, Kay; Hammond...Elvira, Margaret Rutherford...Madame Arcati, Joyce Carey...Mrs. Bradman, Hugh Wakefield...Doctor Bradman, Jaqueline Clark...Edith

CARNIVAL OF SOULS

by Jeff Hillegass

Carnival of Souls opens on the main street of a rural American town. Three young women in a car are challenged to a drag race by a group of young men. The driver of the women's car agrees, and the race begins. On a narrow bridge, the women's car is forced off the road and into murky water. The car sinks into the river as the opening titles undulate over the water's surface. A rescue party arrives, witnessing the figure of one of the women, Mary Henry (Candace Hilligoss), stepping out of the river, covered in mud. When questioned about the fate of her companions, she replies, "I don't remember."

Mary returns to her job at an organ factory long enough to inform her supervisor that she has decided a change of life is in order, so she has accepted a position as a church organist in a distant city. Her co-workers discuss her decision, remarking, "If she's got a problem, it'll go right along with her."

Leaving town, Mary must pass the scene of her accident. With great trepidation, she successfully crosses the bridge. Driving alone at night, she catches sight of an abandoned pavilion which holds her attention. Returning her eyes to the road, she is shocked by the vision of a strange, pasty-faced Man (Herk Harvey) standing directly in her path. She drives off the road in fright, but manages to regain control of her vehicle. Mary does not mention the incident when she stops for gas and directions to her rooming house. She arrives at her rooming house and prepares to retire for the evening, when she again glimpses the Man, this time outside her bedroom window.

In the morning, Mary reports to her new job at the church. The minister (Art Ellison) exclaims that the congregation should be convened to meet their new organist, but Mary begs off. "You can't live in isolation from the human race," admonishes the minister. While Mary practices in the church, the Man makes another appearance. The minister takes Mary on his rounds, and at her request, stops by the deserted pavilion, which has come to fascinate Mary. Upon returning to the boarding house, Mary must fight off the amorous advances of her neighbor, John Linden (Sidney Berger), and deal with another vision of the Man. Mary attempts to sleep, but she discovers that the pavilion is visible from her bedroom window and spends much of the night staring at it.

On her day off, Mary goes shopping. In the midst of a retail transaction, she becomes disconnected from her surroundings. First, storekeepers and shoppers refuse to acknowledge her existence. Then, she begins to lose touch with her senses,

Mary (Candace Hilligoss) finds she cannot sleep.

as she cannot hear any of the sounds of a busy urban street. Fleeing to a park, she manages to regain contact with reality as she perceives the chirping of birds. Mary's reassurance is short-lived, as she mistakes a middle-aged man for the Man she feels is pursuing her, and she becomes hysterical. A doctor (Stan Levitt) passing through the park comes to her aid and encourages her to visit his office.

Mary admits to the doctor that she has no interest in the close company of others. She determines that her unease is somehow precipitated by her fixation on the pavilion and vows to visit the location alone in order to exorcise her neuroses. Acting on her vow, she travels to the pavilion and begins to interpret it as harmless. She fails to see the Man lying in the nearby shallows of the lake.

At church, Mary is compelled beyond her control to play weird compositions on the pipe organ. As she plays, she sees images of the Man and other ghouls rising from the lake and dancing in the pavilion. The minister interrupts her reverie with cries of "sacrilege!" and dismisses her from her post. Mary accepts a date with her neighbor, John Linden, but refuses to dance, drink, or be held close. When they return to her room, she witnesses John's face in the minor become that of the Man. She screams in inconsolable tenor.

The next morning, Mary checks out of the rooming house, to the great relief of her landlady. Mary is determined to leave town, but she is detained in her flight when she experiences car trouble, so she stops for assistance at a local garage. Recognizing the shadowy figure of the Man in the garage, Mary flees on foot. As she attempts to buy a bus ticket, she again becomes disconnected from the world. The ticket sellers cannot see her or hear her cries for help. Mary jumps through the open door of an idling bus, only to find it full of ghouls similar to the Man. She tries to flag down a van and is nearly run down by the driver, who can neither see nor hear her. A trip to the park again brings her back. Mary visits her doctor and confesses,

"I don't belong in the world." Turning to express his reaction, the doctor is revealed to be the Man. Mary screams, which wakes her up in her car, in the garage, and allows her to recognize that everything that occurred after she pulled into the garage was a dream.

Mary drives away from town, straight to the pavilion. Ghouls in evening wear begin to rise from the lake. Power is restored to the pavilion, and outdoor lights illuminate waltzing ghouls. Mary sees herself as a ghoul, dancing arm in arm with the Man. Mary screams and runs; the ghouls chase her to the beach. The scene changes to the pavilion in daylight. The police, the minister, and local townsmen are investigating Mary's disappearance. Mary's car is still at the pavilion. Many sets of footprints lead down the beach and then suddenly stop.

The film ends with a shot under the bridge seen in the opening sequence. The wrecked car is pulled from the river, revealing the dead body of Mary Henry along with her two friends.

Films that become cult classics usually have some feature that distinguishes them from prior efforts. *Last Tango in Paris* broke cinematic taboos by featuring Marlon Brando, a major Hollywood star, in an X-rated production. *Citizen Kane* helped usher in a non-linear form of storytelling. *Eraserhead* presented a bleakness not previously experienced in the cinema. In contrast, *Carnival of Souls* is notorious, not only for its content, but also for the fact that it was produced in the middle of America's Midwestern heartland. All published retrospectives of *Carnival of Souls* note the unlikelihood of Lawrence, Kansas, as the production site for a psychological honor film. In the early 1960s, Southern California was still the dominant locale for motion picture production. So how in the world did some residents of Lawrence, Kansas, come to collaborate on a film that would, years later, inspire comparison to the works of Ingmar Bergman by the New York press?

Herk Harvey and John Clifford had many years of film experience by the time they made *Carnival of Souls,* their first feature. Theirs was the type of experience that paid the bills, but offered little in the way of prestige or acclaim. Harvey and Clifford were co-workers for the Centron Corporation, a Lawrence-based producer of educational and industrial films. Their work on geographical shorts took them all over the world and throughout the United States. On their way back to Kansas from a shoot in California, Harvey drove past an abandoned pavilion in Utah. The Saltair pavilion outside of Salt Lake City had been a grand party spot in the early part of the century, but years of neglect and exposure to the corrosive air had taken their toll. The atmosphere of the location inspired Harvey and Clifford to conjure up a story that incorporated the pavilion. It wasn't long before they got the notion to film a feature, using the production facilities at their disposal. They figured that they could afford to shoot a decent B-movie which could be their break into feature production, enabling them to move on to pictures of a higher grade. They had enough business sense to realize that the only effective B-movie they could produce and sell would be one in the horror genre. Clifford, the writer, set upon the task of preparing a horror script that Harvey, the director, could film on locations such as the Centron soundstage, businesses within the town of Lawrence, and the Saltair pavilion. Three weeks later, the script for *Carnival of Souls* was completed (*Videoscope* No. 16).

In addition to considering the locations at their disposal, Clifford also shaped his script based on other resources that were easily available to the men. Along with the Centron Corporation, another key business in Lawrence was the Reuter Organ Factory, so Clifford deemed that as the heroine's place of business. The soundtrack of the film was also influenced by this decision, as it consists entirely of organ music. When Mary Henry plays the organ at the church, or when the Saltair pavilion is framed by calliope-style music, the sound of a pipe organ originates within the realm of music that is heard by both the characters and the audience. The organ music then continues as an accent perceived by the audience alone. This bit of sophistication belies the modest origins of *Carnival of Souls*.

The total budget for *Carnival of Souls* was $30,000, which was comprised of $17,000 cash and $13,000 deferred. The cash was raised by courting local businessmen for investments in the $500 range. Despite the constraints of a shoestring budget, Harvey and Clifford were determined to imbue their picture with a sense of style that would be more in keeping with the arthouse than the drive-in. The budget necessitated shooting in black and white, which, as many horror film buffs agree, is most conducive to atmospheric storytelling. Harvey was a devotee of the work cinematographer Sven Nykvist provided for Ingmar Bergman, and tried to inspire his cinematographer, Maurice Prather, to light the film in a similar fashion. Given that the budget allowed for only a single take of most shots, Prather managed to turn in an admirably assured work. Clifford fashioned his story in the psychological horror mold of *Psycho*, with touches of *The Twilight Zone*. Such a decision saved money on makeup and special effects, but it also served to propel the screenplay into a more intellectual mode than a formulaic monster-on-the-loose picture. At the outset of his writing, Clifford wasn't sure how he would resolve the storyline. The concept of Mary Henry being dead all along actually came to him midway through the process.

The total production crew for *Carnival of Souls* numbered fewer than a dozen people, with most of the talent culled from the ranks of the Centron Corporation. The advantages to this were obvious; there were fewer people to oversee, but everyone was a craftsman at his job, thanks to his years of toil in the world of industrial filmmaking. A small crew allowed the filmmakers to sneak in and out of settings in order to grab a few shots without having to bother to obtain permits to close streets for shooting. This "guerrilla" style of filmmaking can be a hit-or-miss proposition. *Carnival of Souls* suffers at times from the crudeness of its production, but it also contains some hauntingly gritty imagery that a self-conscious crew would be hard-pressed to duplicate.

Mary is haunted by the strange man (director Herk Harvey)..

Casting for *Carnival of Souls* commenced with the hiring of Sidney Berger in the role of Mary Henry's neighbor, John Linden. Berger was a friend of Harvey's from the University of Kansas, where both taught courses. In discussing further casting with Berger, Harvey requested that he scout New York for a suitable actress for the lead. Linden returned with Candace Hilligoss, the sole professional performer in the film. Hilligoss studied her craft under the tutelage of Lee Strasberg, renowned as the creator and proponent of Method acting. Method actors throw themselves into their roles, striving to become one with their character. Unfortunately, the limited budget of *Carnival of Souls* did not often allow for the luxuries of rehearsals or retakes, and scenes were often grabbed on the fly when a suitable location could be found. In fact, all of the exterior city scenes were shot in Salt Lake City on one single day, with the crew moving from location to location before they could be shooed away. Hilligoss found herself quite frustrated that Harvey could not stop filming to offer her explanations of Mary Henry's motivations for her actions. Unable to connect with her character, Hilligoss spent much of the film acting in a detached fashion, which, as luck would have it, was completely appropriate to the part. In fact, Hilligoss' deadpan delivery and blank gaze go a long way in describing her character and distinguish her from the amateurish theatrics of her co-workers. *Carnival of Souls* marked both the beginning and the midpoint of Hilligoss's feature film career. She subsequently appeared in only one more movie, 1964's *Curse of the Living Corpse*, though one of her co-stars from that film did manage to gain prominence in the cinema; his name was Roy R. Sheider, now better known as Roy Scheider.

Other principal characters in *Carnival* were essayed by local talent Harvey had worked with at Centron. The landlady was played by Frances Feist, who had done some stage work. The doctor and the minister, the film's two authoritarian figures, were respectively played by Stan Levitt and Art Ellison, who had both appeared in numerous industrial films for Centron. The speechless role of "The Man" was played by Harvey himself, who did Alfred Hitchcock one better by not only cameoing in a film he directed, but by making a mark in horror film history as an extremely unsettling filmic presence.

The makeup for the Man and the other ghouls was designed with frugality in mind, and the result was a stroke of genius. The pasty appearance of the ghouls was obtained through the application of egg whites. Since the film was shot on black-and-white stock, the stark white appearance of egg white was reduced to an element of the gray scale, and the flakiness of the egg coating on the actors' skin simulated rotting flesh. For the scenes of the ghouls rising from the lake, greasepaint was substituted for the egg white, as the egg would be washed away by the water.

Stuntwork for the film was similarly economical. While most modern productions are burdened by safety regulations, insurance, shooting permits, etc. *Carnival of Souls* was filmed in the kinder, simpler heartland of America. In order to film the opening scene of the car plunging into the Kaw River in Kansas, Herk Harvey had to agree to pick up the tab for repairing the bridge, which wound up setting the production back to the tune of $16.50. However, filming under the umbrella of a large production does have its benefits: you won't attract the attention of the local constabulary, which is exactly what happened to Harvey! The police wanted to arrest him for attempted murder, until they were informed that the accident they witnessed was, indeed, a simulation for a motion picture.

Filming took a total of one month, and the picture was prepared for release over the course of the next four months. Much of the audio had to be post-dubbed, which led to unfortunate difficulties in sync which remain in the final film. Once Harvey and Clifford finished their opus, which they later evaluated as a combination of "a Bergman look with a Cocteau feel," (Herk Harvey's introduction to Vid America's video edition of *Carnival of Souls*), they premiered it in Lawrence, to a lukewarm reception from an audience obviously not prepared for the improbable combination of horror movie content with arthouse execution.

Disappointed but undeterred (and hardly in a position to be deterred, with $30,000 to recoup in addition to their own deferred compensation), the filmmakers set out to find a distribution company. They initially tried to market the film to the arthouse circuit, but were unsuccessful. They finally turned to Herts-Lion, a small distribution company. Harvey later acknowledged that his inexperience with the distribution market led him to sign a deal with Herts Lion, which would get *Carnival of Souls* into theaters, but which was entirely unsympathetic to the way the filmmakers wanted their work promoted.

"A Picture So Shocking It Is Truly One Step Beyond! A Story So Unusual It Will Burn Itself Into Your Mind!" proclaimed the print advertising for *Carnival of Souls* upon its initial 1962 release. Herts-Lion packaged the film squarely in the B-movie realm, with venues exclusively in the Southeastern United States. The film never reached its intended audiences of urbanites until it was sold to television years later. In the interim, Herts-Lion saw to it that the filmmakers never received any of the profits due them. When Herts-Lion went out of business in 1964, not only were Harvey and Clifford left unpaid, but so was the film lab that struck the release prints. That debt was then transferred to DuArt Labs in Los Angeles.

Topping off the insults rained upon the filmmakers by the distributors was the fact that *Carnival of Souls* was edited for release. Herts-Lion butchered the film, sacrificing mood and script intelligibility for a shorter print which would be easier to double-bill with another picture. The continuity suffered to the point where not only was motivation absent, but so were several minor characters. Despite the cuts, the released version of *Carnival of Souls* slowly gained a cult following, thanks largely to late-night television broadcasts. It was written up in horror genre publications such as *Famous Monsters of Filmland*, *Cinefantastique* and *Black Oracle*, and Harvey and Clifford have recounted many letters received over the years from ardent fans. However, genre-oriented adoration wasn't enough for the two men from Lawrence. They failed to reach their intended audience. An ideal scenario would have been a crossover situation in which both the general public and diehard fantasy film fans would have shared their enthusiasm for the picture, a position enjoyed in the cinema by *Psycho* and on television by *The Twilight Zone*. Unfortunately, the lack of recognition by the mass press, combined with the financial blow of never being able to recoup their modest investment, soured the producers on the concept of remaining in the world of feature films. They continued working quite successfully in the realm of industrials.

Ironically, critical recognition was to become a part of the *Carnival of Souls* story, but it would take 27 years to come to fruition. In the mid '80s, director and film buff Richard Haines was obsessed with the concept of restoring and re-releasing the film, and he managed to convince Panorama

screening and reunion, whose guests of honor included Candace Hilligoss, Sidney Berger, John Clifford and, clad in ghastly egg-white face paint, Herk Harvey, "The Man," himself.

Throughout the brief history of film criticism, a discipline that is only slightly shorter than the history of the cinema itself, the notion of intentionality has been repeatedly prominent. In countless pages of text, film critics and theorists have mulled over what the filmmaker intended to convey with a body of work, a single film, or an individual shot. Often, this is blatant presumption. Other times, intentionality is not mentioned as such, but the critic still tries to get into the head of the filmmaker. For the critic to exist, it is necessary to assume that a work is created for a purpose greater than that of commerce, for the film business is riskier than a slot machine. In particular, the trials of the rogue filmmaker, set against the stodgy machinery of the studio system, presents a trove of material for the critic's work. Why was this film made? What were its influences, and what will it inspire? What is the meaning of this particular shot, or of that juxtaposition of images?

The job of analysis is made much easier in the case of *Carnival of Souls*, due to the fact that its creators set out to make the film with their reasons and intentions firmly delineated, and they have been sure to encapsulate their mission in every retrospective interview they've given on the film's production. With candor, they claimed their goal was to make an art film, which combined the visual style of Ingmar Bergman with the mood of Jean Cocteau. The content of this film would be supernatural. Why make such a film? Their reasoning was simple; they wanted money and recognition which would allow them to make more features, and horror movies are easy to sell. What about the story structure? John Clifford, the writer, has remarked that he made it up in sequence as he wrote it. A simpler, more honest description of a film's birth is rarely heard.

Entertainment to do so, using the original, uncut negative as source material. In 1989, *Carnival of Souls* opened New York's Film Forum, inaugurating the city's third annual fantasy and science fiction festival. The screening sold out and garnered rave reviews in the New York metropolitan press, with accolades coming from *The Village Voice*, *New York Post* and even *The New York Times*. Curious audiences were accommodated as the picture moved to New York's Quad Cinema for an extended run. Throughout the fall of 1989, *Carnival of Souls* opened in art film houses throughout the country. Probably the most significant screening was the one which finally brought recognition and justice to Harvey and Clifford. This was the Lawrence, Kansas,

In 1961, when *Carnival of Souls* was first conceived, art films were not self-consciously produced to the same extent they are today. What might be branded as an "art" film in the United States might be something representative of the standard cinematic output of a European nation. When a foreign film

was screened in the U.S., it would feel different to audiences than their accustomed fare. The additional attention paid to the mode of production in imported cinema differed from the seamlessness of the classical Hollywood cinema, and so such films would be packaged into small venues, usually located in an urban center or a college town. So, the scenario of two neophytes setting out to make a low-budget American film with the look of Swedish cinematography and the feel of French cinema was an unprecedented exercise in self-consciousness.

If a critic is to be honest, the issue of intentionality in *Carnival of Souls* is a moot point. Getting into the minds of the filmmakers would result in little more than a collection of inappropriately grandiose dreams and a desire to get a full-length feature in the can before the expiration of a leave of absence from the day job. What is more interesting in this case are the unintentional moments of true effectiveness in the film, those elements which work despite the sometimes heavy hands of the creators.

Although Harvey and Clifford would have their work classified as a psychological thriller or a surrealist film, their production also falls into the camp of the neo-realists, a school of cinema that saw its heyday in post-World War II Italy. The neo-realists worked within the constraints of a war-torn nation to produce some of the first pictures filmed on real locations with non-professional actors. Now, to be fair, *Carnival of Souls* cannot touch the masterworks of Rossellini and Bresson in terms of gravity of content, as *Souls* is more geared towards eliciting a few chills rather than commenting on the distresses of society. However, the governing factor in the production of Harvey's ghost story and the classics of neo-realism is identical: these were films made with the bare essentials necessary to tell a story. Production money was no less a luxury to two independent producers from the Midwest than it was to survivors of Mussolini's Italy. Every chance to cut corners was embraced, and, in the process, a different look and feel was attained, an immediacy that cannot be reproduced within the protective cloak of recreated sets and trained, experienced actors.

As mentioned earlier, the lead, Candace Hilligoss, was an exception in the roster of non-professional actors. She trained in New York under Lee Strasberg, but had little chance to exercise her abilities prior to this motion picture. Her performance, however, was largely molded by the frenetic pace of the production. She was forced into a role foreign and awkward to one of her training; she was a Method actress devoid of motivation for her character. It is silly to assume that Clifford wrote any back story for the character of Mary Henry, and Harvey was too busy trying to get the film in the can to give her much direction. Hilligoss's response was a cautious, restrained performance, which, serendipitously, was perfect for her character. Mary Henry is alienated from everyone around her, she receives sympathy from no one, and, in the end, she joins the ranks of the dead, an assignation she has been avoiding throughout the narrative, but one that is her fate from the moment her car plunges into the river in the opening scene. How completely appropriate it is, then, to have this role essayed by a blank-faced individual, who seems to glide from scene to scene. Candace Hilligoss' confusion on the set is evident to those who are privy to this bit of behind-the-scenes trivia. The rest of the film's audience are presented with a blank face, on which they can project their own fears, anxieties and insecurities. The essence of acting for movie close-ups is to offer emotions in miniature, and let the viewer fill in the rest of the information by staring at the giant face on the screen and thinking of how he would react in similar circumstances. By virtue of being inadequately prepared by her producers, Candace Hilligoss beautifully performed the function of offering the audience a character of identification.

The element of *Carnival of Souls* which distinguishes it from many other contemporary genre efforts is its mood of creepiness, despair and inevitability. The defining factor in the creation of this mood is the cinematography, which is remarkably assured for such a modest production. Usually, zero-budget pictures are saddled with inexperienced cameramen, poor film stock and limited equipment. Thanks to the industrial film background of the crew, all technicians on the set were familiar with the basic mechanics of moviemaking. Instead of learning on the job, the crew was able to hone their craft through the indulgence of creative impulses that would have to be crushed in their normal capacities on educational films. All of the film gear came from Centron, so the specter of past due bills from angry equipment rental houses never sullied the production. The only way the movie could come in on budget was via the use of black-and-white film stock, which was a definite plus. Although fantasy fans can debate endlessly over the merits of flashy full-color epics versus somber monochromatic horrors, a film like *Carnival of Souls* demands to be shot in black and white. For color films to succeed, a tremendous amount of attention needs to be paid to costuming and set decoration, so that a distinct feel is imparted through the chosen color palette—to avoid the subconscious interpretation that different props, locations and characters have no relation to one another. Also, color is less forgiving than black and white when it comes to concealing inadequate makeup work. While a face in the shadows is effectively chilling in black and white, color cinematography begs for the revelation of every minute detail. *Carnival of Souls'* egg white and pancake makeup combo would appear ridiculous under the scrutiny of Technicolor. Even if we underestimate the ability of the producers to create a moody film on color stock, it is still fortunate that *Carnival* was never filmed that way, as the increased stability of black-and-white stock allowed for the restoration of the full-length version, while color film subjected to the same years of neglect would have faded to a ghastly pink shade.

A few images remain in the mind long after seeing *Carnival of Souls* on the late late show or at the trendy repertory cinema. Mary Henry's emergence from the river in the opening, her face and hair splattered with mud as she staggers on the river bank towards the rescue party, moving under her own power in a mockery of their organized effort of salvation, remains the single most powerful image in the film. First time audiences may notice the beauty of the composition, while repeat viewers recognize the inherent iconography, as the protagonist moves, mute and alone, out of the river's grave she refuses to accept and back into the world of the living. Disheveled and disoriented, she remains separate from the living creatures she returns to dwell amongst. A still of this moment was the primary graphic element of the reissue campaign, replacing the 1962 promotional campaign which featured a garish painting of a busty Hilligoss menaced by The Man at the pavilion. The original campaign played simultaneously on sex, horror and the perceived need to explain literally the carnival of the title, while the reissue advertising emphasized the more cerebral elements of the film.

The quick cuts of the Man are appropriately horrifying, thanks to the lack of gray tones, as his ghastly white face is seen in stark contrast to his evening wear and the dark corners in which he appears. Herk Harvey plays the Man with a subtle arch smile which is far more frightening than any overblown scare tactics would have been. Until the end, we are never sure of exactly what the Man wants, but his omnipresence and his self-assurance indicate that his goal will certainly be attained. He is rarely seen for more than a few seconds, and the editing usually follows a set pattern, in which he is shown in a location, then a cut reveals Mary Henry reacting in fright, and finally the location is shown again, either empty, or with another person in his place. Through the use of this editing convention, the Man then may appear only briefly on film, but he is burned into our minds as an afterimage, as we see from Mary's point-of-view that he really was never there at all... or was he?

The one unfortunate effect that doesn't work at all is the fast action appearance of the ghouls on the pavilion at the film's end. Interestingly enough, this effect was actually a budgetary compromise. It is an established mechanical convention that slow motion is achieved by increasing the camera's shutter speed, and fast action is had by decreasing it. So, if film is shot at 12 frames per second but projected at the standard 24 frames per second, the result is sped-up action. Of course, shooting at a slower shutter speed also serves to preserve film stock. As legend has it, Harvey was running out of film in his camera, and rather than break out a new roll, which would add to the film's expense, he decided to experiment with fast action, betting that a few undercranked shots would work in the context of the scene. Knowing this, it is easier to forgive the use of fast motion, and if this effect had to be used in the film, it is most appropriate in the finale, where the forces of the supernatural are in full evidence.

The appearance of the ghouls is further compromised by the absence of some purportedly effective footage, which was lost in the processing stage. This snafu did not occur until the crew returned to Lawrence, and by that time, the prospect of returning to Utah for a reshoot was out of the question. Since the missing footage was camera original stock, we will never know how the ending of *Carnival of Souls* might have been made even creepier.

The story behind the making of *Carnival of Souls* possesses the bitter irony of an O. Henry tale. The filmmakers wanted a vehicle which would pave their way to a Hollywood career, but were forced to turn their backs on their dreams of success. Years later, their single opus has been elevated to a cult status enjoyed by only a handful of films of its era. It is tempting, in hindsight, to surmise that any subsequent, better-funded efforts would have developed into classics of the horror cinema, or of whatever genre they chose. It is also possible that the artistic success of their first film was a fluke, with effective scenes precipitated by financial necessity, and that freedom from the constraints of a low budget would have produced a string of undistinguished pictures, none of which would have come close to their initial ghost story. Any such speculation is merely an intellectual exercise. At least horror fans can content themselves with the fact that *Carnival of Souls*, the sole effort of Herk Harvey and John Clifford, can now be viewed in the best and most complete form available since its 1962 premiere in Lawrence, Kansas.

CREDITS: Producer/Director: Herk Harvey; Screenplay: John Clifford; Director of Photography: Maurice Prather; Music: Gene Moore; 85 minutes; a Herts-Lion Release; October, 1962;

CAST: Candace Hilligoss...Mary Henry, Sidney Berger...John Linden, Frances Feist...Miss Thomas, Herk Harvey..."The Man", Stan Levitt...Doctor Samuels, Art Ellison...Minister, Sharon Scoville...Girl in Car, Mary Ann Harris...Girl in Car, Dan Palmquist...Service Station Attendant, Bill de Jarnette...Mechanic. Additional Cast: Tom McGinnis...Man in Organ Factory, Forbes CaldweJL Caprenter, Steve Boozer, P Ba)lard, Larry Sneegas, Cari Conboy, Karen Pyles, T.C. Adams, Peter Schnitzler...Ghoul in Water, Bill Sollner

THE CHANGELING

by Kevin G. Shinnick

In the late 1970s, Lew Grade, longtime head of television giant ITC, began releasing theatrical features under the banner of AFD. His hope was to become a major-mini mogul, producing big-time, big-budget films with all-star casts.

For the most part, his grand scheme failed disastrously. While he did produce two bonafide hits (*The Boys from Brazil*, 1978 and *On Golden Pond*, 1981), most of his films, no matter how good or bad, were financial disasters (*Raise the Titanic*, 1980; *Legend of the Lone Ranger*, 1981; *Can't Stop the Music*, 1979). In the early 1980s, Sir Lew quietly folded his tent and slipped back into the medium he knew best, television.

Slipping in almost unnoticed among all those high budget flicks was a superior ghost story, done on a modest (for Sir Lew) budget—*The Changeling*.

Supposedly based on a true story (though I can find no documented proof for this statement), the film is most effective in establishing a mood from the very beginning that remains with the viewer long after the film is over. It has a unifying image—water, an image also prominent in 1981's *Ghost Story*, also featuring Melvyn Douglas, as well as Herk Hervey's *Carnival of Souls*. In all three films the pitiful souls haunting the film were drowned.

The film opens with composer John Russell (George C. Scott) witnessing the death of his wife Joanna (Jean Marsh, in a part that is over before her name appears in the opening credits!) and young daughter Kathy (Michelle Martin) in a freak driving accident (caused by the snow, the first water image).

Several months later, he packs his belongings (including a rubber ball once belonging to his daughter) and moves to Seattle (another water image? Seattle is well known for its rainy weather) where he has accepted a teaching post. Looking for a house where he might compose without interruption, he is shown the old Chessman Park House. According to Claire Norman (Scott's then real-life wife, Trish Van Devere, later to meet more ghosts in Crown International's entertaining *The Hearse*, 1980), the agent for the Historical Preservation Society who shows him the house, the old building has remained unlived in for 12 years. When Russell inquires why, Claire tells him that she has only been with the Society for a year but feels that the Society really hasn't tried to find a tenant for the place.

The building is a grand edifice, a kindred spirit—pun intended—of design that rivals the touchstone of haunted houses, Hill House from *The Haunting* (1963). According to John Stanley in *Creature Features Movie Guide*, "The house was totally created by set designers and you won't forget its eerie corridors, stairway and dark rooms." Claire explains that there were plans at one point to turn the huge structure into a museum, but those plans were abandoned. Claire thinks Russell would like the house because of its music room. He does, and in a short time has moved in. His classes prove very popular. Russell is invited to a fundraiser where he meets Claire and is introduced to her mother, Mrs. Norman (Madeleine Thorton-Sherwood, best known to TV audiences as Mother Superior on *The Flying Nun*). They hear a speech from Senator Joseph Carmichael (Melvyn Douglas), who should have learned to stay away from spooky old houses after *The Old Dark House* (1932). We learn that the Senator is the Historical Society's biggest supporter and is even a member of its board of directors.

Six a.m. the next morning, Russell is awakened by a loud pounding noise that reverberates throughout the house, then stops after half-a-minute. Russell dismisses the event and later begins to compose upon the piano. Turning on his reel to reel tape recorder, he plays the piece, but cannot finish, as one of the keys refuses to sound. When he is called away to accept a new water(!) purifying system for the house, the key depresses on its own, echoing an eerie note.

Later, Russell is listening to the recording when Claire enters and comments that the piece sounds like a lullaby. Admiring his desk, she finds the rubber ball that was his daughters.

That night, he dreams of the death of his family, crying (tears=water) in his sleep, only to be awakened once again at 6 a.m. by the unearthly pounding noise. He has Mr. Tuttle (C.M. Gampel), the caretaker for the Society, check out the boiler. Mr. Tuttle suspects that it was merely trapped air within the pipes. "A furnace is like anything else," Tuttle explains. "It's got habits. It's an old house. It makes noises."

The following (rainy) evening, Russell finishes playing a chamber piece with four of his students. As they leave, he hears water running from within the house. He finds the tap in the kitchen sink on, and shuts it off. The sound of running water continues. Russell is drawn by the noise up into the unused servant quarters on the third floor. In the bathroom there, he discovers that the bath is filled, and the water is still pouring in. He turns off the water and looks away for a moment, only to be startled by the sight of a young boy under the water, staring up at him. Slowly, he backs out of the room. The vision of the young child underwater is truly a frightening moment, one of many throughout the atmospheric film.

Russell visits the Historical Society to see if ghostly events have been recorded in the house previously. Claire believes these things are all in Russell's mind, caused by overwork and the loss of his family. Miss Huxley (Ruth Springford), an older Society member, confronts Russell, and in very cool terms says he should not have been allowed to rent the house, and that Claire did not follow proper channels. "That house is not fit to live in. No one has been able to live in it. It doesn't want people." This statement only confirms Russell's belief that there has been trouble in the past. It also brings to mind the people-hating houses from *The Haunting, Legend of Hell House, The Shining* and *The Amityville Horror* whose spirits went to great lengths to rid themselves of the bothersome humans.

The next time we see Russell exiting his home, a pane of glass from an attic window shatters outward and lands in Russell's path. Russell goes back to the third floor and opens a door next to the bathroom. At first it appears only to be a closet, but he notices that the shelves and the wall behind them are covering something. He tears down the covering and discovers a padlocked door. Taking a hammer, he begins to strike at the lock. Stopping momentarily, he realizes that the unearthly pounding has also begun. With one final blow, the lock breaks.

The Changeling's haunted house rivals other old dark houses of the movies.

He throws himself against the door when it refuses to open, only to have it swing open after a moment on its own.

Russell finds a cobweb-strewn stairwell leading up into an equally dusty and web-covered attic room. Within sits an old fashioned child's wheelchair. That small wheelchair sent shivers down the viewers' spines, much like the seemingly innocent rocking chair in *Psycho*. There is also a desk, upon which he finds a child's notebook dated January, 1909, and bearing the initials C.S.B. Upon the mantle he discovers a music box, that, when opened, begins to play the very piece he thought he had composed! Russell later plays the music box for Claire and compares it to his own recording. It is exactly the same, note for note, right down to the key and tempo. He swears he had never heard the piece before, but that the house has somehow influenced him. Claire has researched the house back to 1920 and can find no record of any extraordinary events during that time. Russell is convinced that Miss Huxley was wrong—that the house is not trying to drive people away, but that it is desperately trying to communicate. He shows Claire the attic room, and then they go to the Society to explore the records of the house.

At the Society, they discover that the last people who lived in the building left after only two years, and that in 1967 the Society took over running the place on a grant from the (Senator) Carmichael Foundation. The files before 1920 are missing, and they ask Miss Huxley if she knows who lived in the house before then, particularly the inhabitants in 1909. Miss Huxley tells them that a man named Bernard lived there with his son and daughter, but sold the house a year later after a tragedy.

They go through the local newspaper files and discover that Dr. Walter Bernard's seven-year-old daughter, Cora (the C.S.B. of the notebook), died after being struck by a coal cart. The couple then visit the family gravesite and view the graves of the parents, of Cora, and of her brother, Lloyd. Could the little girl be contacting Russell due to the similarity of her death and that of Russell's family? Claire urges Russell to leave as his psychic scar is the link to the energy within the house.

65

Russell goes home and looks over photos of his family. As he is looking through the pictures, a new pounding sound is heard. Going to investigate, he is shocked to see the reverberations are being caused by his daughter's rubber ball bouncing down the stairs. A shock to viewers but not as shocking as the next scene. Russell takes the toy ball, drives to a nearby bridge, and drops it into a river. Returning home, he sees the ball once more bound down the stairs toward him, now wet from the plunge it has just taken. This harmless toy bouncing down that eerie staircase is more frightening than any gore thrown at audiences by today's horror directors. Through a parapsychologist from the university (Barry Morse), Russell arranges for Leah and Albert Harmon (Helen Burns and Eric Christmas) to conduct a seance. The couple, she as psychic and he her assistant, sense a presence in the house, the force pulls Leah up to the attic room. They begin the seance. Asking questions of the unseen spirits, Leah begins scribbling furiously, without glancing at the papers or pencils that her husband keeps changing for her. The spirit is that of a child not at peace, but it is not the girl Cora, but a child named Joseph who died in the house and wants Russell's help. The psychic goes into a deeper trance, repeatedly asking the child how it died, but the only answer they get is when a glass that was placed on the table hurls itself across the room and shatters. Director Peter Medak uses the seance scene to advantage, striking even more supernatural terror into the audience.

Russell listens to the audio tape he made of the event and now *hears* a child's voice answering the questions, with a vague mention of a ranch, Sacred Heart, well, "Can't walk," and medal. Suddenly, Russell has a vision of what happened—the young boy was drowned in his hip bath by his father in the attic room. The last thing the child heard as he drowned was the music box that was overturned. The pounding he made with his fist against the sides of the metal hip bath was the sound that Russell heard reverberate through the house. The child's final words, "My name is Joseph Carmichael." Russell phones Claire and faints from the excitement of his discovery.

Russell, Claire and her mother attend a seance conducted by Leah and Albert Harmon.

When Claire hears that tape, she is moved to tears, but explains that Sacred Heart was an orphanage that used to exist in the area. She stares horror-struck up the stairs, and when Russell goes to investigate, we see that the sight that shocked her as well as the audience is the child's wheelchair, which now totters at the top of the landing. The wheelchair should strike pity in the hearts of viewers but somehow we know there is evil there also.

As Miss Huxley notifies Senator Carmichael of the goings, our heroes uncover the fact that Carmichael was born in the house in 1900, and his mother died there during his birth. The child's grandfather on his mother's side hated his son-in-law and made provisions in his will that the father was to be a trustee of the estate. Young Joseph Carmichael was to inherit everything at age 21, but should he die, all the money would go to charity. The problem for young Joseph's greedy father was that the boy was sickly. Rather than chance losing a fortune, he murdered the boy, dumped the body in a well, then substituted a young orphan. The father took the young changeling with him to Europe, supposedly for a rest cure in Switzerland in 1906 and, because of World War I, did not return until after 1918. By then the boy was grown. No one could deny it was the actual Joseph Carmichael, and if anyone questioned that he could now walk, the doctors overseas had "cured" him.

Russell and Claire visit the home of a Mrs. Grey (Frances Hyland), whose young daughter Linda had a disturbing nightmare the night of the seance. Her dream consisted of an almost gnome-like child coming up through the floor boards, and who kept staring at her. Mrs. Grey knows that the pair must tear up the child's room to validate their theories that the house sits atop the old well where the body is hidden, but she wishes time to think about it.

That night while sleepwalking Linda (Janne Mortil) again sees the frightening image of the drowned child floating underwater, staring up at her. The image of the little girl standing there in her nightgown is haunting. Her wide eyes and solemn face convince us she has seen or knows something truly horrible.

In a scene illustrating the good verses evil theme of the film, Russell and a student dig up the floor of the little girl's room and discover the old well and the child's skeleton within. The police are notified, but Claire and Russell only admit to the seance leading them to the body, pretending no knowledge of its identity. Russell feels he needs the baptism medal that the boy was wearing when he was drowned to prove that. He breaks into the house and sifts through the dirt. His task of finding the medal seems hopeless, but the medal pushes itself up through the clay, chain first, so that Russell may have his proof.

The next morning he rushes to the airport to show the Senator the medal, but is stopped by the Senator's guards as

Carmichael flies off. The Senator's aides dismiss Russell as some sort of crackpot (understandable, after seeing how he charged onto the landing field). The Senator, however, has recognized the medal as being an exact duplicate of the one he wears around his neck. He has the pilot radio a Captain DeWitt to await a phone call from the Senator when the plane lands.

The spirit goes into a tantrum when Russell returns home and angrily slams all the doors. "God damn son of a bitch," cries an exasperated Russell. "What is it you want? What do you want from me? I've done everything I could do. There was nothing more than I could do." The audience feels his frustration; they too would go to any lengths to rid themselves of this frightening ghost.

Captain DeWitt pays Russell a visit. DeWitt (John Colicos) knows about the incident at the airport and of the seance that lead to the body being found. He feels that Russell is trying some sort to blackmailing scheme against the Senator and that he has stolen the medal. DeWitt gives Russell a choice: give up the medal or DeWitt will arrange for Russell to be put away. They are interrupted by Claire who rushes in. DeWitt leaves, and Claire tells Russell that she was fired, and that his lease on the house has been terminated. She says she is going off to confront the Board of Directors for answers.

Russell stares into a mirror, which unexpectedly warps and shatters, hurling shards outward, lodging a sliver into his neck. He also has a vision of DeWitt, his face all bloody and a horrified stare frozen on his visage. The phone rings, and it is Claire, who has come across the car wreck in which DeWitt was killed.

The Senator arranges for a meeting between himself and Russell. Russell neglects to inform Claire of this meeting, so when she cannot reach him over the phone, she goes that night to the Chessman Park House. Russell visits the Senator's estate, and presents all the facts—the seance, the child's body, the medal all pointing to the Senator being a substituted Joseph Carmichael. All the Senator's wealth and position are due to the murder of a helpless child.

The Senator will not hear of these attacks upon the good name of his father and feels that it is all part of a blackmailing plot. Russell calmly leaves the tape recording, the papers, and historical notes he was able to find, and most importantly, the medal. He has done what he set out to do, and leaves. The Senator grabs up the medal and compares it to his own. They are identical.

Claire has meanwhile entered the Chessman Park House and begins the search for Russell. When she hears his voice calling from the attic room, she goes up the stairs and into the little chamber. The wheelchair turns suddenly and begins to chase her. This is a miscalculation on the part of the writers and the filmmakers. The chair has no reason to attack Claire, for she, like Russell, is trying to help. The scene, while probably the most famous from the film, often elicits laughs as the chair races along after her. I guess they felt the film needed a visual shock at that point.

She falls down the first floor stairs as the chair nearly rolls over her. Russell comes up behind her, and pulls the understandably hysterical woman out of the house before he rushes back in himself. Russell climbs the stairs to the second floor, but a powerful wind knocks him through the railing back to the ground floor, leaving him dazed, as a large chandelier swings dangerously above him. The house, like the one in Poe's tale of Usher, begins to destroy itself, flames beginning upstairs and racing along the handrails of the stairwell.

The Senator has placed the medal from the murdered child upon a small portrait of his father that rests upon his desk. The desk vibrates violently as the Senator stares trancelike. The spirit wishes for the Senator to see the true story.

Russell, still in a groggy daze, sees the Senator (or is it merely his psychic form?) climb the stairs, which collapse

Greed was the motive for the horrific murder of sickly Joseph Carmichael.

The Senator (or is it?) climbs the blazing stairs to the attic.

spectacularly behind him after he reaches the top. Russell barely avoids the chandelier as it crashes mere inches from where he lay. He rushes out of the building as the Senator climbs the attic room stairs and sees the grim tableau replay once more before him. The strain is too much for Senator Carmichael and he collapses. Back in his office, the physical form of the Senator suffers a heart attack and dies. The attic room of the Chessman Park House explodes as Claire and Russell drive away. They arrive at the Senator's home in time to see his covered form being taken away by ambulance (which drives right by the conflagration). The next day, all that remains are the burnt remnants of the wheelchair and the music box, which springs open and begins to play. Somehow, the tune seems happier.

Hungarian-born director Peter Medak had been responsible for the critically acclaimed Negatives (1968) and *A Day in the Death of Joe Egg* (1970) before helming the brilliant black comedy, *The Ruling Class* (1971). After that, he was responsible for a couple of disappointing comedies, *Ghost in the Noonday Sun* (1974), *The Odd Job* (1978), before helming *The Changeling*. His direction of the actors, as well as the understated way he directs the "hauntings," makes this a memorable film. His handling of the seance places it on a par with similar scenes in the classic *Curse of the Demon* (1958) or *Seance on a Wet Afternoon* (1964). In the 1990s, he began creating marvelously crafted crime dramas like *The Krays* (1990), *Let Him Have It* (1991) and *Romeo is Bleeding* (1993).

George C. Scott was still basking in the glow of *Patton* (1970) as well as the controversy caused when he refused the Oscar. He and Trish Van Devere had costarred in a vanity production, *The Savage is Loose* (1974, which Scott also directed), and his stage work was constantly winning high praise, so it was something of a coup to get him to appear in a horror film. Producers Kassar and Vajna would gain more fame in the 1980s as the producers of the Rambo films.

Critically the film garnered praise. *The Motion Picture Guide* calls it, "One of the most genuinely haunting ghost stories in recent years." *Creature Features Movie Guide* notes, "Superior haunted house story heavy with creepy atmosphere. Ending is far-out but doesn't detract from an otherwise perfect tale of the supernatural." *The Video Movie Guide* states the film "is blessed with everything a good thriller needs: a suspenseful story, excellent performances by a top-name cast, and well-paced solid direction by Peter Medak."

The Changeling is proof that you can make a frightening motion picture without massive special effects or gore. It harkens back to the glory days when you needed much more than buckets of blood to make a good creepy movie.

CREDITS: Producer: Joel B. Michaels, Garth Drabinsky; Executive Producers: Mario Kassar, Andrew Vajna; Director: Peter Medak; Director of Photography: John Coquillon; Composer: Rick Wilkins; Story: Russell Hunter; Screenplay: William Gray, Diana Maddox; Production Designer: Trevor Williams; Editor: Laura Lilla Peerson; Supervising Editor: Lou Lombardo; Associated Film Distribution, 1980, 107 Minutes

CAST: George C. Scott...John Russell, Trish Van Devere...Claire Norman, Melvyn Douglas...Senator Joseph Carmichael, Jean Marsh...Joanna Russell, Michelle Martin...Kathy Russell, Madeline Thorton-Sherwood...Mrs. Norman, C.M. Gampel...Mr. Tuttle, Ruth Springford...Miss Huxley, Barry Morse...Parapsychologist, Helen Burns...Leah Harmon, Eric Christmas...Albert Harmon, Frances Hyland...Mrs. Grey, John Colicos...Captain DeWitt

CURSE OF THE DEMON

by Randy Palmer

Horror film fans are really a pretty fortunate lot. Even though the cinemacabre has been polluted by more than a few hideous horrors over the decades, damning the genre in the eyes of the most unforgiving mainstream critics, there are still gorgeous gems to be sifted from the muck and appraised, admired and enjoyed. One of the very best is Jacques Tourneur's *Curse of the Demon* (British title; *Night of the Demon*).

Initially it may not seem that *Curse of the Demon* has a place in a book devoted to a study of cinematic hauntings, but in fact the film journeys beyond the metaphysical borders separating the physical and spiritual worlds, and many of its elements fit neatly into the category. The film's hero-figure is besieged by such ghostly manifestations of evil as a shape-shifting cat-leopard, an amorphous orb of fire, an invisible monster as well as a *visible* monster, accented in the film by its interloper-producer, Hal E. Chester. (More about this anon.) In fact, in its early pre-production stages, *Curse of the Demon* was known as *The Haunted*, certainly an atmospheric if decidedly nondescript title.

The film does not pander to any particular viewer sensibility or expectation. It unapologetically unspools at its own leisurely pace, rewarding those who stick with it by pumping up the chill factor reel by reel. What I find most interesting is that, for more than 30 years after its debut in 1958 (at which time it played as the lower-half of a double-bill with Hammer's *Revenge of Frankenstein*), Americans were watching a movie that had been emasculated by its own producers! Shorn of more than 10 minutes. it is a credit to the filmmakers that *Curse of the Demon* still managed to fascinate and chill viewers. The missing footage was restored in 1986 when Columbia Pictures released the film to videotape. Not surprisingly, the "complete" version turned out to be even more haunting than the original.

The film's roots are found in a story by Móntague R. James, *Casting the Runes*. Originally published in the 1911 James anthology, More *Ghost Stories*, the tale provides more food for thought for Hollywood's cinematic elaborations of classic horror than any of Roger Corman's Poe adaptations, or for that matter Hammer's retelling of Shelley's *Frankenstein* and Stoker's *Dracula*. In the James tale we meet not only the mysterious and evil Karswell, commander of the forces of darkness, we are also introduced to Edward Dunning (paralleling the film's John Holden character) and John Harrington. (Karswell's first victim in the cinema adaptation is named Henry Harrington. In fact, there is also a Henry Harrington in the short story, brother of the unfortunate John, who meets an untimely death after printing a scathing review of an original work of Karswell's called *The History of Witchcraft*. In the film Karswell is not the author of an original black magic treatise but has successfully translated an existing one called *The True Discoveries of the Witches and Demons*, which had been composed entirely in cypher centuries earlier. This tome takes on an

ominous significance somewhat akin to H.P. Lovecraft's fabled *Necronomicon* in that those who uncover its secrets become privy to dangerous demonic powers.)

The term "casting the runes" refers to Karswell's ability to telegraph long-distance curses via runic symbols inscribed on a piece of parchment, another important carryover from printed page to celluloid. Likewise, Dunning unwittingly takes possession of the cursed parchment when it is slipped into his research papers at the British Museum by a "stout, clean-shaven stranger." And again, we learn that Harrington came into possession of the parchment when the same stranger kindly offered him a concert program. Other particulars that mirror the film version include references to the Ancient Mariner, a woodcut depicting a man on a lonely road fleeing a hideous demon, the conjecture that Harrington may have been killed by an unknown animal (he was running from something in the woods and shimmied up a tree to escape, only to fall and break his neck), the calendar with its pages torn out after the predicted death-day, and a climax that partially takes place aboard a train. Obviously, James's short story provides far more than most Hollywood retellings of Poe, Shelley, Lovecraft, Stoker and even King and Barker, although the fiction's John Harrington is transmorgrified into the film's essential love interest, Joanna Harrington, niece of the late Henry.

The most memorable supernatural elements of Casting the Runes found their way into *Curse of the Demon* thanks to a superb script by Charles Bennett. Although Hal E. Chester also receives screen credit as cowriter, his contributions to the screenplay are virtually nil; in fact, Chester's name was added when the picture was finished, and only after Bennett threatened to invoke arbitration proceedings to have his own name removed from the credits! This all came about because Chester, as the executive producer, insisted there must be some kind of visual underscoring of the film's cerebral shocks. He wanted to incorporate lots of "monster footage" into the picture. This must have rankled Bennett, who had labored hard to infuse his script with the kind of quiet terror that had worked so well for Val Lewton's series of RKO chillers in the 1940s. Having worked with thrillmaster Alfred Hitchcock during the director's British period, Bennett definitely knew how to deliver the goods and had little use for Chester's interlocutors. His scripts for Hitchcock included *Blackmail* (Hitch's first sound picture), *The Man Who Knew Too Much* (first version), *Secret Agent The 39 Steps* and the Hollywood-made *Foreign Correspondent*.

The remainder of the *Curse of the Demon* crew consisted of world-class technicians. Production designer Ken Adam would go on to create some of the most elaborate set designs ever for United Artists's future series of James Bond vehicles. And Wally Veevers, one of the film's three special effects coordinators (the other two were George Blackwell and S.D. Onions), would join the team that blew everybody's mind in 1968 with the groundbreaking visuals of Stanley Kubrick's *2001: A Space Odyssey*.

It's not surprising, then, given the number of talented craftsmen involved, that almost everything about *Curse of the Demon* turned out first-rate. The musical score by Clifton Parker seems as if it were composed on an audible panavision canvas, sweeping from one wide-angle extreme to the other. Often delicately lyrical, the *Demon* theme escalates into a brashly horrifying cacophony as Parker twists his musical vision around a handful of notes, pumping up the volume as well as the complexity; what sounded gentle one moment takes on the most haunting melody an instant later. The opening musical signature with its quadruple-chord heralding death and despair might have become as famous as James Bernard's three-note riff for Hammer's *Dracula* series, if only *Curse of the Demon* had been released with as much fanfare as Terence Fisher's *Horror of Dracula*.

Complimenting Parker's memorable work is the monochromatic lushness of Ted Scaife's black-and-white cinematography. Scaife's prowling cinema eye prefigures the stark effectiveness of Mario Bava's best work, especially in the film's other-worldly centerpiece, when Dana Andrews, alone in the woods in the dead of night, finds himself stalked by a malevolent manifestation from Hell.

Kudos go to the many other technicians who helped to make *Curse of the Demon* a modern day masterpiece, including editor Michael Gordon, whose quick scissors give so many scenes their special frisson. Particularly noteworthy is Dana Andrews's singular exploration of Karswell's Lufford Hall mansion and the children's Halloween party that turns into a wind-torn nightmare. All these technicians worked tirelessly under the expert direction of one of the genre's most talented visionaries, Jacques Tourneur. Tourneur had arrived in Hollywood during the reign of the silents, having emigrated from France with his father Maurice.

Joining MGM as a second-unit director, Jacques Tourneur found work on *A Tale of Two Cities* (1935), collaborating with a fellow by the name of Val Lewton. Tourneur and Lewton seemed to hit it off, and Val would have good reason to recall Tourneur's eye for style and detail a few years later, after migrating to RKO and beginning work on a series of classy horror dramas for the company.

Although he directed a variety of mainstream titles (*Out of the Past*, *Experiment Perilous*, *Easy Living*), Tourneur is best remembered for a trio of films he directed for Val Lewton in the early 1940s.

Lewton contacted Tourneur to offer him the opportunity to direct the first in the new RKO series, but Jacques actually ended up directing three of this new group of fearfilms: *Cat People* (1942), *The Leopard Man* (1943) and *I Walked with a Zombie* (1944).

Many of the elements Tourneur used to craft and sustain moods of unease and fear in his films for Lewton were refined and repeated with even greater success in *Curse of the Demon*. The use of light and shade was especially effective—low-lit corridors falling off into deep shadows evoked a kind of voracious omnipresence eager to descend upon the helpless and defenseless; phantoms, guided by some harmful and as yet unrevealed predator, seemingly lurked around each twist in the roadway and in the corners of every darkened room. Augmented by Clifton Parker's superb music score as well as some imaginative sound effects, these snatches of fear so expertly suggested by Tourneur preyed on the collective conscious of a captive audience and gave the film its special power.

In the film's opening shot, Tourneur conjures an immediate sense of the unearthly with a strange, glowing light that peers from between the trees crowded along a dark country road. But it is only the headlight of an oncoming automobile, after all. As we join the driver of the car, Prof. Henry Harrington (Maurice Denham), we find ourselves trapped inside a relentless, claustrophobic environment. The twin headlights cut a meager swath through the onrushing darkness; trees press inward from the sides of the curving road, shutting out the moonlight. Like something out of Lovecraft country, the road seems to wind forever onward, leading nowhere....

But at last Harrington reaches his destination: the stately mansion known as Lufford Hall. These are the grounds of Dr. Julian Karswell (Niall MacGinnis), an outwardly pleasant fellow who just happens to be an avowed Satanist. Harrington pleads with Karswell to "stop this thing you've started," and for the benefit of the viewer, the sorcerer recapitulates certain recent events. But the bottom line is this: Harrington has publicly ridiculed Karswell and his cult of devil-worshipping followers. Karswell, who claims merely to desire privacy for himself and his group, reminds Harrington, "You said 'do your worst,' and that's precisely what I did." Apparently, Karswell made his move only when backed into a corner, and not without at least some advance warning—hardly the type of behavior one might expect from a self-proclaimed warlock who wields such ungodly power. This is one of the first indications that Karswell is completely atypical of the stereotyped horror movie heavy. Unlike, say, the icily menacing Hjalmar Poelzig (Boris Karloff) of Edgar G. Ulmer's *The Black Cat* (Universal, 1934), or the seemingly civil devil-worshippers of Mark Robson's *The Seventh Victim* (RKO, 1943), evil here is presented as an almost bumbling, clownish inversion—but no less deadly for all that. (A later scene finds Karswell entertaining at a children's party—generously held on his own mansion grounds—while outfitted head to toe in classic clown garb, including X-ed out eyes and bulbous "red" nose.)

Harrington finally departs Karswell's estate satisfied (mistakenly) that the hellish hex has been lifted, but only moments after arriving home he is assaulted by a hideous display of

Karswell's power. Amongst the nearby treetops an envelope of fiery smoke pulses outward, coalescing into the gigantic form of a demon from the netherpits of hell. In his panic to escape, Harrington backs his car into a power line; the downed wires snake back and forth, spitting electricity as Harrington climbs out of the damaged vehicle and scampers away. But he tumbles backward onto the wires as the creature reaches out an immense, clawed talon, and an enormous hoof smashes down beside him....

Tourneur was adamant: he was not going to reveal the fire demon to his audience prematurely, if at all, but producer Hal Chester was just as adamant about showing the creature in the opening reel. Tourneur went on record years ago as saying that he wanted to use "just four or five frames" of the demon during the climax to tease the audience. The frames would flash by so quickly viewers would be wondering if they really saw anything at all. It was a strategy similar to the one Tourneur had used in *Cat People* 15 years earlier, when he spliced in a short, dark shot of a black panther stalking Kent Smith and Jane Randolph in response to RKO's insistence that the audience be shown the "monster." Tourneur and others have claimed that Chester added *most* of the footage of the fire monster to *Curse of the Demon*. In an interview given years afterward, Tourneur admitted it was "a mistake" to show the demon in the opening reel, and this suggests that he may have had more to do with the on-screen presence of the creature than most of us have ever suspected.

Whether or not it's true, here is another bit of food for thought: Charles Bennett's original script draft cites *both* appearances of the title monster, specifically referring to it as "a huge fire demon" and a "hellish creature." Of course it may have been Tourneur's intention to dispense with the demon described by Bennett all along, but there is one especially curious shot in the early sequence described above: the abrupt appearance of a behemoth hoof which appears in the frame after Harrington has been electrocuted. The shot is so different in texture, lighting and juxtaposition of elements from the obvious cut-ins of the longshots (a rather good-looking miniature) and close-ups, that this single composition was most likely a concession by the director to the powers-that-be. Though Tourneur never mentioned it in subsequent interviews, there is the possibility that he had forgotten some of the details after so many years. In any event, the sequence is impressive if slightly marred by the intrusion of the fire demon in close-ups. (The excision of all of the demon close ups and perhaps at least half of the longshots would have benefited the film greatly.)

The introduction of Dr. John Holden (Dana Andrews) as the famous debunking psychologist, sort of a 1958-era Amazing Randi, involves a bit of farfetched, albeit necessary, exposition: attempting to catch a nap aboard an intercontinental flight, Holden buries his face in a newspaper, which just happens to have his photograph and accompanying news item on the upfacing page. It is here that Holden first encounters Joanna Harrington (Peggy Cummins), niece of the late professor.

To Tourneur's credit, *Curse of the Demon*'s love interest is admirably restrained. Holden's and Joanna's preoccupation with one another is minimized, and it never seems forced or unnatural—they are casually attracted to each other when circumstances cause their individual paths to connect, and their mutual affection grows naturally as the film progresses. The word "love" is never mentioned, so the affair takes on a genuineness that is absent in many (if not most) genre productions of the 1940s and '50s. By the end of the picture it is clear they have fallen in love, but neither character is the type to fall madly head over heels for the other. In one of their first and most natural displays of boy-girl interest, Holden purrs, "I never had a kindergarten teacher as pretty as you are" (she, a teacher, has been talking about her kindergarten class) while she tries reading him entries from her late uncle's diary. Joanna's smile as she slips away from Holden, playfully scolding, "You'll listen whether you like it or not," is a barometer of her own feelings, and despite her shifting body language, it's obvious she is interested in him. But rather than play up this angle (as the Columbia suits doubtless would have preferred), Tourneur shifts the characters' attention—and ours—back to the problem at hand, which is: how can Holden sidestep Karswell's curse?

Following Harrington's death, Holden begins an investigation into Karswell's shady devil cult activities. When Holden ignores Karswell's polite warnings to cease and desist, Karswell manages to slip him the cursed parchment when their paths cross in the British Museum. Researching the history of devil worship, Holden has requested a copy of *The True Discoveries of the Witches and Demons*, but the museum's only copy seems to be missing. "It is peculiar," the librarian (John Salew) admits—a clue that the book has been stolen. Karswell, lurking nearby, jumps at the opportunity to put his personal copy of the rare tome at Holden's disposal, but it's all a ruse designed to set the wheels of wickedness in motion. From this point (though neither he nor we discover Holden actually is in possession of the cursed parchment until much later in the film) Holden is on the receiving end of various minor manifestations of the unusual. These incidents, which begin unobtrusively with small, idiosyncratic occurrences (including something as minimal as "a tune running through my mind") escalate into ever and ever larger projections of unreality into the mundane world of reality. In one of the eeriest sequences, Holden is walking through the dark and lonely corridors of his hotel (where are all the other guests, anyway?) when he hears a shrill musical motif followed by a series of thumping beats—the calling card of the unseen demon. Viewers who are particularly attuned to the film have described the sequence as truly "spine tingling." Much of the credit here goes to Ted Scaife's cinematography, Clifton Parker's other-worldly music, and Tourneur's low-key direction, with the camera peering down long, ill-lit hallways that are swallowed up by an omnipresent darkness. We find ourselves wondering—*what* could be hiding in the darkness only a few yards away? The relentless pounding (of hoofbeats?) grows louder as the hauntingly ululant music reaches a crescendo... and of course everything ceases abruptly as a door is pushed open to reveal—not the demon, nor Karswell, nor any manifestation of the supernatural at all, but merely Holden's associates, professors Mark O'Brien (Liam Redmond) and K. T. Kumar (Peter Elliott). There is an immediate cessation of the weird music and thumping footsteps, and our subjective paranormal experience is suddenly over.

In spite of his latest taste of the supernatural, Holden remains steadfast in his refusal to acknowledge the powers of darkness. But the accumulation of not-so-easily explainable events are beginning to take their toll on Holden's psychic armor. The littlest things—a strange tune, a trick of the light, disappearing handwriting, pages ripped from a desk calendar—are combining with other events which cannot be so easily explained. The film's most impressive setpiece—Holden's chase through the woods by a demonic ball of fire—can hardly be discounted as anything other than a manifestation of the supernatural, but the pragmatic Holden tries his damnedest to dismiss it anyway. When Joanna pointedly asks him, "What did you run from in the woods?" Holden replies nonchalantly, "Oh, some trick gadget that Karswell set up." In the same breath he admits he "fell for the bait like an idiot," but only because he has been "stampeded into a state of hysteria" (by Joanna, a steadfast believer in the powers of darkness).

As H.P. Lovecraft knew very well, sanity can be maintained only by an existence firmly rooted in reality. Lose your grip on reality and you risk losing your mind. Without making such a statement, the filmmakers have patterned the John Holden character after some of Lovecraft's own. Holden may feel sanity slipping away from him, which is why it becomes so important for him to find a way to explain away all the supernatural events that happen to unfold in his presence.

Curse of the Demon is not so much a story about a curse or a demon as it is about the psychological make up of a man who must give up that which he holds most dear—that is, his belief in a rational world explainable by science and governed by the forces of nature—in order to accept a reality that has been perverted by the very forces he has been denying throughout his life. Since everything that happens in the film can be explained as either (a) a manifestation of evil, or (b) a coincidence, hallucination, delusion, etc., the story can be interpreted in two ways: as either a supernatural fable or a tale of rationality taken to extremes.

The universe of the story is one set in ordinary, everyday reality. The character of John Holden is an extension of this reality and therefore is the figure most viewers will readily identify with. However, everyone around Holden has either direct evidence of the existence of the supernatural or professes a strong belief in it. This kind of overwhelming contrast goes far in helping audiences overcome their innate sense of disbelief. In fact, whether they realized it or not (and they probably didn't), Tourneur and Bennett were following the criteria established by H.P. Lovecraft in his *Notes on the Writing of Weird Fiction* when they began adapting *Casting the Runes* for the screen. Lovecraft's paper stressed the importance of playing a single element of horror or fantasy against a conservative and realistic background. Without appropriate and ac curate historical and geographical detail and a solid foothold in present-day reality, the viewer/reader must find it difficult to accept a supernatural premise. Thus the universe of *Curse of the Demon* is a universe of the mundane, the ordinary, into which irrationality suddenly intrudes. Holden embodies the viewer's innate sense of skepticism, and as the character's certainty that he lives in a sane and ordered universe slowly erodes away, so does the viewer's.

For contrast consider, say, more recent film fantasy examples such as *Hellbound: Hellraiser 2* or Don Coscarelli's *Phantasm* series. Each picture is woven almost entirely from a fabric of unreality, with numerous outré occurrences happening consecutively or even simultaneously. That all-important suspension of disbelief is much more difficult to achieve, much less maintain, in such a setting.

In *Curse of the Demon*'s universe it might seem as if there are *too many* characters willing to accept the existence of the paranormal. But it's doubtful Tourneur intended his audience to look at the film as a statement about gullibility and the art of the con, because the director himself held fast to certain beliefs which in fact encompass aspects of what most people call the supernatural. However, every unexplainable event that transpires in *Curse of the Demon* is buffered by a completely mundane condition, statement, or explanation that suggests these occurrences are merely coincidences, hallucinations, or the products of sick and/or twisted minds; the door has been left open, if but a crack, for those who desire more down-to-earth explanations. In this interpretation Harrington was merely electrocuted, not mauled by a demon from hell; Holden's subjective experiences are mere "mind games" (instead of literally hearing a perversion of an Irish folk tune, it *really* is just a tune that keeps running through his mind); the medium Mr. Meek (Reginald Beckwith) has no actual spiritual powers but is merely a voice impersonator, as first suggested by Holden; Karswell's windstorm is a freak coincidence whose origin lies in global weather conditions, not his self-professed satanic powers; etc., etc.

Shortly before the mid-point of the picture, Holden, at Joanna's prompting, examines some papers in his briefcase and discovers that Karswell had already slipped him the dreaded parchment. Immediately the thin slip of paper tears from his grasp and, as if guided by some malign intelligence, attempts to destroy itself in the room's raging fireplace. (It's prevented from "escaping" by a screen grate.) Once again Holden piles rationalization upon rationalization: "it's just the wind," he offers lamely while shutting an open window, and when that doesn't wash he insists, "there's a draft from the chimney." Moments later, when the parchment finally "gives up" and falls to the floor, inert, Joanna pointedly asks, "What made them stop?" Holden finally admits he doesn't know— a breakthrough of sorts for a character as stubborn as this.

Prior to this exchange Holden had been besieged only by rather minor occult nuisances. A moment after meeting Karswell for the first time inside the British Museum, Holden's senses begin playing tricks; Karswell's retreating form glimmers oddly, almost as if seen through waves of undulating summer heat. Handwriting on a calling card—"Allowed two weeks"—vanishes on second glance. Holden assumes the card has been chemically treated (Adams' disappearing ink gag?) and has it tested at a local laboratory. When the lab technician assures him the card is "100% clean," Holden writes off the whole thing as a cheap magic trick. (It *is* Adams' ink!)

But later occurrences can't be so easily explained away, and herein lies the great power of this film. At Karswell's annual Halloween party (given in honor of the village children, incidentally—does this sound like the agenda of a wicked devil worshipper?), he reveals wistfully to Holden, "I used to earn my living like this years ago." It's a telling line. Having to forsake the innocent frivolity of an earlier existence in order to enjoy his betrothal to the Prince of Darkness, Karswell seems to recognize that he lost something precious somewhere along the line. But it's a momentary respite, for underneath the cherubic exterior is a deadly, dual personality: the gentle, loving caretaker of childish imagination, the side that seems to almost regret choosing the "lefthand path," and the decidedly evil magician who forfeits sleight-of-hand for the warlock's inverted cross, the kind of person who will conjure a demon from hell merely to prove a point. ("You'd spoil the party," Holden quips.) Moments later Karswell takes umbrage at what he perceives as Holden's pomposity. He poses the unanswerable question, "Where does imagination end and reality begin? How can we differentiate between the powers of darkness and the power of the mind?" The clown abruptly disappears and the evil magician takes its place. To make his point Karswell invokes what he calls "the medieval witch's specialty—a windstorm." As winds gust and howl and begin to build to an uncontrollable rage, the fun and games of the party are obliterated; Holden is taken aback by a bolt of lightning that strikes much too close for comfort, loosening an enormous tree branch that crashes to the ground beside him. When he glances back at Karswell, perhaps expecting to see the elder man running for cover, he sees instead a twisted perversion of the classic clown face: the sorcerer's pancake makeup and bulbous nose take on an eerie malevolence as Karswell stands motionless, hands clasped patiently, smiling incongruously in the midst of raging, cyclonic winds and the terrified screams of panicking children. In the face of the unexplainable, Holden grasps uncertainly at rationality. And no matter how farfetched the rational becomes, he still doggedly pursues it. (To obtain the shrieking wind effect Tourneur was striving for, four airplane engines were employed to generate high winds. Truckloads of leaves were emptied in front of the engines so that the air would be filled with scattering debris.)

Inside Lufford Hall, Karswell apologizes for his "miscalculation" (he hadn't intended to conjure a storm of such intensity) but again Holden scoffs. Karswell is tiring of the game; he turns on Holden and admonishes him to change his mind "before it's too late." (It's interesting to note that, traditionally, it is the female figure who is terrorized or haunted or pursued across the landscape of the horror film. In *Curse of the Demon* it is the male. The character of Joanna Harrington is almost never endangered, except near the finale when Karswell kidnaps her—and even then his intention is not really to harm her, but merely to prevent her from delivering a message to Holden. More on this later.)

Niall MacGinnis, offered the part of devil's advocate Julian Karswell, wrapped his larynx around this plum of a role and ran with it. He is at once delightful and disarming, yet dangerous and not a little demonic. In contrast, Dana Andrews's turn as the down-to-earth John Holden is solid but curiously uninspiring. His recitation of the script's lines is functional and serves Tourneur's purposes, but I suspect Andrews may not have had much of a real interest in playing the part. (He often refused to answer interviewers' questions about *Curse of the Demon*, and it is known that he accepted the film in order to work with Jacques Tourneur, not because he felt any special affinity for the material. A verbal altercation with executive producer Hal Chester probably didn't do much to generate fond memories, either. Andrews even threatened to walk off the picture if Chester persisted in interfering with day-to-day production chores.)

Some horror fans believe that the seance sequence is *Curse of the Demon*'s low point, but in fact there are a few subtleties interwoven into the action and dialogue which make it more interesting than it first might appear. Mr. Meek may be a voice impersonator, as Holden steadfastly believes, but he could just as well be a genuine medium. Tourneur isn't telling, we must draw our own conclusions.

Shortly after Mr. Meek arrives home to greet his guests (including a reluctant Holden and a hopeful Joanna, as well as Mrs. Karswell, who in fact has arranged the rendezvous), he spouts a few lines that do little to endear him to the skeptics on the screen or in the audience. As they take seats around the medium table, Mr. Meek glances rather suspiciously at his wife (Rosamund Greenwood) and says, "Well, Maggie, no use wasting these good people's time The nuance of the vocal inflection, coupled with the surreptitious glance, has the effect of suggesting to the viewer that Mr. Meek is more mimicker than mystic. As Holden later tells Joanna, "Your friend Mrs. Karswell staged the whole thing. She's looking out for her son's interests, not mine." That certainly sounds logical.

On the other hand, there are one or two events which would seem to suggest that Mr. Meek is indeed a legitimate medium with the power to communicate beyond the grave. In the first stages of his trance, Mr. Meek speaks to those in the room with voices that seemingly cannot be his own, including that of a little girl who cries, "Oh mummy, I can't find Frederika!" (This single line was shorn from U.S. theatrical prints.) Finally Mr. Meek speaks in the voice of Joanna's uncle, the late Prof. Harrington, and Joanna sits bolt upright. "That is my uncle, I know his voice!" she insists, as Holden tells her, "Don't be ridiculous, these things are all faked." Nevertheless, Harrington's voice continues to reveal information that Holden will later find important. ("Karswell has translated the old book. The answer is there.") As Holden prepares to reach for the light switch, the voice of Harrington takes on an eerily authentic tone. Re-experiencing his own death in the third person (Harrington's voice cries out, "It's in the trees!"), we hear the unmistakable sound of the unfortunate man's death-cry. Interestingly, he scream on the soundtrack is the same scream we heard when Harrington first saw the demon in the opening reeL (It's a very distinctive scream.) Why would the filmmakers take the trouble to redub this particular scream unless Tourneur wanted to give his audience an (admittedly subtle) clue that Mr. Meek is in fact the genuine article?

Whether Mr. Meek is a true medium or not, Holden decides that the whole episode has been staged by Mrs. Karswell in an effort to pressure him into giving up the investigation into her son's nefarious activities. (Earlier during the seance Mrs. Karswell interpreted Mr. Meek's recitations for Holden. When Harrington's voice is heard to say, "must tell Holden... he can't fight it... it's too strong," Mrs. Karswell whispers to Holden, "he means you must give up the investigation." No wonder Holden figured the seance was a phony!)

Following their experience with Mr. Meek, Joanna is determined to sneak into Karswell's estate to see if he really does have a word key that will unlock the secrets of *The True Discoveries of the Witches and Demons*. Not too surprisingly, this turns out to be a ploy to get Holden involved in the scheme. ("Aren't you even going to try and stop me?" Joanna asks coyly after articulating her plan to a smirking John Holden.) Of course he's not going to let her endanger herself, so he approaches Karswell's sprawling estate from the back. This means he must traverse the woods bordering Lufford Hall in the dead of night—not just once, but twice—and it is here that Tourneur gooses his audience with some of the best cinematic scares this side of *Cat People*, *I Walked with a Zombie* and *The Leopard Man*.

When Tourneur directed those pictures for Val Lewton in the early 1940s, he utilized an audience scare tactic that has since become known as the Lewton "bus." The term derives from a scene in *Cat People* in which the hiss of a bus' air

brakes mimics the growl of a feline predator. There was also the Lewton "walk," so named because in each of his RKO chillers one or more characters experienced an extended walk through lonely and foreboding territory. *Curse of the Demon* combined both techniques for a positively chilling effect during John Holden's trek through the woods outside Lufford Hall.

As Holden carefully picks his way through the dense forest, we notice unearthly lights glowing behind twisted oaks and a layer of background mist. The overall effect is decidedly sinister and otherworldly. Despite our trepidation, Holden arrives safely at the mansion (of course the return trip will prove to be quite different).

In the scenes that follow Tourneur proves he is as much a manipulator of audiences as the masterful Alfred Hitchcock. Repeated "buses"—close-ups of hands intruding into the edge of the frame as Holden takes a Lewton "walk" through the darkened house—provide a plethora of sudden starts (though some of these are lost in non-letterbox television broadcasts). Interestingly, Tourneur also uses these cuts to suggest the presence of a phantom follower: after each shot of the intruding hand, a complementing long shot plainly demonstrates that there is *no one at all* behind Holden!

Holden's battle with Grymalkyn the Cat-Leopard, intended as the highlight of this extended sequence, unfortunately leaves much to be desired. While the camera setup, staging and lighting all are top-notch, the leopard prop compromises the scene's integrity. It is simply much too obvious. Dana Andrews deserves kudos for playing it straight and giving it his best shot, though.

After a brief encounter with Karswell and his mother, Holden retreats and returns to the path through the woods. This time, however, the trees seem almost alive with a kind of otherworldly energy. There is a touch of an *Alice in Wonderland*-ish dilation of time—the return trip takes Holden much longer than his first trek through the woods—and he has difficulty finding the correct path and picking his way through the brambles. Branches seem to cluster together to delay his progress; one snaps downward which he manages to catch in his hands (a great "bus"). Then there is the sound of something awful, something enormous, approaching: thunderous footfalls reverberate in the night, and an invisible entity makes its presence known as its hoofprints appear in the soil.

Now on the very edge of pure panic, Holden blindly stumbles through the forest, a glowing ball of smoke and fire billowing up behind him. The harder he runs, the bigger the fire grows. When it seems as if he is about to be swallowed alive, everything returns to normal, the ball of fire slowly contracting to a mathematical point in the sky above him.

The special effects in this key sequence are superb. The gaseous cloud of smoke and fire, a fairly simple trick of superimposition, is nonetheless quite impressive, as are the hoofprints that appear one by one on the forest floor. These are simple effects, but it's difficult to imagine any way in which they could have been more impressively presented. What really makes these visual tricks work so well is Tourneur's ability to manipulate the audience, creating a state of anticipation that is rewarded by the materialization of the supernatural. The sequence is paced so well, photographed with such verisimilitude and noir-ish technique, and scored so powerfully, the viewer is completely caught up in the fictional circumstances. This really is one of the few times in the history of horror cinema that the required "suspension of disbelief" is virtually *compelled* by the images and action on the screen.

If the viewer experiences such a rush during this nightmarish sequence, what can we expect from the character of John Holden himself? Ahh, typical Holden! Following up at the local police station, he describes the events and even admits, "I could have sworn the smoke came after me." But before long he's back to his old self, rationalizing to Joanna that he merely fell "for some trick gadget Karswell rigged up." When he complains that Joanna has virtually stampeded him into a state of hysteria, she takes off in a huff, setting the stage for the film's final sequences.

As Holden begins preparing for the hypnotherapy demonstration scheduled for that evening, he casually mentions wanting to get back to the United States "as soon as possible." This could just be impatience on Holden's part—he's been in England for several weeks already—but mightn't it also be attributable to an uncharacteristic unsureness on the scientist's part? Perhaps Holden has finally experienced too many coincidences, too many unexplained events, to shrug off the supernatural any longer. Perhaps he hopes that by returning to the States he can sweep the supernatural under the rug, out of sight, and out of mind. Tourneur, of course, isn't saying, but the character's remark could be interpreted either way.

Holden 's uncertainty about Karswell and the devil-cult come to the fore during his questioning of Rand Hobart. While Prof. O'Brien presides over the demonstration designed to unlock the hibernating mind of Hobart, Holden uncharacteristically lunges at a sudden opportunity to learn more about the Karswell curse. Using a combination of chemical stimulants and hypnotherapy, O'Brien breaks through the wall surrounding Hobart's mind, who now recalls the details of Karswell's cult, and what he describes to O'Brien and Holden turns their blood to ice. When Holden reveals the parchment with the runic symbols, Hobart leaps up, scurries down a hallway and through a window, and plummets to his death several stories below. "Oh, this is terrible, really terrible," bemoans Holden's assistant, Lloyd Williamson (Ewan Roberts). Holden, however, isn't listening; his mind is elsewhere. The accumulation of so many coincidences and quirks of fate have rattled him to the point that he is ready to stop taking chances with his future, at last.

Whether Holden has really changed his thinking about the supernatural or is simply taking no chances doesn't matter, because if he was as steadfastly certain about the supernatural as he previously claimed to be, he wouldn't bother doing what he does next: return the parchment to Karswell. It's a little difficult to accept that this last bit of "evidence" is enough to convince Holden of the reality of evil, simply because it would be so easy to dismiss Hobart's statements as the ramblings of a lunatic. Certainly more weight should have been ascribed to physical manifestations of the supernatural such as the pursuing ball of fire outside Lufford Hall?

While there is room for some debate—when exactly did Holden change his mind about the reality of the paranormal?—the point remains that by this time Holden has grown so unsure of his perception of the world around him that he is willing to subvert all his convictions in the face of possible danger. The viewer accepts this as an outgrowth of the character's experiences within the context of the storyline.

Columbia Pictures excised over 10 minutes of footage from U.S. prints to limit the combined running times of *Curse of the Demon* and its co-feature, *The Revenge of Frankenstein*, to under three hours. This ensured that theaters could play the double-bill as many as four times a day. It's remarkable that this emasculated form of Tourneur's film was the version that received accolades from critics, and upon which all favorable fan opinions were based for so many years. In fact, Columbia not only removed portions of the film, but shuffled the order of a couple of sequences (for no good reason that I can think of). In the original version Holden is haunted by an eerie Irish melody (the "distorted folk tune" that keeps running through his mind) and hears the footsteps of the unseen demon after finding the parchment hidden among his briefcase papers. In the 1958 U.S. release version, this scene was moved to an earlier spot in the picture. It's a mystery why Columbia felt the need to switch the running order, but fans are lucky that the original sequencing as well as the missing 10-plus minutes were restored when *Curse of the Demon* was released to home video in 1986.

The footage which had been missing for so many years from American prints of *Curse of the Demon* adds significant background details to the characters of Karswell and his mother. They are a very close pair—perhaps a little too close—and in fact it appears that Karswell has little or no other social contact, except for (presumably) his satanic ringleading activities, which we never see. Mrs. Karswell is the classic doting/interfering mother—wonderfully played by Athene Seyler—who, it would appear, has learned to take her son's dark preoccupation with at least a grain of salt. Until the complete version of the film was made available on videotape it was never very clear whether Mrs. Karswell believed in Julian's powers or not. She ostensibly tried to help Holden intermittently by involving him in such questionable affairs as the seance, but one could never be sure what she really thought of it all. Her priority was getting Holden to halt his investigation into Julian's affairs; whether because she feared for his life or because she thought it was a nuisance (and knew it was her son's wish that Holden leave him alone), we couldn't be certain. When the missing footage surfaced we finally learned that, yes *indeed*, Mrs. Karswell feared for Holden's life. While it is obvious that she loves her son very much, it is equally obvious that she is growing weary of his devil-may-care ways. Halfway through the film she begins feeling anxious to bring Julian's misdeeds to some kind of conclusion. Her hand-wringing line, "All this evil must end, Mrs. Harrington, it must *end*," leaves no doubt that she

has accepted the powers of darkness as a legitimate force that must be reckoned with. The restored footage helped to round out Mrs. Karswell's character enormously.

In the final analysis, it would appear that Mrs. Karswell dotes on her son in the most smothering way imaginable, yet she fears him at the same time. Obviously Mrs. Karswell has interfered with her son's life to the point that he has forsaken a family of his own (he still lives with his mommy, after all), and in fact may have even forsaken life itself. In another bit of dialogue that had been missing from U.S. prints, Mrs. Karswell mentions to Joanna that Julian ought to be married. Almost in the same breath she queries, "*You're* not married, are *you* dear?" Karswell, standing nearby, feigns embarrassment. "Oh mother, mother!" he scolds sheepishly. It's only a momentary vibe, but the interplay between the characters, the timing, and the amplitude of Karswell's line suggests that he might actually approve of his mother's shameless attempt at matchmaking.

The film's traintrack climax is a textbook example of suspense-generating technique. Holden fortuitously catches up to Karswell on the Southampton train. The two sit directly across from one another in a private car, exchanging uneasy pleasantries. Convinced (quite correctly) that Holden is attempting to shift the focus of the curse by secretly passing the parchment back to him, Karswell struggles mightily to avoid any personal contact. But during a brief moment of confusion when two policemen show up (they've been tipped off by Holden, but the cops think *he's* the one who's nuts), Holden is able to sneak the parchment back by hiding it inside the pocket of Karswell's coat. The surprise and fear on Karswell's face as he realizes he's been duped and is now about to become his own victim are priceless. The parchment flies from Karswell's fingers, and the aging, paunchy figure rushes headlong through the train cars in a desperate attempt to retrieve it. It's a pitiable sight, and one can't help feeling for this man who has become entrapped by his own macabre machinations. Jumping offboard when the train pulls to a stop at the next station, Karswell finally catches up to the parchment... too late. It crumbles into ash as the fire demon materializes above the retreating train.

It is here that Tourneur envisioned a quick cut of the demon mauling a diminutive figure of Julian Karswell, and in fact there are brief side and front views of the monster raking its talons down the doll-size magician's chest. However, both cuts certainly total significantly more than the "four or five frames" Tourneur had wanted.

Hal Chester added yet more close-ups of the fire-breathing demon, and recut the film. Charles Bennett was so upset with the film after Chester got through with it, he asked that his name be removed from the credits. Instead, Chester merely added his own name, so that the screenwriting credit ended up reading "by Charles Bennett and Hal E. Chester."

Had Chester kept the added monster footage to a minimum, *Curse of the Demon*'s monster scenes *might* have been acceptable, but so many close-ups are employed repeatedly, intercut with long shots of the miniature demon on the train tracks, that the overall effect Tourneur wanted was ruined entirely.

Yet, even the interference from Chester and Columbia's front office moneymen failed to damage such a ghoulishly great gem too severely. The climax of *Curse of the Demon* remains one of fantasy filmdom's greatest moments—a moment that must have made the late Tourneur (he died in 1977) very proud.

In the film's last scene, when Holden overhears the police detectives and trainmen discussing the mutilated state of the dead man's body ("The train must have hit him," someone remarks), he stops just short of approaching the twisted, smoking human wreckage. Turning back to Joanna, Holden acknowledges, "Maybe it's better not to know." There follows a final surprise "bus" as a roaring train engine screams into the frame, obliterating the forms of Holden and Joanna. When the final train car leaves the frame, the viewer is alone on the tracks; Joanna and Holden have vanished ... presumably into the train station, but then, one can never be too sure....

What makes *Curse of the Demon* such a deliciously frightening film experience? Fear of the unknown is humankind's greatest fear, and Tourneur's film exploits this fear unmercifully. With his many years of motion picture experience, the director had learned how to manipulate an audience, just as Hitchcock and other great filmmakers did. Filling his film with images of darkness and leaving several events unexplained helped enormously in pumping up *Demon*'s scare quotient.

But let's not ignore the hell-beast itself. Admittedly, the power of the demon image is diminished through overexposure, but that which the demon represents—fear, pain, death, hell itself—is finally and irrevocably *irreducible*. As Prof. O'Brien remarks to Holden virtually every culture has its own conception of this creature "whose legend has persisted since the dark ages." Ours is no different.

CREDITS: Director: Jacques Tourneur; Screenplay: Hal Chester, Charles Bennett from the story "Casting the Runes" by Montague R. James; Photography: Ted Scaife; Score: Clifton Parker; Art Director: Ken Adam; Effects: George Blackwell, Wally Veevers; Col/Sabre; 1956; 83 minutes

CAST: Dana Andrews...Dr. John Holden, Niall MacGinnis...Dr. Julian Karswell, Peggy Cummins...Joanna Harrington, Reginald Beckwith...Mr. Meek, Athene Seyler...Mrs. Karswell, Maurice Denham...Prof. Henry Harrington, Liam Redmond...Prof. Mark O'Brien, Ewan Roberts...Lloyd Williamson.

THE HAUNTING

by Bryan Senn

> Adult in concept and wide in scope, *The Haunting* is designed not only to appeal to those who approach the supernatural from an intellectual level, but also to the legions of movie patrons who delight in a genuine ghost story.— *The Haunting* pressbook.

> Silence lay steadily against the wood and stone of Hill House, and whatever walked there, walked alone.—Opening narration.

Ghost Cinema, like horseracing, has its own "triple crown." The first leg comes in the form of a truly haunting tale of love and hate from beyond the grave, *The Uninvited* (1944). The next big event in the apparitional arena is a terrifying study of repressed hysteria and supernatural possession, *The Innocents* (1961). But the undisputed jewel in the ghostly crown, the Kentucky Derby of spectral cinema, is Robert Wise's chilling masterpiece of understated terror, *The Haunting*.

"While I was at the studio doing post production on *West Side Story*," recalled producer/director Robert Wise in *Midnight Marquee* #37, "I read a review of [Shirley Jackson's novel,] *The Haunting of Hill House* in *Time* magazine. The review was so interesting that I went to a book store on Hollywood Boulevard and brought it back to the office to read. I was sitting on the couch in my office reading a sequence that really had me on the edge of my seat. Suddenly, Nelson Gidding, a writer from across the hail, burst into my office and I jumped about four feet in the air! I knew then this book had to be made into a film."

But Wise wasn't sure he'd be the one to make it. "I called nervously to see if it might be available," remembered the director in *Bright Lights* #11, "because usually by the time a book comes out in New York, the big movie companies have scouts back there, story departments, and they grab it up and it's gone. Happily, I found out this one hadn't been picked up."

Wise intended to do *The Haunting* for United Artists, the studio for which he had just completed *West Side Story* [1961] "I persuaded United Artists to buy the book rights for me and finance a screenplay," the director told this author. (Unless otherwise cited, all quotes by Robert Wise are from a 1995 interview conducted by the author.) "And I got Nelson Gidding, who did *I Want to Live!* [1958] for me, to write the screenplay. When we got it done, however, for some reason or another United Artists got a little cold on it and didn't want to proceed with it. So I talked to my agent about it. I had left a contract with MGM a few years before; I got out of the contract early but I had to promise to give them another film. My agent suggested that maybe this could be the script that would fulfill that commitment. So we took it over to MGM."

There the project hit another snag when that celebrated studio balked at sinking big bucks into a horror picture. "They liked it very much," Wise recalled, "but they didn't want to put over a million dollars into it because of the material and the fact that we wouldn't be using big name stars. And the best budget I could get out of MGM Culver City here was one million, four hundred thousand" (nearly half-again what the studio was willing to spend).

Fortunately, fate took a hand. "I was about to go over to London for a command performance of *West Side Story*," recounted Wise, "and somebody said 'well, you know MOM has a studio outside of London [Wood Studios], and maybe they could get you a better budget on the script over there than Culver City.' So I took it along with me when I went to London and gave it to the people at the studio. They liked the idea and came back with a budget of a million, fifty thousand. And so that's why we made it over there, as what we call a runaway production—runaway because I could do it cheaper there."

Though shot in England with mostly English actors, Wise retained the story's American setting. "I was insistent on keeping the New England background," explained the director in *Fangoria* #44, "because Shirley Jackson is a New Englander and wrote in that area. I felt that this kind of story, with an old haunted house, would be fresher material set in America, in New England, than it would in Great Britain, because England abounds in haunted houses. Even though we shot in London, we kept the New England setting without too much trouble." Wise later added that it was no more difficult to transform Olde England into New England than having to "block off the road for a mile or two so I could have [Julie Harris] driving on the right side—that kind of thing. It was very simple, wasn't hard at all."

With the financial difficulties solved, Wise could turn to other problems. "We didn't like that title [*The Haunting of Hill House*]," the director stated in *Fantastic Films*, vol. 2, no. 4. "When I say 'we,' that particularly means me and Nelson Gidding, who did the screenplay. It seemed cumbersome, and the book had not done that well. Jackson is a marvelous writer, but her books were never tremendous sellers, they got most of their acclaim from the critics. We always felt that maybe there was a better title somewhere, and actually, she gave it to us. We had some questions about the story and her intent. Since she lived back in Vermont where her husband was a professor at Bennington, we made arrangements to fly back one weekend and meet with her. We wanted to talk about some things in her story, to get some clarifications on what her intentions were. We had lunch with her that day and during the course of it we asked her if she'd ever had any other title for it. She said, 'Well, I really hadn't. The only title I really ever seriously considered was *The Haunting of Hill House*. But the other one I had thought of for awhile was just *The Haunting*.' It was in front of us all the time, but we never saw it. She's the one who gave us that."

Wise next had to find a cast. He ultimately chose one made up of primarily classically trained and well-respected stars of the stage, including Richard Johnson and Claire Bloom (two British Shakespearean actors), and Julie Harris (an American Broadway star). To round out his leading quartet, Wise chose a young man with whom he had worked on *West Side Story*. But, Russ Tamblyn initially wasn't interested. "You know, I actually turned *The Haunting* down the first time it was offered to me," the actor declared in *Filmfax* #27. "I was living in Paris and Robert Wise, who was in England, sent me the script to read. I thought all the other parts were great but, at that time—and don't ask me why—I didn't like the part that I had in it. I didn't like it at all for some reason, maybe just stupidity. I sent a note back to him 'Thank you very much, but no thanks.' Then I flew back to Los Angeles. I thought that Wise was just offering me the role, no big deal. But when I got back to L. A., once again my agent said, 'The studio called and said if you don't do that film, *The Haunting*, you'll go back on suspension.' Since I really didn't want to go months and months without getting paid, I jumped on a plane for England and did the picture. Of course, now I look back on it, and it's one of my favorite films."

Almost as important as finding the right actors was locating the proper setting for the film's biggest star—Hill House itself. "We wanted a house that basically had an evil look about it," explained Robert Wise in *Fantastic Films*. "Since the film was going to be shot in England, we looked far and wide to find the right house. There are a lot of manor houses and old places in England, but one after the other did not fit our requirements. Finally, we found one [in Warwickshire] about 10 miles down from Stratford-on-Avon. It was an old manor house [named Ettington Park], about 200 years old, and it was being used as a country hotel." Wise felt that its "facing of mottled stone with gothic windows and turrets" were just what the spiritualist ordered. Rosalie Crutchley (who played the morose housekeeper, Mrs. Dudley) credited Wise's deft direction and David Boulton's sinister cinematography with transforming the benign Ettington Park into the malevolent manor of Hill House. "It was a strange house," the actress told this author, "which looked very threatening from the outside but which wasn't actually at all. But it was brilliantly shot, you see, so that it looked very, very threatening." Two other cast members, however, felt that it was threatening enough from the very start. "I went out a day or two ahead with the crew only, the photographic crew," related Robert Wise, "to shoot some of those long shots, the atmospheric shots. I was shooting one morning the second day we were there, and I saw a big Princess limousine coming in at the gateway down the way and drawing up in front, and I knew that it was Julie and Claire coming to report on location. I went to greet them, opened the door of this limo, and they were on the other side of the limo clutching each other, saying, 'Do we have to stay in there?'"

Wise had indeed found the perfect house for his terror tale, one which possessed an unexpected, even frightening, authenticity. Russ Tamblyn agreed: "It was definitely a strange place, especially the grounds. The house, itself, had a history... oh, children who had been murdered, and a 12-year-old who had committed suicide, some other woman who fell out of a window.... There was a bunch of stuff like that which had happened in this house, and there was a little cemetery behind it which was reported to be haunted. People had seen ghosts in this place, even those who had no idea of its reputation. The house was being used as an inn, and you could go in there and have a drink at night— it was a huge library—and the library was set up with tables. The owner—the innkeeper—asked us, 'Please just do me the favor while you're here, and don't spread the word around that this place is haunted.' He said he had people who had seen ghosts there—the same ghosts that people had seen for hundreds of years—without even knowing about the house's reputation" (from *Fearing the Dark* by Edmund G. Bansak).

During the week in which cast and crew stayed there shooting exteriors, none of the production company ran across any resident specters. "The only ghostly goings-on was our acting," laughed Ms. Crutchley.

This may not have been entirely true, however. "I never saw any ghosts," admitted Tamblyn, "and no one else did either, but I did have a chilling experience. One night I went out for a walk in the dark, by the little cemetery about 50 yards in the back of the house, and it was pitch black. I followed a path out there and decided to go out to look for a ghost. The shooting was being done in front of the house so I went in the back where it was so dark you could just make out the silhouette of the house. I walked way out and turned around, and I'll never forget this: I could just hear the noise of the arc lights that were in front, making this great silhouette, and all of a sudden I got this chill on the back of my neck. It was like somebody had laid a big piece of ice there, so much so that my head actually went forward. I had gone out there to look for a ghost, and I knew there was something behind me, but now that I knew it was there I didn't want to actually see it. There was a quick moment when I wondered, do I want to turn around or do I want to walk? And I just walked, walked straight back to the house. I don't know if there was a ghost there or not. But there was something ice cold on the back of my neck, I'll tell you that."

Another cast member, Fay Compton (seen as the elderly owner of Hill House at the film's beginning) went Russ Tamblyn's "chilling experience" one better—by living with a supposed ghost. According to director Robert Wise, the late actress (who died in 1978 at the age of 84) blithely reported, "I have a country house down in Sommerset and I've had to have it exorcised twice—it didn't take the first time."

The Haunting begins with a visual montage (accompanied by Richard Johnson's smooth narrative tones) that reveals the horrible history of Hill House: How a man named Hugh Crain built the house for his wife and daughter "in the most remote part of New England he could find"; how the wife "died seconds before she was to set eyes on the house" when her carriage crashed against a tree; how Crain's second wife mysteriously tumbled down a flight of stairs to her death; how, after Crain died in England, his daughter Abigail "grew up and grew old" in Hill House and eventually took a village girl to live with her as a paid companion; how "it's with this young companion the evil reputation of Hill House really begins" when said servant dallied with a farmhand while her mistress died calling for help upstairs; and how the companion inherited the house only to ultimately hang herself from the spiral staircase in the library ("they say that whatever there was—and still is—in the house eventually drove the companion mad").

In the Boston home of the house's current owner, Mrs. Sannerson (Fay Compton), Dr. John Markway (Richard Johnson), "a trained anthropologist and respected member of the University faculty," speaks with the elderly woman about her possessed property. "All my life," declares Markway, "I've been looking for an honestly haunted house. In the interest of psychic research you must let me have it for a few weeks during my leave of absence." Though Mrs. Sannerson warns that "the dead are not quiet in Hill House," she is won over by Markway's proposed scientific experiment" in which he "will occupy the house with a group of carefully selected assistants" who've "all been involved before, one way or another, with the abnormal."

Back in his office, Markway places a check mark after the name Eleanor Lance on his list of possible assistants, and the scene switches to a small apartment in which Eleanor (Julie Harris) argues bitterly with her overbearing sister and weak brother-in-law. Eleanor (or Nell) is a young-but-rather-spinsterish woman who has spent her entire adult life taking care of her invalid mother. With her mother dead two months and tired of sleeping on her sister's sofa, Eleanor sees Markway's invitation to join the team at Hill House as "the first real vacation of my life." Though her sister forbids it, Eleanor finally takes the family car ("It's half mine," she declares) and escapes her domestic purgatory to drive to Hill House. "At last," she thinks, "I am going someplace where I am expected and where I am being given shelter—and I shall never have to come back. I hope, I hope, I hope this is what I've been waiting for all my life."

Though Eleanor is the first to arrive at the forbidding mansion, she's soon joined by Theo (Claire Bloom), a beautiful, free-spirited young woman possessing acute extrasensory perception. As the pair explore the house, they experience a sudden and terrifying chill. "It wants you, Nell," proclaims the frightened Theo, "the house is calling you."

The moment is broken by the arrival of Dr. Markway and Luke (Russ Tamblyn), Mrs. Sannerson's rakish (and skeptical) nephew, who's come along to inspect the property he expects to inherit one day. The four get acquainted and Theo and Eleanor learn that they are the only ones out of an original six who did not drop out at the last minute ("I suppose they were frightened by the various unsavory stories about the house," admits Markway). Markway explains that "I'm here in hopes of proving [the supernatural's] existence; you're here to keep track of what happens and take notes for an authenticated record." The two women have been chosen because Markway feels that their connection to the supernatural will facilitate occurrences at Hill House, citing Theo's powers of ESP and Eleanor's poltergeist experience when she was a child (an incident the troubled Eleanor vehemently denies).

The frightening occurrences begin almost immediately. That night, Eleanor and Theo are terrorized by horrible sounds and a deafening pounding on their door while Markway and Luke are lured outside by what sounds like a dog running past their rooms.

The next morning Luke finds a message scrawled on the wall: "help Eleanor come home." Turning to the frightened Eleanor, Markway comments, "You do seem to be the main attraction for whatever's in the house."

That evening Markway finds a "cold spot" in front of what he calls "the heart of Hill House," the nursery ("Abigail Crain grew up—and died there").

Later, a new set of ghostly sounds assails the women, and Eleanor chillingly realizes that the comforting hand she'd been holding in the dark did not belong to her corporeal roommate.

Markway's wife, Grace (Lois Maxwell, best known as James Bond's Miss Moneypenny), who doesn't share her husband's belief in the supernatural, arrives the next day and urges him to abandon the far-fetched experiment. When he refuses to leave, she decides to stay as well and jokingly asks for the most likely place to see a ghost. In a fit of pique, Eleanor (who has become enamored of the handsome, attentive Markway and is obviously distressed to learn that he's married) announces, "There's the nursery." Despite her husband's protestations (and those of an immediately repentant Eleanor), Grace insists upon sleeping in the dreaded chamber.

As the hours pass, Eleanor becomes more and more ensnared by the dark forces inhabiting Hill House. "What if he does have a wife?" she thinks, "I still have a place in this house. I belong. I want to stay here. It's the only time anything's ever happened to me. They can't make me leave, not if Hill House means me to stay."

That night, everyone sleeps downstairs in the parlor except for Grace, who insists on staying in the nursery to prove her point. As the quartet dozes fitfully in the parlor, the door suddenly slams shut and the frightening noises begin. The audio assault stops abruptly, but the door itself begins to bow inward—as if some monstrous force was pushing against it from the other side. (Director Robert Wise achieved this frightening effect simply enough by having a burly prop man push on cue against the other side of the laminated wood with a two-by-four, causing it to bend inward to create the "breathing" effect.) While Luke tries to prevent Markway from opening the portal and going to Grace, Eleanor slips out another way, thinking "I'll come, I'll come; whatever it wants of me it can have."

After a terrifying disorienting journey through the meandering passage ways, Eleanor finally comes to the nursery. It is empty; Grace is gone. When the others arrive and begin searching for Grace, Eleanor wanders off, seemingly having fallen completely under the spell of the house. "I want to stay here," she thinks, "I want to stay here always. I will not be frightened—or alone—any more." She ends up at the library and begins climbing the rickety, dangerous metal spiral staircase—the one from which Abigail Crain's companion hanged herself. The structure shakes and sways ominously as the bolts begin to pull away from the wall.

Markway and the rest arrive at the library and entreat Eleanor to come down, but she ignores their pleas and continues to climb the swaying staircase. Markway, risking his own life to go up after her, finally reaches the top and begins to lead Eleanor back down when a trap door suddenly opens in the ceiling and the disheveled, terrified face of Mrs. Markway stares out for a moment before the door slams shut again.

After these events, Markway and the rest decide that Eleanor must leave Hill House—immediately. Though she protests pitifully, Markway insists. "It isn't fair," argues Eleanor, "I'm the one who's supposed to stay here. [Mrs. Markway] has taken my place.... The house wants me. Mrs. Markway can't satisfy it; no one else can."

They bundle Eleanor into her car with Luke. Luke has forgotten the gate key, however, and gets out to retrieve it from

Markway. In the car, Eleanor thinks, "Just by telling me to go away they can't make me leave. They can't shut me out—not if Hill House means me to stay." She starts the car and begins moving down the wooded drive, with Luke, Markway and Theo in pursuit.

Suddenly, something seems to take control of the wheel. At first Eleanor struggles against the force. "Stop it!—please!" she cries. "Why don't they stop me?" she wonders to herself, "can't they see what's happening?" Eleanor quickly grows calm, however, thinking, "But it's happening to you, Eleanor. Yes, something at last is really, really, really happening to me."

Abruptly a shape flits in front of the headlights and Eleanor screams. The car rams a tree—at the very spot where the first Mrs. Crain had died.

When Markway and the others reach the overturned auto, Eleanor is dead. Mrs. Markway staggers out from the bushes—it was her disoriented, terrified form that Eleanor had seen. "That terrible house," Grace stutters to her husband. "I woke up and was frightened so I tried to find your room, but I got lost, almost as though the house was doing it on purpose... I don't even know how I got out here."

As they stand there contemplating Eleanor's fate, Markway intones, "There was something in the car with her, I'm sure of it. Call it what you like, but Hill House is haunted. It didn't want her to leave and her poor bedeviled mind wasn't strong enough to fight it. Poor Eleanor."

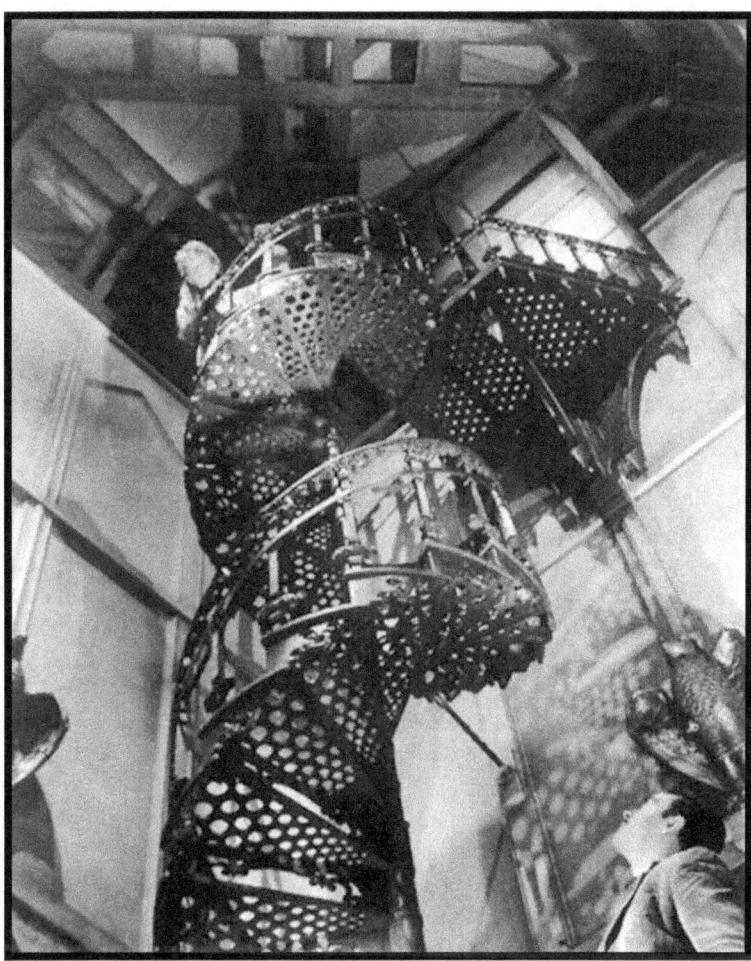

"Maybe not poor Eleanor," adds Theo. "It was what she wanted—to stay here. She had no place else to go. The house belongs to her now too. Maybe she's happier."

Luke only stares at Hill House and declares, "It ought to be burned down and the ground sowed with salt."

As we get one more gloomy look at the malevolent structure, Eleanor herself has the last word as her melancholy voice narrates: "Hill House has stood for 90 years and might stand for 90 more. Within, walls continue upright, bricks meet, floors are firm, and doors are sensibly shut. Silence lies steadily against the wood and stone of Hill House, and we who walk here—walk alone." "It was such a good script," opined Rosalie Crutchley. "As you know, we're all 90 percent as good as our script, most of us. And that was a good script." Robert Wise concurred. "I thought Nelson Gidding did just a fine job on the screenplay," praised the director. "I loved the way he got the whole history of the house, the whole background—which was so important to us before we got into our actual story. That opening, kind of a semi-montage with the carriage turning over and the little girl at the funeral and then in the bed growing older, I thought worked wonderfully well."

The film itself plays much better than a brief synopsis reads. Through realistic and complex characters, superb acting, creative direction, inventive cinematography and terrifying sound effects, the picture deftly sidesteps a gaping pit of haunted house clichés to take the viewer down a darkened path on which every shadow, every unexplained sound, every movement out the corner of one's eye conjures up frightful terrors of The Unknown.

"*The Haunting* is the first film to approach the subject of the supernatural from a mature, adult viewpoint," announced the film's pressbook. While this bold statement cavalierly overlooks the sub-genre's two previous ghost classics, *The Uninvited* and *The Innocents*, it does accurately reflect the picture's attitude—both in its content and its cinematic execution. For *The Haunting* not only explores the possibilities beyond (and terrors of) death, but the complex relationships and interactions in life.

Psychologically, the appeal of ghost stories can be traced to something much deeper than the delicious shivers they induce. A ghost tale can be seen as a way to combat the age-old fear of death. By their very nature, ghosts validate the idea of a further existence after the body ceases to function. Screenwriter Nelson Gidding and director Robert Wise take this a step further in the character of Eleanor Vance. Eleanor doesn't feel comfortable in the corporeal world and so turns to fully embrace the supernatural milieu of Hill House. "I've always been more afraid of being left alone or left out than of things that go bump in the night," she admits. Eleanor takes comfort from that fact that she fits into the spectral scene.

Eleanor is a woman trapped by circumstance, or, more precisely, by her own loneliness and neuroses (arising, no doubt, from her 11-year ordeal caring for her invalid mother and the attendant feelings of guilt over her recent death). When Eleanor first catches sight of the malignant house, she thinks, "It's staring at me. Vile, vile! Get way from here, get away at once! It's my chance; I'm being given a last chance.... Everyone has a right to run away." The tone of her thoughts change suddenly, however, when she realizes, "but you are running away, Eleanor—and there's nowhere else to go." Though recognizing the self-destructive path she's taking, Eleanor sees herself as having no alternative and so intentionally steps into the lion's den.

"It's waiting for me," imagines Eleanor, "evil—patient—waiting." To her lonely mind, something waiting for her—even though she perceives it as evil— is better than nothing. Thus, Eleanor mirrors the attitude of so many people who feel that any attention, even if it comes from a destructive relationship, is better than none at all. *The Haunting* is so much more than a simple (and effective) ghost story; it is a story of human needs, motivations, and frailties.

In the end, Eleanor seems to get what she wants—to remain at Hill House forever. As Theo conjectures, "maybe she's happier" this way. In the bitterest of ironies, however, Eleanor's ultimate sacrifice (her life) in order to attain this "happiness" of belonging at (or, more precisely, to) Hill House fails to alleviate her loneliness. As Eleanor herself narrates at the film's closing, "we who walk here—walk alone."

Though screenwriter Nelson Gidding presents the four main characters as complex individuals, they each function as something of an archetype as well. Along with Eleanor's emotional dependent, Luke serves as the cynical skeptic, worldly and doubting. Theo is the terrified adult/child, who not only cowers before the unknown but becomes instantly petulant whenever she fails to get her own way (such as in her pursuit of Eleanor). Markway is the voice of reason, of the intellect, who holds sway during the bright daylight hours. "When people believed the earth was flat," he explains, "the idea of a round world scared them silly. Then they found out how the round world works. It's the same with the world of the supernatural. Until we know how it works, we'll continue to carry around this unnecessary burden of fear." (Though this sounds perfectly reasonable in the light of day, it doesn't seem to help much when confronted with phantom poundings and spectral screams in the dead of night.)

What brings these well-drawn characters to life, however, are the stellar performances, firmly grounded in reality, provided by the film's principal cast.

According to an MGM publicity article, "Robert Wise has stated that he doubts he would have tackled this picture without a guarantee that he could have the gifted Miss Harris for the demanding role of Eleanor." While this may be a bit of exaggeration on the part of an enthusiastic PR writer (though Wise did tell this author that "I always had Julie Harris in mind; I thought she was just perfect for the lead"), there is no denying the convincing intensity and depth of character the actress brings to her pivotal role. Eleanor is not only the focus of Hill House, but of the entire film itself. Hers is the only life we see outside of the malevolent mansion, and hers are the only thoughts we hear, making the viewer privy to the innermost musings—and torments—of the character. Julie Harris brings Eleanor to life with the utmost conviction, painting a portrait of a sad, lonely woman struggling to find something—anything—to give her life meaning. Through a total command of her craft, Harris makes Eleanor both pitiable and likable, so that the viewer truly does care what happens to Nell.

As Dr. John Markway, Richard Johnson also brings a convincing realism and likability to his role. Due to Johnson's enthusiasm and good humor, his British professor of physical anthropology comes across as a warm human being rather than the stuffed-shirt character he so easily could have become. When Mrs. Sannerson asks Markway what he expects to find at Hill House, Johnson replies, "Maybe only a few loose floorboards, and maybe—I only say 'maybe'— the key to another world?" Johnson ends this rather pretentious (and potentially ridiculous) statement with a deprecating half-smile and a questioning tone, realizing how it sounds but still enthusiastic enough to say it (with apology).

Johnson became something of an exploitation stalwart in the 1970s with roles in Italian-based shockers like Massimo Dallarnano's possession flick, *The Night Child* (1974); Sonia Assoniti 's and Robert Piazzoli's Exorcist-clone, *Beyond the Door* (1975); a pair of Lucio Fulci gorefests, *Zombie* (1979) and *The Gates of Hell* (1980); Sergio Martino's mutant fishman tale, *Screamers* (1979); and the reptile rip-off, *The Great Alligator* (1980). Johnson also appeared in *The Monster Club* (with Vincent Price). In 1965 Johnson met and married his co-

star of *The Amorous Adventures of Moll Flanders*—American screen sex symbol Kim Novak. The union ended in divorce the following year.

Theo, the third point of the interpersonal triangle formed by Eleanor and Markway, may be the most enigmatic and fascinating of the three characters. MGM sidestepped Theo's lesbian overtones by labeling the character an "unconventional girl" in publicity pieces, but there's no denying the undercurrent of alternative sexuality emanating from the woman. This aspect adds a significant depth to the character dynamics evolving within (and involving) Hill House, creating yet another wrinkle in the supernatural struggle over Eleanor. Not only is Theo pitted against Markway (whose feelings for Eleanor remain maddeningly ambiguous—at times he seems to show only a fatherly concern while at others, such as when he gives her face a brief caress, it seems like something more) in a battle for Eleanor's affections, but against the very House itself. Scripter Gidding and director Wise keep these conflicts understated, letting them boil and churn just under the surface. "We actually had another sequence that we cut out at the beginning," recounted Robert Wise in *Bright Lights*, "that sort of hit it too much on the nose. It was early on in Claire's apartment, as I recall, that she was yelling out the window to a girl in a car, and she went over after that to a mirror and wrote 'I hate you!' or something like that, very strong sense of a lesbian relationship. And it seemed to color it too much, so we just dropped that scene."

Beyond offering Eleanor another alternative to her loneliness (albeit one which Eleanor rejects outright, preferring the terrors of Hill House to the terrors of her slumbering sexuality), Theo offers the viewer another perspective—that of the frightened child/adolescent. Not only is she the most severely affected by the various audio apparitions at Hill House (huddling, terrified, in corners and under blankets whenever *The Hauntings* begin), but she's also afraid of herself. When Eleanor asks Theo what she truly fears, Theo answers, "Knowing what I really want."

"Claire has distinction, enormous range, and underneath her sadness there is a bubbling humor, so unexpected, so wistful," admired Charlie Chaplin, who directed the actress in her first screen success, *Limelight* (1952). In *The Haunting*, Bloom brings this "wistful humor" to the fore in order to make what could have become a stock "beautiful bitch" character a fully fleshed out human being, and one who, like her three other compatriots, we come to identify with and like.

Among her nearly two-score film credits are *The Wonderful World of the Brothers Grimm* (1962, which also featured Russ Tamblyn, though the two never met since they shared no scenes), *The Illustrated Man* (1969, in which she acted with her husband of 10 years, Rod Steiger; they divorced later that same year), and *Clash of the Titans* (1981, as Hera opposite her former Shakespearean colleague, Laurence Olivier, who played Zeus).

Of the fourth and final main character, Russ Tamblyn's initial feeling that "all the other parts were great but... I didn't like the part that I had in it," was well founded. Luke, the most worldly—and the most shallow—of the quartet is also the least interesting. Apart from serving as a cynical sounding board and providing the occasional quip about property values, Luke's presence adds little to the story. Tamblyn brings an appropriately wolfish charm to the role, however, and by the end of the picture we find he's grown on us to the extent that we like him as well.

Each of these four main characters shares to one degree or another a common motivation—a desire to belong. Markway feels he doesn't fit into the everyday world (stating at one point, "I didn't want to become what my father called a practical man) and so turned to something decidedly impractical—ghosts. In a way, he too is escaping into the alternative world offered by Hill House. Though married to a lovely woman, Markway's relationship with his wife appears distant. When she arrives, they make no physical contact (not even a polite buss on the cheek), and she insists on sleeping alone in the nursery (despite having been apart from her husband for several days).

The sapphic Theo, of course, seeks her own brand of companionship and unsuccessfully pursues Eleanor to the point where Eleanor finally turns and angrily labels her "unnatural" and "nature's mistake."

On the surface, Luke seems to be the most content of the quartet. His glib tongue and worldly cynicism, however, simply mask his own particular insecurity and loneliness, as evidenced by his sudden silence when one of his quips fails to come off.

Refreshingly, all four exhibit human frailties in their search for acceptance. Unlike Eleanor, however, Markway, Theo, and Luke all manage to resist the unholy temptation offered by Hill House. They choose to continue their healthier struggle to fit in with reality and the rest of humanity rather than succumb, like Eleanor, to a desperate need to belong—anywhere.

The two supporting characters of Mr. and Mrs. Dudley (Hill House's caretaker and housekeeper), though seen only briefly, are immensely important as well, establishing the dour atmosphere of Hill House. These two are the only people who have spent any length of time at the accursed manor (becoming Hill House's human representatives), and they serve as buffers (and portents) to Eleanor's initial contact with the house.

The late Valentine Dyall's (*Room to Let, Horror Hotel*) scornful caretaker, who scowls derisively and spits, "You'll be sorry I ever opened the gate," is perfectly matched by Rosalie Crutchley's (*Creatures the World Forgot, Blood from the Mummy's Tomb, And Now the Screaming Starts*, et al.) gloomy Mrs. Dudley. Ms. Crutchley's knife-edged features ("I think Robert Wise just thought I had the right face for it," commented the actress on why she won the part) and thin frame serve to enhance her mortician's mannerisms. She answers Eleanor's knocking without a word, then soundlessly leads the nervous woman upstairs. When finally she speaks, Mrs. Dudley only recites her dinner routine and notes that she and her husband leave before it gets dark so that "we couldn't hear you—in the night." Eleanor asks about Dr. Markway, but Mrs. Dudley interrupts, pressing on with her speech as if not hearing Eleanor—or as if working within the morbid house has somehow severed her connection to other people. "No one could," she continues flatly. "No one lives any nearer than town. No one will come any nearer than that. In the night. In the dark." At this, a mirth-

Russ Tamblyn was not happy with his role in *The Haunting*.

less grin splits her previously solemn and expressionless face, as if enjoying a private, unhealthy joke. With her head titled slightly to the side like some strange bird, Rosalie Crutchley's cold, inappropriate smile (accompanied by a muted, jarring trumpet note on the music track) becomes downright unsettling.

A moment later, when Theo arrives, Mrs. Dudley repeats her litany about dinner and her leaving before nightfall while Theo seemingly ignores her prattling as inconsequential. When Mrs. Dudley comes to the point in her routine when she states, "I leave before the dark comes, so there won't be anyone around if you need help," this finally gets Theo's attention. As the housekeeper turns to go, Eleanor pipes up, half in jest, "No one can hear you if you scream in the night, isn't that right Mrs. Dudley?" The housekeeper turns and smiles her chilling smile before repeating (as if for the first time), "No one lives any nearer than town. No one will come any nearer than that. In the night. In the dark." At this, her face takes on her usual solemn cast and she exits, quietly closing the door. In Hill House, even the servants are slightly off-kilter.

"We were all fairly experienced theater actors," Crutchley (still active in films and television at age 74) told this author. "Most of us had done an awful lot of theater. That was how films were cast in those days; they saw you in the theater or they saw you in another film."

The entire talented cast of *The Haunting* gave their all to the production. ("I remember my husband making *The Haunting*," Valentine Dyall's widow reported, "as he spent hours closeted with tapes of New England dialect!") "I think we all knew it was very good and very interesting," agreed Rosalie Crutchley, "and not at all like the usual film of the time."

Though at one point Markway tells his skeptical wife that "[Hill House] is a deadly. serious place," there's plenty of wry humor in *The Haunting* (much of it of the apropos whistling-in-the-dark variety). Beginning with the opening narration in which Johnson intones, "[Hill House] was built 90-odd—very odd— years ago..." (you can almost see the twinkle in his eye), low-key humor finds its place among the stolid brick and mottled stone of Hill House. Even the house's elderly owner manages to joke, "As an old woman due shortly to enter the next world, I should like to know if there is one." There's even one instance toward the beginning which comes very close to a pratfall. Showing off for the ladies his knowledge of Hill House's bizarre layout, Markway declares, "I've studied a map," then promptly opens a door and steps into a broom closet.

But the well-placed humor never quite alleviates the picture's overwhelming mood of unease, and at times the jokes actually augment the barely suppressed atmosphere of terror. When Luke finally experiences *The Haunting* firsthand, for instance, he stands, stunned, as the parlor door bulges obscenely toward him of its own accord. Letting his half-empty whiskey bottle fall unheeded from his hand and unable to tear his eyes away from the horrific sight, he faintly whispers to Markway, "Doc, let you have the house cheap." The obvious fear in his voice and awe etched into his face shows the crack to be nothing more than the false bravado it is—which serves to heighten rather than lessen the tension.

"I can't tell you," declared Robert Wise, "how many people have said to me, 'Mr. Wise, you made the scariest picture I've ever seen and you didn't show anything!'" Even jaded modern monstermakers admit to the film's frightening power. FX expert Mark Shostrom (*From Beyond, Evil Dead 2, A Nightmare On Elm Street 2 & 3*, et al.), for example, who makes his living creating astounding and gruesome visual effects, recalled in *Deep Red* #2 that *The Haunting* "scared the shit out of me one night when I was working late in my studio and I had it on the VCR. I started to get really freaked out. It still holds up; it's a great film." Makeup maestro Tom Savini (who needs no introduction to modern-day horror fans) asserted in *Deep Red* #3 that "one of the greatest horror movies around had absolutely no makeup effects or monsters—*The Haunting*. That was a scary, scary film. It was all in manipulating the audience and then scaring them with the stuff you planted in their brains early on."

At one point in *The Haunting*, Markway states, "Ghosts are a visible thing." Not at Hill House. *The Haunting* is perhaps the only ghost film in which the specters are never seen. Horror specialist Stephen King in his *Danse Macabre* observed that "what we have in the Wise film is one of the world's few radio horror movies. Something is scratching at that ornately paneled door, some thing horrible... but it is a door Wise elects never to open."

I remember viewing the film as a young child and feeling cheated because I never saw a single ghost, especially at the very end when Eleanor seemingly struggles with a disappointingly invisible force inside her car. Fortunately, *The Haunting* wasn't made for children and there's nothing childish about it. Now, as an adult, I can fully appreciate Wise's restraint and applaud the artistry with which he applies it. For some viewers, however, this lack of visual confirmation of the supernatural becomes a major stumbling block, not realizing that it is the ambiguous, mysterious, unseen nature of the inhabitants of Hill House which gives the film its chilling power. To put it bluntly, sometimes what is not shown makes the most impact, an axiom modern filmmakers have seemingly forgotten. Robert Wise's mentor, producer/screenwriter Val Lewton, in his string of subtle chillers from the 1940s, forged a career out of employing this principle in films like *Cat People* (1942), *The Leopard Man* (1943) and *Isle of theDead* (1945). Wise, having cut his directing teeth under Lewton's tutelage on *The Curse of the Cat People* (1944) and *The Body Snatcher* (1945), knew full well the power of this "fear of the unseen." "For the horror films," explained Wise in *The Perfect Vision*, "it was Val Lewton's thesis that people really feared the unknown. You see that shadow over there! What's that?! That noise over there! What's that?! That's what he played on. Darkness and shadows."

"In doing *The Haunting*," continued Wise, "which was my last film in black and white, I was returning to my beginnings as a director, going for the same feeling and philosophy we had at the Lewton unit." Time after time Wise places his audience in literally hair-raising situations, not by exposing us to pasty-faced ghouls, but by playing upon the terrors of our own individual imaginations. Through clever use of lighting, camera movement, sound and actor reactions, Wise terrifies with pure atmosphere, frightening us with what is not seen. "It's kind of an homage to Val," declared the director.

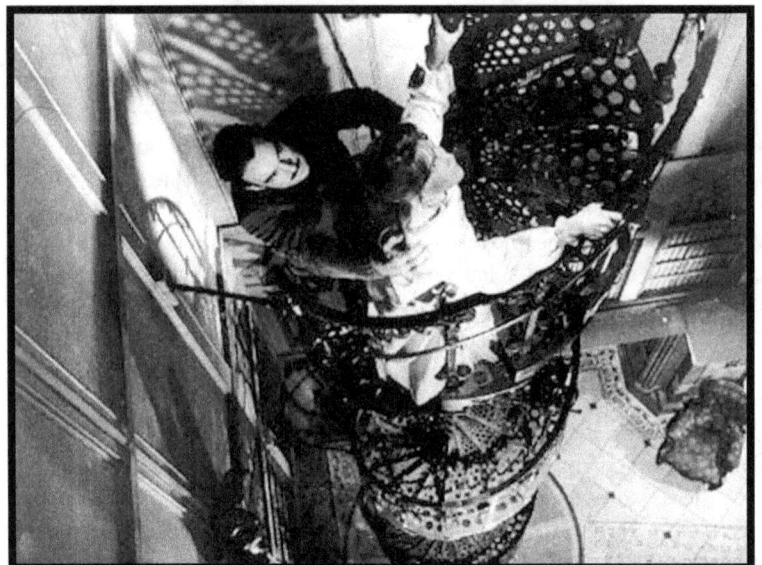

The film's centerpiece, and its most terrifying sequence, is a testament to this very power of suggestion. Taking place in Eleanor and Theo's bedroom in the dead of night, it begins with a brief shot of the shadowy chamber, then cuts to a close-up of Eleanor's face, half-shrouded in darkness. She suddenly opens her eyes and lifts her head slightly as if something has disturbed her slumber. The camera cuts to a section of textured wallpaper and we hear a low, unintelligible mumbling seemingly emanating from behind the wall. Unlike the loud "cannonball" poundings of the previous night's haunting, the rather quiet, otherworldly noise now heard is an incoherent, agitated, eerie voice. In her bed, not daring to move, Eleanor whispers to Theo (whose bed sits beside her own), "Are you awake? Don't say a word, Theo, not a word. Don't let it know you're in my room." While she speaks, the camera creeps in tighter until Eleanor's anxious face fills the screen, saturating the space with her fear. Abruptly, a high-pitched laughter joins the assault, and Eleanor places her hand tightly across her mouth—as if to stifle a scream. Once again we see the textured wall and the camera moves in—ever so gently—on the pattern while the unnatural laughter continues. The camera stops its subtle movement and... is that a demonic face discernible amongst the curlings and ridges of the pattern?! Suddenly, our suppressed-but-not-entirely-forgotten childhood fears come rushing back to us—fears of dim, horrible faces reflected in glinting bedroom door knobs or of clothing draped across chairs that take on the shape of terrible monsters.

Wincing from fear, Eleanor takes her hand from her mouth to extend her arm and implore, "Hold my hand, Theo. And for God's sake, don't scream." The weird raving sounds increase in volume, then fade away. "Is it over?" breathes Eleanor hopefully. "Do you think it's over? Theo, you're breaking my hand!" Before Theo can answer, the noises begin again, this time in the form of a crying child, whose sobbing quickly evolves into high-pitched shrieks.

As Eleanor lies in the dark, unmoving, her face grimacing in fear and loathing, she thinks, "This is monstrous, this is cruel. It is hurting a child and I will not let anyone or anything hurt a child. I will not endure this. It thinks to scare me. Well, it has—and poor Theo too. Honestly, it feels like she's breaking my hand!" As the child's cries merge with the returned deep-voiced mumblings, Eleanor thinks, "I will take a lot from this filthy house for his sake but I will not go along with hurting a child. No, I will not! I will get my mouth to open right now and I will yell, I will yell, I will yell!"—"In extreme close-up, we see (and hear) her mouth shout "STOP IT!" Abruptly, Eleanor sits bolt upright in the dimness. With a click, a light comes on and Eleanor glances to her left. The camera spins quickly, panning with a dizzying speed to the right to stop on the startled Theo sitting up and asking, "What—what Nell, what?!" Theo is in her bed—across the room. Eleanor, now realizing she's been sleeping on the couch rather than in her own bed, looks wonderingly down at her outstretched arm, at her now-empty hand. An extreme close-up of her face shows her eyes widen slightly before she lurches upright, holding her hand out in front of her like some alien thing, and asks tremulously, her horror barely held in check, "God! Whose hand was I holding?!" The harrowing cacophony has stopped, but we hardly notice as the terror of the unseen washes over us.

This sequence, taking place almost entirely in near-darkness, with only a few square feet of wall and one woman's shadowy face dimly visible, perfectly encapsulates the fear of the unknown. Though I've viewed this particular sequence a dozen times—and know exactly what is coming—it never fails to raise the hackles on my neck and literally send shivers down my back. It is truly one of the most chilling moments in cinema history—and one which shows absolutely nothing.

Since sound (and the actors' reactions to it) was so very critical to the picture's success, Wise spared no expense in that department. The director sent a six-man sound crew, headed by dubbing editor Allan Sones, to an empty 17th-century manor house where (related a studio article), "working in shifts day and night for a week, they recorded every sound which developed, as well as a few synthetic secrets of their own. Doors, they reported, do slam for no apparent reason and floorboards do creak when no one treads on them."

So that his actors would receive the full impact of the terrifying sounds (and react accordingly), Wise employed for his on-set audio hauntings the same type of sophisticated playback system filmmakers use for musicals during the song and dance numbers. "Usually when you have a sound effect in a film you have a prop man offstage making noise or something," explained the director in *Bright Lights*, "but I realized the importance of the sound effects of whatever's out there. So I had prescored sound effects, and I had a regular playback machine. Like with the door where the two women are reacting to it, I had a big playback machine and it was banging away with the sound effects there. And later, those sniffing noises. I improved it a little bit before we got done, but what you heard was pretty much what they were reacting to." (Those "sniffing noises" were Wise's favorite audio effect: "I remember the shot where the girls are in bed. It's the first time they hear it, and the sound is kind of like a sniffing outside the door—all around the door. The feeling's like, 'If there's a little crack, I can get in.' I loved that. It was handmade for the film.")

As a photographic experiment, Wise used a special film stock in order to obtain the dark, moody and (pardon the expression) truly haunting image of the house itself. "I made it look a little bit more monstrous than it might have been," explained the director, "because I shot all the exteriors with infrared film, which brought out the kind of exaggerated striations of the rock and turned the skies blacker and turned the clouds whiter. It added an eerie feeling to it."

Wise's experimentation extended even to the camera lens. "*The Haunting* was filmed in Panavision anamorphic—that's the widescreen," the director recalled. "And at that time, the widest angle that they had was about a 35mm, and I was just wishing I had something wider for some more extreme angles. So from London I called Bob Gottschalk, who was the head of Panavision and whom I knew very well. I said, 'Bob, don't you have anything wider than 35 that I could use in the film to get some special angles?' He said, 'Well, we're working on a 28mm but it's still got distortion in it.' I said, 'Jesus, that's just what I want! I want that distortion.' He finally, after much persuading on my part, agreed to send it over to me. But I had to sign a document saying that I would not come back at him and complain about distortion in the lens. I used that for some of the shots down the long hallway, upstairs, along the stairwell—the spooky shots. That lens really helped me to milk those sets and create atmosphere."

With Eleanor's (and the viewer's) first clear sight of Hill House, Wise's wide-angle lens creates a subtle distortion that gives the towers and turrets a bent, off-kilter appearance. The house looms over us, its edges seeming to curve inward slightly like the encircling arms of some monstrous beast. Coupled with the stark texture and dark hues produced by the infra-red film stock (in which the recessed gothic windows become solid black masses like the empty eye sockets of some gigantic skull), the sight becomes a subliminally unsettling vision. Upon seeing the grotesque structure, the alarmed Eleanor thinks, "It's staring at me! Vile, vile!" Due to Wise's innovative techniques, the viewer feels the very same thing. "One of the things I liked about the house," recalled Wise, "and I was able to really use it that way to make a character out of it, was that it had that tower there with those windows. So I could cut to the windows and then down to Julie getting out of her car and going in, like the house was watching you. I tried to capitalize and use the house just as much as I could."

"I remember working with Robert Wise as an excellent experience," remarked Rosalie Crutchley. "He was a very brilliant director. And I seem to remember he was terribly kind and friendly. I think we all felt it was rather like working in a theater company, we were all working together, you know what I mean? You didn't just turn up and do your bit and disappear. I mean we all kind of worked together."

"I have to be immodest and say I really like *The Haunting* because that's one of my best directorial jobs," opined the director himself. "I really think it worked well." Indeed, *The Haunting* is filled with so many examples of Wise's dazzling direction (and David Boulton's creative cinematography) that it could be used as a veritable film school course in cinematic technique. Fortunately, Wise uses his skills intelligently and to precise purpose—always to advance the story, explore character, or create mood (not to mention scare the daylights out of his audience). He deftly sidesteps the trap so many filmmakers fall into (even such luminaries as Woody Allen with his endless and pointless circling camera in *Shadows and Fog* or Martin Scorsese with the wild aquatic ballet at the close of *Cape Fear*) when they sadly misapply "clever" cinematic tricks to no real purpose. In *The Haunting*, Wise sees to it that technique remains a means rather than an end.

To suggest Mrs. Crain's carriage crashing against a tree, for instance, Wise begins with a close-up of the two horses rearing, then cuts to a series of disorienting and frantic shots of the sky and tree flashing by before the camera focuses in on the tree trunk itself and the image shudders violently—as if experiencing a sudden impact. The next shot shows a ruined carriage wheel slowly rotating on its side. Suddenly, a woman's limp hand drops down into the frame in front of the spokes. As a final touch, her bracelet, which wraps about her middle forearm, abruptly slides down her arm to rest on the heel of her dead hand—symbolic of the life draining from her body (a more subtle and effective device than had Wise employed the usual clichéd rivulets of blood dripping from the fingertips).

Wise makes the death of the second Mrs. Crain even more involving, inter-cutting shots of her tumbling down the stairs with spinning POV images. The world seemingly flips end over

end and the banister races past as if the camera itself had been hurled down the stairs. Wise closes the scene with an extremely dramatic and disturbing low-angle view of the woman lying on her back at the foot of the stairs, her mouth open, eyes staring. With the camera at floor level, her head seems to rest at an impossibly unnatural angle.

The first chilling encounter involving Eleanor and Theo is another impressive exercise in lighting, camera movement and sound. As the two women try to find their way through the maze of Hill House, they experience a sudden chill. Theo exclaims, "The house wants you, Nell. The House is calling you!" In medium close-up we see Eleanor, gripping herself tightly in fear, begin to slowly retreat backward down the hall away from the camera. Rather than follow with her, however, the camera begins to move in an odd, elliptical pattern while subtly sliding forward then back, so that Eleanor's image becomes unstable and appears to be slipping away into the dark recesses of the house. "Don't let me go!" she cries, backing into complete shadow so that she nearly disappears. Suddenly, a shaft of light from a door opened by Markway extracts her from the clutches of Hill House, and (at least temporarily) vanquishes our terror of the dark.

"Do you recall the shot in the film where we're at the bottom of the library stairs, just a loose camera, and it climbs up the circular stairway, going all the way to the top?" asked Robert Wise about another of his impressive camera tricks. "Well, we had that whole stairwell railing designed specially to take a little dolly that would hold a hand-held camera. There was a wire underneath to guide it. So all we did was light the whole set the way we wanted it, started the camera at the top, turned it on, let it wind all the way down to the bottom, turned it off, and then when we printed the film, we just reversed it.

I thought that staircase was a particularly wonderful piece of construction. There was a man at the studio there called 'Terry the Tinsmith' (I don't know his actual name). That was his department. He designed and constructed that whole thing, a marvelous piece of work."

As each successive supernatural incident becomes more and more overtly frightening, so too does Wise's camera come more and more into play. While the horrific noises reverberate through the hall outside the women's bedroom, the camera pans across the wall, following the sounds to show that the unholy clamor is alarmingly mobile. Then as the sound gives way to a deathly silence, a sudden raucous pounding begins and the camera violently lurches forward toward the door, the frantic visual movement suggesting—and intensifying—the terrifying presence just behind the wood.

As the audio assault continues, a quieter (though no less frightening) sound of scuffling and sniffing emanates from behind the door. The camera becomes a roving, probing animal as it tilts and moves around the edge of the doorjamb or abruptly drops down to the crack at the bottom in a visual representation of the sinister sound's unseen presence and exploratory movements on the other side.

Even during calmer moments, Wise will unexpectedly tilt the camera so that the ghostly white face of a marble statue abruptly enters the frame (Wise's own version of a Val Lewton bus). Or, as Eleanor takes panicked flight through the house, he'll move the camera back and forth like the rolling of a ship—making the house itself seem to come frighteningly alive with a malevolent motion. All these cinematic tricks serve to effectively heighten our fear of what's behind the door or of things that go bump in the night—in other words, the fear of the unseen.

Reviews of *The Haunting* were nearly all positive, an impressive accomplishment for a horror film considering the holier-than-thou attitude frequently taken by critics regarding the genre. Judith Crist of *The New York Herald Tribune* (September 19, 1963) labeled the film "a thoroughly satisfying ghost story for grown-ups done with a style and professionalism that has long been denied spook-story addicts.... Shirley Jackson's nastily eerie *Haunting of Hill House* has been given its due by Robert Wise and his associates and emerges again as a top-notch ghost story, old-fashioned and therefore filled with the horrors of the unseen and the unexplained, and completely contemporary in its psychological overtones and implications."

Across town at the *New York Times* (September 19, 1963), even the anti-horror stuffed shirt Bosley Crowther seemed pleased (with reservations, of course). "Believe me," he wrote, "before this antique chiller drags to an ectoplasmic end, you'll agree that it does have just about everything in the old fashioned blood-chilling line except a line of reasoning that makes a degree of sense. It is great as long as Julie Harris and Claire Bloom are huddling in a room in that luridly off-kilter mansion, waiting in paralyzed terror for they know not what.... This film makes more goose pimples than sense, which is rather surprising and disappointing for a picture with two such actresses, who are very good all the way through it, and produced and directed by the able Robert Wise."

Variety's "Tube" (August 21, 1963), though impressed with the picture's "cinematic savvy," tended to agree with Mr. Crowther's complaint about the storyline. "The artful cinematic strokes of director Robert Wise and staff are not quite enough to override the major shortcomings of Nelson Gidding's screenplay.... Audiences will respond to the film's intermittent terror passages, thanks to the skill of Wise, his cast and his crew, but are apt to find the whole unsatisfactory." Apparently, Tube was disappointed by the rather enigmatic ending. "After elaborately setting the audience up in anticipation of drawing some scientific conclusions about the psychic phenomena field, the film completely dodges the issue in settling for a half-hearted melodramatic climax that is a distinct letdown." (No doubt this reviewer could identify better with the outlandish but more obvious conclusion of *The Legend of Hell House*.) Tube observed that "the acting is effective all around," and "the picture excels in the purely cinematic departments" while "J.B. Smith's acutely sensitive and fluid sound is of enormous value to the mood, as is Humphrey Searle's chilling, tantalizing music score."

The only significant pan the picture received was from a singularly unilluminating review in *Time* magazine (October 4, 1963) which (incredibly) labeled the film's specter "the usual commercial spirit. Whenever it appears, the violins on the soundtrack start to didder, doors open and shut by themselves, people stare about in terror and squeak: 'The house, it's alive!' The picture, it's dead."

Fortunately, most reviewers fell more in line with Hollis Alpert's assessment in *Saturday Review* that "it has all the eerie chilliness, the icy little shocks that such a film should have.... *The Haunting* represents another considerable achievement for Mr. Wise."

The passage of time has not dimmed *The Haunting*'s brilliance. Recent reassessments vary only in the height of the praise heaped upon this

Robert Wise directs on the set of The Haunting.

undisputed classic. Paul M. Sammon in 1994's *Video Watchdog* Special Edition, called it "The greatest contemporary, quiet ghost story."

Horror filmmaker Wes Craven (*A Nightmare on Elm Street*, *The Serpent and the Rainbow*) recently paid the film its greatest compliment when he voiced a desire to remake *The Haunting*. In *The Perfect Vision* (vol. 5, no. 20) he wrote, "The power of *The Haunting* is in its evocation of the ancient link between home and head. It's among the first American films to exploit this connection—that structures reflect not only the architecture of their builders but the minds of their inhabitants as well—and it not only did this with class and restraint, but with such power and conviction that it scared the pants off its audience as well. For that reason, it's stayed in my mind since I first saw it, and is the reason why I want to remake it myself." (Craven is not the only modern genre director to openly recognize the power of *The Haunting*. Stuart Gordon [*From Beyond*] showed *The Haunting* to his cast and crew preparing to shoot his film, *Castle Freak*. "Stu wants us to get a sense of the evil presence the castle will represent in this film," reported *Castle Freak* star Jonathan Fuller in *Fangoria* #149. "From now on," added the actor, "I will never feel totally safe at night here.")

Despite such laudatory critical appraisal (both past and present), *The Haunting* was not a financial success upon its initial release. "I don't know that it ever broke even," reported Robert Wise. "It just didn't take off to the degree that it has

attained over the years. Now it's become a real favorite of so many people."

The film's lack of financial success may have been due in part to it being shot in black and white at a time when color features were all the rage. Filming in black and white was a conscious choice for Wise, and the director has no regrets. "I love the fact that I shot *The Haunting* in black and white," ex claimed Wise. "For that kind of film, the mood and quality of it and the look of the thing, you could only get from black and white."

In 1989 Robert Wise discovered (purely by chance) that *The Haunting* was in the process of being colorized. Furious, the director went back to his original contract and found that it specified that the picture would be filmed in black and white (an unusual clause to be included in a contract of that time), making it "an important component of the film." With contract in hand, Wise threatened legal action and the colorization project was (thankfully) dropped.

While the subject of specters may not quite be in the same league as the primal issues of sustenance, reproduction and religion, so long as insightful writers like Shirley Jackson and talented filmmakers like Robert Wise tackle the topic with sensitivity, intelligence, and skill, the subject of ghosts will (ahem) never die.

"I'm very pleased that young people are still interested in *The Haunting*," concluded Rosalie Crutchley, "because it's worth it when a film is good; it's worth remembering these things." Thanks to digital releases (not to mention frequent theatrical revivals) of *The Haunting*, this "mother of a ghost films" will be remembered for a very, very long time.

CREDITS: Producer/Director: Robert Wise; Screenplay: Nelson Gidding; Based on the Novel *The Haunting of Hill House* by Shirley Jackson; Director of Photography: David Boulton; Camera Operator: Alan McCabe; Music: Humphrey Searle; Special Effects: Tom Howard; 1963, Metro-Goldwyn-Mayer; 112 minutes

CAST: Julie Harris...Eleanor Vance, Claire Bloom...Theodora, Richard Johnson...Dr. Markway, Russ Tamblyn...Luke Sannerson, Fay Compton...Mrs. Sannerson, Rosalie Crutchley...Mrs. Dudley, Lois Maxwell...Grace Markway, Valentine Dyall...Mr. Dudley, Diane Glare...Carrie Fredericks, Ronald Adam... Eldridge Harper, Freda Knorr...2nd Mrs. Crain, Janet Mansell.. Abigail (6 years), Pamela Buckley... 1st Mrs. Crain, Howard Lang...Hugh Crain, Mavis Villiers...Landlady, Verina Greenlaw. . Dora, Paul Maxwell...Bud, Claud Jones... Fat Man, Susan Richards...Nurse, Amy Dalby...Abigail (80 years), Rosemary Dorken...Companion

Special thanks to Robert Wise, Rosalie Grutchley and Kay Dyall for their participation.

The "why bother" remake of *The Haunting* left nothing to the imagination but offered no real scares.

THE HAUNTING
1999, Director Jan de Bont

You know how you experience chills down your spine when you hear that Hollywood is remaking a classic. Well, shivers galore occurred when the news broke they were daring to remake *The Haunting*.

DreamWorks lined up a much more impressive cast than the original: Liam Neeson (as Markway, now called Marrow), Catherine Zeta-Jones as Theo, Owen Wilson as Luke, Lili Taylor as Nell and Bruce Dern as Mr. Dudley.

The film grossed $177 million worldwide, but 1999 tickets cost a lot more than 1963 tickets did.

While the original film's director Robert Wise was nominated for a Golden Globe for best director, the only awards the remake could garner were a slew of Razzie Awards including worst picture, actress, couple, director and screenplay.

Roger Ebert actually recommended the film, "To my surprise, I find myself recommending *The Haunting* on the basis of its locations, its sets, its art direction, its sound design, and the overall splendor of its visuals. The story is a mess, but for long periods of time that hardly matters. It's beside the point, as we enter one of the most striking spaces I've ever seen in a film."

The *San Francisco Chronicle* was not as kind. "There's no excuse for *The Haunting*. It's based on a great book, *The Haunting of Hill House*, by Shirley Jackson. A 1963 adaptation of the book was scary and intelligent. The only thing scary about the new version is realizing that someone keeps giving director Jan De Bont money to make movies."

Liam Neeson and Lili Taylor in the 1999 *The Haunting*.

HIGH PLAINS DRIFTER

by David H. Smith

"I don't believe in ghosts, but I've been afraid of them all my life."—Charles A. Dana

Is the electron a particle or a wave? It's *both*. In other words, the answer to one of the most fundamental questions about the nature of reality is cheerfully contradictory.

The larger implication is that the correct response to any question might be two apparently opposing explanations. With one particular ghost movie, this dichotomous way of thinking opens the gateway to debate—in the form of *High Plains Drifter* and the question of whether or not it's a ghost story at all.

Purists may contend *High Plains Drifter* isn't a ghost story in the given sense. Belief in ghosts means to some people an unequivocal acceptance of the souls of the dead in sheets and chains, squeaking and gibbering in Gothic ruins. On film, headless horsemen and lifelike apparitions, ghostly dogs and spectral trains: the wide range of ghostly manifestations makes it difficult to find a stereotype which will encompass them all.

"The heart of any classic ghost story focuses upon the ambivalence between whether the ghosts are real or merely figments of the imagination," Gary J. Svehla wrote in *Midnight Marquee* #48. Ipso facto, two inarguable classics of ghostly cinema, *The Innocents* and *The Haunting*, as well as their source novels, let their audiences decide whether the ghosts are substantial or imagined.

Now, while *High Plains Drifter* leaves no doubt as to whether the title character truly exists, it's the question of exactly what he truly is that leaves the film open to interpretation.

There are as many ideas about Clint Eastwood's character in the movie as there are film scribes, it seems. Archie P. McDonald, in *Shooting Stars: Heroes and Heroines of Western Film*, was ambivalent and offered three possibilities, "whether he is a ghost, the dead Marshal [come back to life, or a stranger passing through." Each theory has merit, and an analysis of the film lends credence to all of them, and more.

Today, Clint Eastwood needs little introduction to movie fans. Born in San Francisco in 1930, he had toiled as a contract player for Universal in the 1950s, starting with those oft-cited bits in *Revenge of the Creature* and *Tarantula*, both for director Jack Arnold in 1955.

Bigger parts and even screen credit began with *Francis in the Navy* that same year, where he played Jonesy; as George Moseley, in William Weilman's *Lafayette Escadrille* (1958), Eastwood garnered some positive reviews at last. Those earned him the part of Rowdy Yates, righthand man to trail boss Gil Favor (Eric Fleming), on TV's *Rawhide* for seven years.

The three iconoclastic Westerns Eastwood was hired for in Italy (filmed in Spain), based on his popularity from imported episodes of *Rawhide* edited into feature form, came at a fortuitous time, as the television series had just about run its course (he even did a guest shot on *Mr. Ed*). Beginning with *Per un Pugno di dollari* (*A Fistful of Dollars*, 1964), director Sergio Leone made Eastwood an international superstar and, according to *Italian Films* by Robin Buss, at the same time "revived a dead (or, at best, dying) genre in Hollywood, pepped it up, added realism to the violence, and more than a hint of sadism."

With Eastwood, Leone, the master chef of the Spaghetti Western, created the "The Man With No Name" character for a trio of films, though none were really sequels to one another. "Making Eastwood's very lack of acting expressionism an asset, Leone made him a fixed state of order in a storm of violent chaos," *MediaScene* #7 elucidated. "The character molded by Leone created Eastwood the loner, the hunter, the conqueror, the embodiment of masculine fantasy, using and cherishing women, food, drink, money, and justice without depending on any of them."

Traditionalists were aghast. These "severe and sparse Spaghetti Westerns put a harsh glare on the innocence of the John Ford–John Wayne Western era," Barbara Lester essayed in *XS*, "... from rotting teeth on cretinous villains, to bodies being hurled in and out of swinging saloon doors, to the worship of the almost phallic-like six-shooter."

Yet it was this laconic persona that endeared Eastwood to audiences around the world and became virtually his alter ego. "Eastwood played the deadliest, most cold-blooded, most unkempt cowboy heroes ever on screen," Thomas G. Rylesworth and John S. Bowman wrote in their *World Guide to Film Stars*. "His thin-lipped, unemotional style was perfect for the scruffy brutal hero of those violent films."

By the time of *High Plains Drifter*, Eastwood's 10th film as a star, the actor was established. It was to be his second film as a director. His first, *Play Misty For Me* (1971), was acclaimed as a suspenseful thriller, abetted by Jessica Harper's intense portrayal of an obsessed fan of Eastwood's disc jockey character.

Wanting to, rather than being invited to, take up the director's reins again, Eastwood searched for a suitable vehicle, hoping to incorporate his love of the Western as stylized by Leone and the more straightforward action films he had made with Don Siegel, among them, *Dirty Harry* (1971). He read a nine-page idea for a screenplay inspired by the real-life case of Kitty Genovese, a girl murdered in front of 38 indifferent witnesses. "What if that happened to a Marshal in a small town?" Eastwood wondered, and commissioned Ernest Tidyman to flesh it out

Novelist Tidyman, who created the character of and wrote the scripts for the *Shaft* movies, had just won an Academy Award for the screenplay for William Friedkin's *The French Connection* (1971). Peter Douglas, in the deferent *Clint Eastwood: Movin' On*, related, unsurprisingly, how Tidyman "created the principal role... especially with Clint Eastwood in mind." Under the banner of his own Malpaso Company and the aegis of Universal, Eastwood went to work.

High Plains Drifter was shot on a specially constructed set on the shores of Mono Lake in California, some 300 miles from Hollywood, east of Yosemite National Park. Logistics involved a 46-man crew of technicians and 10 laborers working 12-hours a day for 10 days, using 150,000 board feet of lumber for the job. They built 14 houses and a two-story hotel in their entirety, rather than as facades. Production went smoothly, and the movie was completed two days under a six week schedule; as Iain Johnstone concluded in *The Man With No Name*, "Eastwood took an inventive and cleverly written script and, with a sure sense of pace and purpose, directed a classic Western."

The first indication of a ghostly nature to the title character comes even as the opening credits roll. With the heat rising in shimmering waves, Eastwood, as "The Stranger," suddenly appears in the distance, galloping across the plain. The music, by Dee Barton, starts eerily enough, but there are no distinctive leitmotifs, such as those composed by Ennio Morricone for the Leone films; the soundtrack soon shifts to innocuous and rather nondescript background music as the camera follows The Stranger. He rides through some woods, then to a ridge overlooking expansive salt flats and a town called Lago that abuts a huge lake.

Mono Lake has been referred to as the Dead Sea of California for, despite its inviting blue-gray calm, it is too salty to support even fish life. Mark Twain called it "one of the strangest freaks of Nature found in any land." The word mono means "fly" in the language of the native Yokut Indians and, accordingly, with 87 square miles of water, it also supports 85% of the total California gull population, which feasts on the one small species of saltwater shrimp and the larvae of brine flies that breed there.

Screeching seagulls do make their presence felt throughout the movie. Symbolically, a white bird is a portent of death in some places in the United States, and, around the coasts of the British Isles, seagulls are said to be the souls of drowned seamen. More apropos to *High Plains Drifter* as we later learn, among the Bantu in Africa there is a belief that the spirit of a murdered man haunts his killer as a bird.

Perhaps significantly, The Stranger's horse canters through a graveyard as he approaches the main street. Whimsically, as in-jokes to Eastwood fans, among the visible tombstones there are inscriptions for "S. Leone" and "Don Siegel."

The soundtrack goes to dead silence, save for the amplified hoofbeats of the horse and the animal's snuffling. All eyes in town follow The Stranger's procession, from the lolling sheriff (Walter Barnes) to the curious patrons of the saloon. At one point he passes two men climbing on a buckboard; when one of the men (John Guade) cracks a whip to start the horses, The Stranger jerks violently at the sound, as though it holds some deeper meaning for him.

The Stranger goes the full length of the main street, ending at the undertaker's. He turns back and tethers his horse in front of the saloon, goes in and orders a beer and a bottle of whiskey, all the while being glared at by the patrons therein. Three roughnecks heckle him, but The Stranger ignores them and takes his bottle and leaves the saloon.

Crossing the street to the barbershop, The Stranger asks for a shave and a hot bath. The nervous barber (William O'Connell) quotes him a price and hesitatingly asks for the money in advance as The Stranger doffs his overcoat and flat-crowned tilted black hat. The three roughnecks watch from across the street.

As the barber is dabbing on the shaving lather, his fearfulness grows as the trio of miscreants enters and resumes badgering The Stranger. In a quirky foreshadowing of Eastwood's 1992 epic *Unforgiven* (he played a widower on a pig farm), they complain of his smelling like "pig shit." Still being ignored, the leader (Scott Walker) of the three grabs the barber chair and spins The Stranger around to face him, only to be shot between the eyes by a gun hidden under the sheet. The Stranger fires twice more in quick succession, hitting the other two in their chests, the last crashing through the front window. Wounded, he tries to pull himself up on the hitching rail, but collapses dead.

The Stranger gets up, wipes the lather from his face, and puts on his hat and coat. The townspeople, hearing the ruckus, all come to stare, but only a midget (Billy Curtis), seen earlier at the saloon, comes forward. The little man offers The Stranger a cigar and asks, "What'd you say your name was again?"

"I didn't," The Stranger replies, not missing a beat.

"No, I guess you didn't at that, did you?" the little man mutters as The Stranger walks away. Iain Johnstone, in the aforementioned biography of Clint Eastwood, called this "the most dramatic opening sequence of any Western"; obsequious overstatement perhaps, but what has transpired so far is wildly effective, drawing viewers into the narrative as much as offending them with its abject violence.

The Stranger walks down the street, the townspeople giving him a wide berth as they come out to see the carnage up close. Callie Travers, a strumpetlike townswoman (Mariana Hill), purposely bumps him, then chides him for his appearance and manner. Though he balks at first, her continued pestering pushes him to his limit, whereupon he drags her kicking and screaming into the nearby livery stable and rapes her.

The scene is grossly misogynic: her cries of protest give way to moans of pleasure, and her flailing hands begin to caress his back. Paul Higson, in *Samhain* #17's "The Even Wilder West," was correct in calling the scene "especially disturbing in that the rapist is the undoubtable hero of the film," but he doesn't go nearly far enough in expounding its repugnance.

Glowering at the woman, The Stranger rises and fastens his pants in an extreme low angle shot to denote his power. The midget has spied on them throughout and proffers another cigar to replace the one she batted out of his mouth; The Stranger ignores him, has the stableman board his horse, and goes to the hotel. He takes a room, refuses to sign the guest register, takes off his coat and hat, and lies down on the bed.

Here, in what can be construed as either a flashback or a dream, we witness a man (Buddy Van Horn) being whipped to death in the street outside. It is night, and despite his pleadings for help, the townspeople ignore him as three villains continue their assault. Bleeding, and resigned to his fate, the dying man groans, "Damn you all to hell," before expiring. The prophecy of those words will soon manifest itself.

The Stranger awakes the next day and, for only a moment, looks at himself in the hotel room mirror. Here one of the theories as to his true identity can be explicated. He traveled through the graveyard earlier, where, we later learn, the murdered man in the "dream" is buried.

Is it possible the spirit of the dead man entered The Stranger as he passed the graveyard, thus, possessing him? He reacted to the whip crack by the roustabout, and perhaps only now, after a period of unconsciousness, has the spirit taken full control. It only takes a second, but the look in the mirror, far from narcissistic, might be the curiosity of the murdered man looking to see what his new visage looked like.

He returns to the barbershop, tidied up from the violence of the day before. The barber orders the midget to fill the tub with hot water. Chewing on another cigar provided by the diminutive Mordecai, The Stranger reclines in the steel bathtub as the diffident sheriff assures him no charges will be filed in the deaths of the three troublemakers the day before.

Callie bursts in brandishing a rifle, cursing The Stranger, who sinks beneath the water's surface. She gets off four shots into the tub before the sheriff wrestles her out the door, telling Mordecai to have The Stranger wait around town for a business proposition.

The Stranger rises from the water, the cigar still clenched in his teeth. "Wonder what took her so long to get mad?" he muses.

"Because maybe you didn't come back for more," Mordecai offers. This sequence of events provides another clue toward revealing The Stranger's true nature. The bullets clearly hit the water, yet he emerges unscathed. He may be a ghost prone to the pleasures of the flesh, but not susceptible to the weaknesses of it.

Meanwhile, the town elders discuss the necessity of hiring The Stranger to defend Lago against three convicts being released from a territorial prison that day.

The sheriff brings Callie in, who, despite her cries for justice, is told she must let a man like that have his way for the good of the town. "There's too much at stake to throw away on hysterics now," Drake tells her. "Hysterics" she says incredulously. "Well, I can remember some hysterics one night not too long ago!" Her allusion to the man being whipped to death is obviously a secret shame of the men gathered.

The Stranger rejects the sheriff's offer to safeguard the town, claiming not to be a gunfighter and bearing no grudge

against the three men they all fear. The Stranger asks for the details of the trio's misdeeds. The sheriff tells him they had been troubleshooters for the mining company, but had become glutted with braggadocio, and had to be taken into custody. In fact, they had taken a gold ingot that had been left in the mining company office, and the sheriff himself had been the arresting officer.

The Stranger expresses his doubts as to the truthfulness of the story, but insists the sheriff arrest the three again should trouble start. "Look, I'm no lawman," the sheriff protests. "They just hung this thing on me when that young Marshal Duncan was killed. Y'know, he was whipped to death? Right here in this street. Bullwhipped. Damnedest thing I ever saw."

"Now, why would anyone want to do a thing like that?" The Stranger ponders, drawing the sheriff out.

"Well, I don't know. Wasn't anybody from this town anyhow." "How do you know?" he prods.

"This is a good town, these are good people," the sheriff rationalizes haplessly. Obviously uncomfortable with the line of questioning, he again asks The Stranger to act as the town's defender. Acquiescing, he details a rudimentary plan of ambush the townsmen themselves could carry out. The Stranger is offered carte blanche, unlimited credit "with no reckoning" to all Lago if he will oversee the proposed ambush.

Intrigued, The Stranger tests the peoples' generosity, first by giving away candy and blankets to an elderly Indian man and the two children with him who were being insulted a moment before. Next, he helps himself to a fistful of cigars, then has three pairs of boots, a belt and a new saddle specially made.

The Stranger's burgeoning entourage trundles along with him from shop to shop, guffawing at the proprietors' reactions to the giveaways. They end up at the saloon, where a round of drinks is ordered for all, and Mordecai is presented with the sheriff's badge and the mayor's hat. Save for the friendly midget, everyone in town has been knocked down a peg.

Meanwhile, the three convicts, led by Stacy Bridges (Geoffrey Lewis), are released from prison, and begin their slow journey toward the town.

With the gunsmith providing everyone a new rifle, The Stranger sets up an exercise for the townsmen. He places them on strategic rooftops and has a wagon pulled through town with three dummies perched on a sawhorse, with orders for the people to shoot them off. Their marksmanship is pathetic, and The Stranger, sipping a beer in disgust, takes off the "heads" of all three with as many shots.

The Stranger sets in motion his scenario for Lago's defense. As with the earlier scene in the store with the Indians, The Stranger is "politically correct" as he comes to the defense of two Mexican carpenters he has put to work building giant picnic tables, appropriating the needed lumber from the walls of the hotelier's barn. Irate at his property being dismantled, Lewis (Ted Hartley), the hotel owner, is further incensed by being ordered to surrender 35 bed sheets to serve as tablecloths.

The trio of villains comes across some campers on the range, kills them, and continues their trek on horseback.

Outraged by the course of events, Lago's elders begin to quarrel amongst themselves about their decision to hire The Stranger, hoping against hope the three convicts they fear might be "blind-drunk in some Nogales whorehouse," and forgiving of the town's prosecution of them.

Here we learn the reasons for the Marshal's murder: the mine is illegally established on government land, and Duncan was going to go to the authorities. The three villains, killing the Marshal under orders, have kept silent for fear of incriminating themselves as well the mining company powers-that-be.

The Stranger orders the hotelier to evict all his residents, that he might have the entire building to himself. The preacher is outraged, and confronts the town's "guardian angel."

"See here, you can't turn all these people out into the night," he rails. "It is inhuman, brother. Inhuman!"

"I'm not your brother," The Stranger reminds him.

"We are all brothers in the eyes of God!"

Chased underneath a porch by the disgruntled town elders, Mordecai has his own flashback of the murder from that same vantage point, as the villains call Duncan out and begin whipping him to death, with the townspeople looking on from the shadows. Some appear indifferent to the scene, while others seem to be reveling in the cruelty. Only the hotel owner's wife Sarah (Verna Bloom) is seen objecting, and she is quickly hustled away. Mordecai, watching again the death of the Marshal in his mind's eye, cries silently in the darkness.

Perhaps the most unconventional postulation about *High Plains Drifter* comes from a book entitled *Clint Eastwood*. After a plot synopsis, author Neil Sinyard makes a précis of the whole film as nothing more than a fantasy dreamed up by Mordecai. Mordecai becomes the hero of the film, Mr. Sinyard asserts, because it is "a dream that gives the dwarf [sic] heroic stature."

One of the villains' horses goes lame, so they double up.

Back in Lago, the townspeople gather in the church to bemoan The Stranger's presence. Lewis declares it "couldn't be worse if the Devil himself had ridden right into Lago," another possibility, albeit a slim one, as to The Stranger's identity. In folklore, the Devil has often appeared as a man, often a dark man, befitting his role as leader of the powers of darkness

The town elders have had enough, so they go to the hotel that night as The Stranger sleeps after sex with Callie. She slips from his bed and leaves the door open for them—they burst in with clubs and two-by-fours, pummeling the bed in the dark room. Outside, on the ledge, The Stranger lights a stick of dynamite with his ubiquitous cigar and tosses it back through the window. The gang scrambles to escape before the blast.

Biding his time, The Stranger picks each man off with his gun as they scurry. He even seems to shoot through a hostage, Sarah, without ill effect, to wound one (Jack Ging). Bleeding from the shoulder, the man makes it to the stable, mounts up, and rides off into the night.

Lewis is dumbstruck at the ruin of his hotel: The Stranger orders him to help dig graves for the dead men posthaste. Drake, plainly terrified, promises a large bonus for The Stranger to see through the town's defense.

"I knew you were cruel, but I didn't know how far you could go," Sarah berates The Stranger.

"Well, you still don't," he remarks. All of the other hotel rooms in ruin, The Stranger goes to Lewis and Sarah's to bed down for the night. Inevitably, she joins him.

The next morning, he looks out the window to see the impromptu funeral ceremonies for the men killed the night before. From the bed, Sarah asks him, "Have you ever heard the name Jim Duncan?"

"I've heard a lot of things. Why?"

"He was town Marshal here," she explains "He's lying out there in an unmarked grave. They say the dead don't rest without a marker of some kind. Do you believe that?"

"What makes you think I care?" he asks nonchalantly.

"I don't know," Sarah shrugs. "He's the reason this town's afraid of strangers." Sarah's theory forms the basis for the possibility of the ghostly nature of *High Plains Drifter.*

Sudden death, and especially death by violence, has often been cited as a reason for murder victims' known hauntings. In classic literature, ghosts often remain to harass the living, like Hamlet's father, until vengeance is done. Also, ghosts remain when their bodies have been improperly buried, or not buried at all, as with Odysseus's friend Elpenor.

As The Stranger starts to leave, Sarah stops him short. "Be careful," she urges. "You're a man who makes people afraid, and that's dangerous."

"Well, it's what people know about themselves inside that makes 'em afraid," he adds, furthering the idea of his supernatural omniscience. The Stranger rides out to the graveyard and repaints the town sign to read HELL in dripping red letters. He tells Mordecai, ex officio, to have the people begin painting the entire town bright red.

Following the wounded man's blood trail, The Stranger starts off into the wilderness. Sarah announces to her husband Lewis she's leaving, disgusted at the town's concealment of Duncan's murder. Lewis feebly tries to dissuade her, but cannot.

The wounded man comes by the approaching villains, who, delighted at getting an early start on their revenge, finish him off by jamming a stick into his throat. Suddenly, shots ring out, making them scramble for cover. The Stranger's uncanny aim (he clips one of the men's ears off), plus a few sticks of dynamite, effectively pins the trio down.

Stacy calls out a challenge, thinking it's only Drake or one of the other bureaucrats. Mysteriously, in an incredibly short time, The Stranger is able to get all the way around the ridge above them and toss another stick of dynamite. Shards of pulverized rock embed themselves in Stacy's face, infuriating him. The Stranger takes off back to Lago.

Every building has been painted bright red, even the frameworks of those under construction. The Stranger warns the

people that the three are on their way, and sends the stableman up to the bell tower to act as a lookout.

The Stranger helps himself to some whiskey as Mordecai approaches him. "What about after?" he asks, his voice trembling. "What about after we do it? What do we do then?"

"Then you live with it," The Stranger replies knowingly. He gets on his horse and rides out of Lago the opposite way the three villains are coming. The bell starts to toll.

Significant in this scene is the history of the tolling bell in superstition. A common inscription on church bells of the 19th century was, "I call the quick to church and dead to grave"; it was also generally accepted that, until the passing bell had been rung, the soul remained earthbound, since it only "rose to heaven on the sound of the bell."

The trio rides up, pause at the vision the town presents, draw their guns, and charge. They pull down the WELCOME HOME BOYS banner as well as the picnic tables set up in their honor, and lasso the former sheriff, dragging him through the streets. Despite Mordecai's urging, none of the ensconced riflemen fires at the three, and most are picked off by the villains' guns. Drake comes out of the mining company office with a valise, but is chased down by Stacy and shot dead, falling into the alkaline lake.

That night, with a goodly portion of Lago aflame, the villains herd the remaining populace into the saloon. As Archie P. McDonald wrote in the source cited earlier, first The Stranger has put "the town folk through the wringer...never letting them forget what cowards they really are"; now, their spirits crushed, those folks are utterly defeated, at the mercy of the villains.

Callie begs for Stacy's forgiveness, pleading her love, which he dismisses. At last feeling sated with revenge, the trio prepare to leave, when one of them wonders who it was that waylaid them that morning.

Before Stacy can begin questioning the survivors, a whip cracks outside and pulls one of the villains out of the saloon into the street. There, The Stranger whips him to death.

Inside, the remaining two are plainly terrified. Mordecai smiles at the turn of events as the whip is tossed over the transom. As everyone moves outside to check out the body, a lighted stick of dynamite tossed nearby causes the townspeople to flee in terror. It fizzles out, and the remaining two stalk the town in search of their partner's killer.

Another whip snakes from a rooftop and snags another of the villains by the neck, hoisting him up and strangling him. Only Stacy is left. An oil lamp is thrown, and Stacy fires wildly at it and into the alleyway from where it seemed to emerge.

From that darkness a voice pleads, "Help me," echoing the final sibilant cries of the Marshal the year before. Stacy smiles, thinking he's wounded his unseen enemy. The Stranger suddenly appears across the street and Stacy is shot dead. Lewis tries to sneak up and kill The Stranger, but Mordecai shoots him in the nick of time. The Stranger nods approvingly.

The next day, as the town is cleaning up, The Stranger rides out of town. Some meet his steely gaze, including the reinstated sheriff, who manages a smile despite his scarring. Sarah gets on a buckboard with a suitcase and smiles at The Stranger, who concedes a smile himself. He gallops to the graveyard where Mordecai is seen working on a headstone.

The midget squints, looking up at him. "I'm just about done here," Mordecai tells him. "I never did know your name."

"Yes, you do," The Stranger states.

Mordecai's mouth opens slightly in shock as he watches The Stranger ride off. The camera swivels around to show the marker the man had been working on, which reads "Marshal Jim Duncan - Rest In Peace." The Stranger gallops into the rising heat waves and, as in the opening scene, vanishes. Interestingly, just before the credits roll, the camera pans slightly to the right, as if searching for The Stranger, to make sure our eyes haven't tricked us.

Unprepared audiences, teased throughout with hints of the supernatural, no doubt felt a chill at this denouement. The eerie content is paid off so much at the end that it's difficult to imagine any interpretation of The Stranger other than as a ghost.

Still, it is this element of preternaturalism that has inspired the greatest commentary from critics and scholars, and not necessarily those with affinities to the genre of ghostly or horrific cinema. Jay Hyams, in *The Life and Times of the Western Movie*, called it "a very unusual Western with a very unique style [that] goes well beyond the boundaries of traditional Westerns, becoming almost surreal."

In *The BFI Companion to the Western*, Edward Buscombe declared it an "extraordinary Gothic Western" and that "a weird aura of exorcism hangs over the film."

Brian Garfield, in *Western Films*, discoursed, "At the end there's a peculiar surrealist plot. It goes past realism into the abstract, sometimes effectively, and those are interesting ghostly touches, but it's by no means a good movie: it's a sex-and-violence fantasy, faddish and empty, very self-conscious, but in its weird visual structure it's sometimes fascinating."

Most comments are brief, with little elaboration. *TV Guide*'s Judith Crist called it "the usual S & V orgy," while *Halliwell's Film Guide (Eighth Edition)* said it was "very watchable, but irritating."

Leave it to *Variety* to sum it up, "A nervously humorous, self-conscious near-satire on the prototype Eastwood formula," discoursed Murf. "Tidyman's untidy patchwork script.., has some raw violence for the kinks, some dumb humor for audience relief, and lots of arch characterizations befitting the serio-comic-strip nature of the plot.., mechanically stylish music lends an eerie feel at the right moments... artsy."

Variety also made astute commentary on the other actors, saying, "Ryan, Ging, Gierasch and Hartley are good... Barnes is very effective... Lewis, the prime heavy, is excellent." Remarkably, only one review made special note of what must be the best performance in the movie. In the *Blockbuster Guide to Movies and Video 1996*, the unnamed writer said the film had "extreme violence appropriate to its genre, with a sparkling supporting turn by Billy Curtis."

Curtis, at four-feet-two-inches, is best known among film aficionados for his starring role as the hero in *The Terror of Tiny Town* (1938), the infamous midget Western. As a supporting actor, Curtis had better parts in a host of movies, from *Saboteur* (1942) to *Planet of the Apes* (1968). Mordecai is the most sympathetic character in *High Plains Drifter*, and the 63-year-old Curtis' winsome performance is worthy of far more praise than has yet been conferred. The films other performers had, or have since, achieved a comfortable familiarity with audiences, both of mainstream and of fantastic cinema. Mitchell Ryan, even mustachioed, struck a familiar chord with fans of the early days of TV's *Dark Shadows*, wherein he enacted the hero's part of Burke Devlin; and, more recently, played the part of Commander Riker's (Jonathan Frakes) father on *Star Trek: The Next Generation*.

Jack Ging had been in *Play Misty For Me*, as Frank, with Eastwood earlier. John Hillerman, before gaining

widespread familiarity with *Magnum P.I.*, was in the reincarnation thriller *Audrey Rose* (1977) as Scott Velie. One of the three villains was played by Dan Vadis, the bodybuilder star of several Italian-made sword-and-sandal films, among them *Ursus the Gladiator* (1962) and *Son of Hercules in the Land of Darkness* (1963), as well as a Euro Western of his own, *The Stranger Returns* (1967). He did work with Eastwood again, playing the American Indian member of a traveling Wild West show, in *Bronco Billy* (1980). Vadis died in 1987.

Stefan Gierasch and Mariana Hill had a reunion of sorts when both were cast in *Blood Beach* in 1981, where they encountered, as L.R. Morse's *Video Trash & Treasures* described it, "an animate artichoke." Geoffrey Lewis, perhaps more notable today for fathering award-winning actress Juliette Lewis, had a successful association with Eastwood for many years, turning up as the best friend in the comedy *Every Which Way But Loose* (1978) and its sequel *Any Which Way You Can* (1980) (both with John Guade as the leader of an inept motorcycle gang), as well as in *Bronco Billy*.

Also, the very familiar face in muttonchop whiskers tending bar in *High Plains Drifter* belonged to Paul Brinegar. To fans of horror and science fiction, little introduction need be made, what with his parts of Willie in *The Vampire* (1957) and of Vida in *World Without End* (1956); his most well-known role was that of the fidgety Rivero, assistant to Robert H. Harris's mad makeup artist in *How To Make A Monster* (1958). In a nod to Eastwood (the two had costarred in *Rawhide*), his character in *The Creature Wasn't Nice* (1981) a.k.a. *Spaceship* was named Dirty Harry. He died in 1995 at 77.

No discourse on *High Plains Drifter* would be complete without some mention being made of two other films. Most commonly cited as a remake, *Pale Rider* (1985) was Eastwood's first Western since *The Outlaw Josey Wales* (1976), and, in the words of *TV Guide*, "a very respectable homage to countless sagebrush sagas that preceded it." The weekly magazine continued, "Riding to folks' aid is something Eastwood has done better in *High Plains Drifter*." *Cinefantastique* also made comparisons to *High Plains Drifter* in its review, saying "the supernatural touches here are nicely understated, but never really mesh." Alan Dean Foster's novelization, based on the screenplay, shed no light on his origins.

When a motley group of gold prospectors is harassed by an unscrupulous land baron (Richard Dysart), a teenage girl (Sydney Penny) paraphrases the 23rd Psalm over the grave of her dead dog. As if on cue, a mysterious "Preacher" (Clint Eastwood) appears to take up their defense. He even rides a dappled gray horse like The Stranger did. After dispensing a few homilies and exhibiting some martial arts skills with an ax handle, he divests himself of his clerical collar and retrieves a gun and holster from a safe deposit box. The agnominal Pale Rider, so-called for Death, the Fourth Horseman of the Apocalypse, then goes about giving the tycoon and his cronies their comeuppance.

The venal sheriff (John Russell, TV's *Lawman*) thinks he recognizes the clergyman, believing him dead, but never gets a chance to confirm this before the climactic shoot-out. Five bullet-shaped wounds on the Preacher's back remain unexplained, and, once justice is meted out, he rides off into the mountain snow. More politically correct than ever, this nigh angelic (as opposed to *High Plains Drifter*'s demonic) character forgoes the ubiquitous Man With No Name cheroots, and even comes out against the tycoon's method of "raping the land" in mining it.

To be sure, *High Plains Drifter* is an imperfect film, clumsily bifurcated into a prosaic Western and a tenuous ghost story. Eastwood insisted to Universal that he did not want to utilize the studio's rustic back lot locales, that for the finale's conflagration new setpieces were compulsory. Lago's newness actually works against itself, however. Whether it is historically more accurate is not the point; the right "look" is all-important in cinema, no matter the genre, and *High Plains Drifter* falls short in that department. The town scarcely looks lived in, and there never seems to be more than a score of people populating it.

There are only a few women, no children or dogs, and no one ever seems to put in a day's work. The mine, the very pith of the town, is never even shown.

Tidyman's dialogue is rife with anachronisms, perhaps in an effort to inveigle a younger audience. At one point the high-strung barber asks, "What's the diff?", a contraction familiar to adolescents of the 1970s. Drake, the mining company executive, reminds his accomplices that hiring The Stranger is the solution to "saving your ass." Callie wonders if there is anyone left in the town "with a full set of balls."

And there is that camouflaging of the ghostly aspects, too obvious to be anything but intentional, as though Eastwood the director was afraid to venture into the macabre outright. This theory is confounding, though, in that Don Siegel, one of his mentors, had earlier directed him to critical success in a sublime Gothic horror tale, *The Beguiled* (1971), without hesitating to evoke an otherworldly ambiance. It may also have been a reaction to the actor's leaner days in 1965, when he had a small role in the justly obscure Italian comedy *Le Streghe* (*The Witches*) for director Vittorio de Sica. The movie flopped when it was finally released in Europe in 1967 and did the same in the U.S. two years later.

Eastwood and certifiable ghost movies didn't stay strangers forever, though. In 1995's *Casper*, Dr. James Harvey (Bill Pullman), possessed by "The Ghostly Trio," metamorphosed into Eastwood (making an unbilled cameo) for a few seconds' screen time.

Virtually every action taken by The Stranger can be explained away without resorting to the supernatural. His shimmering appearance and disappearance that bookend the movie can be the result of desert heat; his seemingly inexhaustible supply of dynamite sticks might have been appropriated from a mining company supply shack; his aim in the barbershop and out on the range might be as good as Callie's is bad at the bathtub.

Is The Stranger a ghost then? There is no concrete evidence either way, and, as in classic literature, the imagination of the audience is the best venue to inspire fright. After all, in Charles

Dickens' *A Christmas Carol*, Marley's presence in Ebeneezer Scrooge's bedchamber may indeed be the result of nothing more than "a undigested bit of beef, a blot of mustard, a crumb of cheese, a fragment of underdone potato."

This sort of subjectivity has worked frequently in ghostly cinema. The title *High Plains Drifter* itself masks the ghost content, as have several others of the same ilk, particularly in recent years. *The Girl in A Swing* (1989), *Truly Madly Deeply* (1990) and *The Force* (1994) have all been released deliberately evasive about their content, all of them simply, or complexly, ghost stories. The fact a film sometimes makes known that it is a ghost movie, whether with a hackneyed title or via eerie promotion, doesn't lessen its predestined impact, but rather inures the audience for what is to come, e.g. *Ghostbusters*, *The Wraith* (1987) and *Ghost*.

In one early scene, The Stranger tells an intimidator that he "is a lot faster than you'll ever live to be," a challenge that works just as well when aimed at Eastwood's cynical peers in the film industry. For years little was thought of Eastwood the actor, sentiments recapitulated by prolific film scribe John McCarty who described him in *Psychos: Eighty Years of Mad Movies, Maniacs, and Murderous Deeds* as "a likable actor with virtually no range," while Eastwood the director continued to earn accolades and respect.

After winning an Oscar for his direction of *Unforgiven* in 1992, Eastwood received the Irving G. Thalberg Memorial Award from the Academy of Motion Picture Arts and Sciences in 1995 and the American Film Institute's lifetime achievement award in 1996. AFT chairman, Frederick S. Pierce announced the award by saying, "Eastwood's career has epitomized talent, integrity and vision."

For some of us, the vision of The Stranger vanishing into the heat of the new day will haunt forever, and *High Plains Drifter* stands as a classic ghost movie that seems reluctant to admit to being one.

CREDITS: Producer Robert Daley; Director: Clint Eastwood; Written by Ernest Tidyman; Director of Photography: Bruce Surtees; Technicolor; Filmed in Panavision; Running Time: 105 minutes; Universal Pictures and The Malpaso Company; released in 1973

CAST: Clint Eastwood...The Stranger, Verna Bloom...Sarah Belding, Mariana Hill...Callie Travers, Mitchell Ryan...Dave Drake, Jack Ging...Morgan Allen, Stefan Gierasch...Mayor Jason Hobart, Ted Hartley...Lewis Belding, Billy Curtis...Mordecai Fortusse, Geoffrey Lewis... Stacy Bridges, Scott Walker... Bill Borders, Walter Barnes...Sheriff Sam Shaw, Paul Brinegar...Lutie Naylor, Richard Bull...Asa Goodwin, Robert Donner...Preacher, John Hillerman... Bootmaker, Anthony James...Cole Carlin, William O'Connell...Barber, John Guade...Jake Ross, Jane Null...Townswoman, Dan Vadis...Dan Carlin, Reid Cruickshanks...Gunsmith, James Gosa...Tommy Morris, Jack Kosslyn... Saddlemaker, Russ McCubbin...Fred Short, Belle Mitchell...Mrs. Lake, John Mitchell...Warden, Carl C. Pitti...Teamster, Chuck Waters...Stableman, Buddy Van Horn...Marshal Jim Duncan

Special thanks to Craig Ledbetter for his immeasurable assist, Todd Tjertland and Simon Upton for, respectively, having a stronger stomach and a longer attention span than I, and to my wife Lynn for reining me in when necessary, but still letting me think I reign.

THE INNOCENTS

by Don G. Smith

The Innocents is based on *The Turn of the Screw* (1898), a novella by Henry James (1843-1916), one of the most highly acclaimed authors in the English language. James, however, is also heralded for his ghost stories, of which *The Turn of the Screw* is rightfully the most renowned. James' other important supernatural stories are the often-anthologized classics "The Romance of Certain Old Clothes," "Sir Edmund Orme" and the lesser known "The Friends of the Friends."

In *The Guide to Supernatural Fiction*, author Everett F. Bleiler writes:"[*The Turn of the Screw*] is unquestionably the most studied and 'interpreted' story in the corpus of modern supernatural fiction, with an almost unbelievable range of interpretations, often in the most fanciful modes. It has been read by Edmund Wilson and others as an anticipation of Freudian sexuality; by others as a restatement of the Creation and the Fall; and still by others as a contra-narrative of various figurative sorts."

Despite its rich reputation, *The Turn of the Screw* was not adapted as a motion picture until 1961, when it attracted the interest of director Jack Clayton. Having directed the award winning *Room at the Top*, Clayton turned down numerous projects over the next two years because he considered them too similar to his previous successful venture. Clayton explained in a pressbook interview:"I wanted to do something different. I started preparing a couple of films—one for Ingrid Bergman and a second for Laurence Harvey—but one clashed with the other and I did neither.

"About 18 months ago I suddenly remembered the Henry James classic, *Turn of the Screw*. I first read the psychological thriller when I was ten and it made a great impression on me. I was surprised to learn that although it had been a great success as a play, as an opera by Benjamin Britten, and as a television presentation, it had never been made into a motion picture.

"20th Century-Fox owned the film rights and was not prepared to sell it. So I asked if I could make the picture for them and they agreed."

Fox assigned noted author William Archibald to write the screenplay, but upon its completion, Jack Clayton begged Truman Capote to undertake a rewrite. Since the story was one of Capote's favorites, he accepted the challenge. As Capote later recalled, "I thought it would be a snap because I loved *The Turn of the Screw* so much. But when I got into it, I saw how artful James had been. He did everything by allusion and indirection." In 1954 Capote worked with Jack Clayton on the film *Beat the Devil* (with Humphrey Bogart and Peter Lorre). During the filming, the diminutive Capote surprised everyone by defeating Humphrey Bogart at arm wrestling, Bogie being the most surprised of all. In 1958 Capote enhanced his literary reputation with the successful lighthearted novella *Breakfast at Tiffany*'s. When Capote got Clayton's call to rewrite *The Innocents*, he was at work on the book that would make him a household name—the powerful *In Cold Blood*. Putting *In Cold Blood* aside, he traveled to London. After the cold and drizzle of a London winter, the author later used his money from *The Innocents* to buy a two-room condominium in Verbier.

The starring role of Miss Giddons went to six-time Academy Award nominee Deborah Kerr. It was the British actress' first film with a 19th-century setting since *The King and I* (1956), though all similarities between the two films end there! Kerr indeed came to *The Innocents* on the strength of a splendid career, her most heralded films being *Black Narcissus* (1946), *From Here to Eternity* (1953), *The King and I* (1956), *Tea and Sympathy* (1956), *An Affair to Remember* (1957), *Separate Tables* (1958) and *The Sundowners* (1960).

According to the pressbook, while on the set of *The Innocents*, Miss Kerr offered her opinion on ghosts and governess:"I do not believe in ghosts. I think women who are afraid to be left alone in their house or imagine there's a man under their bed, are either mighty conceited or just pulling feminine tricks to keep a man around the house. Or maybe, they're hopeful. As for Miss Giddons, I'm sure she sees ghosts, but she's the only one who does. After reading the Henry James classic *Turn of the Screw*, I was convinced that the governess, a sheltered girl, was neurotic. She had no outlet for her frustrations and therefore had to create an outlet. The ghostly visions are a product of her disturbed imagination."

The role of the uncle went to Sir Michael Redgrave. Though he appears in the film for only five or six minutes, his grand reputation earned him second billing. Redgrave's only horror film before *The Innocents* was the classic *Dead of Night* (1945), in which the actor turns in an unnerving performance as a ventriloquist.

Jack Clayton chose 12-year-old Martin Stephens to play young Miles. The boy had already appeared in the highly acclaimed horror/science fiction film *Village of the Damned* (1960), for which he topped a list of 178 youngsters who interviewed for the parts of 12 alien-spawned children with supernatural powers. Posters for the film featured the face of Stephens with glaring, unearthly eyes: "Beware the stare that will paralyze the will of the world!"

Screen tests for the role of Flora produced seven candidates. Though Tokyo-born British youngster Pamela Franklin had no acting experience and was studying to be a dancer, her natural talent and receptivity to direction convinced Jack Clayton to hire her.

Clayton chose Freddie Francis as cinematographer. Francis had handled the camera for Clayton's *Room at the Top* and had won an Academy Award for his work on *Sons and Lovers* (1960).

The Innocents proved to enhance the careers of all concerned. Deborah Kerr would go on to further acclaim in such films as *The Night of the Iguana* (1964). Michael Redgrave would star in such critically acclaimed films as *Nicholas and Alexandra* (1971) and *The Go-Between* (1971). Martin Stephens would turn in good performances in *The Battle of Villa Fiorita* (1965) and the Hammer horror film *The Witches* (1966). But it was Pamela Franklin who would go on to carve out a minor place in the pantheon of horror film performers. She would appear with Bette Davis in Hammer's *The Nanny* (1965), flee from a mad killer in *And Soon the Darkness* (1970), resist being turned into a witch by Orson Welles in *Necromancy* (1972), assist Roddy McDowall as a psychic in *The Legend of Hell House* (1973), and battle giant rats with Ida Lupino in *Food of the Gods* (1976). Her best performance, however, would be in *The Prime of Miss Jean Brodie* (1969) at the end of which she "puts a stop" to Maggie Smith.

Jack Clayton would go on to direct the critically successful *The Pumpkin Eater* (1964) and the underrated *The Great Gatsby* (1974). He would return to the horror genre as director of Ray Bradbury's *Something Wicked This Way Comes* (1983), only to prove that Bradbury's horror/fantasies are very difficult to translate successfully to the screen.

On the success of his journalistic novel *In Cold Blood*, Truman Capote would become the darling of the jet set, a frequent guest on late night talk shows, and one of America's most critically acclaimed writers. Unfortunately, his powers weakened by drug addiction and alcoholism, he would die in 1984, an outcast from the rich who once adored him, but still a formidable figure in American literature.

Cinematographer Freddie Francis would later turn horror film director on such projects as *Paranoiac* (1963), *Nightmare* (1963), *The Evil of Frankenstein* (1964), *Dracula Has Risen from the Grave* (1968) and *The Doctor and the Devils* (1986). Though his films often boasted stars the status of Peter Cushing and Christopher Lee, the final products, with a few notable exceptions, were mediocre. Returning occasionally to cinematography, however, he guided the camera on such well-received films as *The Elephant Man* (1981) and would win an Academy Award for *Glory* (1989).

Apparently realizing they had a potential winner, 20th Century-Fox promoted the film with a well-executed trailer, an attractive pressbook, and an intriguing set of posters. The key line in the ads was "Do they ever return to possess the living?" Borrowing hints from Alfred Hitchcock and William Castle, some ads read: "BE FOREWARNED In your own interests, see this picture from the beginning. BECAUSE This picture creates a tension and an atmosphere never experienced in a motion picture. BECAUSE You must savor every spine-chilling moment without interruption. BECAUSE The only way to fully enjoy this masterpiece of macabre love is to see it from the very begining to the mind-stunning end." Though this rather poorly written piece of exploitation could be taken by cynical (or experienced) readers as just another example of overblown hyperbole, in this rare instance it is not. *The Innocents* is an artistically constructed film, and the viewing experience would indeed be marred or destroyed by walking in at the mid-point or by incurring several interruptions (like bathroom breaks or frequent kisses in the balcony). In other words, *The Innocents* was advertised for what it is—a serious work by true professionals.

On the ads and posters, certain evocative words appear in eerie italics: "whispers, witchcraft, evil, depravity, aberrations, apparitions, corruptions." Only "witchcraft" is misleading as *The Innocents* is replete with all the rest! Viewers were challenged to experience "a strange new experience in SHOCK from Jack Clayton, director of *Room at the Top*."

Ultimately though, it was the quality of the film itself that promised to attract audiences. On that point, 20th Century-Fox was on very solid ground.

We hear the chirping of birds. Still the screen is dark. Then we see hands in supplication, and the face of Deborah Kerr as the governess: "All I want to do is save the children, not destroy them. More than anything I love children. More than anything. They need affection, love…someone who will belong to them."

The scene fades, and we hear the voice of Michael Redgrave as the uncle:"Do you have an imagination?"

"Oh, oh yes," the governess bubbles. "I can answer that yes!" The uncle goes on to explain that he needs a governess to look after his orphaned nephew and niece, Miles and Flora. He explains that he is a selfish man and does not want to be saddled with orphaned children. Little Miles is away at school and Flora is at Bly House, where she is currently under the care of Miss Grose, the housekeeper. The uncle relates that Flora was very fond of Miss Jessel, the former governess, and that it came as shock when she died. "It was all very odd," he says, without further explanation.

When Miss Giddons accepts the position, the uncle reiterates, "You are in supreme authority. Whatever happens, you must handle it alone."

These opening scenes set a mood and foreshadow what is to come. The haunting song "Willow Waylee" introduces the theme of a bereaved lover preparing to die of a broken heart as she awaits the return of her dead mate. But the song is sung by a child, not an adult, suggesting the problem that Miss Giddons is to face at Bly House.

In establishing Miss Giddons as the highly imaginative daughter of a country parson, the early scenes suggest that the governess is probably heavily influenced by religion, somewhat sheltered, possibly naive in the ways of the world, and definitely fanciful—characteristics that will later call into question the reliability of her perception and interpretation of events.

Of course, her words regarding her love of children foreshadow her motives and credibility will somehow be called into question under painful circumstances. The mood is conjured, the clues are left, and the stage is set for the unfolding of probably the greatest ghost story of all time.

The scene shifts to Miss Giddons' arrival at Bly House. Then the music darkens a bit as Miss Giddons hears someone calling the name of Flora. The governess comes upon Flora by the edge of a pond and asks if she did not hear someone calling her. The girl responds that she did not. Miss Giddons introduces herself to Flora, and the little girl shows the governess Rupert, her pet tortoise. Flora expresses her joy at Miss Giddons's arrival, saying "We will have fun together, won't we!"

Upon meeting Mrs. Grose, Miss Giddons expresses her pleasure with Bly House: "I never imagined it would be so beautiful. It's a Heaven for children."

"Miles is away at school," Flora tells Miss Giddons. "He'll be coming home soon."

Alone with Mrs. Grose, the governess asks what her predecessor was like. "A young woman," Mrs. Grose answers. "Some would say pretty." Then in reference to some man, the housekeeper says, "He has the devil's own eye." When asked who she is referring to, Mrs. Gross unconvincingly says that she was referring to the master.

Flora informs Mrs. Grose and Miss Giddons that Miles will be coming home soon, and again they tell her that Miles will not be home until the end of the school term. When Miss Giddons walks Flora to her bedroom, the little girl volunteers that, unlike Mrs. Grose, she likes to keep her eyes open in the dark. When the governess asks Flora what she sees in the dark, the precocious youngster changes the subject.

Flora then perfunctorily repeats the Lord's prayer, after which she asks where the Lord will take her soul if she dies in her sleep. "To Heaven," Miss Giddons tells her. "Are you certain?" Flora asks. "Yes, of course," Miss Giddons replies, "because you've been a very, very good girl." "But I might not be," Flora persists, "and if I weren't, wouldn't the Lord just leave me here to walk around? Isn't that what happens to some people?" Before Miss Giddons can answer, the cries of an injured bird emanate from beyond the bedroom window. "You must pretend you didn't hear it," Flora responds. "That's what Mrs. Grose always says." "Pretend?" Miss Giddons asks. "Then you won't imagine things," Flora explains. Miss Giddons replies pensively, "Sometimes one can't help imagining things."

The first day and night at Bly House establish Mrs. Grose as a middle-aged, goodhearted, simple woman. They also establish Flora as bright, cheerful, evasive and secretive. But secretive about what? Who did Miss Giddons hear calling Flora out near the pond—if anyone? Was it a ghost calling to her at the pond? What does she see when she keeps her eyes open in the dark? Then there is the recurring matter of imagination. When Miss Giddons insists that sometimes one can't help but imagine thing. What is she saying? Obviously, the screenplay suggests that ghosts might indeed exist. However, it also suggests that Miss Giddons has an over-active imagination that might be influenced by Flora's references to evil people walking the earth after death. Though Miss Giddons might be highly imaginative, who or what was Flora looking for out her window in the dead of the night? The lyrics of "Willow Waylee" certainly suggest possibilities. At this point the situation is completely ambiguous, but since the audience sees and hears what Miss Giddons thinks she sees and hears, we are prone at this point to suspect the existence of ghosts at Bly House. The next day, a letter arrives from the uncle. Enclosed is a message from Miles' school informing the uncle that Miles has been expelled. When Miss Giddons presses Flora as to how she knew Miles was coming home so soon, the little girl changes the subject by directing attention to a "lovely spider" about to devour a fly. When Flora leaves, Miss Giddons discusses several disturbing aspects of the letter with Mrs. Gross. It seems that it was impossible for the school to keep Miles because he is "an injury to others." Miss Giddons wonders how the school concludes Miles "contaminates and corrupts" the other students. Mrs. Grose dismisses the expulsion explanations. "Oh, Miss," she laughs. "Are you afraid he'll corrupt you?"

These scenes suggest a supernatural link of communication between Flora and Miles, a link that the little girl is unwilling to discuss. They also suggest that the fly caught in the "lovely" spider's web might symbolize Miss Giddon's situation at Bly House. If Miss Giddons represents the fly, who or what represents the spider? Further, the scenes introduce the themes of contamination and corruption. Is Miles a bad influence on other

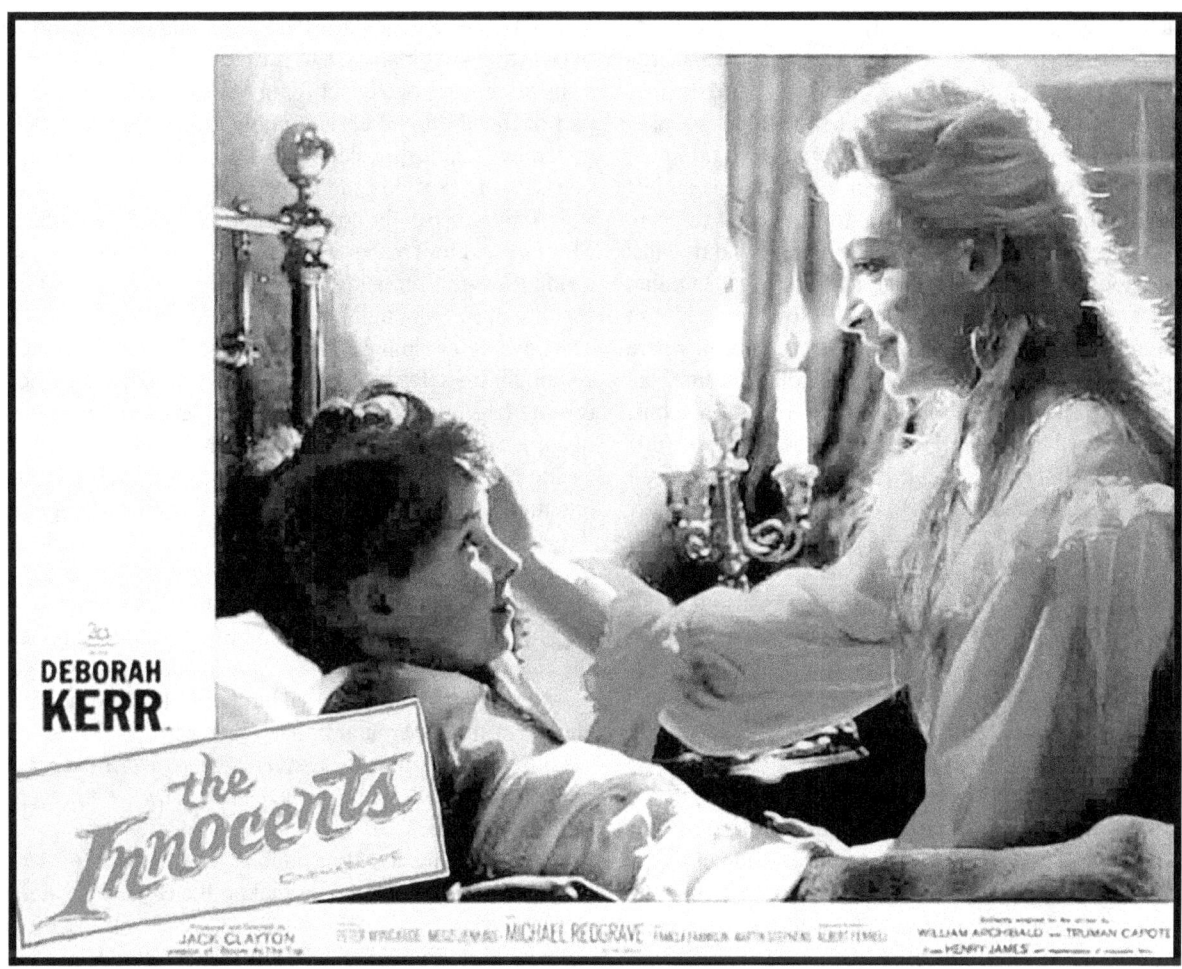

children? Mrs. Grose doubts the charge, but Miss Giddons is concerned. Though Mrs. Grose is joking, she plants the idea that Miles, a 12-year old boy, might (sexually?) corrupt Miss Giddons.

Upon arriving by train, Miles presents a bouquet of flowers to Miss Giddons. On the carriage ride to Bly House, the following conversation ensues:

Miles: May I tell you something?
Miss Giddons: Yes, Miles, of course.
Miles: I think you're far too pretty to be a governess.
Miss Giddons: And I think you're far too young to be a deceitful flatterer.

Is Miles just a precocious child? Mrs. Grose probably thinks so. Or is Miles truly capable of contaminating and corrupting others? Innocent though the exchange between Miss Giddons and Miles appears, it suggests that Miles' ability to corrupt may indeed be of a sexual nature. The boy certainly engages in dialogue with Miss Giddons that makes one question his "innocence."

After meeting Miles and watching the children run out to the field to see the horses, Miss Giddons concludes that the letter must have been a horrid mistake. That night, Miles invites Miss Giddons into his bedroom. When Miss Giddons tells Miles he should already be asleep, he replies that he is much too excited to sleep. He adds through words and texture of voice that meeting Miss Giddons made a meaningful impression on him. He then adds that he likes to lie awake in bed anyway. "That is a very bad habit," Miss Giddons tells him. When Miss Giddons raises the subject of Miles' expulsion from school, the boy matter-of-factly states that his uncle "doesn't care about me or Flora. He doesn't care what happens to us... It's a bit sad when people don't have time for you." Miss Giddons leans forward to comfort Miles, assuring him that she has time for him and Flora, and that she cares. She brushes her hand against the boy's cheek, and he turns his teary eyes toward her. Suddenly a noise startles Miss Giddons. "Don't be frightened," Miles says softly. "It was only the wind, my dear."

The relationship between Miss Giddons and Miles is becoming problematic. When Miles includes his meeting with Miss Giddons among the exciting events of the day, he does so as a young man might speak of meeting a young woman with whom he is seriously impressed. When Miss Giddons tells Miles that lying awake in bed is a very bad habit, she is speaking, of course, of the old admonition that under such conditions a child's mind can easily turn to sexual matters leading to masturbation. Miss Giddons is subtly acknowledging Miles' sexuality. The boy's loneliness and sense of abandonment leads Miss Giddons to comfort him, but when a noise breaks the silence, it is Miles who comforts Miss Giddons.

The next day, Miss Giddons is in the garden cutting roses as Flora plays nearby singing "Willow Waylee." The sun is shining, and the governess is peacefully smiling. She then parts the roses to find a statue of a little boy. As she watches, a large black insect crawls from the statue's mouth, disturbing her contentment. Suddenly all is quiet, and Miss Giddons senses that something is amiss. Slowly her eyes are drawn up to the tower of Bly House where the figure of a man moves amidst the flutter of pigeons and against the harsh rays of the sun. Miss Giddons squints her eyes for a clearer view and walks toward the house. Looking up again, she finds that the man has disappeared. Flora resumes singing "Willow Waylee," and Miss Giddons enters the house and ascends to the spot where she thought she saw the figure. Instead of finding the man she thought she saw, she finds only Miles and a flock of pigeons. When asked if someone has been with Miles, the boy replies that he has been quite alone with his birds. Perhaps, he suggests, it was he that Miss Giddons saw. But no. Troubled that she may have experienced an hallucination, the governess confides, "I haven't been sleeping well." "I know," Miles replies. "Flora told me. She says you make little moans and groans all night. Of course, one can never believe Flora. She invents things. She imagines them." Later, when Miss Giddons asks Mrs. Grose if there is anyone else in the house she hasn't met, the housekeeper says that there is no one.

The insect crawling from the mouth of the stone statue suggests that what may appear young and innocent on the outside can be corrupted on the inside. Does this startling moment lead the governess to imagine the figure of a man on the roof of Bly House? Certainly the audience sees the man along with the governess. But when the governess looks up a second time, the audience also sees that the man is gone, thereby raising doubts about his actual existence. The audience, as well as the governess, is led to question the experience. Is the figure an hallucination? The scene leaves open the possibility. When Miles tells Miss Giddons that Flora "invents things," he again places before the governess and the audience the theme of over-active imagination. But is over-active imagination really a sinister excuse or a cover for more troubling activities on the part of the children? Or is it really the chimerical root of the governess' inability to sleep soundly and of her general growing unease—or all of this and more?

At the close of the conversation between Miss Giddons and Mrs. Grose, Flora rushes in and invites Miss Giddons to witness a riding exhibition being performed by Miles. Miss Giddons accompanies Flora to the field where Miles is riding his horse. The boy begins riding so fast that Miss Giddons becomes concerned for his safety. Then, when Miles expertly rides the horse over a hedge, the wind in the trees produces a sound evocative of applause. "That was very clever," Miss Giddons tells Miles as she glances nervously at the trees. As they leave the field together, Miss Giddons is obviously relieved to be going.

This scene is interesting because of the ambiguity inherent in Miss Giddons' reference to Miles' "cleverness." Is the governess referring to the boy's equestrian feat or to the uneasy phenomenon of the "applauding" trees? Her eyes tell us that she is speaking of the trees. Yet, how could Miles arrange such a clever trick without supernatural aid? It is clearly the possibility of the supernatural that unsettles Miss Giddons. Still, coming shortly after her conversation with Miles involving imagination and invention, she questions her own perceptions, as does the audience.

That evening, as Miss Giddons and the children share conversation, the governess says that unlike Bly House, her home was very, very small. "Too small to have secrets?" Miles asks, casting Flora a knowing glance. "Much too small," the governess replies. The children then suggest a game of hide and seek.

As Miss Giddons walks the darkened hallways in search of the hiding children she sees the figure of a woman slowly cross a doorway. Confused, Miss Giddons walks upstairs and into

an attic where she finds a music box that plays "Willow Waylee." Beside the music box is the miniature photograph of a man. The doorknob slowly turns and Miles rushes in, playfully wrapping his arms around Miss Giddons' neck. When she complains that he is hurting her, the boy ignores her plea and continues to squeeze. Miles' rough play is interrupted when Flora rushes in and tells Miss Giddons to go hide. When the governess obeys, the children remain in the attic counting, a preternatural gleam in Flora's eyes.

Miss Giddons is hiding behind a curtain when she is startled by the face of a man at the window. Mrs. Grose appears and asks Miss Giddons if anything is wrong. The terrified and confused governess blurts out that she has just seen the man she earlier saw on the tower: "He was staring past me into the house as if he were hunting someone.... He had dark curling hair, and the hardest, the coldest eyes.... It is the man in the miniature upstairs."

Mrs. Grose informs her that the man in question is Peter Quint, the master's former valet. But Peter Quint is dead! Mrs. Grose is worried for Miss Giddons, who is confused and frightened. Upstairs, the children laugh mockingly as they look down upon their two caretakers.

These are key scenes. First, both we and Miss Giddons see the figure of a woman who is not supposed to be in the house. Then, a "playful" Miles comes dangerously close to injuring Miss Giddons. How are we to interpret Miles' aggression, and what are we to make of Miss Giddons' lackluster attempt to free herself? Finally, both we and Miss Giddons see the hard, handsome face of the deceased Peter Quint, staring into the house as though he is hunting someone. The music box links the tragic song "Willow Waylee" and its lyrics of the returning dead with Quint. The chain of events ends with the children laughing as though they enjoy Miss Giddons' confusion and terror. Or is their laughter merely that of children having fun? The ambiguity increases.

Can we believe Miss Giddons? We are obviously seeing what she sees, but are we seeing what is really there? Disturbing is the fact that Miss Giddons immediately states that the man whose face she saw in the window is that of the man she saw on the tower. But the man on the tower was very distant and washed in sunlight. Looking up from the perspective of Miss Giddons, we, the audience, could not see his face plainly; so how could she? Did Miss Giddons' runaway imagination make her jump to the conclusion that Quint and the man in the tower were one and the same? Still, if there really was a man in the tower with Miles, who was it if not Quint? Further, could Miss Giddon's overactive imagination have produced the female specter? If Miss Giddons did see the ghost of Peter Quint at the window, for whom was he hunting? If the ghost is real, then Miles must have lied to Miss Giddons that day on the tower. The film again links the ghosts with the children, though Miss Giddons has not yet made the conscious connection.

At Miss Giddons' urging, Mrs. Grose tells the story of how Quint came home drunk on a dark winter's night, presumably slipped on the ice, sustained a head wound, and died. "I can't forget his eyes," she says. "They were open, filled with surprise, with pain, like the eyes of a fox I once saw, a fox that the dogs had hunted down."

When Miss Giddons inquires if Quint's death could have been something other than an accident, Mrs. Grose will say only that Quint probably had enemies due to his vicious life. Furthermore, she warns that no one should mention Quint to the children. It was Miles, after all, who discovered Quint's body, screamed, and begged the dead man to speak. Miles worshipped Quint. The two were always together.

This conversation is interrupted when the children come downstairs dressed as royalty. Flora, who is carrying the music box, playing the haunting "Willow Waylee," announces that Miles will recite a poem.

"Look at that..." Miss Giddons whispers to Mrs. Grose. "I was afraid for them. What if Miles knows?" "Knows what?" inquires Flora.

Later, when Mrs. Grose expresses her view that Miles was just playing a game, Miss Giddons will have none of it. As their exchange continues, Mrs. Grose reveals that she could do nothing to separate young Miles from the wicked Quint because the master had left Quint completely in charge. Besides, she was afraid of Quint. But what of Miss Jessel? Miss Jessel was not afraid of Quint at first. She was a happy woman upon arriving at Bly House. She loved music and dancing. She and Flora would dance together for hours. But Miss Jessel changed. The educated lady somehow fell under the spell of the ruffian Quint. When Miss Giddons presses for more, the housekeeper says that all of that is over and done, and there is no use in telling tales of the dead. "Over and done with," Miss Giddons darkly muses. "Yes, but is it?"

These scenes allow Miss Giddons to make the connection between the apparitions and the children. When Flora says the word "horrible" (in reference to the weather?), Miss Giddons is ready to assign the adjective to Flora's knowledge of the specters. When Flora explains that she was using the word in relation to the weather, Miss Giddons does not pursue her own suspicions.

That Miss Giddons still believes she has seen ghosts is evinced by her trepidation at letting the children go upstairs by themselves. The down-to-earth Mrs. Gross, however, continues to attribute Miss Giddons' fears to suggestibility and an overactive imagination, but the governess will have none of it.

Mrs. Grose's revelation of how Quint died suggests to Miss Giddons the possible existence of a supernatural tie between the boy and the deceased valet. Mrs. Grose's comparison of Quint to a fox suggests that the former valet was sly and animalistic. These references lend credence to the suggestion that a diabolical plot might be unfolding. The governess' suspicions are strengthened by Miles recitation of the poem about his lord's return, certainly a morbid and well-wrought poem to have been written by one so young. The lightning during Miles' recitation is eerie, and the camera profile of Miles staring out the window as he utters the final words of the poem are unnerving. When Mrs. Grose reveals the close relationship between Flora and Miss Jessel, Miss Giddons continues to make (imaginary?) connections between the dead and the children. One might only reflect upon Miles' behavior in this scene and others to make a similar connection based on circumstantial evidence. Like Quint, Miles can be verbally cruel to his sister as well as successfully manipulative of Miss Giddons. In other words, like his "lord," Miles can handle women. But is Miles evil or just precocious? Flora certainly loves her brother and deeply resents his taunts. Are the children developing a relationship mirroring that of Quint and Miss Jessel? Tensions now abound, and the audience is eager for definitive evidence. If Miss Giddons is right, then the childrens' lives and souls are in danger. On the other hand, if Miss Giddons is wrong, the children are potentially threatened in as yet unspecified ways by the emotional and mental state of the governess herself.

Next day, alone together beside the lake, Miss Giddons asks Flora where she learned the song she is humming ("Willow Waylee"). Flora is noncommittal. Suddenly Miss Giddons becomes aware that two voices are humming the song, and that Flora is staring across the pond at the figure of a woman. When Miss Giddons asks Flora who the woman is, Flora appears puzzled. When Miss Giddons again looks across the lake, the figure is gone.

That night, Miss Giddons confides to a credulous but polite Mrs. Grose that there are two "of those abominations." The children, she says, "are playing, or being made to play, some monstrous game [that is] secretive, whispery, and indecent." The children, she continues, are in dreadful peril. Miss Giddons then gets Mrs. Grose to aid her in saving the children by helping discover what the ghosts want. This elicits some further history from Mrs. Grose. It seems that Quint and Miss Jessell were "in love," much in the way that sadists and masochists are in love. Quint physically abused Miss Jessel, and she crawled to him as though asking for more. The two used "rooms by daylight as though they were dark woods." The children trailed behind Quint and Miss Jessel, whispering. "There was too much whispering in this house," Mrs. Grose says, to which Miss Giddons replies, "Yes, I can imagine!"

The turn of the conversation prompts Mrs. Grose to defend the innocence of the children. Miss Giddons concludes, however, that it was Quint's and Miss Jessel's goal in life and in death "to corrupt" the children. Confused, Mrs. Grose confides that she sometimes wondered if Quint and Miss Jessel were just using the children. Miss Giddons repeats the word "Using" as though it carries great significance. Mrs. Grose concludes her history lesson by revealing that Miss Jessel died after a period of mad grief following Quint's death.

Miss Giddons then hints that she intends to discuss the problem with the village vicar, but Mrs. Grose strongly discourages the plan. Mrs. Grose is not truly convinced of the soundness of Miss Giddons' perceptions.

Miss Giddons then informs Mrs. Grose that she intends to relay her suspicions to the Master. Miss Giddons then extracts from Mrs. Grose that Miss Jessel died "in wickedness" by drowning herself in the pond.

Later, as Miss Giddons awaits a carriage to take her to London, she wanders into the schoolroom. There at the teacher's desk is the pitifully sobbing specter of Miss Jessel. When the ghost disappears, Miss Giddons approaches the desk and wipes a tear from its surface. She will not go to London, she decides. The children are definitely being possessed, she tells Mrs. Grose. "I could feel pity for her," she says of Miss Jessel, "if she herself were not so pitiless... and hungry... hungry for him." Miss Giddons decides that if the children can be forced to admit the existence of the ghosts, the haunting spirits can be banished forever.

The walk to church illustrates Mrs. Grose's recollections of the children whispering secrets together and allows for Miss Giddons to elicit more damning information concerning Miss Jessel. The scene in the school room is important because of the controversy surrounding it. Screenwriter Truman Capote recalled: "I made only one mistake. At the very end, when the governess sees the ghost of Miss Jessel sitting at her desk, I had a tear fall on to the desktop. Up until then it wasn't clear whether the ghosts were real or in the governess' mind. But the tear was real, and that spoiled everything." Actually Capote is too hard on himself. The scene ruins nothing. Throughout the film we have seen the specters and everything else through the eyes of Miss Giddons. When Miss Giddons "sees" a tear, why must we assume that it is real? We need not, of course, and the ambiguity is preserved.

That night, the sound of whispering and giggling draws Miss Giddons out of her room as the wind howls and the house creaks. Through eerie light and shadow, Miss Giddons makes her way upstairs to Flora's room to find the little girl watching her brother, who is down in the garden. Miss Giddons believes Miles is looking up at the tower where she first saw Quint. Later Miles explains that it was all a prank. Having returned Miles to his bed, Miss Giddons finds a broken-necked pigeon under the boy's pillow. Miles claims that he was only trying to keep the dead bird warm. Suddenly Miles says, "Kiss me, Miss Giddons." And they kiss, a long protracted kiss that leaves Miss Giddons shaken.

These are all key scenes in the film. At one point, as Miss Giddons searches for the source of the whispering, she whirls in circles as though completely confused and distraught. Freddie Francis shoots this brief moment from above, making it reminiscent a similar camera angle capturing Lillian Gish's terror in *Broken Blossoms* (1919). Perhaps the success of these two scenes influenced cinematographer Ernest Haller briefly and similarly to photograph the horror and confusion of a wheelchair-confined Joan Crawford in *What Ever Happened to Baby Jane* (1962).

Next day, as rain pours down, Miss Giddons and Mrs. Grose find Flora missing and trace her to a gazebo across the pond. As the little girl dances alone (she always used to dance with Miss Jessel), Miss Giddons spots the specter of the former governess on the opposite shore. When she tries to force Flora to acknowledge the existence of the ghost, the little girl begins screaming hysterically. Though Mrs. Grose tries to comfort Flora as best she can, the girl continues to scream, even after the three have returned to Bly House. In a tense confrontation, Mrs. Grose confesses to Miss Giddons that she did not see the ghost of Miss Jessel across the water. Mrs. Grose goes on to express her fear that such awakening of old memories may cause Flora harm. Feeling betrayed (and/or desperate?) Miss Giddons then decides that everyone must leave the house except for herself and Miles, at which point she will try to get the boy to admit the existence of Quint's ghost. Mrs. Grose is very reluctant to leave Miles in the hands of Miss Giddons, but protests cease when the governess makes her request an order.

Mrs. Grose's failure to see the ghost is the strongest evidence yet that Miss Giddons is delusional. The audience has counted on Mrs. Grose to reach some firm conclusion, and now we have it. Still, ghost lore would insist that some people are able to see what others are not. All things considered, however, I think the scales tilt against Miss Giddons at this point, though not decisively.

Next day, as Mrs. Grose and Flora leave Bly House, Miss Giddons be comes convinced that Miles has stolen a letter intended for the uncle. The daylight hours pass uneventfully. That night, Miss Giddons begins to press Miles for confessions and explanations. Miles finally admits that he took the letter, but only to find out what she had written about him. He never finished reading the letter he says. Miss Giddons (at long last) then tries to extract from Miles the reason he was expelled from school. Miles answers that he heard things at night and frightened the other boys. When Miss Giddons continues to press, Miles "snaps" and sarcastically calls the governess "a damned hussy, a damned dirty-minded hag." "You never fooled us." he laughs. "We always knew!" As Miles berates her, Miss Giddons sees the ghost of Quint behind the boy, as though guiding and encouraging him. Miles runs out into the garden and into a terrace of statuary. Miss Giddons follows. Grasping him in her arms, she begs Miles to say the name of the man who is haunting him. Miles staggers toward the statuary where Miss Giddons sees the ghost of Quint, blurts out the man's name, and collapses. Sure that Quint has been exorcised, Miss Giddons holds the fallen Miles in her arms and kisses him on the lips, only to discover that he has died. She cries out Miles' name and cradles him in her arms. He is lost to her forever, but is he lost to "them?" The birds chirp as they did during the film's dark prologue. The end.

The film received favorable reviews upon release and continues to enjoy critical praise today. In *Horror in the Cinema*, Ivan Butler concludes: "Clayton has been criticized for making use of old tricks of suspense such as billowing curtains, faces pressed to windows, ticking clocks, shock cuts and the rest. It is not the fact that such effects have been used in the past and will be used in the future that matters, however, but how they are used in the present. Here they are handled superbly, and it is difficult to imagine a better film version of the famous ghost story."

So, do ghosts walk the grounds of Bly House, or is Miss Giddons as tortured as the children? Has Miss Giddons uncovered a diabolical plot of possession, or is she, as Miles charges, "a damned dirty-minded hag"? Henry James, William Archibald, Truman Capote and Jack Clayton leave the questions unanswered.

Clayton's direction is certainly successful in allowing multiple interpretations. Consider, for example, the contrasting perceptions of Butler and Pine. Butler writes that Clayton obviously means us to take the ghosts literally: "Both Archibald and Clayton show us the ghosts and thus indicate their opinion of the governess' state of mind." Pine, on the other hand, takes the

exact opposite view: "Perhaps Clayton gives too much weight in his direction to the psychological interpretation (making the ghosts a figment of Deborah Kerr's imagination....)"

Ample evidence exists for one to argue either perspective, which is just one reason why the film invites and rewards repeated viewings.

Finally, all performances are impeccable, particularly those of the children and Kerr's vulnerable, underplayed governess. There have been other great and near great cinematic ghost stories. *A Christmas Carol* (1951), *The Uninvited*, *The Haunting*, *Don't Look Now* and *Lady in White* come immediately to mind. I would argue, however, that *The Innocents* rates slightly above these others. It is, to be precise, the perfect cinematic haunting.

But what of the ghosts? Are they real, or is the governess delusional? To answer that question, I would like to offer an interpretation of the story and film as yet unventured. I believe Miss Giddons is emotionally disturbed. She is sexually repressed and she is a pederast. I also believe that the ghosts are real and that they *are* indeed attempting to possess the children. The children's behavior is sometimes difficult to explain any other way. For example, how *does* Flora know that Miles is going to return so soon to Bly House? Why must the interpretation be an either/or proposition? Both interpretations are defensible, and they are not mutually exclusive. Indeed, both interpretations are necessary if we are actually to reconcile what we see and hear. The combination is both gothically explosive and eminently arguable based on the evidence. Ghosts really do walk the corridors and grounds of Bly House. Believe me.

CREDITS: Producer and Director: Jack Clayton; Executive Producer: Albert Fennell; Screenplay: William Archibald and Truman Capote, Based on *The Turn of the Screw* by Henry James; Director of Photography: Freddie Francis; Editor: James Clark, 1961, 20th Century Fox, 100 minutes

CAST: Deborah Kerr...Miss Giddons, Michael Redgrave...The Uncle, Megs Jenkins...Mrs. Grose, Peter Wyngarde...Peter Quint, Martin Stephens...Miles, Pamela Franklin...Flora, Isla Cameron...Anna, Clytie Jessop...Miss Jessel

The Turn of the Screw
2009, BBC TV

In 2009 the BBC TV presented a new version of *The Turn of the Screw*. TV critic Tom Sutcliff said in his review, "The blunt verdict on BBC1's *The Turn of the Screw* is that Henry James's powerfully unsettling tale had been comprehensively vandalised. The qualification one would have to add is that the author himself might not entirely have disapproved. In the preface to the New York edition, after all, James made it clear that he didn't want mimsy, out-of-the-corner-of-the-eye-style ghosts–the sort of things that he found in the psychical research literature and which could easily be dismissed by the rationally minded as a mere trick of the light. 'Good ghosts, speaking by the book, make poor subjects,' he wrote, 'and it was clear that from the first my hovering, prowling, blighting presences... would have to depart altogether from the rules. They would be agents in fact; there would be laid on them the dire duty of causing the situation to reek with an air of evil.' Whatever legions of subsequent readers have thought, then, James seemed to happy to accept that Quint and Miss Jessel were really there and it was their job to make your flesh creep.

But James surely knew precisely what he was doing when he ensured that the evidence for the ghosts' existence is all hearsay, and never independently corroborated by a second witness. Indeed, there's a point in the story when the governess attempts to get someone else to see what she's seeing and fails. The terror of the story is a second-hand terror, even third-hand arguably, and that distance between perceived apparition and description is essential to its mood. Awkwardly for anyone adapting a work for cinema, film unavoidably makes eyewitnesses of us all, and neither Tim Fywell, the director, or Sandy Welch, the writer, had felt it necessary to find some visual equivalence for the careful ambiguity of the literary text. When the governess sees Quint on the tower for the first time so do we, and the thing that really haunts us as we read the story–uncertainty–vanishes to be replaced by a much duller kind of fretfulness, about when something is next going to pop out at us.

Whatever Henry James intended, *The Turn of the Screw* is a psychological case study or it is nothing, but by changing the frame so that it was a clinical case study, Welch effectively turned it into a rebuke against psychiatry, while at the same time ramping up a sense of the governess as a bundle of repressed sexual hysteria. Part of the DNA running through this adaptation was all those horror films in which a cocky young man of science has his certainties upturned, the instructee in this case being Dr Fisher, who even ended up seeing Quint himself, darting round a corner at the asylum. Add to this the decision to have one of the tweenies hurled off the roof shortly after muttering dark warnings at the governess and you should get some measure of how the terrifying indeterminacies of the original had been turned into a slightly shabby ghost-train ride.

Josef Lindsey, Eva Sayer as the children and Michelle Dockery as the governess star in the BBC1 production of *The Turn of the Screw*.

LADY IN WHITE

by Robert Alan Crick

"Restraint" is a word seldom linked with horror films of the 1980s, films far removed from the low-key chills of *Dracula* (1931), *Frankenstein* (1931) and *The Wolf Man* (1941), and nearly as distant from the subtle thrills of Hitchcock, just a few years back. After such gut-wrenching hits as *The Exorcist* and *The Texas Chainsaw Massacre* in the 1970s and *Friday the 13th*, *A Nightmare on Elm Street* and *The Fly* in the 1980s, Hollywood seemed obsessed with grit and gore, apparently leaving the simple, clean-cut terrors of old-world moviemaking behind for good.

And yet the old-fashioned pleasures of horror's glory days were not altogether forgotten, for the 1980s still delivered an occasional production whose gentle touch and tasteful elegance recalled the gentler, seemingly forgotten graces of classic directors like James Whale, Tod Browning and George Waggner. It is into this tradition of tasteful shivers that Frank LaLoggia's 1988 ghost saga, *Lady in White*, was born. Hardly a big hit financially—scores of lesser films that year fared far better at the box office—*Lady in White* nevertheless remains one of the l980s' most engaging offerings, a simple little tale of murder, the supernatural, and, equally important, growing up.

This last element, along with the early-1960s nostalgia accompanying it, is perhaps the film's happiest surprise, splendidly separating it from other works of the decade. Whereas most 1980s fright films suffer an appalling lack of emotional depth, characters in *Lady in White* emerge as warm and nurturing. Its hero, nine-year-old Frankie Scarlotti, lives in a world bathed in love, where fathers are firm yet tender, siblings tease and taunt yet never with a mean spirit, and grandparents enforce discipline while baking cookies and taking temperatures. Even its villain—a *child molester*, of all things, and a serial killer— emerges as much pitiable as perverse, for while LaLoggia never soft-pedals the man's sick inclinations, our disgust comes as much from a dear friend's betrayal as gut-impulse revulsion. In *Lady in White*, even killers are three-dimensional people, not cardboard stock figures.

Indeed, while *Lady in White* calls upon countless horror and suspense movie and literary traditions for inspiration—at times, it recalls *The Turn of the Screw*, *It*, *The Other*, *The Uninvited*, *The Window*, *The Curse of the Cat People*, and endless others—the works it echoes most have little to do with such genres at all. Harper Lee's *To Kill a Mockingbird*, for example, with its loving father rearing two children—one of whom, like Frankie, describes her childhood initiation into her quiet hometown's dark secrets—has been noted by John McCarthy in *The Modern Horror Film* for parallels to *Lady in White* (as in Lee, racist whites are all too eager to blame a black man for a sex-related crime, and a peculiar recluse both terrifies and aids local children). According to McCarthy, in fact, the 1962 film version has been alleged to be one of LaLoggia's favorite films.

Yet *Lady in White* also recalls less weighty works, among them Bob Clark's *A Christmas Story* (1983), a film likewise showcasing an adult's memories of childhood holidays, Woody Allen's *Radio Days* (1987), with a grown-up Allen recalling a boyhood amid an odd yet loving New York family during radio's Golden Age, and many other big-screen nostalgia pieces. In ways, it even resembles Charles Dickens' *Great Expectations*, a novel featuring not only an adventure begun for its adult nar-

rator as a boy, but also the unsettling yet matter-of-fact presence of a graveyard close by (adjoining the boy's home in Dickens, his school in LaLoggia's film), a villain who both alarms and nurtures a naive, ambitious youth (a terrifying convict-turned-benefactor in Dickens' tale, a family-friend-turned assailant in *Lady in White*), an eccentric old woman who is agonized by life-changing heartbreak, preserves keepsakes of better days, and dies in a blazing room, her treasures burning about her, and other familiar motifs.

At times, the film recalls TV even more, notably ABC's much-admired *The Wonder Years*, in which Daniel Stern narrates the Vietnam-era life lessons of young Fred Savage. It brings to mind the CBS classic *The Waltons*, with creator Earl Hamner, Jr. as budding writer John Walton, Jr.'s wise older self, recalling his Virginia upbringing during the Great Depression (like John-Boy, *Lady in White*'s Frankie is also an aspiring writer). Perhaps it ultimately resembles nothing so much as Gary David Goldberg's short-lived CBS series *Brooklyn Bridge*, which likewise features a warm, caring relationship between brothers and a pair of endearing immigrant grandparents. The list of other such parallels is endless, but the point is clear: *Lady in White* is easily the most *human* ghost movie of the 1980s. It also happens to be one of its best.

Despite its exhaustively detailed closing credits, most of *Lady in White*'s refreshing warmth and tenderness must be attributed to one man. Frank LaLoggia's work would merit praise even had he only helmed the movie— *Lady in White* is easily one of the 1980s' most expertly directed genre efforts— yet LaLoggia also co-produced the movie with Andrew G. LaMarca, provided its sure-footed musical score, and, best of all, authored its highly engaging script, merging mystery, suspense, the supernatural and nostalgia into something new and charming. A talent largely lost amid the Carpenters, Cravens, Barkers and Hoopers of the age, LaLoggia did not become a household name on the basis of *Lady in White*, yet he proved beyond doubt he was a storyteller with whom to be reckoned.

The present-day adult Frankie narrates—it is the Halloween of 1962, "The year she came into my life."

Panning to the house, we see Frankie's grandmother, the Italian Mama Assunta (Renata Vanni), hanging clothes, and the boy scampers to his bike in a Lugosi Dracula mask, cape about his neck. He starts to peddle off for school when his father Angelo (Alex Rocco) steps onto the porch, Frankie's forgotten jack-o'-lantern in hand and, after retrieving the item, Frankie lifts his mask for a warm hug (the boy's love is obvious in a close-up over Angelo's shoulder) and kiss on the cheek. Just as a few scenes capture the quiet innocence of a 1960s small town, so has this brief but tender exchange exquisitely paints the essence of this close-knit family's affection. Clearly LaLoggia has a real knack for depicting the tone and texture of old-fashioned virtues, recreating the simple pleasures of community and home with so much charm and humanity the viewer can't help feeling a tad nostalgic himself—and maybe even a little homesick.

Teenage brother Geno (Jason Presson), after kissing Angelo in mid-scamper, slams into Frankie. "You've got the prettiest brown eyes!" he taunts. We also meet Angelo's father, Papa Charlie (Angelo Bertolini), a comical old man whose attempts to smoke without his wife's knowledge provide one of the film's chief running gags.

An early sequence helps to establish Frankie's character. We cut to the now candlelit jack-o'-lantern, one of many in a class full of costumed children (the wildest, Donald, is dressed as Satan—an appropriate outfit considering Donald's persistent role of tempter throughout the film), giggling and cavorting to "Mr. Bassman." Prim, frantic teacher Miss La Della (Lucy Lee Flippin) switches off the 45 r.p.m. insanity and blows a whistle to announce one final treat: Frankie has written a story just for Halloween. A few chuckles arise, and wise-guy Donald (Jared Rushton) and his pirate-costumed pal Louie (Gregory Levinson) roll their eyes.

LaLoggia and Haas are in top form here. Stepping "on stage" with a Shakespearean flourish, like some nine-year-old Olivier, the caped Frankie recalls some preteen Phantom of the Opera, or Zorro, or Hamlet, or Romeo at Lord Capulet's party. His ominous introduction—"*The Beast that Destroyed London*," he begins, "by Frankie Scarlotti"—opens a tale crude and clichéd yet genuinely engaging (and cleverly recalling store window alligators Frankie saw earlier—a truly inspired idea). We grin as his giant monster is called a "pre hysterical beast," yet the attempt at vivid adjectives reveals a promising talent. True, Donald and Louie mock his efforts, but cute little Mary Ellen (Lisa Taylor), dressed as an angel (superbly foreshadowing coming events), sits captivated.

Frankie's tale may be roughhewn, but he (like LaLoggia) has a knack for drama, killing his beast in an enormous fissure, "eaten up by the only thing bigger than him—the earth." Better yet, his hearers no sooner think him finished ("And there was nothing to be frightened about anymore," he says) than he offers one last worry. "That is, of course," he whispers, "unless the monster had a baby." All gasp, and he adds, "But that's impossible—or is it?" The camera moves in on his eyes now—he savors his tale's effect—and an openmouthed boy dressed as a pig (and eating like one) sits awestruck while in a simple yet endearing special effect, one piglet ear descends. Finally the bell rings, jolting all, especially Miss La Della, who goodheartedly thanks Frankie for his "very *unusual* story."

In another winning scene, Frankie carries books for his teacher as they talk of greeting cards he has sold her and Mr. Lowry, the mailman, and how the cards must come "all the way from Nebraska." (Pleasantly, the moment somehow calls to mind similar scenes in Thornton Wilder's *Our Town*.) "Frankie, you should be very proud of yourself," his teacher says. "You're a very enterprising young man for your age, and that's very unusual." This second "very unusual" wins a smile, but what makes the scene such a joy is his half-gasp, half-chuckle answer. "I know!" he says breathlessly, and both laugh. The line is pure nine-year-old honesty perfectly selected by LaLoggia, and thanks to the gifted young Haas, pricelessly delivered.

After she drives off, Donald and Louie casually "notice" Frankie is missing his new cap (a gift from Angelo), and they suggest he try the cloakroom.

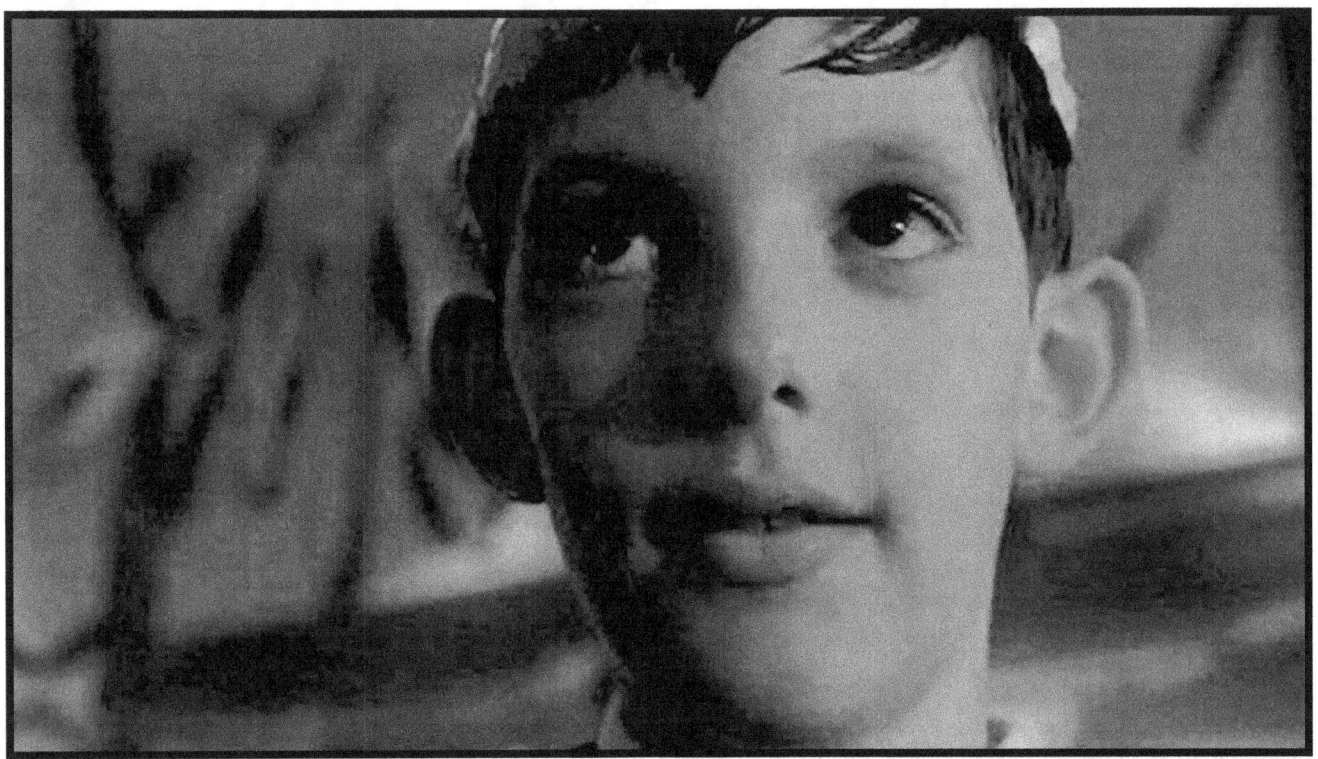

Frankie (Lukas Haas) finds real horror during Halloween in *The Lady in White*.

Furious, he sends Donald sprawling, and a witty ground-level shot echoing Hitchcock's *The Trouble With Harry* (1955) shows Donald's shoe soles as Louie and Frankie enter the frame, after which Frankie decides he will find his cap, and Louie helps up Donald to follow.

In the classroom, Donald's hands open his teacher's desk drawer, removing a key. As Frankie seeks his cap in the cloakroom, Donald turns off the light, reaches in, and slams the door. Young hands lock it outside (again, all this attention to objects and body parts has a distinctly Hitchcockian feel to it), and Frankie gasps—first as darkness descends, then again as a second door slams. Another pair of hands—Louie's—locks it too, and the laughing boys flee. Frantic, Frankie tugs at each door, pounding on one, to no use.

The cinematographer fills the frame with blackness, then Frankie nears the window and climbs to it. He finds his cap on the way, and calls to the boys through the semicircle window. He sees them below, running through the cemetery, and—in an extraordinarily fine shot underscoring the futility of the boy's efforts—we see Frankie as if from outside and below, mouthing unheard pleas until, helpless, he huddles in a corner atop the shelf. The camera moves in on the window, then freezes as night falls in what seems like a single take until, retreating, it shows Frankie asleep, mask atop his head. In a scene sure to carry a great deal more significance later on after the appearance of a real lady in white and the child from whom she too has been separated, he dreams of his mother's funeral, a behind-the-back shot following him to the coffin where his lovely, flame-haired mother lies in a pale dress as the camera circles, then lingers, on the sad child.

Her warm voice beckons (affectionate, light-garbed women do a great deal of beckoning to children in this film), and, turning, the screen fills again with Frankie's dark suit, then emerges to find a lively, cheery Mrs. Scarlotti just as she was. She sits in her living room (well-lit for wish-fulfillment surrealism), doors behind opening to show Dad and Geno playing baseball before a sunlight-bathed field. She has made him a new plaid sportcoat, and he tries it on, hugging her as—still filming the reunion in one take—the camera circles her. "Don't leave," he begs tearfully, but she dismisses the very idea: "How could I *ever* leave *you*?" He grins, but despair hits as he turns suddenly, his gaze followed swiftly as he is swept back to the funeral, where, gasping, he turns back to the coffin. Yes: she *is* dead, and the lid slams shut, waking him. In close-up, Frankie sobs, his greatest crisis renewed. It's a powerful moment exquisitely depicting a mother-son relationship reaching from beyond the grave—and foreshadowing a similar mother-daughter bond which defies death even in a far more literal sense.

His grief is postponed, however, as wind sweeps through the sealed room—evidence, in such tales, of a visit from the dead (as well as a pleasant, old-fashioned reminder of the days when such simple traditional effects as a snuffed-out candle, extinguished by a ghostly wind, suggested more than enough unexplained eeriness to give fans of a good ghost story the shivers). Filming just behind the boy's head, LaLoggia supplies a shelftop view of one door below, a floor furnace grating nearby. To Frankie's astonishment, a playful, ghostly little girl (Joelle Jacobi), about his age and in pink, steps backwards through the locked door, addressing some unseen adult—coming in, one senses, as once she did in life. "Where is it?" she asks eagerly.

"Where's my present? Where'd you hide it this time?" From these over-eager words, we suspect something is disturbingly amiss, for what adult offers gifts to a naive schoolgirl in a secluded cloakroom after school? (It is, incidentally, in moments like this that *Lady in White* most resembles Henry Jones' *The Turn of the Screw* for there, not one, but two children, each of them captivated by a beloved grownup's seductive allure, becomes in some way tainted by his dark corruption.)

The apparition, oblivious to Frankie's stunned, silent presence, reenacts exactly her final secret visit, singing her unseen tempter's favorite song, "Did You Ever See a Dream Walking." "Because you're always singing it," she responds to an inquiry Frankie cannot hear. "That's how I know."

During her interaction with the figure, splendid close-ups (again rather Hitchockian) reveal Frankie's wide-eyed stare. When at last she spins about and skips his way, spirit and physical worlds meet as she gasps upon seeing Frankie high on the shelf above. "Who are you?" he asks, wonderstruck, but she returns to the door and her unseen "friend." "I'm scared now!" she says, tenor rising. "No. I don't want to play anymore. I want my mommy! I want to go home!" Her young fingers grasp the doorknob to escape, but—another close-up shows Frankie's terror—invisible hands suddenly yank her back by the hair, spin her about, and rip her dress. An unseen something falls to the floor, and Frankie's eyes follow as it rolls to the grating and falls through. Hitchcock fans may regret much of the battle is seen from Frankie's viewpoint well across the room, limiting viewer involvement (only three shots during the struggle—the girl's grab for the doorknob, the harsh yank at her hair, and the tearing of her dress—appear in close-ups), though the shots intercut of Frankie's stunned reaction are vivid enough to help quite a bit. Flinching throughout, he begs, "No. Don't hurt her. Don't!" with superb frozen helplessness, his hands gripped tightly within his twisted cap. More powerful still are the girl's screams as she beats her fists against the man's chest without effect as he begins strangling her. Her shrill, chilling "Oh, Mom-my!" is truly disturbing, and poor Frankie's heart aches. "Please. No," he begs, but by now it seems too late, for the girl has fallen limply to the floor. It's a splendid scene, setting up everything else *Lady in White* will now be about: first, uncovering the supernatural significance of the ghostly little girl, and second, unveiling the true identity of the murderous Willowpoint Falls adult whose depravity has caused the girl's death.

In the silent aftermath of the strangulation, Frankie hears footsteps move from the body to the grating. Invisible fingers try prying it up for the fallen item—or items—but to no avail. Giving up, the man returns to the body, lifts it, and carries it through the locked door. A shot of the town clock shows the time is now 10, and it strikes gloomily. Frankie will later recover the ring lost so long ago.

Then, amazingly, the footsteps return—only now the body they belong to comes also. A shadowy adult appears through the door glass, rattling the knob as the camera moves in. Giving up, he shatters the glass and the man—face obscured by darkness—enters with a flashlight. He turns a beam of light into the grating, a shot from his viewpoint revealing a shiny object within. Frankie recoils in terror, and LaLoggia, always one to keep us on out toes with unexpected variations on the sizes and perspectives of his images, supplies an enormous close-up of a screwdriver put to work.

A rat squeaks, and Frankie's eyes turn to it—as do the intruder's, his gloved hand taking up the flashlight to toss a beam in its direction. The beam barely misses Frankie, but as work resumes, the rat scuttles Frankie's way. Two great close-ups of his frantic eyes capture his dread—it's really quite an effective little moment of good old-fashioned movie suspense— and as the rat crawls up his legs and for his lap, he all but swallows his cap to stifle a scream. Shoving the rat away, he alerts the man, who grabs his flashlight and discovers him—an instant *after* Frankie yanks down his mask. It is an amusing reflex (and a thoroughly believable bit of child psychology), as if his young mind thinks the mask somehow makes him still able to hide.

The intruder rises, the camera following his approach just behind. "Who are you?" he asks. "What do you know?" (Whether LaLoggia intended it or not is hard to say, but, astonishingly the voice sounds much like Angelo's; could Frankie's own father be the killer?) "I got locked in," the trembling child stammers. "My friends locked me in after school, and—"

The trembling child tries to explain, but abruptly, the man slams down his screwdriver, narrowly missing Frankie, and a fierce struggle begins that is pure Hitchcock in its quick shots of flailing body parts. Grabbed for, the boy falls onto the wall behind, then is yanked down and pushed into another. Repelled by Frankie's kick, the man strikes his head, drops the boy, and falls too. Frankie crawls off, but is gripped by one leg and dragged back, then flipped over, two hands bearing down on his neck. We see the attack from the viewpoint of both parties, and Frankie feels his life draining away. A black-gloved hand seen through his eyes moves in to squelch all breathing, and a cosmic light burst appears as the giant hand darkens the screen.

"I was dying," Frankie's adult self narrates. "I could feel my eyes close shut, and yet I continued to see." Now we see a vivid dream sequence—it recalls other childhood "flying dreams" in *Explorers* (1985), *The Boy Who Could Fly* (1986) and even *The Wizard of Oz* (1939)—in which an over-the-shoulder shot has Frankie soaring above the cemetery, cape and mask floating off.

As he is drawn to a gravestone, we see its words seen through his eyes: "IN LOVING MEMORY, FRANKLIN T. SCARLOTTI, 1953." Feeling the same wind from before, he is bathed in soft light. Ahead is the girl, her back to him before two tombstones (like the adult Frankie earlier—a rather neat parallel). As he approaches to question her, a snow of sparkles fall, and she places flowers on her parents' brightening graves.

Her name, he learns, is "Melissa," and she asks him, "Don't you know where you'd like to be going?" "To my home," he decides, "in my own bed," and she weeps, for she too longs for home. "My mommy's lost, and I can't find her," she sobs. "Will *you* help me find her?" Then, breathing in the aroma of her flowers, she extends them, and he leans in to inhale.

In a masterful "breathing scene" transition, LaLoggia cuts suddenly to a close-up of Angelo giving Frankie mouth-to-mouth resuscitation. The boy coughs awake, reassured that "Daddy's here: It's okay." Yet again, because of the familiar tone of that threatening voice we heard, we worry: has Angelo attacked his son, realized his error, then tried to revive him? It seems unlikely, however, for in the lit room Sheriff Saunders (Tom Bower) is with him even now. Next, two white deputies rush into the dark boiler room, where they arrest Mr. Williams, a black man who sits at a static-filled TV—perhaps wittily suggesting his own alcoholic haze, yet it is hard to enjoy the humor. True, the man has been on duty and is thus the most likely suspect, yet one senses somehow he is innocent, and the law's racist supposition that a black man must be responsible is deeply unsettling.

Later, Angelo seems troubled by the Williams case, and—assuming he was home during the attack—we sense again this is a truly good man. How many other 1962 small town whites would keep faith in a black man charged with hurting their child? Indeed, suspicion turns briefly to family friend Tony because he, like others, is so quick to pass judgment, even spewing a harsh racial slur before he leaves.

We discover now that Angelo's parents brought up an orphaned Phil, Angelo's closest friend. "You know," Angelo says, "when we were kids, nothing frightened me more than the thought of losing my parents. Then I watched it happen to you—both of them within a year." Losing a wife and nearly a child has been no easier. "I used to think fear was something you grow out of," he admits, "like being afraid of the dark. But now with Marion gone, I'm more fearful than ever. You know, Philly, the thing that scares me the most is the thought of losing one of my kids." His worst fear nearly reality, he weeps, Phil hugging him just as Geno might hug Frankie. The porch scene forms one of *Lady in White*'s best moments, not only echoing Frankie's devastation at the loss of his mother, but also beautifully exploring such themes as friendship, betrayal, loneliness, bigotry and secret fears—all of which make *Lady in White* a far cry from the usual "lunatic on the loose" tale. Most horror films are about stalking and slashing; *Lady in White* is about relationships, about *people*.

Once Frankie sleeps, the camera shows a spinning weather vane model at a closed window, then pans to a *Frankenstein* comic (perfect for budding horror writer Frankie), its pages turned by unseen fingers. It is Melissa, playfully singing "Did You Ever See a Dream Walking." Opening a drawer, she tinkers with scissors, a toy car, a photo and a Slinky, and we next focus on Frankie's slippers, into which she slides both feet and, giggling, shuffles to the window above the toy chest. As its cushioned lid compresses beneath her, the curtains part, and her breath clouds the glass, onto which she draws a heart. (Once again, LaLoggia's grasp on what children do and how they act is absolutely uncanny; somehow this seems like exactly the sort of creative play some real-life Melissa might engage in.) The camera travels around Frankie's bed now, a rocking chair nearby moving fast. Outside another window is a mysterious, white-gowned old woman (Katherine Helmond) peering in. Is this the Lady in White?

In one of the film's most creative scene shifts, LaLoggia draws us to the toy weather vane for a clever low-level shot of the spinning item, replaced by the real thing on an area farm. We next see the old woman moving like a ghost through a misty forest, followed by a shot of the ocean as seen from a high cliff, then another look from over the woman's shoulder.

Frankie stops Geno (Jason Presson) from crying out.

As she departs, we see she is crying, and as she nears a small farmhouse and enters, one sees the real weather vane spinning.

Later, at the Eastside Iron Works, labor continues on the cemetery gate. Frankie climbs to Angelo's office, and we see a peephole as he peers in. Sheriff Saunders tells Angelo Mr. Williams is "the perfect scapegoat. He's *black*," and while both know it is unfair, Saunders says 10 years ago he found blood in the cloakroom matching Melissa's type. "I know that she was killed there," he reveals. Outside, Phil sees Frankie, who naively tells him about the furnace items he found on a return trip to the cloak room. "It was all kid stuff," he says, then realizes, "except for the ring. It was *his* ring. Maybe that's what he came back to get." Before he can finish, Angelo and Saunders appear.

In his bedroom, Geno sits to remove his shoes—and spies the ring Frankie had found. LaLoggia traces his gaze to it, shows him take it up, then pans to his impish grin. Frankie, Geno decides, is up to something.

In bed later, Geno lies in thought. Is he wondering if his father is a child molester? Since we have worried too, we forgive his sneaking to the basement to inspect a trunk of Angelo's keepsakes—yet surely he knows Angelo was *home* during Frankie's assault, and he must have seen Angelo's ring earlier. In any case, the rings are from the same year, as we see in point-of-view close-ups, including one through a magnifying glass revealing the initials "A.R.S." in Angelo's ring.

When Geno enters his room, he is shocked to see Melissa and nearly screams before Frankie clasps a hand to his mouth. "She wants her mother," he says. A glimpse shows it is 10—the time of her murder years ago. Floating through the window like Peter Pan (or some harmless variation on the child vampires in TV's *Salem's Lot*), she alights and skips off to join her "friend," whose unseen hand she takes. "She's with him," Frankie senses, and he slips into shoes and a coat to follow. Geno comes too, but without shoes, and soon they are peering in at the front school door. We see the boys from within, then their view as a limp Melissa is carried by her killer downstairs, through the locked door, then through the cemetery—and finally toward the cliff. Frankie follows, but Geno steps on glass and, in a grisly scene, must remove it.

At the cliff, he is shocked to learn Melissa was not dead when hurled over in 1962. "Mommy?" she asks, then, panicking, wildly kicks and screams. "She's alive!" he calls, and, eyes hidden, his painful "No!" blends with her death scream. We see her dead hand on the rocks, waves crashing atop it, then the *real* Lady in White, her mother, exits the cottage, nightgown flowing—a beautiful image. Her approach is in slow motion, and as she nears the edge, we see the body as she sees it, her utter collapse, and her anguished leap. An incredible shot of her fall as her gown spreads like white wings is viewed atop Melissa's hands, and we recall the porcelain angel Frankie held at his Christmas tree. Frankie rolls over, and a close-up of his eyes makes her seem to fall towards him, viewed in his pupils. He shuts his eyes, then opens one for a giant close-up of the old woman there, beckoning. Devastated, he rolls onto his elbows, closing both eyes and opening them as Geno arrives. Seeing the cottage and weather vane, he buries his head in his arms as Geno takes one last look and we fade out.

Reporters are now seen before the courthouse, where Mr. Williams has been freed for lack of evidence. As the press rushes for the story, we see the Cilaks (the mother and father of Richie, one of the murderer's victims) in the crowd. Mr. Williams, relieved, joins his wife as they exit the "Gabriel Courthouse" (furthering the angel motif), planning to go get his belongings from jail. Nearby, Angelo looks grateful, the sheriff accepting and Mrs. Cilak, stealthy reaching for an item at her feet, tells her husband, "I want to apologize." Mr. Williams and his wife kiss, and as he climbs into a squad car, through the left rear, Mrs. Cilak appears, and he lowers the glass. With pretend piety she apologizes, and he accepts with greater grace. Seemingly pleased, she calls him "kind—very kind," then adds, "And as for my Richie... here she lifts a pale scarf—it hides a gun— and shoots him in the head, cracking the opposite glass with a red spatter (a powerful effect). Mr. Williams, martyr to racial injustice, slumps dead. It's a remarkable moment, thoroughly unexpected in a ghost movie, yet here again we see why *Lady in White* is so special. LaLoggia's film isn't merely about the supernatural; it's also about human beings, exploring the devotion and tenderness they give one another in their quiet moments, as well as the unspeakable atrocities they commit in fits of passion, from bigotry to brutality, from molestation to murder.

Later in the film, Angelo's trunk opens as Geno removes an old yearbook and closes it again. Through his eyes, we see the Washington High School 1934 yearbook as he examines the "A.R.S." of Angelo's ring, then the "M.P.T." found in the other. He then finds the name and photo he seeks: "Michael P. Terragrossa" (perhaps by accident, the last name suggests "gross terror"). The "P" is for "Philip"— Phil—whom Frankie is with right now!

We cut to an arrow shot by Phil hitting the bullseye—amazing Frankie, who is assured with what is, from a child molester, eerie advice: "You have to train your mind not to think about anything else except your target." A beautiful distant shot has them overshadowed by a passing cloud—similar gloom soon engulfs their friendship—and Phil hopes to talk on the ride home. As Frankie takes a final shot, one cringes when Phil's hand touches Frankie as he pulls the bow, the killer's cheek is pressed close with the arrow aimed. Is he going to kill Frankie?

The arrow hits its mark, and as they pack up, Frankie climbs into the rear of Phil's stationwagon (the last time he was alone with Phil, the vehicle he left in was an ambulance—and nearly a hearse), where, humming, he casually takes up the tune Phil whistles. Then, slowly, he realizes the song is the favorite of Melissa's killer. Phil, smiling, peeps in through the rear window and senses something is wrong when Frankie stares back with sick little gasps (Haas is superb at conveying growing terror); even as we fear Phil, we pity the pain of lost faith.

Frantic, Frankie scrambles into the front seat (cleverly, LaLoggia here plays upon our fear of entrapment, capturing Frankie—and, by extension, us—in an enclosed space from which we can see no immediate means of escape), his fist slamming down the left door locks. Phil tries calming him, but Phil's anger boils, and when he vanishes, the gasping boy pounds the right door locks. Reappearing, Phil has snapped, and he tries the rear window. Frankie's hands rush to insert the key, and the rear glass rises, trapping Phil, who breaks free. As Frankie flees the car, Phil grabs his bow. The camera follows the chase through the sunlit woods, and when Frankie stops at a tree, the camera shows a chilling shot of something zeroing in. It is only a crow zooming by, though soon Phil arrives. Laying down his weapons, he vows not to hurt Frankie, and he speaks calming reassurances.

Had he known it was Frankie in the cloakroom, says Phil, he would not have hurt him, and as the boy runs again, Phil's "No. Frankie! Don't!" registers real pain. During their standoff, daylight has fallen into bluish gloom too fast for realism, yet forgivable—and Frankie runs to the cottage, a crane shot capturing his helpless frailty below.

A descending crane shot has Frankie moving to the door. It is locked, but after he spies a shadow, aged hands within remove the bar. He gives up, the shadow retreats, and the door opens, and as he rounds a corner he is grabbed by Phil, who—as the camera tilts—pushes him to the ground (again, as in the car scene, we feel cornered, cut off from all means of escape). "I don't want to hurt you," he says, demanding the ring, and, claiming Angelo need not know, cries heavenward, "Oh, God! I could never face him if he knew!" Yet soon he is raving again, strangling Frankie and snarling, "Where is it? Give me the ring!" Seen behind him, however, the old woman strikes him with a heavy stone, and both Frankie and Phil collapse, blackness descending.

Frankie wakes in Melissa's bed at the old seaside cottage, hundreds of candles about him, Amanda Harper (the old woman) seen down a hall at her piano. As she enters (we share her view of a sea of burning wicks), she offers to teach him piano as she did Melissa and her mother. Like her sister (Meslissa's mother), she has also tried suicide, and cries, "What's the point of living, when all that you love is gone?" Claiming her sister's spirit is not at rest, roaming about for Melissa, Amanda has kept the room as it was, and offers Frankie eerie comforts. "Now, now, child," she says of Phil, "I've killed him—see?"

Frankie—attacked by one lunatic, another hovering above him—lies paralyzed, tears rolling. His fear rises after her kiss, for as he sees her withdraw, LaLoggia craftily reverses her attack on Phil as she is strangled from behind. As Phil yanks her away, candles spill, and the room is engulfed by flames. War rages between the adults, seen mostly in shadow, and Phil beats Amanda to death, his fist, seen twice up close (as with so much in LaLoggia's film, one is again reminded of well-cut close-ups in the violence scenes of Hitchcock), crashing down amid cuts to burning items, including a photo of Mrs. Montgomery, glass cracking.

Lugged to the cliff, Frankie locks his legs about Phil and hangs on, biting Phil's face. Balance lost, Phil hurls him over, but the boy grabs a branch and crawls up atop the fallen man as we see cold waves below—and the spinning weather vane. At last the hand of the Lady in White appears, lightning from her index finger striking the device (for no reason made clear). Wailing, she swoops at an upright Phil, who falls—we think—to his death. Frankie hides his eyes, and waves crash below (vaguely recalling 1940's *Rebecca*). Eyes open, he sees (as do we) the Lady in White above, grateful as she floats back to the cottage. We see her next through the fire, then through her eyes Melissa floating from the blaze. Echoing effects films like *Superman*, *Star Trek: The Motion Picture*, and *E.T*, the two unite in midair, hugging, and Melissa offers a happy "Thank you" to Frankie, who smiles; reunion with his mother is what he wants too. The pair spin gleefully, enveloped by cosmic sparkles, until with a flash they shoot star-like into the sky, part briefly for two playful spins, then reunite and soar off.

Angelo arrives with Geno, the sheriff, and a slew of officers and dogs. Frankie tries rising, but pain strikes, a gash seen in his torn pants leg, and a hand grips his ankle. He screams as Phil climbs up, but Angelo's firm hand shakes Phil's free. Relieved, he exchanges tearful hugs and kisses with Frankie, but his face changes as he (as do we) sees Phil clinging to a branch. Nobly, Angelo offers his hand. "Take it!" he shouts angrily. Phil does, but cannot bear having hurt his dearest friend and lets go of the branch. Angelo cries "No. Philly, no!" but Phil releases Angelo as well, and—in the film's weakest, most needless effect—plummets to his death in one long take not entirely dissimilar to a famous fall in Hitchcock's *Saboteur* (1942).

Though a great film and filled with enjoyment, *Lady in White* is hardly a flawless film, as countless scenes make clear. Frankie's failure to tell Angelo about Melissa (at least, we assume he doesn't, but it's not easy to tell) never seems sensible, for one thing, even if he *isn't* likely to be believed. Likewise, unless LaLoggia *wants* us to suspect Angelo as a murderer and child molester, it might have helped to establish that Angelo was indeed home during Frankie's attack—something a few simple lines from Sheriff Saunders could easily answer. True, doing so would render foolish Geno's fear that Angelo may be the killer, but then we are never really sure Geno has this fear anyway. Is Geno curious about the ring just because he has fun poking about in Angelo's "stuff," is he sleuthing to uncover the killer's identity, or does he truly suspect Angelo of the crime? The issue never quite comes together, and it helps little that once we decide Angelo *is* innocent, all mystery dissipates; we know Phil barely five minutes before his guilt seems painfully obvious. *Citizen Kane* and "Rosebud" this is *not*.

There is also the matter of the Lady in White herself, for there are really *two* such figures—three if one counts Frankie's own pale-garbed mother. Frankie's mistaking Melissa's aunt (the haunting Katherine Helmond) for her mother with the aunt's debut as the first white-garbed cliffs-wanderer adds to the mystery, yet it also creates needless confusion. Similar ambiguity plagues the whole grating situation. Do two items fall into the vent during the murder—the ring and a barrette—or was the barrette there *before* the murder? (Presumably, it's the former, but again, it's hard to tell.) Does Frankie open the grating with Miss La Della's blessing, or is he just sneaking about on his own? Why does he not show the objects to his father, or Miss La Della, or Sheriff Saunders, or *someone* instead of keeping them on his person? Add to this several rather gratuitous effects shots (Phil's fall, for example, or that inexplicable fingertip lightning bolt) and a few more scenes which just don't quite work (the cliff sequence draws out its melodramatic "Phil's dead!" "No, he's alive!" game to no end), and one has a film with more than its share of disappointing artistic missteps.

And yet at its best, *Lady in White* also bears marks of sheer brilliance, Throughout the film, LaLoggia surprises us at every turn by varying the size of his images and the viewpoint from which they are seen. Giant close-ups of everything from barrette boxes to ring engravings, and our perspective is persistently challenged with inventive camera shots filmed through heating ducts and window panes. The camera crawls along floors like baby alligators and soars through forests like crows, and quick cuts from image to image lend speed and suspense to moments of action and conflict. There is, in short, very little in the way of effective camerawork which LaLoggia cannot do.

He's also quite good when it comes to character development and symbolism. Making Frankie and Melissa soulmates, for example, sharing a heartfelt yearning for a lost mother, is a real masterstroke, making the plight of each, especially Frankie, truly touching; we not only know the boy better, we feel for him too. (Again, LaLoggia's script slips a bit. Why Melissa and her mother can *separately* prance about woods and farmhouses at will yet can't meet is never clear; Phil isn't even dead yet when they reunite, so if unfulfilled "justice" isn't what is keeping these two apart, what exactly has Frankie done meriting Melissa's grateful "Thank you"?)

Nice too are the leaves, glitter, snow and sparks forever floating and fluttering from the heavens (the imagery lends the film great visual beauty), and LaLoggia's use of masks and trickery provide both humor and pathos at key moments. The director's angel motif is also remarkably effective, appearing in forms as varied as Mary Ellen's Halloween costume to the Scarlottis' Christmas tree ornament. Even better is the ingenious use of the old Harry Revel/Mack Gordon tune "Did You Ever See a Dream Walking," its walking, talking and dancing dream idea a clear nod to not only to Melissa, her mother and the alive-yet-ghostly Amanda Harper, but also Frankie's late mother. Also, in light of how often the Scarlottis exchange hugs, kisses and verbal "I love yous," the

line "Did you ever see heaven right in your arms, saying, 'I love you. I do' ?" takes on special power. Add to this the fact that the line "Something that I feared somehow is now endeared to me" echoes Angelo's words about not having outgrown his fears and Frankie's about no longer fearing what he cannot see, and one realizes *Lady in White* is quite an impressive bit of storytelling.

Chief among the film's many pleasures is its marvelous team of actors, for however jarring an occasional visual or logic flaw might first seem, one need only wait a heartbeat before LaLoggia's gifted cast tugs one right back into the movie's magic all over again. Child actor Lukas Haas merits particular acclaim as Frankie, turning in a performance so winning and so forthright that one instantly sees in him an actor whose sheer earnestness puts the average mugging, hipster child star from TV and film to shame. Clearly, Haas' much-heralded breakthrough work at age six in 1985's *Witness* was no fluke; this lad is a natural actor. Likewise, veteran actor Alex Rocco, whose closest brush with fame came as smarmy Hollywood agent Al Floss in the one-season CBS satire *The Fabulous Teddy Z*, could hardly be better, creating in Angelo a figure so wise and warm that, could his integrity and love be bottled and sold to real-life fathers, teenage bums, addicts and street hoods might be a thing of the past. Also quite strong is actor Len Cariou, whose family friend-gone-mad Phil is by turns caring and crazed, sympathetic and sinister. True, it is all too easy to recognize Phil as the Cliffside Killer, yet in the hands of a lesser actor, Phil might have been nothing but an eye-rolling, hand-wringing freak. Amazingly, though, Cariou makes Phil seem all the more deadly because outwardly he appears so respectable, so kind; since he has in effect "seduced" the entire Scarlotti family for so many years, one can easily see how a young, trusting child like Melissa might fall prey to his charms.

As Frankie's brother Geno, actor Jason Presson (so winning in his early work opposite a young Ethan Hawke and River Phoenix in 1985's *Explorers*) strikes just the right note of free-spirited fun and wise-guy playfulness; thanks to Presson's upbeat, goodhearted performance—and LaLoggia's delicate handling of the character on paper—one genuinely *likes* Geno instead of finding him annoying. Of course one could argue that Angelo Bertolini and Renata Vanni's work as the boys' grandparents veers close to ethnic stereotyping, yet they comprise such a lovable old twosome that all is quickly forgiven; besides, who *doesn't* have such a set of comically quarrelsome elders in the family?

The rest of the cast is equally good, from TV veterans Tom Bower as Sheriff Saunders (Bower was Mary Ellen's husband Curtis Willard in *The Waltons*) and Lucy Lee Flippin as Miss La Della (she played a similar

spinster teacher role, Miss Eliza Jane Wilder, in *Little House on the Prairie*), both of whom turn potentially flat parts into figures of surprising warmth and humanity, to Joelle Jacobi as Melissa (the very picture of childlike curiosity) and Katherine Helmond (whose own TV work in shows like *Soap* and *Who's the Boss*? quickly eclipsed a rich career of big screen roles) as tragic Miss Amanda Harper, a figure frightening and touching all at once. Henry Harris is also quite memorable as the deeply misjudged Harold Williams (thanks to Harris, we sense at once that this is a good man horribly wronged), as is Rose Weaver as his long-suffering wife, Matty (her emotional collapse upon her husband's death is truly extraordinary), and Rita Zohar as despairing Mrs. Cilak, grieving to the point of murder over the loss of her child. Actually, all the roles in *Lady in White* seem superbly cast, right down to the small parts scripted for ministers, spouses, children and coworkers.

The story goes that LaLoggia—basing *Lady in White* on his own upbringing and the eerie local legends of his boyhood—raised two million of his film's nearly five million dollar budget from 4,000 investors in the Lyons, New York area, not far from his hometown of Rochester. Perhaps this "community project" feel (some investors allegedly appear in scenes filmed in Lyons) lends the film much of its comfortable, small town flavor. In any case, critics were generally kind to *Lady in White*, *L.A. Weekly*'s Michael Dare labeling it "one of the most intelligent and riveting ghost stories since *Poltergeist*," and *People*'s Peter Travers seeing it as "something rare: a ghost story that truly haunts." *Newsweek*'s David Ansen, declaring the film "the rare genre movie that seems inspired by personal experience," expressed pleasure that LaLoggia avoids "cheap displays of gore," and *The New Yorker*'s Pauline Kael admired the "poetic feeling" she felt compensated for an otherwise "overcomplicated plot," along with its many "touches that charm" along the way. She also praised Haas, noting how his "rapt belief in his visions lends credibility to the events." As she put it, Haas "loves acting so much that when he's miming spooked terror he's tickled to be doing it. He gives himself the shivers, and probably grins when the director calls for retakes."

Lady in White may not be the perfect ghost film—too many events remain inadequately explained, and the final quarter-hour strives too hard for melodrama and spectacle—yet its human element is so pure, so earnest, so real, that it transcends its minor weaknesses to become something truly special. The Scarlottis are a family worth knowing, and Willowpoint Falls, racist undercurrents notwithstanding, a town meriting a brief stay. Thanks to LaLoggia, *Lady in White* may be visited again and again. It is, beyond question, a trip well worth taking.

CREDITS: Executive Producer: Charles M. LaLoggia, Cliff Payne; Producer: Andrew G. La Marca, Frank LaLoggia; Director: Frank LaLoggia; Screenplay: Frank LaLoggia; Visual Effects Supervisors: Ernest D. Farino, Gene Warren, Jr.; Director of Photography: Russell Carpenter; Music Composer/Arranger: Frank LaLoggia; A New Sky Communications, Inc. Picture; 1988; 113 minutes

CAST: Lukas Haas...Frankie, Len Cariou...Phil, Alex Rocco.. Angelo, Katherine Helmond...Amanda, Jason Presson...Geno, Renata Vanni...Mama Assunta, Angelo Bertolini...Papa Charlie, Joelle Jacobi...Melissa, Jared Rushton...Donald, Gregory Levinson...Louis, Lucy Lee Flippin...Miss La Della, Tom Bower...Sheriff Saunders, Jack Andreozzi...Tony, Sydney Lassick...Mr. Lowry, Rita Zohar...Mrs. Cilak, Hal Bokar...Mr. Cilak, Henry Harris...Mr. Williams, Rose Weaver...Matty Williams, Karen Powell...Lady in White, Lisa Taylor...Mary Ellen

THE LEGEND OF HELL HOUSE

by Robert Alan Crick

The much admired 1971 haunted house novel *Hell House*—filmed in 1973 as *The Legend of Hell House*—is one of the more off-putting Richard Matheson works, no less imaginative than the fantasy master's greatest creations yet somehow, at the same time, one of his least approachable. Its characters are fascinating psychological studies, though simultaneously remote and single-minded, making them less embraceable than, say, the warm, romantic lovers in *Bid Time Return* (brought to the big screen as *Somewhere in Time*) or the lonely, pitiable hero of *The Shrinking Man* (retitled on film as *The Incredible Shrinking Man*). Its subject matter—four visitors to a haunted mansion, three of whom differ on the best method of vanquishing the deep-seated evil therein—is offbeat and compelling, yet less emotionally involving than more personal Matheson stories such as "Nightmare at 20,000 Feet" (a troubled, suicidal airline passenger must prove to himself his own sanity), "Duel" (an ordinary driver is targeted for death on a lonely highway for no apparent reason), or "Little Girl Lost" (a loving father seeks to rescue his young daughter, who has inexplicably vanished into another dimension). Even its very title, not to mention its somewhat explicit language and detailed moments of depravity, make *Hell House* a rather difficult Matheson work with which to warm up. This is certainly not, by any means, in the same vein as Matheson's whimsical L. Frank Baum tribute, *The Dreamer of Oz*.

Even so, haunted house stories have always been great fun, and on film even *Hell House*—its rather unpleasant title softened ever-so-slightly as *The Legend of Hell House*—proves remarkably winning despite its darkest impulses. Yes, Matheson's screen adaptation still dabbles in the perverse; yes, its dialogue still offends those who prefer even good horror to exercise self-restraint; and yes, its characters are still as remote and all-business as Matheson originally conceived them. Still, *The Legend of Hell House* is a surprisingly engaging little film, its grim, often unpleasant tone more than offset by a splendidly paced script by Matheson himself; earnest, heartfelt performances from a cast who must have felt themselves straitjacketed by dialogue heavily laced with psychological, scientific and religious references; a deeply affecting electronic score by Brian Hodgson and Delia Derbyshire; topflight scene-cutting

from editor Geoffrey Root; and a dazzling display of disorienting visual tricks from director John Hough.

Hough's opening shot prepares us for what is to come, for already the creative camerawork is underway. The film begins with an impressive look at the ceiling of an elaborate mansion, an ornate religious painting seen from below—a winning shot into which steps Ann Barrett (Gayle Hunnicutt, whose character is named Edith in the novel). A prim, rather matronly woman, Ann takes a seat beside her physicist husband Lionel (Clive Revill, whose character in the novel suffers the effects of childhood polio but here seems in fine health). Almost instantly, Lionel Barrett is summoned for his meeting with a figure identified in the novel as publishing giant Rolf Rudolph Deutsch, a crotchety, ailing old man (played by Roland Culver) who seeks an answer to one of life's great questions—and thinks Barrett, "one of the best five" in his field, can uncover the truth.

What Deutsch seeks is something his own tabloid-style periodicals have speculated about for years—positive proof that "survival after death" is either a reality or a fraud. He offers Barrett £100,000 to bring him "the facts" (in the novel, Hell House is in Maine, not England, and Deutsch's offer is in dollars, not pounds). The facts he seeks can be found in the legendary Belasco House—"the only place I know on earth," says Deutsch, "where survival is yet to be refuted." For years the Belasco House has remained sealed, but Deutsch plans to send Barrett and two other experts for an in-depth study. The old man's unreasonable time limit—"I expect an answer within a week!"—displeases Barrett, but the offer is too tempting to pass up: £100,000 to put to the test his own theories in the notorious landmark referred to with both disgust and reverence as "Hell House." Almost immediately, the deal is made. (in Matheson's novel, Deutsch's pressing need for word about "survival after death" seems a bit more urgent than here, for in the original the 87-year-old tycoon dies before Barrett's week at Hell House is up. In the novel, Matheson suggests that Deutsch, his own death closing in, seeks proof that perhaps he too—like the spirits of Hell House—will outlive his decaying body. Such omissions are unfortunate, though one cannot fault Matheson's expositional skills; the entire scene between Barrett and Deutsch takes barely two minutes of screen time. It's a marvel of storytelling efficiency.)

Barrett arranges to have a machine he designed delivered to the house; he will approach the investigation from a strictly scientific viewpoint—whatever phenomena have manifested themselves can be subdued through wires, electricity and mechanically generated energy. None of this, however, means Barrett disbelieves the house contains some dangerous, even lethal force. Driven away from the mansion in a Deutsch limousine, he warns Ann that perhaps she should not join him on this latest enterprise. "Isn't it just another so-called haunted house?" she wonders. "It's the Mount Everest of haunted houses," declares Barrett, who recalls that in the last two attempts to rid the edifice of its evil, eight people died, and one of the survivors, Ben Fischer, returning now for the Deutsch venture, was left "a mental wreck." "I don't want to be left alone," Ann says: whatever the risk, she will be at her husband's side.

Monday morning (just minutes into the film), the limousine containing the Barretts picks up medium Ben Fischer (Roddy McDowall) at a train depot. Hough manages to make even this minor moment visually interesting, placing his camera *inside* the limousine and shooting out one window, watching Fischer approach as the car slows for him (Hodson and Derbyshire's intense, pulsating music add immeasurably here). Instantly afterward, a shot of a church is interrupted as medium Florence Tanner (Pamela Franklin) steps before it and into the frame. As the car pulls up, Florence smiles and gets in, leaving the church behind in more ways than one as it is overtaken by fog.

The limousine is seen through the iron gates of Hell House as the vehicle drops off its four passengers, leaving them there for a week during which anything—*anything*—is likely to happen. It is only now, as the four visitors push open the front gates and examine the house through the fog, that the credits appear, the film's driving, disturbing score creating an atmosphere of dread even in daylight. As the quartet enter the gates, they are shot slightly from below, making the house seem to loom before them like some enormous brick-windowed mountain, then—after an unsettling image of a black cat loping up, then crouching as if lying in wait—they are shot from even farther below as they gaze up at the mansion, intrigued. "It's hideous," Florence observes, to which Barrett, clearly no believer in mere instinct, points out, "We're not even inside yet, Miss Tanner." Even so, Florence's perception is too strong to be dismissed so easily. "I don't have to be," she insists.

Director Hough's first look at the mansion's interior—a terrific long shot of inky darkness dispersed as the front door opens to admit a stream of light— is just the first of many moments underscoring the mansion's immense size. Indeed, throughout the film, even in the opening scenes at the Deutsch estate, Hough places a persistent emphasis on high ceilings and distant walls—an inspired idea, really, for three reasons: first, such long shots of oversized rooms dwarf the characters themselves, somewhat limiting audience involvement with them as people but focusing attention primarily on their investigation (thereby reproducing remarkably well the same cold, analytical tone of Matheson's novel); second, this same dwarfing effect makes the characters seem disturbingly helpless and alone, mere playthings for the awesome, all-powerful force which at times will assault them as individuals, at other times pit group member against group member; and, third, though never undermining the necessarily claustrophobic nature of Matheson's story (the action occurs almost entirely indoors), frequently placing the camera far from the actors guarantees that the audience will not find themselves squirming in their theater seats, longing for a change of pace from the same old drab, dusty interiors. This latter benefit is secured as well through Hough's frequently off-kilter camera angles, not to mention Root's imaginative editing. From moment to moment, one never quite knows what to expect—whether for the next shot the camera will be filming from the ceiling, some distant wall, or the floor. Any number of horror movies are warmer, more sensitive, more human; few, however, are more visually interesting, something *The Legend of Hell House* invariably remains from beginning to end.

Even as the group first enters, one senses that Lionel Barrett and Florence Tanner will be at odds over how best to handle the investigation. When Florence declares, "This house—it knows we're here," Barrett offers a gentle glance of disapproval. It is Fischer's reaction, however, which proves most interesting. Quiet, restrained and cheerless from the first moment we meet him, Fischer is, as the only previous Hell House visitor in the group, the true expert among them, yet it is this very expertise which makes him now the least vocal; it will take some time before Fischer can force himself out of his "shell," revealing him to be not the team's weakest link, but perhaps its strongest. For now, however, Barrett is the group's clear leader, with Florence just behind, competing with him while Fischer "plays it safe" like some glum, fearful child.

If Barrett's wife is the Hell House visitor least prepared for whatever horrors may soon befall them, it is Fischer who knows best how truly insidious Hell House can be—and, therefore, it is he who is most frightened.

At present, the only courage Fischer can muster is a faint smugness; his colleagues are in deadly danger, yet only he seems to see it coming. When Barrett recalls that original Hell House owner Emeric Belasco "left millions when he died," Fischer asks softly, "Died?"—a single word, barely given utterance, yet from it there can be no doubt about his point of view: Belasco's evil is very much alive, and unless Barrett accepts this as fact, he himself may turn out to be the mansion's next victim. Asked about his previous stay, Fischer seems even now 20 years later— still too unnerved by the events to share them freely. "What's to tell?" he whispers. "The house tried to kill me. It almost succeeded."

If Fischer's reaction to Hell House is one of coiled, silent dread, Florence's reveals her overwhelming fixation upon matters religious (in the novel, it is made far clearer that "the Reverend Florence Tanner" has been a minister for the past six years at the church where she is picked up). To her revulsion, Hell House has its own blasphemous version of a chapel—"a church in Hell," notes Barrett—a chapel within which she senses a disturbance she cannot bring herself to confront. "Her system's attuned to psychic energy," Barrett explains to Ann—evidence again that Barrett *does* believe the structure has imprisoned residue from all the violent, hostile energy of those who once dwelt there. In time, once his machine has arrived, he will dispel this mindless, soulless energy, freeing the mansion of the terrible force still housed there.

In the dining hall that evening, Florence theorizes that Belasco's mansion is being haunted by "multiple surviving personalities," Belasco's among them. Only now does the usually silent Fischer bring himself to reveal something of the mansion's history. Hell House was built in 1919, he recalls, after which it was lorded over by Emeric Belasco, a six-foot-five pleasure-seeker and deviate known as "the Roaring Giant." Asked how Belasco earned his reputation for barbarism and cruelty, Fischer offers only a glimpse of the dark, demented figure described in Matheson's novel. Belasco was, says Fischer, a practitioner and proponent of "drug addiction. Alcoholism. Sadism. Bestiality. Mutilation. Murder. Vampirism. Necrophilia. Cannibalism. Not to mention a gamut of sexual goodies." "How did it end?" Ann wants to know. "If it *had* ended," says Fischer, "we would not be here."

He does note, however, that an end of a sort occurred in 1929, when 27 people were found dead in the house, though Belasco himself was not among them; the creator of this private Hell was nowhere to be found. The novel states that Belasco formed a secret society called Les Aphrodites, socialites who lived by the principle of "total self-indulgence." By 1929 (interestingly, the year the whole world's "party" ended with the stockmarket collapse) the group had become so mired in open perversity as to be beyond redemption. Having become so self-absorbed with satisfying their own animal pleasures that even personal health and cleanliness were secondary to the drug-like power of human depravity, Belasco's guests, by now wallowing in physical filth as well as mental, died of influenza, pneumonia, and of "killing each other for food or water, liquor, drugs, sex, blood, even for the taste of human flesh, which many of them had acquired by then."

Barrett, confident that science can overcome the deadly forces trapped within the mansion's walls, maintains that the situation will end for good in a matter of days—optimism with which Fischer obviously disagrees. Asked if he will exercise his prowess as a medium for a "sitting" soon, Fischer is noticeably

fearful of the outcome. Mental medium Florence, however, agrees to an informal sitting that night, during which her preoccupation with religion is very much in evidence. In the midst of her trancelike state (in Matheson's novel, Florence speaks in the stereotypically stilted phrases of an Indian spirit she calls "Red Cloud"), she quotes the Biblical passage "If thine eye offend thee"—seemingly a meaningless reference, but eventually a key to solving the Hell House puzzle. Seconds later, Florence speaks in a deep, eerie voice, one by turns pleading and helpless ("I don't want to hurt you, but I must! I must!"), then harsh and threatening ("Get out of this house or I'll kill you all!"). Far more exciting cinematically is the sudden shimmering and rattling of objects on the table before her— unwittingly caused by Florence. The unnerving disturbance is a brief one, but its significance lays still more groundwork for the growing conflict within the group.

Florence, in her bedroom, becomes witness to a strange phenomenon. Seemingly under its own power, the door to her room opens, and one registers the sensation of some unseen figure entering. "You're not Belasco, are you?" Florence questions her visitor. "Who *were* you?" Amazingly, the invisible being yanks her bedclothes from the bed. A split second later, like some strange, windlike power, her guest overturns a chair, table, and vase, flings open the door again, seemingly exits, and slams the door shut.

The next morning—Tuesday—Florence (in a splendid shot, making her entrance reflected in a silver teapot being held by Barrett) is cheerful and upbeat reporting her encounter the night before. "He's Belasco's son," she tells Barrett, explaining that if she can persuade Daniel to leave the house, much of the mansion's "haunting force" will be eliminated. Barrett is clearly only humoring her. He requests a second sitting—"under scientific conditions this time," of course.

Florence, wearing a formfitting, skimpy black outfit to eliminate any chance of fraud, sits behind a netted screen as Barrett, documenting the event with a tape recorder, meticulously monitors his subject's pulse, temperature, and breathing. His instruments register the presence of "electromagnetic radiation," as well as ozone in the air. In the film's strangest visual effect, pale ectoplasmic threads form from Florence's fingertips, the filaments from each hand uniting into separate strands. "Leave a sample in the jar, please," Barrett requests, and indeed a sample does move into the glass jar atop the table until suddenly—Crack!—an abrupt miniature explosion from the container startles Ann, who screams. Almost simultaneously, Florence shrieks horribly.

Ann apologizes to her husband for having "spoiled" his research with her outcry, but Barrett, examining his specimen under a microscope, assures her he is quite satisfied. The ectoplasm, he claims, is mere "organic externalization of thought"—Florence's own mental processes given physical substance. It is, to his mind, all explainable by science, and thus certainly no cause for him to start believing in ghosts—not even in Hell House, the one place on earth where ghosts just might exist.

Later, Florence has a second encounter with the force she has identified as Daniel Belasco. Beneath the covers of her bed, a human shape is clearly outlined, yet when she yanks the bedclothes away, nobody is there, though "Daniel" does abruptly open the door and slams out. Florence reports the incident at breakfast with Barrett and Fischer the next morning—Wednesday—but again Barrett's appreciation for her speculation is minimal. Insulted, Florence's temper flares. "Will it never end?" she snaps suddenly, and Barrett is dumbfounded by the outburst, despite the fact that his own patient condescension has triggered it.

Barrett, responding with kindness, attempts to address Florence's sudden fury, but he never gets the chance. With an abrupt BANG!, his coffee cup explodes in his hand (a masterful bit of editing, by the way, guaranteed to make any viewer flinch), followed by a shattered goblet which launches its jagged edge into Barrett's palm. In practically the same instant, a china plate begins to rattle, then hurls itself at him, followed by a metal platter. The entire table now begins to leap up, bucking wildly, chandeliers rattle, and Barrett's chair—he is standing now—slides roughly beneath him. Caught by the impact, he falls backward in the chair and a chandelier plunges toward him. Rolling away just in time (and as a horrified Ann enters), Barrett is besieged by a sudden burst of flame from the fireplace, after which a wall mirror bathes him in broken glass. It is a splendidly well-edited sequence, thrillingly executed and ending only when Florence, seemingly the cause of the assault, screams "No!" at the top of her lungs. In an instant, almost as if on command, the attack upon Barrett ends.

Astonishingly, Florence urges Fischer—who, typically, has not uttered a word during the entire scene, cross or otherwise—to leave Hell House at once. "You're the physical medium," she points out. "You're obviously being used! You're not in control!" Naturally, Fischer is flabbergasted; true, he is capable of "manifesting physical phenomena," but since Florence is the angry one here, laying the blame for the barrage on him makes no sense, as Barrett quickly points out. "Trying to get rid of us *both* now!" he shouts accusingly, and in seconds both he and his wife have exited to nurse his wounds. Alone with Florence now, Fischer, ever the voice of soft-spoken solemn reason, reassesses the situation for Florence's benefit. "You're the one who should leave," he tells her calmly. "You're the one who's being used—not me." With this pivotal scene in the film, "the gloves are off," so to speak; from this point on, professional courtesy will remain secondary to each individual expert's need to defend his own position. In their room, Barrett's hand is bandaged while he offers his interpretation of the assault to his wife. "There's a lot of power in this house, Ann," he admits. "She was the one who used it, though—directed it at me." Entering, a now calmer Florence still insists their conflict is precisely what Daniel Belasco was after to begin with. "He's trying to separate us," she maintains. "We're less of a challenge to him that way." Barrett insists Florence is wrong in blaming his injury on Emeric Belasco's son. "There is no such person!" he tells her, but she is unmoved.

In one of the film's more eerie scenes, a black cat lopes by the house, after which Ann joins her husband in bed. As he sleeps, Ann takes note of a statuette of a man and woman embracing—and is startled to find their silhouettes on the ceiling coming to passionate life! Ann discovers a book called *Autoerotic Phenomena*. As if strangely compelled somehow, the normally reserved, modest Ann begins to read.

Downstairs, Fischer discovers Ann watching him from upstairs. Descending the staircase with a provocative "come hither" slink, the emotionally liberated woman caresses a female statue, approaches Fischer, and makes brazen overtures—even suggesting that all four Hell House visitors engage in drunken passion. To Fischer's amazement, she even disrobes before him, and he slaps her hard across the face. Coming to from her somnambular intoxication, Ann awakens to embarrassment and horror. "You were walking in your sleep," Fischer explains gently, but, ashamed and revolted, she rushes upstairs.

Shortly afterward, Florence enters the "chapel" alone for the first time. Here she locates two metal crutches—a significant clue to the tale's climax. Touching them, however, she senses something, and is drawn by the sounds of suffering (real? imagined?) to a stone wall. Opening a secret door there, she appears briefly triumphant. "Daniel, I've found you!" she says proudly, but within seconds she emits a chilling shriek as some unseen force sends her reeling backward, strangling her. The Barretts, hearing, rush downstairs, but Fischer is already at her side. She has found Daniel Belasco, Florence insists, and when Barrett looks doubtful, she shows him the gruesome scratches acquired just moments before. "Well, I'm not *imagining* it!" she cries defensively, then gestures to her discovery behind the secret door. "Did I imagine *this*?" she asks, and indeed, within are a male's remains, chained to a second wall—some poor soul left to die during the days of Emeric Belasco's barbaric experiments in pain and torment. Florence and Fischer bury the body outside, she believes Daniel Belasco has received the love and respect merited him.

The funeral is not enough, however, for the scene slowly merges into one of Florence tossing and turning in her sleep, haunted by Daniel's lonely laments. "Help me, Florence," the voice begs. "You should have gone on. You've been given your release." But her encouragement goes unheeded, the voice maintaining that she is his only hope—and urging her to embrace him with physical passion. In the end, Florence is shaken awake by Daniel's influences, sitting bolt upright with an angry "No!" as the film's sound effects and Daniel's urgings reach a fever pitch. There remains only silence now, but Florence notices her bedroom door brushed open as a black cat enters. To her astonishment, the cat hisses at her threateningly, then abruptly leaps atop her and begins mauling her. Terrified, Florence flings the animal away, but it leaps again, then again, refusing to give up even as she hurls the crazed beast into lamps and clubs it with a heavy decorative piece from a table nearby. The entire scene is superbly constructed, shot from so many different angles and edited with such swiftness that even a few glimpses of a stuffed cat clutched about Florence's neck and shoulders are so fleeting that the overall effect is truly gripping—especially when capped by a truly terrific shot from the cat's point of view as it races along the carpet after her. The viewer experiences a tremendous relief as Florence reaches the bathroom first and slams the door behind her, though the sight of the frustrated cat's paws swiping at the space under the door is still unsettling.

The next morning the completed machine Barrett has requested is delivered. As Barrett and Ann examine the box-like device, an excellent over-the-shoulder shot reveals Fischer looking down from upstairs (the mansion appears truly tremendous from this angle). He offers news of Florence's injuries. Barrett examines Florence's wounds—"It was possessed by Daniel Belasco," she says of the cat—and, in light of this second mauling, he advises her to leave the mansion at once. "I don't want you," he explains, "to be another victim of Hell House." After the Barretts exit, a concerned Fischer has to agree.

Fischer looks over Barrett's machine with little confidence—and for the second night, he is joined there by Ann Barrett, who descends in her nightgown, hair down again, intoxicated. Fischer urges her to go back upstairs, but Ann does her very best to seduce him. "Touch me or I'll find somebody

who will!" At these words, director Hough offers another unexpected over-the-shoulders shot, this time of Ann's husband, who has arrived on the balcony just in time to witness her attempt at seduction. As both spot him on the balcony, Ann is suddenly overwhelmed by guilt and passes out—her disorientation and collapse captured beautifully with a remarkable point-of-view shot utilizing a convex lens effect as she hits the floor.

Later, Fischer warns Barrett about the "grave danger" facing Ann. "It was not her fault," he explains, to which Barrett, even if comforted, registers embarrassment. "Doctor, I don't think you know what is going on in this house." "I've noticed quite a number of things, Mr. Fischer," Barrett says flatly. "One of them is that you're blocking yourself off completely."

As Barrett stalks off, his criticism echoes in Fischer's head, followed by his own thoughts in voiceover. "I am not blocking anything," he tells himself. "I'm just not sticking my neck out the way I did in 1953." Taking Barrett's words to heart, Fischer sits alone, head back, closes his eyes in an attempt to "open himself up," and suddenly sits bolt upright with an anguished scream. Another clever use of lens distortion, shot from different angles (including overhead), gives the scene a nightmarish, disorienting quality, as the agonized Fischer collapses on the floor.

Thursday morning Fischer is visited by Florence, whose efforts to remain hopeful about the outcome of the investigation fall upon deaf ears. "Give up," Fischer tells her and relates the tale of the 1953 catastrophe—how a medium leapt from a Hell House balcony and shattered both legs; how a physicist literally crawled out of the house to die; how a chemistry professor left the mansion paralyzed for life; and how a psychic investigator survived only to remain "crippled and insane to this day." The picture of a man who had all the fight knocked out of him at 15 and has never recovered, Fischer admits that he hasn't been very helpful to the investigation and has no plans to try.

"I *am* obstructing. You're quite right. I'm shut off. I'm going to *stay* shut off until I am far away from this place. I am going to collect my 100,000 and I am never going to come within a thousand miles of this house for as long as I live, and I suggest you do the same." We've never heard Fischer sound quite so selfish—yet we forgive him even as he exits because he has been through so much.

The next scene offers a clever shot of a pacing Florence reflected in her bedroom's mirrored ceiling (appropriately, Florence's bedroom boasts a brazen scarlet color scheme, indicative of her intense relationship with the vulgar, seductive "Daniel"). The camera next pans down to the real Florence, drawn to the sound of running water in the bathroom. A female silhouette is visible through the shower door, and a trickle of blood spills onto the floor. Florence opens the shower door, and looks down with a gasp of horror as the camera zooms in for a truly repugnant shot of the cat, one eye torn from its socket, floating dead in a pool of water and blood. The scene, accompanied on the soundtrack by both a ghostly scream and an electronic squeal, makes for such a real "shocker" that at first one is tempted to discount the scene as gratuitous, cheap and manipulative. In time, however, the viewer "on his toes" will come to realize that the cat's missing eye—like the metal braces discovered by Florence in the chapel, the religious references in her first sitting, and other such moments—actually provides a clever clue to the ultimate solution to the Hell House mystery.

Downstairs, Barrett readies his machine for the big event: the freeing from Hell House of the awesome power trapped there. "It's a real power, Ann," he says. "A field of measurable energy—energy that can be reversed." Thus, even after all he has seen, Barrett still holds there is no consciousness within the mansion, no evidence of a sentient, scheming force plotting against them. "By this time tomorrow," he assures Ann with confidence, "Hell House will be drained." "That pile of junk you have there, Barrett?" Fischer says. "It isn't going to do a thing. Get her *out* of here! You haven't got a chance!" "Have you?" Barrett wonders. "Yes. Yes, I know the score," Fischer insists. "You do not fight this house!... What it doesn't like is people who attack it. Belasco doesn't like it."

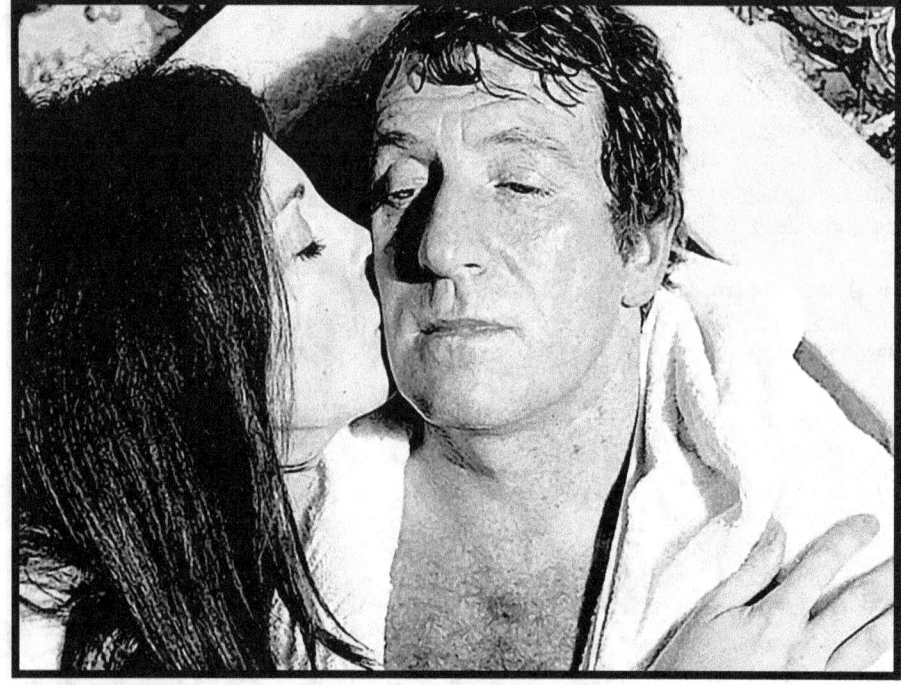

"He won't listen, will he?" he asks Ann, and then declares solemnly, "I was the only one to leave here alive and sane in 1953, and I will he the only one to make it out of here alive and sane this time."

Florence is drawn to the chapel by ghostly whispers ("Help me!"), shrieks and noises. She covers her ears as the bombardment becomes almost deafening, and at last she flees. A trio of distorted camera angles reflects her intense confusion as she ascends to the balcony, where Hough's camera begins to spin wildly, the entire scene turning topsy turvy until finally Florence reaches her bedroom and slams the door shut. As Daniel continues to whisper longingly ("Please... help me. Love me"), Florence prays for his "tortured soul" and, undressing fully, climbs into bed. The covers are drawn back as "Daniel" joins her, and close-ups of Florence, eyes closed, reveal her misguided devotion to the plan she has conceived. "I give you now the love you've never known," she tells Daniel. "I give it freely so that you will gain the strength to go on from this house."

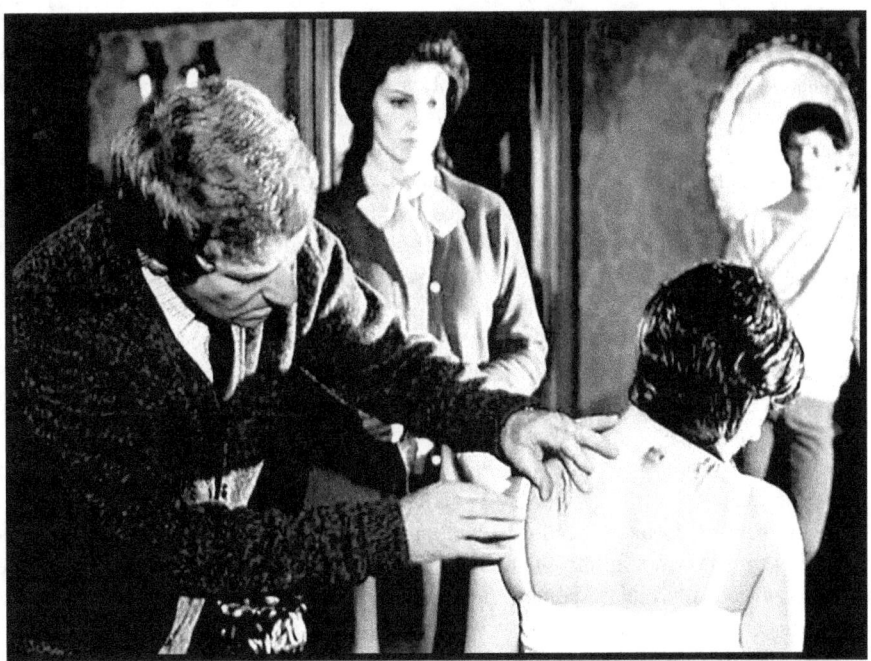

Mercifully, there is a brief cut to Fischer in his room, then a return to Florence as she gives herself over completely to her outrageous plan. The scene is appropriately repugnant, ending with Florence opening her eyes in revulsion and horror, screaming wildly. Fischer hears, runs to her door, joined by the Barretts, and attempts to break through. Finally, as if by itself, the door opens. The trio enter and find Florence, lying in bed, her naked body mauled yet again—and, as if possessed, she emits a demented, vulgar laugh at her associates.

Friday morning she wakes chuckling, telling Fischer seductively, "You could have slept with me." Then, with sudden terror, she realizes the words are not her own. "He's inside me!" she gasps, hugging Fischer close. "I can feel him just waiting in there to take over." Fischer, comforting her, vows to take her away this morning, but she insists Daniel can stop her departure.

"I'm taking her away," Fischer tells Barrett, who suggests there is no point in his returning. "By this afternoon the house will be clear." Suddenly, realizing Barrett intends to send Daniel Belasco "from one Hell to the next," Florence tries to destroy the machine, smashing a few gauges before anyone can stop her. Fischer is clubbed senseless when he attempts to intervene, but Barrett, protecting his machine, knocks Florence unconscious.

A short time later as Barrett repairs the damage done to his machine. Florence slips off—the camera takes on POV as she strides to the chapel—where, bombarded by wind, groans and painful shrieks, she hears "Daniel's" whispered "Florence." Still moved by pity, she urges him to leave at once, warning him against Barrett's machine.

The force manipulating Florence, however, has no need for her now, and suddenly a heavy wooden cross tumbles atop her, crushing her legs and pinning her underneath. Florence lies writhing in anguish beneath the enormous weight of the cross. A whispered "Florence" is heard again, and a flicker of light and shadow in the direction of her gaze suggests the powerful force stalking Hell House is now quite close. "You tricked me!" she gasps. "You tricked all of us!" and, as the presence chuckles cruelly, she uses her last ounce of strength to leave a clue for the others. When discovered, Florence lies dead, a bloody "B" drawn in a circle on the cross above her.

Barrett activates his machine, and he, Ann and Fischer exit the mansion as the device emits its dull, droning hum. As they wait outside, dust billows within the house, lamps rock gently, and tragic, painful cries echo from within. Once it is safe, the trio return. Hough keeps his camera far back, the interior of the house distorted slightly as the door opens, letting in a stream of daylight—and Fischer seems perplexed as he "opens himself up" to put Hell House to the test. As Barrett enjoys his apparent victory, Fischer is absolutely ecstatic. "Barrett, the house is clear!" he cries from upstairs. "It is completely clear! And I called that machine a pile of junk!"

Later he is startled to find his devices going haywire—registering high levels of energy within Hell House. Abruptly, one of his gadgets explodes in his face, and he grips his eyes in pain.

A cheerful Ann comes downstairs, but finds the work area in disarray. When she calls to Barrett, his voice responds, "In here!" from the chapel. Reassured, Ann—seen once through a slightly distorted lens again—makes her way there, only to scream in utter despair as she finds Barrett's body crushed beneath a chandelier, a close-up showing he has been blinded in one eye. Running in panic to the accompaniment of unearthly soundtrack screeches and echoes, she at last blunders into the arms of a shadowy figure seen only from behind and, struggling wildly, collapses to the floor. The figure is Fischer. Ann begs him to take her away, but to her surprise—and ours—he tells her he cannot leave, "I'm going back to the chapel," he says. "Ann, listen," he says warmly. "It's for Florence. It's for your husband. If I leave Hell House now, my whole life is going to be a failure." "You can't solve it," Ann tells him. "It cannot be solved. You're going to die—like Lionel. Like Miss Tanner." Fischer is polite but resolute. "Then I will," he says.

Ann goes with Fischer into the chapel; pleasingly, the unlikely pair is now a team. "It's here," Fischer is certain. "The entire house is clear except for this one place. Why?" Examining Florence's encircled letter "B" on the cross again, he begins piecing the puzzle together, realizing now that both Barrett and Florence had misinterpreted the source of the evil from the start. "Belasco," he whispers. "She was trying to tell us that it was only Belasco all along. It isn't mindless, directionless power. It isn't multiple hauntings. It's only one."

Fischer turns his attention to Florence's crushed legs, then Barrett's. Through a soundtrack voiceover, he hears Florence's words during her first sitting— "Extremes and limits," she said—and slowly it comes clear. "Of course," he realizes. "That's what she meant. Extremes. Limits. *Legs*." Again, he recalls the victims of his first stay: the investigator with the shattered spine and legs; another crawling from the house; one paralyzed; still another crippled. We hear Florence's voice again, whispering, "If thine eye offend thee," and suddenly Fischer, invigorated, sees it all now and bravely calls to Belasco in challenge.

Confronting Belasco head-on, taunting him, Fischer is narrowly saved from a falling chandelier by Ann. He torments Belasco cruelly. "Tell me something, Belasco, why didn't you ever leave this house when you were alive? Why did you despise the sunlight? Was it better hiding in the shadows?" Fischer grips his head in pain as pulsating waves of hatred and wind gusts assault him. "You weren't a genius!" he cries. "You were a deviate! A sawed-off little—." A sudden whiplike burst of energy launches him backward several feet, but soon the newly confident medium is at it again, lashing out now at Belasco's mother's morality and Belasco's illegitimacy. A second whiplike burst hurls him backward. "You're no genius!" he bellows. "You're no roaring giant!" A third attack sends him reeling again, but this time Fischer does not fall and brings it all out into the open. "What size *were* you, Belasco?" he cries. "Five- foot-two? One? I *know*! You weren't even five-foot tall!"

And now Belasco cries out in pain and fury, defeated, his voice fades into nothingness. With Ann at his side, Fischer shatters the stained glass behind the fallen cross, revealing another wall. They open a door and find themselves face to face with the *real* Emeric Belasco—an elegantly dressed corpse, seated in a comfortable chair, wine goblet in hand, looking as fresh and relaxed as if it were still 1929! Ripping the cloth of Belasco's trousers, Fischer reveals Belasco's legs to be made not of flesh and bone, but 1920s' plastic and metal. "He so despised his own shortness that he had both his legs cut off and wore those instead to give himself height," Fischer observes. "If thine eye offend thee, pluck it out."

Equally impressive is Fischer's discovery of the secret room. "Maybe he was a genius after all," he realizes. "These walls are sheathed with lead. He built himself a fortress to protect his spirit." Both Florence and Barrett were partially correct: Belasco did indeed remain conscious after death, and operated like a general from a safe position, just as Florence believed; and his own energy truly could be harmed by modern science, just as Barrett had claimed all along.

Fischer turns on Barrett's machine. "Your husband and Florence helped us to rid this house of Belasco," he tells Ann. "Let us hope that their spirits guide him to everlasting peace." Director Hough offers one final shot of Belasco's corpse in the open room as the EMR machine hums, and a voice—Florence's, perhaps?—whispers to him from beyond the grave. Finally, as Fischer and Ann leave the house, walking toward the camera and through the gate, director Hough inserts one last look at a black cat sitting, as if watching, from nearby.

In 1994, years after writing *Hell House* and *The Legend of Hell House*, Matheson was asked by *Filmfax* interviewer Matthew R. Bradley how much influence Shirley Jackson's short story "The Lottery" and her 1959 novel *The Haunting of Hill House* and Robert Wise's *The Haunting* had on his own haunted house story. Matheson was quick to praise Wise's film, but he dismissed the notion that *Hell House* was intended as some sort of companion piece to Jackson's tale. On the contrary, while *The Haunting* may have inspired him to finally take a stab at his own ghost story, *Hell House* was not really meant as his answer to Jackson's effort. "I wasn't trying to parody *The Haunting* or anything like that," he explained; he just wanted to write a good ghost story, and seeing *The Haunting* added fuel to a fire that was already starting to kindle. How could the man who had tackled vampires in *I Am Legend*, gremlins in "Nightmare at 20,000 Feet," otherworldly dimensions in "Little Girl Lost," and the terror classics of Edgar Allan Poe for filmmaker Roger Corman not turn his attention to writing a haunted house story one day?

On the other hand, Matheson acknowledged that seeing *The Haunting* left him slightly irked since, like another classic ghost tale, Henry James' enigmatic *The Turn of the Screw*, the film left the audience as perplexed as they were frightened. "I think *The Haunting* is a marvelous film," Matheson told Bradley, "very scary, but I didn't like the idea that you never really knew what did it—was it actress Julie Harris' hallucination or was it really her? I thought, 'I'm going to do a haunted house story where you damn well know it's haunted, and there's no question in your mind.'"

Ironically, Matheson's story does precisely what he intended—removes all doubt that its four heroes are being pummeled by a hard-hitting physical evil—without overindulging in the usual heavy-handed tricks of the genre. Matheson wisely sidesteps the obvious, avoiding the typical pitfalls of big screen horror.

In fact, the single best moment of *The Legend of Hell House* comes in its last big scene, as Fischer and Ann find Belasco's' corpse inside his lead-lined tomb. The sheer idea of a human being taking action to protect his own spirit not only against death but against science that is still dozens of years away is truly astonishing. It is sheer awe which makes this sequence work so well—not blood, not gore, not even sudden shocks.

Happily, "subtle terror" is one of *The Legend of Hell House*'s real strengths, a feature helped immeasurably by the intricate performances of its four lead actors. As the cautious, whisper-voiced Fischer, the always extraordinary Roddy McDowall strikes just the right balance of anxiety and heroism, foreshadowing his cowardly lion turns hero role in 1985's *Fright Night* by well over a decade. McDowall's Fischer is the most skittish member of this hastily assembled team, yet it is he who ultimately summons up the courage and resourcefulness to finally defeat the monster in the film's final moments. Pamela Franklin's casting was equally inspired, bringing to mind her role as Flora, one of the too good to be true siblings in 1961's *The Innocents*. Her behavior here is by turns noble, stubborn, heroic, and irrational, making Florence much like the film itself: with Florence, one never knows quite what to expect next. As Barrett, the always professional Clive Revill turns in yet another distinguished, winning performance. Like McDowall, Revill is a master of subtlety; with the faintest flicker of a grin or twinkle of an eye, he makes Barrett in a single moment polite yet condescending, warm yet aloof, driven yet low-key. Finally, Gayle Hunnicutt proves quite the chameleon as Ann, for no sooner are we convinced the conservative, mild-mannered woman with her old-fashioned, almost 1950s' dependence upon her husband is the antithesis of spunky, liberated Florence, then suddenly there she is at Fischer's side, a full-fledged woman of the 1970s, looking younger and more dynamic than we could ever have imagined. Indeed, the newly widowed Ann seems oddly *right* teamed with Fischer, and one is surprised by how well-suited this unlikely pair now seems.

In his *Filmfax* interview, Matheson recalled that he had envisioned Ben Fischer and Florence Tanner as somewhat older than they appear in the final film. "Later on," noted Matheson, "my dream casting at the time might have been feasible. Right after *The Legend of Hell House* was made, *The Exorcist* was made, and all of a sudden the horror film became an "A" product, which would have reflected well on *Hell House*. Not that it was badly done, but I would have liked to have seen Elizabeth Taylor and her [then] husband, Richard Burton, as the two psychics, and Claire Bloom and her [then] husband, Rod Steiger as the parapsychologist and his wife."

To be sure, post-viewing reading experiences leave one mildly annoyed at the loss of the novel's intriguing "back stories" for each character: the teenaged Fischer's tragic exploitation by an overbearing mother and his pitiable loss of confidence after his first Hell House stay; Florence's acting background, her turn to religion, and the devastating loss of her beloved brother; Barrett's insecurity about himself as husband and lover as a result of his polio-ravaged body; Barrett's wife's skittishness about alcohol and marital relations, brought on by an alcoholic father and prudish mother. One misses, too, several highly effective scenes lost in the transition to film—the nightmarish assault upon Barrett in a Hell House steam room, for instance, or Ann's somnambular attempt to drown herself in the tarn beside the mansion. Even so, one hesitates to suggest that *The Legend of Hell House* would somehow be a better film were another 15 to 20 minutes added to its 94-minute running time. On the contrary, the film is so well-paced and crisply told that demanding that it drag its feet by forcing a series of needlessly distracting flashbacks or a slew of tacked-on dinner conversations seems a surefire way to sabotage what is, after all, still an extraordinarily well told story.

In the final analysis, perhaps Matheson's film lacks the emotional depths of a true masterpiece, but its strong reputation among horror fans is nevertheless richly merited. *The Legend of Hell House* is, at the very least, a minor horror classic, surely one of the best genre films of the 1970s, and as such deserves a far wider audience than it has earned thus far. In a genre known more for self-indulgence than self-restraint, the "subtle terror" Richard Matheson expressly aims for seldom gets better expression than this.

CREDITS: Producer: Albert Fennell, Norman T. Herman; Director: John Hough; Screenplay: Richard Matheson Based on his Novel *Hell House*; Director of Photography: Alan Home; Photographic Effects: Tom Howard; Editor: Geoffrey Root; Released by 20th Century-Fox Film Corporation; 1973

CAST: Pamela Franklin...Florence Tanner, Roddy McDowall...Ben Fischer, Clive Revill...Dr. Barrett, Gayle Hunnicutt...Ann Barrett, Roland Culver...Mr. Deutsch, Peter Bowles...Hanley

NOMADS

by John E. Parnum

To begin with—and to set the mood—I'm going to tell you a ghost story. A true ghost story, so bear with me. Our family was friendly with the caretakers of a museum called Howell House in the historic Germantown section of Philadelphia. My two daughters played with the caretakers' children several times a week, and the occasions were particularly exciting for them since they were sometimes allowed to spend time in the museum that housed a rather extensive collection of antique toys.

Howell House was built before the Revolutionary War, but the caretakers and their two children lived in a newer section at the back. Their job was to keep the museum clean and to act as guides for tourists. The wife, Suzanne, would misplace items... dust cloths, mops, brooms, etc., or at least when she put them down they would disappear, only to be found later in other parts of the house. She would lie awake at night and hear doors open and close, as if someone were moving from the third floor to the first. When she told her husband Joseph about these occurrences, he pooh-poohed the idea of ghosts and told her it was all her imagination.

Then came the evening that Joseph had to go to the museum's third floor to retrieve some tools he had left there. When he entered the darkened room, he felt a presence in the corner where the tools lay on the floor. As he picked up the hammer and screwdriver, he saw a milky mist move toward him and envelop him—a definitely hostile apparition that warned him he was not welcome there. As he fled the room, he could feel the presence unwrap itself from his body. He never went back to that room after dark again.

Several weeks later, Suzanne was showing a group of visitors the museum. Among them were two spiritualists who were visiting Howell House for the first time. As they entered the museum, one turned to the other and said, "There're dead soldiers in here!" And Suzanne hadn't even begun her tour talk that described how Howell House had been used as a hospital during the Battle of Germantown.

Whatever moved about the rooms at night would often pay visits to the neighboring house... also an historic museum, tended to by different caretakers. One night these people had a dinner party that lasted well into the night. Rather than clear the table and clean up, they decided to retire and take care of those chores in the morning. When they came down the next day, they found the wine goblets on the dining room table had been crushed into powdered glass, with only the bases and stems remaining.

Not many of us have experienced a visitation from a ghost, but I'll wager that we all know of someone who has had such an encounter. Ghosts seem very elusive to most of us...as allusive as the 1986 low budget, cinematic haunting *Nomads*. And just as only a handful of lucky people have actually seen this truly frightening little ghost film, so too have only a handful of—should I say lucky?—people encountered a spectral sighting. No one in my family ever saw anything unusual during our many visits to Howell House.

Suzanne and Joseph and their children no longer live there, but when they related the above incidents to me, icy chills ran up my spine... especially the parts about the spiritualists and the crushed wine glasses. It is curious that of the many horror, fantasy, and science-fiction films I have seen, only ghost-story films have sent those chills through my body. Sure, other movies have scared or shocked me, mostly by cheats when, for example, an actor in an ugly mask jumps out at the audience unexpectedly. But to me, the ultimate frightening scene is one that sends those cold fingers up the spine by creating an eerie atmosphere as opposed to a bombastic surprise. *The Uninvited*, one of the greatest ghost films of all times in my opinion, can still produce those chills even if I'm watching it on a small TV set in the middle of the afternoon. When Ray Milland and Ruth Hussey are awakened just before dawn by a woman sobbing in the house they have just purchased, the stage is set for mind-numbing fear in this classic 1944 black-and-white film.

And those same tingles down the central nervous system occur in *The Haunting*, when Julie Harris and Claire Bloom cling to each other as "something" bangs on their bedroom door. Or when Deborah Kerr sees the ghostly face at the window in *The Innocents*. Both of these movies were filmed in black and white, a medium well-suited for macabre moods, but not necessarily exclusively so. Another chill-producer, *The Changeling*, was shot in Technicolor with George C. Scott, alone in the house he has rented, watching a child's ball bounce down the stairway one night—*after* he has tossed the same ball off a bridge into the river earlier in the day.

Nomads, released spottily in 1986 by Atlantic Distributors, was the last movie I've seen to send those chills up my spine, a credit to first-time movie director John McTiernan, who also wrote the script (based on a novel by Chelsea Quinn Yarbro). McTiernan is now known primarily as a director of action films (*Predator, Die Hard, Die Hard with a Vengeance, The Hunt for Red October* and the much-maligned *Last Action Hero*), but he has also shown he can handle more serious drama with *Medicine Man* starring Sean Connery.

There are various types of scares that occur in *Nomads*: The sudden appearance of something unsuspected, usually accompanied by an abrupt sound, like an automobile screeching to a stop or a loud musical chord; the discovery of people in places where they shouldn't be, such as the spectral nun in the deserted building or a punk rocker standing next to the protagonist atop a Los Angeles skyscraper; the impending fear of contemporary street gangs is heightened immeasurably upon discovery that the gang members are actually the aimlessly wandering dead; vulnerability to an unrelenting and indestructible force, such as someone hiding under a car—and realizing that the pursuing evil knows he is there and is just toying with him; or an onslaught of zombie cyclists, that no one else can see, storming your home and leaving you with no way of escape. As I relate the scenario of *Nomads*, I will cover these in greater detail. Also, I will occasionally refer back to Suzanne and Joseph's ghost and indicate how their experience gives credence to the film's spirits.

McTiernan had the good judgment in filming *Nomads* to avoid excessive blood and gore, especially since he made it at a time when other directors were trying to outdo each other with more and more inventive ways to skewer and disembowel their slasher's victims. *Nomads* is a ghost story and ghost stories derive their effectiveness from the subtle treatment of the unknown, whether it be through dreams and hallucinations or the transfer of memory from a dead person to a living. The film succeeds admirably in this department, suggesting that McTiernan may have been influenced by the films of Val Lewton and Rod Serling's *Twilight Zone*.

Nomads opens with a black-and-white photograph of an Eskimo, the fur-hooded face shrouded in darkness. The camera moves slowly into the blackness of that hood and dissolves into a night scene of Los Angeles, the lights of the city seen from a distance, and the occasional wail of a police siren interrupting the stillness. This is the first of many clever transferences that McTiernan uses to take us from one place to another or from one person to another in a different timespan. A phone rings and interrupts the distant sounds of the city. A light goes on. A startled cry. A close-up of a woman's face. That sudden appearance of something unexpected, followed by an equally unexpected sound. This is the first shock the audience experiences, albeit a minor one but enough to alert us that we may be in for quite a ride. Dr. Eileen Flax (Leslie-Anne Down), a new doctor on the midnight detail in a large city hospital, has been napping on a table in an examining room. It is 3:30 a.m. In a daze she answers the phone: "Oh, yeah. OK, I'll be right down," and she heads for Emergency. Ms. Down was quite active in films for about 15 years, sharing the screen with some of filmdom's classiest superstars: John Gielgud, Elizabeth Taylor, Laurence Oliver, and Harrison Ford. One of her two other horror roles came early in her career when she played Countess Elizabeth Barthory's imprisoned daughter in the 1970 Hammer film *Countess Dracula*. The second was in the 1973 omnibus movie *From Beyond the Grave*.

She hears a strung-out patient shouting in French and follows a bloody trail to the curtained partition where he lies babbling on an emergency room bed. She proceeds to examine the bearded victim (Pierce Brosnan), but as she presses her face close to his to examine his eyes with a flashlight, he suddenly rears up screaming (second unexpected shock) and bites her ear. As nurses and the intern rush to her aid, she laughs and says, "I guess he got me." She is led away in shock and in the background someone says, "Jesus Christ! He's dead!" Brosnan, of course, played James Bond in the 1995 *Goldeneye*, the fifth actor to play the part in the highly successful series. During the filming of *Nomads*, however, the Irish actor was starring as the lead in the popular television series *Remington Steele*. His other genre picture was *The Lawnmower Man*, a 1993 science-fiction thriller based on a Stephen King short story.

As Eileen is being stitched up, she rambles about how she left her husband back east to pursue a medical career in Los Angeles, but that she misses seeing trees. She remarks how the city is so barren, that it appears that every last bush has been installed just like Disneyland. The surgeon informs her that what people don't realize is that Los Angeles is a city built on a desert. "Just think of it as extended parking for the beach," he jokes.

When Eileen is leaving, the doctor asks her what her patient said before he died. She replies, "Nothing." The intern laments, "That's a pity; the last thing a man says is supposed to be significant."

After a shower, Eileen falls asleep in her bedroom apartment. Suddenly she sees the word "Kill" in bloody letters on the wall and a French woman staring at her and saying, "What are you doing?" Another unexpected shock for the audience. McTiernan wastes no time in setting up these little jolts. Flax flips on the light and sits up. It was a dream. Or was it?

The next morning she breakfasts in the hospital cafeteria with her salty-tongued friend, Cassie (Jeannie Elias as the film's only comedy relief). The intern joins them and remarks that Eileen's nut case from the night before was not a drug addict, but rather a respected anthropologist named Jean Charles Pommier, a new teacher at the University, and who, with his elegant-looking wife Niki (Anna-Maria Montecelli), just recently moved to the United States. As it turns out, Eileen does

remember Pommier's last words and she asks Cassie "What does *N'ils sont pas... des enas* mean?" Cassie translates, "They are not there... they are," but she stumbles over the last word. "Sounds like a place."

That evening on duty, Eileen absentmindedly answers a nurse's question about medication by saying, "No, the carpet's fine; I like the color." Puzzled, the nurse watches her walk slowly down the hall in a daze. In her mind, Eileen hears a voice say "The old carpet was yellow" and then sees the French woman of her dreams being shown a house by a real estate agent (Nina Foch), who informs her that the original owner was there for only a short time but that they did a great deal for the house.., that the old carpet was yellow. As they check out the rooms, the French woman turns to the person accompanying her and we see it is the anthropologist, Jean Charles, and that the woman is his wife Niki. It is a nice transference of time, place, and people, but we are immediately drawn back to the present when Eileen trips and falls onto the bed of a hysterical elderly patient.

Eileen Flax is still trapped in the hallucinatory world of the strange house, hearing the real estate agent asking Jean Charles about his work and the anthropologist explaining that he is a counselor, that he watches people instead of digging around for bones. As they check out the frontyard, they see a black van with leather-clad passengers pull away from the curb and careen down the street. The agent sarcastically comments, "Goddamn freaks!"

Nina Foch's real estate agent is a tough old bird. Foch starred at Columbia in the early 1940s in two grade-B horror programmers, *The Return of the Vampire* and *Cry of the Werewolf*. She remained active into the late '80s in television chillers such as *Lights Out*, *The Outer Limits*, *Suspense*, etc. and as a regular on *Shadow Chasers*, usually playing hardened-women roles. A television director I know told me of a cast party he attended where the booze flowed freely and where Nina Foch loudly vocalized about her predicament. "They're always putting me in bitchy roles," she shouted across the floor in a raspy voice. "Why the fuck don't they give me a soft part?"

Back on her tour of duty, Flax is still acting peculiarly. She stumbles against an IV set-up. It falls in slow motion, as does she, with the glass bottle breaking and the staff running to her assistance in slow motion. Doctors and nurses wheel her away and tend to her cuts as black-and-white photographs flash upon the screen... photographs of African natives, Alaskan Eskimos... photos it turns out that Jean Charles is tacking to the walls of his workroom. The anthropologist and his wife talk about their new life in America and she shows him a picture taken of him at a family gathering when he was a boy. He wrestles her for it, demanding to know where she got it, and she tells him his mother gave it to her.

Jean Charles goes to the car to get some supplies. On the garage door he sees the words "pigs" and "kill." Niki who has followed him out says, "What are you doing?"—a *deja vu* statement from Eileen's first hallucination. And we are returned to the hospital where Eileen is hemorrhaging.

Jean Charles drives the car into the garage. The headlights illuminate more graffiti: "Hero." He unrolls a yellow carpet that belonged to the previous owner and which had not yet been discarded. It is stained with blood and he finds a clipping about a dead rock star and a picture of the scene-of-the-crime house. A black van roars up the street and the anthropologist goes to look. He checks the photo of the house again and then, when he looks back at his own house, he realizes they are the same. He exclaims, "*La maison les attires!*" Eileen, lying in a hospital bed repeats the same phrase—"They're attracted to the House!"

The tests on Eileen have all proved negative. And even though she appears comatose she has the brain functions of a person who is wide awake, active, hearing, seeing. Suddenly Cassie is shocked to hear Eileen laugh. But the scene shifts and it is Niki listening to her husband laughing with Eileen's laugh. This is an extremely jarring effect for the audience, who either shiver at the contradiction or laugh nervously. Here we have Eileen, recently possessed by Jean Charles, himself possessed by something not yet explained, now laughing in the anthropologist's body—and at an earlier time when no possession had yet taken place. The mind boggles.

Then comes Jean Charles's haunting pursuit of the occupants of the black van, with appropriate musical accompaniment—"Strangers" sung by Dave Amato, with words and music by Bill Conti and Ted Nugent. He follows them constantly snapping pictures. He photographs them as they hang out in dives, demolish a car and torment its owner. He continues to tail them the next day as they prowl the beaches. He also realizes that they may be watching him. In the meantime, Cassie discovers that Eileen has left the hospital and we see that the doctor is also wandering those same beaches where she comes upon a bizarre totem pole sculpture. This is to remind us that all these flashbacks are being experienced by Eileen Flax who, through his bite, has been possessed by the dead anthropologist.

In a darkened alley, Pommier watches his adversaries kill someone and dump the body in a trash bin. He screams at them. Jean Charles flees with the punkers in hot pursuit. Seeing a parked automobile, the only refuge around, he crawls under it. This is a particularly nightmarish scene. The gang approaches the car. Jean Charles has chosen one of the most vulnerable places to hide. Obviously he can be seen from a distance.

His avenues of escape are the four sides of the car. But these same avenues are also available entrances for his attackers. His lying on the ground in the claustrophobic area beneath the automobile is certainly not conducive for a struggle. The suspense is agonizing, similar to that which I experienced as a teenager while watching *House of Wax* when Phyllis Kirk was trying to hide in a fog-shrouded doorway from Vincent Price's phantom-like madman.

The "strangers" circle the car. A woman laughs. A match is dropped inches from Pommier's face. McTiernan uses lots of close-ups in this film, which can be a disadvantage when watching it on video since action just outside the close ups is often cropped. But as mysteriously as the gang arrives, they simply leave. Jean Charles runs out of the alley. A car appears out of nowhere and screeches to a deafening halt, nearly running over Eileen and reminding us that this is her nightmare. Val Lewton, noted for his atmospheric chills, would sometimes surprise us with these sudden unsuspected noises, like the air brakes of the bus in *Cat People* or the whinny of a horse in *The Body Snatcher*. It can be very effective when used correctly, but so many times it is predictable like when a young woman explores a deserted shack in a *Halloween*-type film and backs slowly toward the camera and we know that Jason or some other fiend will immediately bellow forth and jump out at her. Lewton's atmospheric horrors were created by his appreciation and knowledge of light and shadows. McTiernan also excels at this in *Nomads*, especially in the alley scene where the shadows of a fire escape play upon Pommier like bars of a prison, symbolizing his trapped situation.

Of course, Jean Charles finds no body in the trash bin. He continues to follow the gang, snapping pictures of them. Concealed in the darkness, he photographs Ponytail (Hector Mercado) playing with a knife... Number One (rock singer Adam Ant) shifts positions in profile, almost as if he were posing for the camera. Then he turns, looks directly at the camera, and smiles. Whatever they are, these beings are toying with him. Like the playful ghosts at Howell House who would hide the caretaker's dust cloths and mops. But these ghosts are far more deadly; Pommier had seen them kill a man.

Jean Charles returns to his house. He has been away for a day and a half and Niki is furious. He explains that he has spent 30 hours following people who do not live anyplace, who do not work anyplace, and whose vehicle is not registered. He tells Niki they are nomads. "Yes, nomads. Like all of them. Every place we have lived for the last 10 years. Here in Los Angeles, in the middle of a modern city." He relates how he observed them going from one party to another, from gas station to restaurant, how they live in parking lots, and how in 30 hours they didn't stop moving. He describes how they have no structure, how they do not participate. There are no exchanges or constraints, "there is no provocation and they get away with it. To the official world they do not exist." He holds Niki and tries to comfort her by saying, "I didn't tell you because I didn't want to frighten you."

Cassie, meanwhile, has the police break into Eileen's apartment. The phone is ringing and she is able to answer it before the party hangs up. It is a researcher in Boston who is calling with information on the French phrase Eileen has asked him to decipher. He tells Cassie that "*des enas*" is not a place—that perhaps the word is "Innuat," an Eskimo word referring to a nomad myth about wanderers in the desert. Cassie is confused because she identifies desert with sand. The researcher tells her there can also be deserts of ice. Further more, he explains that the Innuat are "...hostile spirits capable of assuming human form. Thought to inhabit places of past calamity, they brought disaster and madness to any human who fell in with them. Only a myth, of course, but observers well into the 20th century marked how cautiously older Eskimos approached strangers on the ice." The song *Strangers*, played during Jean Charles's pursuit now has a deeper and more sinister meaning. Cassie repeats the French phrase: "*N'ils sont pas... des Innuat*. They are not there... They're Innuat."

Pommier develops the film, but of course they do not appear in any of the pictures. When he goes to the bedroom he is startled to see and hear a shadowy woman laugh. It is the same laugh he heard while hiding under the car. When he turns on the lights, the room is empty. Hearing that laughter is quite unsettling for the viewer, especially since it is more of a mocking laugh than a sinister one. Jean Charles then jogs through the park. He sees a figure step behind a tree, but when he checks it out there is no one there.

Senseing the black van is following him, he breaks into a run and the van picks up speed. He dashes over a bridge and down a flight of stairs to another street below.., the van is there too. It pursues him to a narrow alley and when he emerges at the other end, the van is waiting for him. There is no escape. It is the stuff of nightmares and the tension and suspense are excruciating.

Pommier takes refuge in an abandoned building. Suddenly he hears a voice say, "I have a light here if you prefer." In the shadows is a nun (Frances Bay). She says her name is Bertril, and when he inquires where the others are, she explains that she will be following them eventually. "I have been left here to look after things, as it were, although I'm not sure they saw the humor in it." Then she startles him by calling him Mr. Pommier. As he follows her, she shines the flashlight on her face and the way the bright beam illuminates her causes her to appear quite spectral.

"Won't you have tea, Pommier?" He replies, "You know about them, don't you?"—to which she answers, "There are places with pasts, Pommier, places with secrets. Things collect. You just looked too closely. Most people are luckier—they never know that a certain percentage of what they see is not there." Frances Bay imbues the part of Sister Bertril with unsettling eeriness, yet we are never terrified by her. She has graced such genre films as *Blue Velvet* and *Arachnophobia*.

Bertril then advises Jean Charles. "The problem now is not what you know; it's what they know." She speaks more softly: "They know about you." She tells him he must go away, change his job, sell his house. If he hides, he can still survive, but under no circumstances should he try to fight them. "If you've ever run from anything in your life, run from this. They're leading you to another world." Pommier argues that the nomads are not real and that they can't do anything. Bertril looks around, casting furtive glances to see if anyone is listening: "They brought you here, Pommier!" It is a chilling scene because we realize that Bertril is herself a nomad.

Bertril persuades him to leave, and as he runs down the hollow corridors, he comes upon a body hanging from a rafter: it is Bertril, a suicide. His vision is then assailed by hysterically fleeing nuns and rotting corpses.

He screams and hits his head on the windshield of his car, shattering the glass. "*Un cauchemar*!" he repeats over and over. "Nightmare!" But has the encounter with Bertril been a dream? As he adjusts the rearview mirror to examine his cuts, he suddenly sees a woman in the backseat and hears her laughing.

Director McTiernan is unrelenting in these jolting surprises, and this particular shock is especially nasty.

He leaps from the car. The nomad Number One waits for him across the street. Jean Charles takes a tire iron from the trunk of his car. He walks up the steps of his house... Number One follows. As the nomad prepares to strike him, Jean Charles turns and smashes the iron against Number One's skull. He continues to pummel the creature, even as it smiles up at him. Number One is the rock star in the newspaper clipping who was jailed for murdering someone in the Pommiers' house.

In the security of his bedroom, he strips off his clothes and looks out the window at One's body. Jean Charles then moves to the bed where he makes love to Niki. The next morning he arises and looks out the window to see that the body is gone. Niki awakens, smiles, and sleepily asks, "What are you looking at?" The figure at the window turns and we see it is *not* Jean Charles, but Eileen, with a sheet wrapped around her nude body. This is perhaps the most jarring of the Eileen/Jean Charles transformations. Not only is this a case of possession, but it extends to one of sexual possession.

Niki speaks softly to Eileen, filling us in on how Flax has shown up at the house. "You come up here last night; you seem very ill. You also seem to know a lot about my husband." When Eileen stares quizzically at the rumpled bed, Niki offers: "You slept on the couch." But we know differently, don't we, since we have seen Jean Charles perform cunnilingus upon Niki during their lovemaking. So that the "cheat" surprise that McTiernan foists upon us becomes more meaningful as we see that Pommier's spirit has transcended death by possessing Eileen so he can continue to physically love his wife. Eileen realizes this also when she tells Niki later that her husband cares for her more than anything else in the world.

Eileen slips into another past event vision. Jean Charles and Niki are taking in a view of Los Angeles from the roof of a skyscraper. Pommier speaks sadly to his wife: "Did you ever have a dream and not know when it started?" He tells her of the Eskimo elders who used to spin tales about the dangers of traveling too far... of hunting alone on the ice. How one might no longer know what was real. "We are so very far from home, you know. All of us. We have wandered so very far from home." It is a sad lament; almost as if the anthropologist knows he is going to die violently. Niki tries to cheer him up. He pats her stomach and talks about their plans for the future—perhaps a family. Out of the corner of his eye, Jean Charles observes other sightseers on the roof. One of them is a nomad woman. He turns to look over the roof. Standing next to him is the leather clad side-burned Ponytail. The creature looks slowly up at him and pulls down his sunglasses. Ethereal music drifts through the air. The punker moves slowly between Pommier and Niki who is oblivious to the intruder. Suddenly, with a burst of superhuman strength, Jean Charles lifts Ponytail over the railing and hurls him to the street below. The nomad drops quietly down the side of the building, smiling up at Pommier as if to say, "This will do you no good; it's all a game, I'll be back." Niki, of course, has witnessed none of this. It is her husband's nightmare that has been transferred to Dr. Flax.

As Eileen washes up, she tells Niki that she thinks Jean Charles "is losing his sanity. He's hallucinating." She looks in the mirror, realizes her error in tense, and corrects herself: "Was hallucinating." The phone rings; it is a call from Cassie. As Eileen speaks with her, she sees the clipping of the rocker's death by suicide in his jail cell. Cassie tells Eileen she is coming to pick her up but is warned against doing it. When she hangs up, Flax tells Niki that when the police found her husband he had been running—as if he were trying to take the old woman's advice, but how something wouldn't let him. This gives further credence to Eileen's possession since only Jean Charles knew about the nun. "Oh, Niki. What if he wasn't insane!"

Meanwhile, Cassie has stopped at a light. A woman selling flowers approaches her car. She peers in the window and grins. Another nomad opens the passenger's door and tries to climb in. Cassie floors it and the car careens out of control and smashes headlong into an oncoming truck.

Eileen tells Niki to start packing, that they've got to get out of the house. "If they know about Jean Charles, then they know about us." So the horror of the Innuat now extends from Pommier through Eileen to Niki. "You can't come back here—ever!" There is a quick shot of the nomads holding up the bloodied body of Jean Charles—obviously Eileen's hallucination. Niki stands at the window repeating "Who are these people?" When Eileen looks out, the street in front of the house is filled with nomads. More arrive on motorcycles. Eileen stares at Niki and says, "Oh, God. You can see them too." They try to phone for the police, but the line has been cut.

Now this is a classic climactic confrontation, the most suspenseful sequence in the entire film. It mirrors other famous horror movies where a group of people have been trapped in a place from which they can't escape by creatures who are invulnerable: *Night of the Living Dead* with its survivors holed up in a farmhouse surrounded by George Romero's zombies; one of Cronenberg's earliest—*Shivers* (*They Came from Within*) where the tenants of a high-rise apartment keep turning each other into plague-ridden monsters; and *Demons*, the Lamberto Bava film where theatergoers trapped in a Italian cinema are prey to vicious monsters. So, too, is the scenario set for *Nomads*. The Innuat have surrounded the house. They are on the roof. They smash in the front door. One drops in through the skylight. A creature on a cycle roars into the living room. As Eileen and Niki try to escape up the stairs, they see a nomad, Dancing Mary, on the roof outside the window. They climb the ladder to the attic. Dancing Mary slashes out at Eileen with a knife. They make it through the attic trap and secure it with ropes. But Mary splinters the door. She looks into the attic at the cowering women and smiles at them. And then she leaves.

Eileen and Niki wait for an eternity. A new fear arises. How long do you stay hidden? How do you know if they're really gone and are not lying in wait for you. What will be found once you leave the security (if you can call it that?) of the attic.

Slowly they make their way back down the attic ladder steps. The house is in shambles. Graffiti covers the walls. Niki picks up something off the floor. It is the shattered picture of Jean Charles with his family when he was a young boy. The significance of this is enigmatic. Many primitive tribes do not want to be photographed since they feel the camera will take away their soul and put it on paper. Do the pictures hanging on the Pommiers' wall contain the souls of their Eskimo and African subjects? Is this what has drawn the Innuat to Jean Charles? Is the reason that the photos Pommier took of his pursuers are blank because the creatures are already soulless? And could it be that when the nomads invaded the house and found the picture of the young Jean Charles, they broke the glass to capture his soul, and then retreated from the house leaving Eileen and Niki unharmed because they had gotten what they wanted? The film leaves room for many questions. And many answers.

But there is a surprise ending. An ending which sent more chills up my spine than any other scene in the film. And here I must caution the reader who has not seen *Nomads* (and it appears there may be many of you) and who does not like to have surprise endings revealed. Do not read the next two paragraphs. They reveal the climactic surprise and my interpretation of it.

Stealthily the two women get into Eileen's car and drive away. Hours later, the sun is rising, and they are leaving the city. Niki is driving as Eileen awakens on the backseat. They approach the mountains and Eileen looks out the back window at the receding skyline. She sees a cyclist in a black jacket and sunglasses following them. He roars past them and motors directly in front of their car as if leading them. Eileen leans over the front seat and warns Niki, "Don't stop! No matter what you see, don't stop!" The cyclist slows down, circles the car, and pulls to the side. As he faces their vehicle, he raises his goggles and we see it is Jean Charles Pommier! Niki screams and Eileen urges her again, "Don't stop." The car roars away up the mountain, Eileen's face at the rear window a mask of terror. Pommier watches their car disappear in the distance, his face a mixture of sadness and longing. He places his foot on the accelerator and motors slowly back down the road toward the city. The camera pulls back and we see a sign by the road pointing to where the motorcyclist has gone: "Entering California."

This ending is open to as many interpretations as the puzzle about Jean Charles' childhood photograph. There are some who might say that Pommier pursued the women out of the city the way the Innuat relentlessly chased him, or at the very least made an appearance as a warning not to return. I believe that he was actually leading them away from the other nomads. Eileen told Niki that Jean Charles cared more for her than anything else in the world. This was the way he showed it: to get her away from the city... the city built on a desert. Away from the nomads who roamed that desert. It is obvious from the expression on his face that he is sad to lose her. It is an expression that has haunted my own dreams for nine years now. One thing is clear: Pommier is now a restless spirit himself, condemned to join the Innuat. But because of that, he no longer inhabits the doctor who tried to save him. He no longer inhabits her body. Eileen Flax is free.

The cast of *Nomads* does a commendable job making the supernatural aspects of the story believable. Brosnan is particularly impressive and, for an Irishman, affects a decent French accent. His beard makes him appear more mature than his new Bond image, even though it was filmed nine years earlier. Lesley-Anne Down doesn't come off quite as well. Her initial scene of being awakened from her catnap is a bit stilted and there are moments when it appears she doesn't understand the script and puts wrong interpretations on reactions. Anna-Maria Montecelli is a delight as Niki. Her warmth and concern for her husband come across with complete naturalness, and she is perhaps the most believable actor in *Nomads*. Her film career was incredibly short, as was that of Jeannie Elias who provided comic relief as Cassie. This young actress lightened the tension of the film with much needed humor, and it seems a waste that this talent hasn't brought her greater fame. Adam Ant, as one of the sinister nomadic spirits, imbues the role with a kind of sadness that seems appropriate since ghosts that roam the earth do so because of some calamity at the time of their demise, like the revolutionary soldiers that haunt the toy-filled rooms of Howell House. But after all, we learn that he was a suicide in prison, damned to walk the earth as a spirit in the same manner as the spectral nun. And while Bertril certainly was more benevolent than Number One and the other punkers, the character, as portrayed by Frances Bay, comes off as more frightening, perhaps because her encounter with Pommier is more personal. Hector Mercado, Josie Cotton and Mary Woronov elicit the proper hostility as the other nomads, but Woronov is especially sinister through her lascivious smile and laugh and provocative, almost obscene, dance.

Director McTiernan does a laudable job as a first-time director, his training at New York's La Moma and the Juilliard School (with a class under John Houseman) providing him with proper background for the task. Leonard Maltin in his 1995 *Movie Encyclopedia*, calls McTiernan "a visually oriented craftsman who relies more on fluid camera work and tight cutting than on fluid performances and tight scripts. In an article in the February, 1992, issue of *Premier* ("Strong Medicine" by John H. Richardson), McTiernan describes his introduction to movies: "I was nineteen. I sat in the Symphony Space theater in New York eight hours a day for three days watching *Day for Night* until I wasn't involved with the actors or story, until I could just see the shots." His attention to composition is quite evident in *Nomads*. Hooked by the moviemaking bug, he next attended SUNY on Long Island as a film major. After graduation, according to Richardson's article, he took $10,000 which his family had given him for a house, and produced *The Demon's Daughter*, a Viking epic that he shot on his grandfather's farm, where he put wigs on ponies and built a replica of a Viking ship. He took the completed project to Hollywood where it was turned down. He started writing scripts, one of which was *Nomads*, and he won the chance to direct it.

Premiere also states that critics panned the film, but with the exception of *Cinefantastique* (which claimed it "plays like a tedious *Twilight Zone* episode with a predictable ending that appears tagged on"), all reviews I read were positive. *Variety* stated that *Nomads* "comes off as the most stylish supernatural-theme chiller since Brian DePalma had his breakthrough with *Carrie*," and that it "avoids the more obvious ripped-guts devices in favor of dramatic visual scares.... In fact, everything seems to come naturally in a tale that even has the supernatural ring true." Contrary to *Cinefamntastique*'s critique, the magazine states, "The denouement is as truly a surprise as the suspense is sustained throughout." They also concur that Jeannie Elias is "bitingly funny even within the suspense framework." Alan Jones, in the a 1986 issue of *Starburst*, explains, "What gives *Nomads* its major lift, though, are the dual personality changes between Brosnan and Down which keep occurring to constantly knock you off your guard, and which ensure interest is kept up."

Film critic Judith Crist was impressed enough to label *Nomads* "A chiller thriller. Complex and fascinating. Brimming with menace and suspense. Pierce Brosnan proves himself a top talent." But perhaps the most positive review appeared in the March 11, 1986, edition of *The Philadelphia Inquirer*...positive in a sense because the reviewer, Desmond Ryan, usually hates horror films and constantly puts them down. In

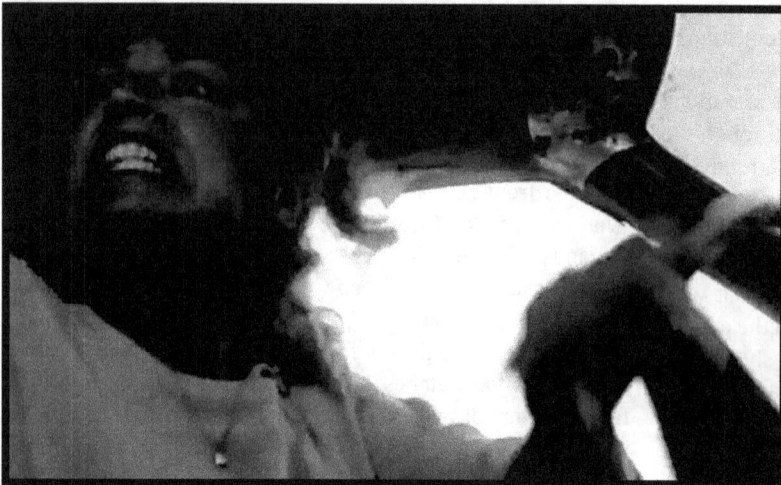

considering how possession and paranoia were making a comeback in films at the time, Ryan praises McTiernan for doing something "more intelligent and adult" and making a "dark, unconventional movie that stays clear of the clichés." He does complain that the film "has a purely technical problem that is becoming more of an annoyance in movies. Because of the way the sound has been miked and recorded, it is often impossible to understand what the actors are saying. Whole scenes come into the theater as an inaudible and exasperating mumble. The same problem afflicts movies as diverse as the current *Pray for Death* and *9 1/2 Weeks*...." Ryan, usually the film curmudgeon, sums up thusly: "The conclusion of the film is defiantly different and downbeat, and McTiernan has an original way of putting real and imagined terror on the screen. It's a pleasant surprise to discover a horror movie that isn't a silly bore. *Nomads* deserves to be seen, and it would certainly help if it could be heard properly."

The film did not do well in the theaters, although it's my belief that this had more to do with the poor distribution and advertising by Atlantic than audience word of mouth about the poor quality of sound. Just try to find any press material on *Nomads*. Just try to find anyone who has seen the film. Atlantic Distributors finally faded away, with the video rights to *Nomads* being picked up by Paramount.

It seems that ghost films, the elite of chiller movies, are not widely accepted by the general public. How many of them have been top moneymakers? The original *House on Haunted Hill*, maybe, but that was promoted by the king of showmen, William Castle, ballyhooing a new screen gimmick called Emergo. *The Haunting* and especially *The Innocents* were based on stories by famous writers. They were promoted strongly by Fox and MGM, two super studios who did not like to lose money on a film, so they touted them for all their worth. But with all their publicity, did they really make a huge profit for these companies? And, as for *Carnival of Souls*, it has only been since its availability on video that the film has been labeled a minor classic.

Perhaps it's the subtleties of these cinematic hauntings that prejudice potential distributors. Let's face it, some folks don't like to be scared. Some audience members cover their eyes when something unpleasant appears on the screen, just as some distributors cover their eyes to release contracts for high-risk films. Probably most of you reading this book do like to be scared, but may have covered your eyes at a particular scene at some point in your life. It's like a roller coaster ride: there's the thrill of the anticipation as you make the climb, and the thrill of the plunging descent that takes your breath away. *Nomads* is a pretty scary movie, a lively ride that takes your breath away. And, like the spiritualists and the broken wine glasses at Howell House, it sent chills up my spine.

Inspired while writing this, I reflected more on the events at that toy museum nearly 20 years ago. Suzanne and Joseph and their children have long since moved from that eerie establishment with its Revolutionary ghosts. But I was curious as to whether the new caretakers were tuned into the infinite.

I reflected upon what Sister Bertril told Jean Charles: "There are places with pasts. Most people never know that a certain percentage of what they see is not there."

After some final fact checking for the *Nomads* chapter, I climbed into my Toyota and drove to Germantown. The old neighborhood had been deteriorating 20 years ago, and it was worse now. Graffiti, a perpetual problem in Philadelphia, covered most available surfaces. I drove slowly down the cobblestones of Germantown Avenue and pulled up in front of 5218—Howell House. Looking at the graffiti sprayed fence surrounding the museum, my eyes caught the words "kill" and "pigs" spraypainted nearby. I opened the ornate iron gate, walked to the porch, and knocked on the door. No answer. Perhaps the new caretakers were out. Wait. Was that a movement from within? The family dog? A woman? In a habit? In my mind I heard Sister Bertril whispering softly to me, "They know about you. If you've ever run from anything in your life, Parnum, run from this. They brought you here!" I turned, walked quickly through the gate, and drove away from Howell House as fast as I could.

CREDITS: Executive Producer: Jerry Gershwin; Producers: George Pappas and Cassian Elwes; Associate Producer: Stanley Mark; Direction and Screenplay: John McTiernan; Editor: Michael John Bateman; Music: Bill Conti; Pro duction Manager: Susan Baden-Powell; Production Coordinator: Mary McLaglen; Director of Photography: Stephen Ramsey; Color by Technicolor; Released March 1986 by Atlantic; 95 minutes; Rated R;

CAST: Pierce Brosnan...Jean Charles Pommier, Lesley-Anne Down...Dr. Eileen Flax, Anna-Maria Montecelli...Niki Pommier, Adam Ant...Number One, Hector Mercado... Ponytail, Josie Cotton...Silver Ring, Mary Woronov...Dancing Mary, Frank Doubleday... Razors, Frances Bay...Sister Bertril, Tim Wallace.. Intern, Reed Morgan...Cop, Freddie Duke, Josse Beaudry, and Anita Jesse...Nurses, Dana Chelette...Orderly, Alan Autry... Olds, Jeannie Elias...Cassie, Nina Foch.. Real Estate Agent, J.J. Saunders...Cort, Kario Salem...Schacter, Helen Vick...Young Nurse, Gayle Vance.. Older Nurse, Athan Karras. . Apartment Manager, Paul Anselmo and Michael Gregory...Cops in Apartment, John Vidor...Kid in Park, Elizabeth Russell...Cathy, Junero Jennings...Gas Station Attendant

PORTRAIT OF JENNIE

by Steve Vertlieb

Moments before dawn, the heavens spy the stirring of an island, blanketed by layers of clouds, an ethereal universe coming to life slowly, reluctantly 'neath a dreamlike mist. Floating slowly, gracefully, the mist begins to lift as a curtain rising upon the opening moments of a theatrical presentation. The players, upon closer examination, are marionettes, pawns knowingly manipulated by an invisible presence. It is dawn now and the inhabitants of Manhattan Island are waking from a dreamless sleep, phantoms not yet solid, scattered thoughts, random particles of memories of the past and hope for an undetermined future. Birth comes with dawn and yet, we are told, "Nothing ever dies but only changes. Time itself does not pass but curves around us. The past and future are forever at our side... together. That Existence begins and ends," wrote Richard Matheson, "is man's concept, not nature's." Or, as Jack Finney succinctly phrased it... "Time is just a place."

Eben Adams was his name, as if names matter. He was an artist and a struggling one at that. Depressed, lonely, he endured a "winter of the mind," a bleak landscape in which the harsh winter light shone mercilessly upon his singular countenance. As written by Robert Nathan and enacted by Joseph Cotten, Eben Adams was an empty soul, longing for happiness and success. He had found neither and so, on that bitingly cold winter day as he walked aimlessly through the snow-covered park, a terrible fear consumed his heart, a fear that the emptiness might consume him. It was then that he saw the little girl playing in the snow. She was building a snowman as children often do. She waved to him happily and began talking. Her name was Jennie, Jennie Appleton. She was playing in the park while her parents were playing the matinee. They were circus performers, aerialists, playing the matinee at Hammerstein's Victoria. Adams was perplexed. Hadn't the theatre been demolished years ago? He told the little girl that Hammerstein's had been torn down, but she told him that that was silly. She'd left her parents only moments ago as they were preparing to perform their high wire act and that it frightened her whenever they would climb to the top of the tent.

She was a funny kind of a kid carrying an old newspaper. Even her clothing seemed somehow dated. He thought no more about it as they walked together across Central Park and sat for a time on a wooden bench. She talked excitedly about her life and about her friend, Emily. "I know a song," she said. "Would you like to hear it?" As she sang, the sun seemed to fade from view, replaced by shadows and clouds. It was a strange, haunting song that he couldn't forget. "Where I come from... nobody knows.., and where I am going... everyone goes... The wind blows.., the sea flows.., nobody knows... and where I am going... nobody knows." And then she asked the funniest question. It didn't seem strange when she first asked him and yet, as time evaporated in shadow, her request seemed to take on a more desperate note. "Would you wait for me, Mr. Adams?" she asked so innocently. "Would you wait for me to grow up?" It seemed a harmless enough question and yet he was startled somehow. It was impossible, they both knew, but there was a distant sadness about the child that threw his senses off-kilter. She said, after all, that she'd try to hurry. As Jennie left to return home, she left her parcel and scarf. He raced to the bench to retrieve her belongings, but when he turned again, she had disappeared into the evening mist... as though she'd never been there at all.

Swallowed by time, Jennie (Jennifer Jones) had left him alone once more. She wasn't a phantom. He'd seen her, talked to her.., but there was something strange, other-worldly, about the girl. As Eben walked thoughtfully back to his room the song that Jennie sang echoed in his mind... "Where I come from nobody knows and where I am going everyone goes."

So begins the timeless stretching of canvas that became known as *Portrait of Jennie*, David O. Selznick's obsessive love sonnet to his own Jennie, Jennifer Jones. Selznick was a romantic of the old school and was drawn instantly to Robert Nathan's fragile tale of ghostly longing. Jennie Appleton was, you see, a spirit and spirited girl whose life was cut short years earlier in a tragic accident at sea.

So, Jennie wasn't real. She was, after all, an apparition. And yet there is a longing in the human soul for love and definition that will not be denied. And so, in the skating rink in Central Park where Eben first spied her building a snowman, Jennie appears once again out of a mist. "Instinctively I found myself approaching the bench in the park and, as I did, I was conscious of an unaccustomed atmosphere, as though time were melting with the snow." Eben is noticeably startled as he sees her. "You've grown." "Of course I have," she responds. "I'm hurrying." When Eben pulls her scarf from out of his pocket she seems confused and disoriented, as though it were part of a distant memory. She senses that it isn't time yet and asks Eben to "keep it for me until I grow up." Eben and Jennie make plans to see one another again at 2 o'clock on Saturday. Jennie turns back sadly, sensing somehow that she is a helpless pawn rising or falling with the tides of time, and says, "At least... I'll try."

When Jennie fails to return to the park at the appointed time on Saturday, Eben seeks out anyone in the theatrical community who might remember Jennie or her parents. Old Pete at the Rialto has difficulty remembering but suggests to Eben that he contact Clara Morgan, a former wardrobe mistress who has kept scrapbooks on all of the old acts from years gone by. There, amongst the musty press clippings, photographs, and treasured memories, is a browning playbill featuring the names of Mary and Frank, The Flying Appletons. There was an accident, Clara remembers. It was tragic. The wire broke and both Mary and Frank fell to their deaths while Jennie watched from the audience. When Eben finds Jennie in the park once more, she is crying. "Something happened," Eben tells her. "Yes," cries Jennie. "The wire broke," Eben states while Jennie

continues sobbing. But how could this be, he wonders. All of this happened so many years ago. The newspaper that Jennie had carried with her scarf the first time they had met was dated 1910. And yet Jennie was here with him now on that same bench in the park. What was time, for each instant he saw her, she had grown older, more mature. Was he going mad? He didn't know. He didn't want to know, for he was falling in love with her.

Tantalizing, mysterious, Jennie's appearances had become addictive to Eben. The enigmatic spirit had woven a wondrous web from which the struggling artist had grown unwilling or unable to break free. When weeks, then months go by without an appearance by Jennie, Eben grows depressed and increasingly bitter. Beginning to lose his grasp on sanity, he wondered if she were ever real at all, or if he had conjured her out of a deep spiritual longing and emptiness. And just at the moment between midnight and dawn when reason and his own sanity seemed most illusive, Eben returned from a nocturnal outing to find the door to his room ajar.

With anxious heart he hurried to the door and there, looking excitedly over his paintings, was Jennie, his Jennie. She had come back to him. He had been given another chance. Eben realized that he must capture her on canvas so that she may never escape his gaze again. As he set about stretching a new canvas for the task, Jennie appeared nervous, frightened. One of his paintings had unsettled her. It is a landscape that he had painted up at Cape Cod, an old abandoned lighthouse known as Land's End Light. She can't explain her reaction to him. "I don't know, Eben. It just frightens me," she says.

The night passed quickly as Eben began work on his project, the visualization of his obsession. As the hours passed, Eben grew consumed by his work, scarcely noticing that all had grown quiet. Turning to Jennie, Eben was filled with dread. Jennie wasn't breathing. His dream had become a nightmare. Frozen in time, a still life enraptured in a spectral mist, she had become the painting. Eben was terrified. Had she died while he was painting her? His mind wouldn't let him believe. Time, it seemed, had stood still once more, imprisoning Jennie within the newly painted canvas. He panicked, crying out her name and racing to her side. "Jennie," he cried, shaking her and sobbing. Awakening from her stupor, the vision in the light sighed deeply as though returning from beyond the veil of eternal sleep. "I must have fallen asleep," she smiled. "Oh, Jennie," he sobbed... "Please...don't ever leave me."

They walked and talked for hours, and as midnight met the dawn, an enchantment seemed to hover over the couple, embracing Jennie and Eben. "Look, Eben," she said, "It's

tomorrow." Eben grew thoughtful. "When is tomorrow?" he mused. "Does it matter? This was tomorrow once:' Looking into Jennie's eyes he recalled what the old gentleman at the art gallery had said... "There ought to be something eternal about a woman, something not of the present... not of the past. What you see in the face is without age, without time." As the words echoed in his mind, he began to realize that he was "caught in an enchantment beyond time and change," and that love is endless.

Eben knew only that he wanted to spend the rest of his life with Jennie. He couldn't allow her to slip through his fingers again. One further boundary stood between the lovers, however. Jennie's aunt was ill and asked the child to spend the summer with her in Cape Cod. "It's only for a few months," she told him, "and then we can be together for always." Eben was increasingly edgy, reluctant to let her go, sensing that something ominous, larger than the two of them might separate them forever. "I feel that there is a balance of yesterday and tomorrow, and it frightens me," he told her, "that there is no way to bridge it." There seemed a conspiracy of time and space, and neither Eben or Jennie was strong enough to resist its influence.

Earlier Eben had accompanied Jennie to her graduation from the convent. Sensing that he might lose her once and for all, he journeyed back to the holy order, searching for a glimmer of hope from the sister who had inspired his little girl lost. The nun recalled Jennie fondly. There was a special quality about Jennie, she remembered. Yes, the child was possessed of an inner warmth, a loving light. Eben pressed the sister for information on Jennie's present whereabouts. It was then that the old woman frowned. "Why, Jennie's dead. She drowned years ago off the coast of Cape Cod while visiting her aunt for the summer." "That's impossible," Eben cried, "for I saw her yesterday, spoke to her, held her in my arms. You say Jennie died years ago while visiting her aunt, but I was with her *last night* before she left on her trip." Eben recalled his last words to his love... "When is tomorrow? Why, it's always. This was tomorrow once."

Jennie had told him that "the strands of our lives are woven together, and neither the world nor time can tear them apart." He resolved to find her. "What if for a while," he had told her, "we had lost our way. Yesterday rose again ahead of us. We had found beauty together and we could never lose it."

Eben journeyed throughout the night, arriving in Cape Cod on October 4th. Jennie had drowned, he learned, as a terrible tidal wave slammed the New England coast back in the 1920s on October the 5th. He had arrived a day ahead of time in order to beat her to the scene of the tragedy. If only he could be there to meet her, he reasoned, he could change time and the course of events and save Jennie's life. Two elder seamen were talking of old times and old battles when Eben arrived at the cove asking to charter a boat to the lighthouse. The men thought that he was crazy when he spoke of an impending hurricane.

After all, they said, the weather was calm all along the coas. Calm seas and warm weather had been predicted for the next few days. "Wasn't that the prediction," Eben asked, "those many years ago back in the '20s when the great storm had hit?" Yes, the men agreed. It was a day much like today. It was this very day, in fact, those many years ago, October the 5th.

The fisherman was old, as old as time itself, but he owned a rowboat and promised to rent it to Eben. With a little prompting, he too recalled that terrible day from out of the scriptures. "I was a boy," he remembered, "but I can see it like it was yesterday... a great wave. Sometimes I think I've never seen it, that I just read about it, like something in the Bible. It come up from out of the sea.., like a mountain coming toward the land... like the day of judgment."

Eben tried carefully to navigate the tiny craft through the increasingly choppy seas, finding the lighthouse at Land's End Light and pulling the boat ashore. "Jennie," he cried again and again. It was a lonely cry, echoing his desperation through the lonely night. Entering the deserted lighthouse, he climbed the spiraling staircase round and round until at last he reached the top. Walking cautiously to the edge, just beneath the light, he rubbed his eyes of rain and sea, trying to catch a glimpse below of Jennie's craft. Then, as the mist began to clear and the sea to calm, he spotted a lonely sail nearing the island. It was her. "Jennie," he cried, "Jennie."

He raced down the rickety stairs, his heart pounding with joy. He had found his beloved Jennie again. The boat reached the shore and Jennie tied her tiny craft to the rocks. "Eben," she cried, and in moments they were in each other's arms. "Jennie, I've found you again and I'll never let you go." But she knew better. She'd been drowned before her life had even begun, and she'd searched eternity for the love that might free her from the depths of loneliness and despair. Condemned to wander infinity unloved and unfulfilled, she'd been given another chance. She had found Eben and now everything was right once more. Time was but a place and when this time had passed there would be another where Jennie and Eben would be reunited and spend eternity in each other's arms. "We were lonely, unloved. Then time made an error.., but you waited for me, Eben, and we found our love. There is no life until you love and have been loved.., and then there is no death."

Eben grew frantic. He knew only of worldly goals and reached out to pull Jennie toward him. "We've found each other again and I cannot let you go." But it was out of his hands. The winds of time had grown restless and demanded their prize. The sea reached out to reclaim what it had lost. Eben clutched desperately at her hand as the terrible wave filled the sky, blocking out reason and the sun, and looming like some prehistoric monolith. It froze above them for an eternity and then crashed to earth, claiming its prize. Eben sobbed uncontrollably, for Jennie was gone.

Eben awoke days later in the cabin of the old fisherman. He lay in a coma, his body wracked with fever. No one believed his story of seeing Jennie again, He was desolate. Had it all been a dream, a feverish delusion? Had Jennie ever really existed outside of his tortured mind? And then Miss Spinney, the old woman who had been his patron at the art gallery back in New York, reached into the torn pocket of his coat and dropped an old, weather beaten scarf to the floor. "What's this?" she asked, stooping down to pick it up. Eben stared at the scarf in stunned silence and then smiled. Spinney was sobered by the realization of his expression. Almost afraid to speak the words, Spinney asked "Was this Jennie's?" "It's all right," he said, "I haven't lost her. Everything's all right now." He smiled again, clutching the precious garment, relaxing as his head and shoulders lay back upon the pillow where he slept peacefully for the first time since it had all begun.

Portrait of Jennie is, quite obviously, a ghost story yet not of the usual paranormal variety. Rather than the spectral monstrosities of Steven Spielberg's *Poltergeist* or the vengeful apparition seeking retribution in Lewis Allen's *The Uninvited*, *Portrait of Jennie* was and is a gentler, more sublime exercise in spectral gymnastics. The film is, after all, a love story. Eben Adams is frustrated in virtually every aspect of his meager existence. He seemingly hasn't the talent, perseverance, or inspiration to create anything lasting or meaningful. He lives an empty life, taking a room he can scarcely afford. He has only one friend to call his own, a wise and wily Irishman who himself seems more a crafty leprechaun than a supportive influence. Consumed by more than a hint of bitterness and despair, Adams is a singular and solitary individual, a white zombie walking between the joys and accomplishments of a successful life.

Into this shadowy existence floats a sweet, vibrant little girl named Jennie Appleton, eager to taste each of the many nectars and fruits that life may offer. Yet, Jennie too, for all her excitement and exuberance, seems to pursue a phantom existence, walking above or below life's pleasures and rewards. Where Eben has only to reach out and touch the fulfillment of his dreams yet is unable to raise his arms, Jennie continually reaches out her hand only to find that what she sees and desires is eternally just out of reach. Jennie is frustrated too, a spirit who died too young to savor the joy, success and love that come with blossoming maturity. She roams the earth a phantom, neither young nor old, unexpressed... a joy waiting to be shared. Eben becomes the man of her dreams and the purpose of her being if only she can remain in one timeframe long enough to emerge from within the shadows and make a difference. The lonely painter becomes the man of her sensual and mortal awakening. He is as much a phantom to her as she is to him, for her grasp on what we call reality is tenuous at best, fading in and out of time as a wisp of smoke. She hurries through time to become the woman he desires, the pathway to his salvation, sensing all the while that once this magical transformation has occurred she must once again succumb. Like an insect that dies upon completion of its own mating ritual, Jennie's longing and eventual fulfillment must culminate with her own expiration.

And yet there is an inner knowing, a realization by Jennie that death is only a beginning, a doorway to a deeper dimension of love and joy. For as Eben fights desperately to save her life, Jennie is resigned to her fate, serene and at peace. Unlike Eben, she knows that time is infinite and that once they had found each other, they could never truly be separated again. That Existence began and ended was man's notion, not God's. She would always be with him and he with her for now their lives meant something and now they would never be lonely again. In another time and place, they would meet and love again.

David O. Selznick had read and fallen under the spell of Robert Nathan's romantic fantasy, *Portrait of Jennie*, paying $15,000 for the property in the latter part of 1944. Published in 1939, the book seemed an ideal prospect for the love of Selznick's life, Jennifer Jones. The producer had already fallen in love with the book's title before he had read a single word. Due to the delicacy of the story and its frequent manipulation of time, the novel posed a formidable challenge to any writer who might attempt a coherent screenplay. Indeed, MGM had optioned the book some years earlier and allowed their option to lapse when the job appeared insurmountable. One of the many suggestions proposed by Selznick's production department in 1944 was to cast Shirley Temple as Jennie and film the story in pieces over a period of several years so that Jennie's growth patterns would appear more natural. While the publicity potential of such a stunt appealed briefly to Selznick, he wisely decided on a more mature actress who might more subtly convey the changing look of his timeless heroine.

While Selznick had conducted a highly publicized search to cast Scarlett in *Gone With the Wind* for MGM some years earlier, he was adamant about Jennifer Jones for the title role of *Jennie*. After all, he'd purchased the project for her. Eben Adams was another matter entirely. With all of his powerful publicity wheels cranking, Selznick launched a massive media blitz to whet the public's appetite for the male casting of the second lead. When the results were in, three names topped the polls and all three had worked for Selznick before. Gregory Peck headed the list, having worked with Selznick in *Spellbound*, *The Paradine Case* and *Duel in the Sun*. Joseph Cotten weighed in next with Laurence Olivier coming in a strong third. Peck, however, had already committed to a picture at Twentieth-Century Fox, and while Olivier might bring more prestige to the picture, Selznick decided on Joseph Cotten. Cotten had made three pictures thus far with Jennifer Jones, and the two genuinely liked one another. The most romantic of the three previous pictures had been without question *Love Letters*, directed by William Dieterle, and so Dieterle appeared the perfect choice to helm *Jennie*. Aside from his romantic predilection, Dieterle had a strong visual style, thriving on dark, other-worldly thematic material. RKO's 1939 production of Victor Hugo's *The Hunchback of Notre Dame* was a stunning depiction of Dieterle's cinematic style, making him the natural candidate to work once again with the two stars on *Portrait of Jennie*. Dieterle was delighted with his selection and accepted the assignment immediately.

Filming began in New York's Central Park in February, 1947. Selznick wanted the picture filmed entirely on location because, as he wrote, "It will have an atmosphere it won't have here in the studio, thereby improving the quality of the picture immeasurably." He planned to shoot the lion's share of the story in New York, moving on later to Boston Harbor for the climactic sequence involving Adams' struggle to save Jennie from the giant tidal wave. Bad planning, however, delayed filming for weeks while production costs soared. Locations were being scouted in Manhattan during production, leaving the cast and crew sitting idle. Scripting was still incomplete when production began, causing many scenes to be shot and reshot while "improvements" to the script were made and revised daily. To make matters worse, Selznick disliked the early rushes, saying that the harsh winter light presented the two stars unattractively, robbing the picture of its essential aura of fantasy. Selznick began castigating both his director and cinematographer, Joseph August. The pressure finally became too much for August, who died of a heart attack on location while filming in September, 1947.

Selznick had already shut down production once that year in April. The stoppage had lasted for five weeks while the producer brought in Paul Osborn, who completely rewrote and restructured the difficult script. Selznick wasn't about to shut down production again. Lee Garmes and Paul Eagler were flown in from California in order to shoot the remainder of the picture. The final frame of film was shot on October 9, 1948, some 18 months after *Portrait of Jennie* had begun filming. The script had been rewritten twice, every member of the supporting cast had been changed, and each scene had been shot, in some cases, up to five times. The entire production had been called back to Hollywood finally where the bulk of the picture's exterior shooting could be accomplished on the Culver City lot under the protective eyes of Selznick.

The biggest disappointment to Selznick was, perhaps, the lensing of the climactic scene in which the lighthouse is enveloped by the great tidal wave, and Jennie is returned to the sea whence she came. Selznick wanted a wave of Biblical proportions, and, like Merian C. Cooper who had reputedly shouted "Make it bigger... Make it bigger" to the production crew on *King Kong*, decided to reshoot the wave in 70 millimeter and open up the screen in the final moments of the picture.

Composer Bernard Herrmann had been associated with the picture from the beginning and was apparently hired to write an original score. However, production and filming had dragged on for so long that Herrmann was forced to leave the picture for other assignments. At the conclusion of the film there remains a title card thanking Bernard Herrmann for his contribution to the music. It is known that Herrmann wrote the odd, haunting little tune that Jennie sings to Eben early on in the story. Information has recently come to light, however, that Herrmann may have contributed significantly more than that little tune. Amongst the Bernard Herrmann archives has recently been discovered what may have been a complete finished score for *Portrait of Jennie*. Reportedly there are plans now afoot to restore and record the missing music for posterity, if not for the picture.

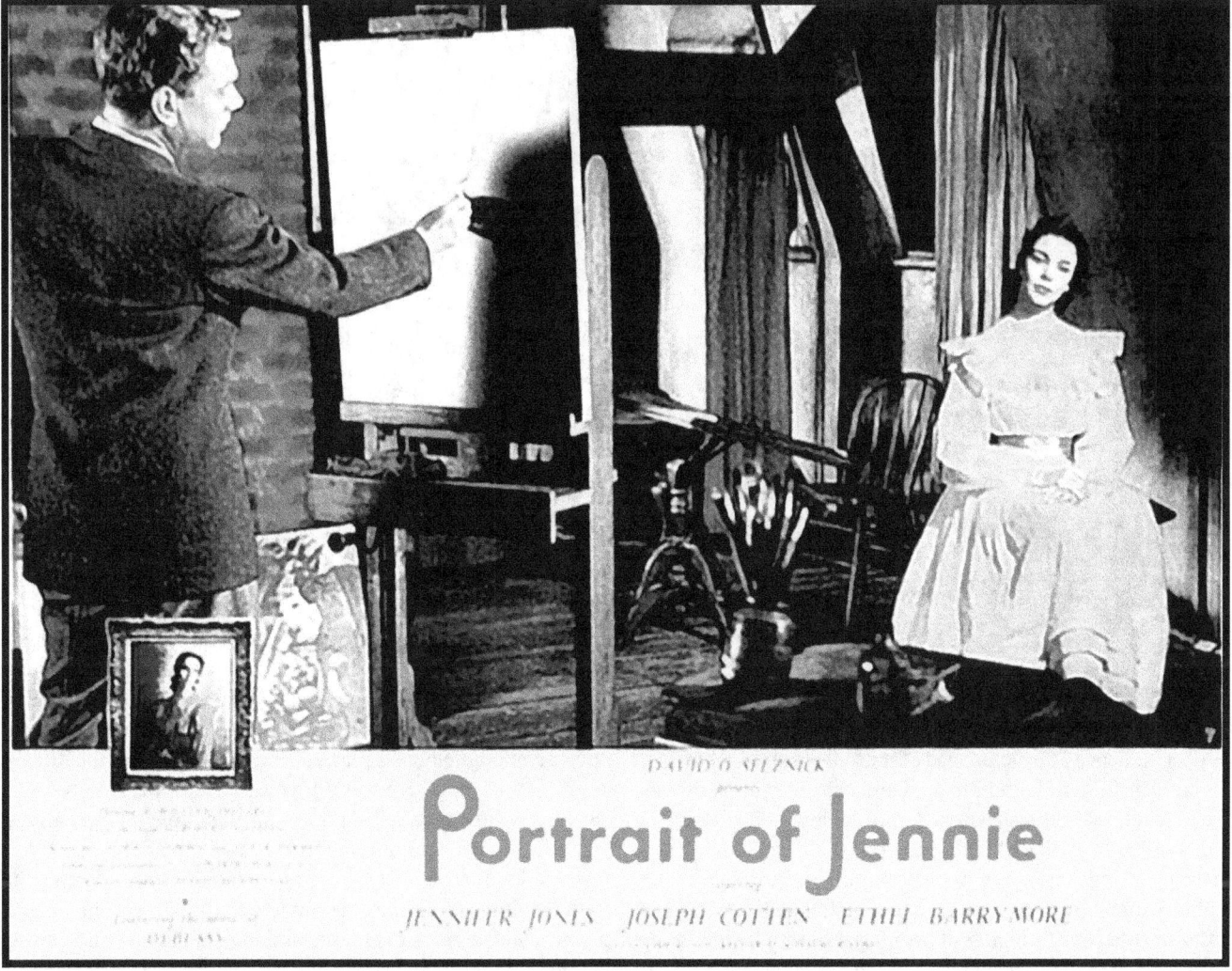

Arturo Toscanini was contacted by the studio and asked if he might consider conducting a new soundtrack comprised of various appropriate classical pieces. Toscanini, a purist who scorned motion picture music, was reportedly "appalled" at the suggestion. Finally Selznick began serious discussions with the estate of the late French composer, Claude Debussy, to bring his music to the screen for the first time. When the rights had at last been secured, Selznick announced it to the press with considerable hoopla. Dimitri Tiomkin was asked to prepare the music for the screen and to conduct the soundtrack. The orchestra was comprised of 74 players and 28 voices. Six scoring sessions had been scheduled, but, true to form, this aspect of production itself soared way over budget, consuming 20 separate scoring segments before completing the soundtrack of the picture. Elements from "Clouds," "The Maid with the Flaxen Hair," "Arabesque," and "Prelude to the Afternoon of a Faun" were chosen as the musical components of Debussy's posthumous contribution. Tiomkin's original intent, judging from press releases of the period, suggests a strict adherence to using the musical extracts exactly as originally written. Selznick, however, believed that the music should be "adapted" to fit the picture. He wrote at the time that "music, like everything else that pictures make use of to achieve their effects, sometimes has to be adapted. The film medium is not a pure medium. There is nothing in it that is not derived from something else, and its collaborative nature precludes anything about it not undergoing some sort of alteration, because everything is subservient to the dramatic needs of the story. Nothing matters except the finished picture." The recording of the music for the picture reportedly took six months at a final cost of $160,000. Purism aside, Selznick had a point and was not afraid to make it.

Another of Selznick's radical conceptions was to film the picture *almost* entirely in black and white. There is an otherworldly quality in black and white cinematography, somehow vaguely spectral and distant, that is shattered when colors are introduced, ripping away its simplicity and exposing that fragile innocence to a harsh, more realistic interpretation. Artist Robert Brackman was hired to portray Jennie's timeless beauty on canvas. As haunting as his conception appeared in black and white, its magical loveliness reached fruition in a startling transformation to full color at the film's completion as present day art lovers stare adoringly at the painting at Spinney's Gallery while Ethel Barrymore looks on.

Portrait of Jennie opened amidst a media blitz to generally complimentary reviews early in 1949. The Cycloramic screen and Cyclophonic sound, however, all but submerged the fra-

gility of the tender ghost story which never seemed to find a proper audience The picture had cost its investors $4.04 million dollars. Its financial return totaled less than $2 million dollars. Selznick, tired and disheartened, closed down his production units in Hollywood and left for Europe with Jennifer Jones in what would become a lengthy, self-imposed exile from the cold, callous world of motion picture production. A brief 10 years after the planetary triumph of his masterpiece, *Gone With the Wind*, Selznick crumbled under the staggering weight of a $12 million dollar debt owed to creditors and banks. In Europe he could find solace, seeking shelter from the Hollywood storm within the comforting arms of his beloved Jennie, his bride, Jennifer Jones.

If time is the ultimate gauge of success, then *Portrait of Jennie* has proven itself a timeless classic. For anyone who has ever longed for love, for anyone who has ever yearned to be embraced in his time, *Jennie* has painted an enduring canvas of love and acceptance. Certainly, ghost stories date back thousands of years. In our own time, cinematic renderings of supernatural hauntings have painted their own indelible portraits of life and love beyond the veil of light. In Paramount's *The Uninvited*, a venomous spirit, consumed by hatred for those who continue to live and breathe, seeks revenge for her own untimely demise while plotting the murder of her apparent offspring. MGM's *The Canterville Ghost* delivered Oscar Wilde's comedic/quasi-tragic tale of a coward condemned to wander this mortal plane, a stranded apparition marooned on earth until such time as he is set free by an act of heroism by a willing ancestor. Both *Peter Ibbetson* (Paramount, 1935) and Samuel Goldwyn's classic romantic tragedy *Wuthering Heights* (1939) explored the tantalizing potential of supernatural coupling, love powerful enough to transcend mortal boundaries, escaping time and space.

There is an undeniable fascination with love, life, and death that is shared by all humanity. Is love ultimately transitory, and therefore empty and superficial, or is it profound and enduring, coming but once in a lifetime, leaving an imprint as deep and eternal as the moon and the stars? Are we reborn and reincarnated again and again throughout time and infinity, loving and beloved by a singular spirit, or is love an illusion, and commitment a momentary expression of transparent involvement? Is love as eternal as time and space, or is it a self-serving lie, forgotten and reborn at will? As society grows more cynical and commitment assumes increasingly insurmountable proportions, the ideal of romantic love has assumed its own dual identity, as both a curse and an ethereal plateau. In a simpler time, the attainment of enduring love was a joyous, uncomplicated goal. On screen, in literature, and in the wistful, simplistic imaginings of most human kind, it remains the loveliest of dreams. If the ideal of love and marriage have fallen into hopeless disrepair in life, the movies continue their magic journey, a spiritual plane upon which dreams come true and love is the most powerful, compelling force for good in the universe. It is an increasingly illusory universe in which Cathy and Heathcliff walk through the clouds toward infinity, while Mrs. Muir and her patient captain hold each other's hands as they confidently traverse time and space. Who's to say which world is more tangible or more important? This is, after all, the stuff that dreams are made of, and where would inspiration and achievement lie in the absence of dreams? If time is, indeed, only a place, then might not this innocent canvas, this *Portrait of Jennie*, become a pathway to reward and contentment, engraved upon a tapestry of revelation.., a stairway to heaven on which the truth lies not in the stars but in our dreams?

CREDITS: Executive Producer: David O. Selznick; Producer: David Hampstead; Director: William Dieterle; Screenplay: Paul Osborn, Peter Berneis From the Novel by Robert Nathan; Adaptation: Leonardo Bercovici; Director of Photography: Joseph August; Music Score Adapted from the Works of Debussy by Dimitri Tiomkin; Selznick Releasing Organization; March 1949; 86 minutes

CAST: Jennifer Jones...Jennie Appleton, Joseph Cotten...Eben Adams, Ethel Barrymore...Miss Spinney, Cecil Kellaway...Mr. Matthews, David Wayne...Gus O'Toole, Albert Sharpe...Mr. Moore, Florence Bates...Mrs. Jekes, Lillian Gish...Mother Mary of Mercy, Henry Hull...Eke, Clem Bevans...Captain Caleb Cobb, Felix Bressart... The Old Doorman, Anne Francis...Teenager

SCROOGE

by Tom Johnson

The ghost story has been a staple of literature practically since the beginning, and no country has provided better examples of the genre than England. Many authors have tried their hand and some—M.R. James, for example—became specialists; but few stories have captured the public's imagination as has Charles Dickens' *A Christmas Carol*. With its combination of sentiment and sensationalism, humor and horror, the story has fascinated audiences for over a century and a half, both in book and movie form. It's no accident that the story is one of the favorites written by one of England's most loved authors.

Charles Dickens was born in Landport, Portsea, on February 7, 1812. His special gift as an author was the ability to combine vivid comedy, strong moral sensibility and social criticism into one seamless whole. Like most social critics, he was unable to provide solutions to the problems he saw, but, through his entertaining writing, he at least exposed them.

Dickens' family moved to London in 1822; their impoverished situation forced him to leave school and work in a warehouse. His father was sent to debtor's prison in 1824, and Charles was soon supporting himself in a rented room. He wandered among London's poor who, like himself, lived in hopeless ness, and he never forgot the experience—in fact, it was the backbone of his later writing.

In 1832, Dickens became a reporter for *The Morning Chronicle* and was soon contributing articles to magazines. Most of his novels were first published in serial form, where far more people had access to them than would have been possible in book form only. He became a national figure after the publication of *Pickwick Papers* (1836-37) and *Oliver Twist* (1837); *Nicholas Nickleby* (1838-39) and *The Old Curiosity Shop* (1840-41) followed in quick succession. *A Christmas Carol* appeared in 1843 and proved to be one of Dickens' most enduring works, aided, a century later, by the film versions.

The success of *A Christmas Carol* pushed Dickens to even greater heights, with *David Copperfield* (1849-50), *A Tale of Two Cities* (1859) and *Great Expectations* (1861) among his finest achievements. His luxurious lifestyle forced Dickens to write at a manic pace and, combined with his extensive touring to read his works, his health was soon broken. He died in Kent on June 9, 1870 with *The Mystery of Edwin Drood* unfinished.

The first sound version of *A Christmas Carol* was filmed in Britain, retitled *Scrooge*, and starred Seymour Hicks. It began production in March, 1935, at Twickenham Studios under Henry Edwards' direction. As one would expect, it was released in December. Reviewers found the picture to be an excellent Christmas present: *The Daily Herald*: "I defy anyone to remain unmoved at its sheer human appeal"; *The Daily Mail*: "A great performance by a great actor"; *The Daily Sketch*: "A first rate production"; *The Sunday Express*: "Fine family entertainment"; and the *Sunday Dispatch*: "A universal story with a universal appeal."

The success of *Scrooge*, both in Britain and America, prompted a U.S. version only three years later. Backed by MGM's production gloss, Joseph L. Mankiewicz's film, directed by Edwin L. Martin, again rang the bell. Reginald Owen (who, oddly, previously played both Dr. Watson and Sherlock Holmes) scored as Scrooge. However, the definitive version of the story had yet to be filmed.

George Minter's film of *Scrooge* was first announced in the British trades on May 10, 1950. *The Kinematograph Weekly* revealed that Minter's production team from *Tom Brown's Schooldays* (1951) was reassembled for a May 21, 1951 start on the Dickens classic. Returning were two key members of Minter's previous production.

Director Brian Desmond-Hurst was born in Castlereagh, County Down, Ireland, on February 12, 1895. After fighting in World War I, he stayed on in Paris, where he studied art at L'Academie Julién. In 1925, he went to Hollywood to paint a mural for a wealthy owner of a luncheonette chain and met fellow Irishman John Ford. Claiming to be a distant cousin,

Hurst joined Ford's film unit as an art director. He later repaid the favor when he introduced Ford to Liam O'Flaherty, author of *The Informer* which became one of the Ford's best pictures.

Hurst returned to Ireland in 1933 where he directed two low-budget movies, one of which—Poe's *The Tell-Tale Heart*—received good notices. He was picked up by Associated British/ Elstree in 1935 and, during World War II, worked on some of Britain's most prestigious pictures (*The Lion Has Wings,* 1939, *Dangerous Moonlight* ,1941 and *Caesar and Cleopatra,* 1945). After, the war, his first major film was *Tom Brown's Schooldays* for George Minter, which led directly to *Scrooge*, the highlight of his career. A veteran of 27 features, either as producer or director, Hurst died on September 26, 1986.

South African novelist and playwright Noel Langley was given the unenviable task of adapting one of the best known and loved English novels, He was born, appropriately enough, on Christmas Day, 1911, in Durban. He emigrated to London in the early '30s and, by 1934, had two of his plays staged. In 1935, Peter Bull, who acted in *Scrooge*, produced two of Langley's comedies in Cornwall. Langley soon went to Broadway, then Hollywood, where he wrote the screenplay (with Florence Ryerson and Edgar Allan Wolfe) for *The Wizard of Oz* (1939). He joined Minter's team for *Tom Brown's Schooldays*, *Scrooge* and Dickens' *The Pickwick Papers* (1952), which he also directed. He retired from screenwriting in 1961 after *Snow White and the Three Stooges* (no wonder!) and died on November 3, 1986.

Any version of *A Christmas Carol* is no better than its Scrooge, and in Alastair Sim, Minter found the prototype. Sim was born in Edinburgh, Scotland, on October 9, 1900. He was a Lecturer of Elocution at the city's New College, and it was there that he turned his hand to directing amateur plays. He attracted the attention of poet/critic John Drinkwater, who suggested he try acting—as a professional. With Drinkwater's help, Sim landed the prime role of Iago opposite Paul Robeson as Othello in 1930 and became typed as a villain.

Sim showed his flair for comedy in the Old Vic season of 1932 and made his first real impression on theatregoers in *Youth at the Helm* (1935). He appeared in his first film in 1935, after having to turn down two previous offers due to his stage commitments. Sim's film career caught fire with the *Inspector Hornleigh* series (1939/1941), and he became a major character star after *Green for Danger* (1946), a creepy comedy/thriller. His stock-in-trade character was described by Pauline Kael in *The New Yorker* as being "so gentle, unctuous, and tragic of demeanor that he suggests the modern epitome of agonized culture: the undertaker."

After his huge success in *Scrooge*, Sim scored again as the otherworldly "policeman" in J.B. Priestley's *An Inspector Calls* (1954). He reached his peak of comedic mayhem as a clockmaker/assassin in *The Green Man* (1956) and, in drag, in *The Belles of St. Trinians* (1955). He reprised his 1948 stage role as Dr. Robert Knox in *The Anatomist* (a 1962 movie), then left the screen for 11 years, returning in *The Ruling Class*.

An enthusiastic chess player and swimmer, Alastair Sim was a very private person. "All the public needs to know about me is what they see," he said. "Let their opinions be formed by my performances." He gave audiences many good opinions before his death on August 19, 1976. Awarded The Order of the British Empire in 1953, Sim was one of the country's most highly regarded actors. Hard-to-please critic Bosley Crowther (*New York Times*) wrote of Sim's performance of Scrooge, "He exposes much more than the grief and despair of a nasty old man. He exposes a sort of wretchedness of the soul.., a holloweyed horror of the void that is not only before him, but on all sides because of his long-time indifference to affectionate associations with other men."

London's nastiest old man of 1830 is Ebeneezer Scrooge, a financier without friends or any recognizable human emotion except greed. Either hated or feared by all in his orbit, Scrooge is a man to beware. On Christmas Eve, as he leaves the stock exchange, he passes two businessmen. "Old Marley was dead as a doornail," we are told by the first (Peter Bull). "This must be distinctly understood or nothing wonderful can come of the story I'm going to relate." When he asks Scrooge (Sim) if he's hurrying home to "keep Christmas," he answers "Christmas, sir, is a humbug." Carolers scatter as Scrooge enters his office where he is accosted by two men seeking donations for the poor. "Are there no prisons?" asks Scrooge. "And the Union Workhouses. Are they still in operation?" When told that many would rather die than enter a workhouse, the miserable Scrooge responds, "If they would rather die, they'd better do it and decrease the surplus population."

Alastair Sim is the ultimate Scrooge.

Scrooge's nephew, Fred (Brian Worth) arrives to wish his uncle a Merry Christmas (disregarded) and to invite him to Christmas dinner (refused). Scrooge begrudges Fred for his marriage to an "unworthy" girl, and for far more...

At closing, Scrooge chides his underpaid and overworked clerk, Bob Cratchit (Mervyn Johns), for—again—requesting Christmas as a paid holiday. "It's a poor excuse," snarls Scrooge, "for picking a man's pocket every 25th of December." As "poor" Cratchit bounces off, smiling, to his family, Scrooge stalks off to no one.

"Home" to Scrooge is lonely and forbidding, like the man himself. As he pauses on the doorstep, he sees the image of Jacob Marley (Michael Hordern), his dead partner in business. As he mounts the staircase, Scrooge hears Marley calling to him and, soon, heralded by bells, his spirit enters the bedroom. Marley is weighted down by chains and weights which he forged during his miserable life. "Why do you doubt your senses?" he asks his skeptical host. "You might be an undigested bit of beef, a fragment of underdone potato," says Scrooge. "There is more of gravy than the grave in you."

Jacob Marley (Michael Hordern) warns Scrooge of the fate that awaits him.

Due to his misspent life, Marley walks the earth, witnessing the joy in which he could have shared. "I am doomed," he wails, "to wander without rest or peace. I come tonight to warn you... you have a chance... and hope... of escaping my fate." Scrooge will be visited by three spirits who will try to put his life—and soul—in order. Terrified, Scrooge takes to his bed, and waits... The First Spirit (Michael Dolan)—the Ghost of Christmas Past—transports Scrooge to his childhood to relive a heartbreaking moment. Accompanied by the Spirit, Scrooge cannot be seen but sees far more than he would like. A youthful Scrooge (George Cole) is comforted by his sister Fan (Carol Marsh), who has come to reunite him with his estranged father. "You're never to be lonely again," she says. Always delicate, she soon dies as a young married woman giving birth to Fred, whom Scrooge cannot forgive. The Spirit points out to Scrooge that his own mother died giving him life…as if it were Scrooge's fault.

Scrooge then relives a party given by his first employer, Mr. Fezziwig (Roddy Hughes). "Was there *ever* a kinder man?" asks Scrooge. He is stunned when he realizes the joy Fezziwig has given for so little money... "It was as great as if it had cost a fortune," he muses, thinking of Cratchit.

Scrooge becomes engaged to Alice (Rona Anderson), but both his love and personality turn cold as he advances his business. When Mr. Jorkins (Jack Warner), something of a visionary, attempts to buy out Fezziwig, the kindly gentleman demurs, wanting to remain true to the old ways. "There's more to life than money," he says. Young Scrooge, however, is not so sure.

Called to Fan's deathbed, the young Scrooge stalks out before hearing her ask him to care of her newly born son... but the old Scrooge hears her all too clearly. "Forgive me, Fan," he says through his tears. "Forgive me."

After taking up with Jorkins, Scrooge meets young Marley (Patrick MacNee); the two soon buy out the broken Fezziwig and begin their lives of greed. Alice and Scrooge soon part. "Our promise is an old one," she says, "made when we were both poor and content to be so." The young Scrooge strides out as the old Scrooge watches her cry.

Scrooge (Sim) and Marley (Hordern) bail out Jorkins, who has embezzled from his shareholders, by taking over the business. Years pass; one Christmas Eve, Scrooge is told by Mrs. Dilber (Kathleen Harrison), Marley's housekeeper, that his partner is dying, but he waits until closing to see his "friend." At the stroke of seven, Scrooge brushes off Cratchit ("We've all got to die sometime"), berates him for wanting Christmas Day off, and heads for Marley's. The Undertaker (Ernest Thesiger) is already there, and Scrooge enters the death-chamber. As Scrooge leans over the bed, Marley croaks, "While there's still time... Wrong... Wrong..." Shaken, Scrooge replies, "Well, we can't be right all the time. We've been no worse than the next man." With his final effort, Marley gasps, "Save yourself."

The Spirit forces Scrooge to see a final disturbing image. "Jacob Marley," says the Ghost, "worked at your side for 18 years—he was the only friend you ever had. But... what did you feel when you signed the register and took his money, his house, and his few mean sticks of furniture?" Scrooge is saddened as he looks at his younger face, tight with greed and devoid of pity.

Scrooge, in his bed, is startled by the laughter of the Second Spirit—the Ghost of Christmas Present (Francis DeWolff Robed, bearded and jovial, the Spirit asks, "Is your heart still

unmoved?" Scrooge moans, "I'm too old... I'm beyond hope." But the Spirit will not be put off. "We Spirits of Christmas do not give only one day of our year. So is it true of the Child born in Bethlehem. You have chosen not to seek him in your heart... therefore, you shall come with me and seek him in the hearts of men of Goodwill." Scrooge touches the Spirit's robe, and...

At the Cratchit's home, Bob enters with his son, the crippled Tiny Tim (Glyn Dearman), and is overjoyed to see his daughter Martha. The Cratchits are satisfied with very little and want only that the sickly Tim's condition not worsen. Scrooge, uneasy, asks the Spirit, "Will Tiny Tim live?" The Spirit hints that this will be the boy's last Christmas. "Oh no—no!" moans Scrooge. "Say that he will be spared!" "Why?" asks the Spirit. "If he be like to die, he better do it and decrease the surplus population." Mrs. Cratchit (Hermione Baddeley) and her children set the table and the family enjoys its simple pleasures, as Bob proudly announces that he's found a job for Peter, the oldest son. "God bless us everyone!" toasts Tim. "I give you Mr. Scrooge, the founder of the feast," echoes Cratchit. The family voices its disgust, as Scrooge turns away.

At Fred's, a gala party is in full swing with Scrooge the topic of discussion. At a soup kitchen for the poor, a middle-aged Alice serves a stricken woman. Scrooge is horrified to see her. "Spirit," he stammers, "are these people real, or are they shadows?" "They," he answers, "are real—we are the shadows. Did you not cut yourself off from your fellow beings when you lost the love of that gentle creature?"

Scrooge and the Spirit stand outside. "Will you profit from what I've shown you of the good in most men's hearts? If it's too hard a lesson for you to learn, then learn this lesson." The Spirit parts his robe... at his feet sit two bedraggled children. "Spirit," asks Scrooge, "are these yours?" "They are man's," the Spirit answers. "They cling to me for protection from their fetters. This Boy is Ignorance, this Girl is Want. Beware them both—but most of all, beware this Boy."

"Have they no refuge... no resource?" asks Scrooge. "Are there no prisons'?" shouts the Spirit.

Scrooge's flight is halted by a hooded figure, the Spirit of Christmas Yet To Come... the most forbidding of the three.

"Spirit of the Future," sobs Scrooge, "I fear you more than any other specter I have seen. But even in my fear, I must tell you that I'm too old!" The Spirit motions him ahead.

At the Cratchit home, Peter reads from the Bible as his mother and sisters listen sadly. Bob returns home—alone. He has been to Tiny Tim's grave. Scrooge can only stare.

At a disgusting "rag-shop," Old Joe (Miles Malleson), Mrs. Dilber and The Undertaker paw through the belongings of a recently deceased man. "Eight shillings for the lot," sneers Old Joe. The trio joke about the meager cache: "It's poetic justice," says The Undertaker. "He frightened everybody away from him when he was alive; now he benefits us when he's dead!" Scrooge watches with growing horror.

At the Stock Exchange, the businessman discusses attending a funeral service. "I must be fed, or else I stay at home." Scrooge recognizes the man...and that his own place under the clock is empty. "I ought to be there this time of day—but I'm not. I'm not!"

At a cemetery, Scrooge implores the Spirit. "Before I draw nearer to that stone, answer me one question. Are those the shadows of things that must be?" The Spirit directs Scrooge to his tombstone; with a horrified wail, he falls upon it. On his knees, he tells the Spirit, "I'm not the man I was. Why show me all this if I'm beyond all hope? Pity me, Spirit. Help me. I do repent. I'll change. I'm not the man I was."

Scrooge awakens in his own bed—it's Christmas Day. Mrs. Dilber brings his tea, and Scrooge is beside himself with joy. He dances about the room, frightening the poor woman as he wishes her a Merry Christmas. He gives her a gold coin.., and a kiss.., quadruples her salary, then sends a small boy to the butcher to buy a turkey for the Cratchits. Somehow, Tiny Tim realizes who has sent the anonymous gift.

Fred's dinner party has a late-arriving guest. Beaming, Scrooge asks his niece (Olga Edwardes), "Can you forgive a pigheaded old fool who had no eyes to see with and no ears to hear with all these years?" She leads him into the parlor and to the other guests.

The next day, Cratchit—late—tiptoes into the office. "What do you mean by coming in here this time of day! Step this way, Mr. Cratchit. Well, we won't beat about the bush. You leave me no alternative but to... raise your salary."

He laughs at Crachit's stunned expression. "I haven't taken leave of my senses, Bob—I've come to them." He promises to help the family and in the words of Dickens, "was better than his word. He became as good a master and as good a man as the good old city ever knew. It was always said that he kept Christmas well."

As with any film based on a literary classic or on a previously successful picture (or in *Scrooge*'s case, both), there was probably some apprehension as to its reception by audiences and critics. If so, it was unwarranted.

Retitled *A Christmas Carol*, the movie was previewed in America a month before its general release in Britain. *The Kinematograph Weekly* (December 6, 1951), under the headline "*Scrooge* a Hit in America," quoted the following reviews: "The film glows anew." (*N.Y. World Telegraph*); "Rich in atmosphere, fascinating sets and costumes." (*N.Y. Journal American*); "There is simply nothing to criticize." (*N.Y. Post*); "Fine motion picture." (*Daily News*); "Sim is one of the greatest actors of our time." (*Saturday Review*); "By far the best version ever made." (*Cue*).

British reviewers were no less impressed. *Scrooge* was trade-shown in London on October 15, and *The Kinematograph Weekly* (October 18, 1951) said, "The inspired casting of Alastair Sim in the name part is a sure guarantee of its success. Sim dominates the tale without stealing the limelight from the rest and smoothly rounds off his superb portrayal with comedy. *Scrooge* has such wide appeal that it can be billed with equal confidence during a heatwave or when snow is on the ground. Great story, tour de force by Alastair Sim, accurate detail, moving sentiment, quiet laughs, sterling moral, and box office star and title."

That reviewer said it all, but was not alone. "Sim is truly magnificent, filling his part to the brim with every drop of energy, pathos, humour, and intelligence it demands." (*The Spectator*, November 23); "Brian Desmond-Hurst has had to pad it out a good deal. This he has done by many magical, mystical and ghostly inventions." (*Daily Herald*, November 11); "It is a brave film with the courage of its romantic convictions." (*London Times*, November 11); and "Very useful and welcome it is." (*Daily Worker*, November 25).

As noted by the reviewers, *Scrooge* manages to elicit many emotions in the viewer, any one of which would have been enough to sustain the average film. The picture's gentle comedy provides well-spaced laughs—often in the midst of "straight" scenes. Many moments—Fan's death, Scrooge's realization of his own degeneration, his joyful redemption—are enough to bring tears to even the title character's eyes. The ghost scenes, while not there specifically to terrify, often do just that—especially if one is able to closely identify with Scrooge. Marley's pitiful wails and ominous chain-rattling are not easily forgotten, nor is the pitiless demeanor of Scrooge's spirit guides as they

take him through his miserable life: past, present and future. Perhaps *Scrooge*'s most horrifying moment is when he is forced by the Ingmar Bergmanesque Ghost of Christmas Future to see his own grave. While the viewer is hardly surprised at this development, the scene works precisely because it manages to shock us even though we are more than aware it's coming.

Alastair Sim gives one of the screen's great bravura performances, but it's far more than that. He makes Scrooge touchingly real—we feel his meanness, loneliness, terror and joy. Despite the others who have played the part, Sim makes it his own. A big budget 1970 musical starring Albert Finney failed to do for Dickens what the Oscar-winning *Oliver!* had done two years earlier. Although the 1989 made-for-TV version with George C. Scott was well-meaning (and well-made), it failed to move the 1951 picture from the top spot. Bill Murray turned in his typically amusingly sleazy performance in *Scrooged* (1988), which succeeds in a "guilty pleasure" sort of way... but no more.

Perhaps *Scrooge*'s true impact wasn't realized until 30 years after its release. By 1981, the picture was a Christmastime staple of American TV, but...

"They're calling me Scrooge," said Bob Muller, head of Gold Key Entertainment (*N.Y. Daily News*, December 16, 1981). "It's an unfortunate situation. There was nothing I could do about it." The "unfortunate situation" was that for the first time in 25 years, *Scrooge* was not available for showing on U.S. television. It took until November for Muller to renegotiate the rights from a British copyright holder—too late to finalize the Gold Key's paperwork with American TV. "I'm not trying to be the bad guy. I love the film myself, and so does my family."

There was a huge outcry from viewers who were not willing to be pacified with lesser versions. The situation was little better in 1982 when the rights were acquired by pay-cable. The film went back into domestic syndication in 1983, which did little to console those who had to endure the unthinkable— two Christmas Eves without *Scrooge*. That was a situation almost as heartbreaking and terrifying as the one the old miser himself had to endure.

CREDITS: Director: Brian Desmond-Hurst; Producer: Brian Desmond-Hurst; Screenplay: Noel Langley, Based on Charles Dickens' *A Christmas Carol*, Director of Photography: C. Pennington Richards; Black and White; 86 minutes; UK Certificate "U"; A Renown Production; Released December 24, 1951 (UK); Presented by George Minter. Released in the United States as *A Christmas Carol*

CAST: Alastair Sim...Scrooge, Kathleen Harrison...Mrs. Dilber, Jack Warner... Mr. Jorkins, Michael Hordern. . Jacob Marley, Mervyn Johns...Bob Cratchit, Hermione Baddeley...Mrs. Cratchit, John Charlesworth...Peter Cratchit, Glyn Dearman...Tiny Tim, George Cole...Young Scrooge, Rona Anderson.. Alice, Carol Marsh...Fan, Brian Worth...Fred

THE UNINVITED

by Gary J. Svehla

Why does everyone enjoy the campfire ghost story? What is there about these communal tales of disembodied spirits, revenge from beyond the grave, and shadows on moonlit bedroom walls that so many people find attractive? And why has Hollywood generally avoided making such archetypal cultural experiences a larger part of the ever-popular horror film genre? Vampires, zombies, werewolves, Frankenstein Monsters, etc. are all very essential to the fear film genre, but ghosts, on the other hand, are more often the ectoplasmic creations of camp and ridicule, seldom being taken seriously or maturely in most Hollywood productions. A.I.P's *The Ghost of Dragstrip Hollow* and *The Ghost in the Invisible Bikini* seem to sum up Hollywood's glib attitude toward ghosts. Perhaps because they quickly became the caricature of human beings wearing a white sheet in two-reel comedies or the comical howling spirits of Disney cartoons, the ghost in Hollywood has never been taken seriously enough.

Hollywood's attraction to the ghost movie genre has largely been tongue-in-cheek with early 1930s encounters between spooks and Laurel and Hardy, The Three Stooges, and the robust, demented Little Rascals. Even the MGM late '30s version of *A Christmas Carol*, while featuring disembodied spirits of the spookiest nature, still managed to keep the proceedings moralistic, tidy and safe (even fun). At least the spooks offered up to Mr. Scrooge were played seriously for their chills and horrific impact! But the Halperin Brothers' deadly serious *Supernatural*, one of the first mature ghost movies, is barely remembered today. Perhaps very few people accept the paranormal and the supernatural, while at the same time, movies that deal with ghosts, spirits, and things-that-go-bump-in-the-night hit a tad *too* close to home to be merely dismissed as filmic foolishness. The honor film genre is basically a genre of the fantastic, of the netherworlds of the imagination; they generally do not skirt with reality. And while the ghost subgenre is definitely an important, traditional part of the horror film genre, it is one that manages to touch a nerve because of its inherent, subconscious belief that ghosts might be real and closer to reality than we dare admit. People generally scoff at the thought of the existence of ghosts, yet at the same time, our religious doctrines teach of the re-animation of spirits and the existence of otherworldly life beyond this realm of the living.

Thus, even after Hollywood took the ghost movie seriously with Paramount's major 1944 release *The Uninvited*, (remember, four years earlier Paramount released the Bob Hope comedy classic, *The Ghost Breakers*), the subgenre soon reverted to lighthearted levity with the "it's all explained away... almost" antics of *House on Haunted Hill* and the over-the-top fun of *13 Ghosts*, in the late 1950s and '60s. Simply stated, with very few exceptions (*The Innocents* being one), Hollywood has released very few serious ghost films between the years 1944 and 1963 when *The Haunting* was released. For every *Curse of the Cat People* or *Dead of Night* in Hollywood history, there are four or five comic treatment of ghosts in movies such as *The Ghost Catchers*, *The Ghost Chasers* and *Ghosts on the Loose*. Hollywood discovered once it had created and encouraged the silly stereotyping of ghosts in films, it was increasingly more and more difficult to turn things around and make Casper the Friendly Ghost appear terrifying.

Thus, *The Uninvited* deserves credit for turning things around, and in a major Hollywood way, reinventing the image of the ghost as something malignant, insidious and horrible.

Secondly, as experienced in great literature, such as Henry James' *The Turn of the Screw*, the ghost genre is a very adult one whereby the ghosts and hauntings themselves often become metaphors representing the external manifestations of a character's inner turmoil. Therefore, the ghost genre allows the filmmaker to explore the inner workings of a central character or characters by manifesting their inner struggles, fears, yearnings, failings, etc. through the external manifestation of ghosts. Simply stated, in ghost cinema, the filmmaker confronts the internal (character motivations which generally are not verbalized for the audience's benefit, sometimes motivations only understood via the subconscious mind so the character him/herself is left partially or totally in the dark) by revealing the external (the haunting spirit, the ectoplasmic mist, the ghost manifestations) and then all so subtly links the two together. Such subtleties generally are a result of complex plotting or, minimally, complex character development, which means the end product is generally very adult or multi-layered. thus making the motion picture a harder sell for the generic cinemagoer. This may be the reason why the majority of ghost movies are humorous or stereotyped and why serious, mature ghost movies are few and far between. At heart the ghost movie is powerfully character-driven and psychological in nature, tending to focus primarily upon the internal journey of self-discovery resulting in the destruction or disappearance of the haunting spirit once that internal journey has been successfully completed. The external "spirit" becomes a metaphor for the hellish demons which we all sometimes harbor in our minds, and once those psychological demons have been exorcised, the external ghost also vanishes. Unlike vampires, Frankenstein Monsters, and creatures from black lagoons, the substance of ghost cinema resides well within the domain of the human psyche and solutions are never as easy as a wooden stake through the heart.

Paramount's *The Uninvited* (1944) along with MGM's *The Haunting* are perhaps the two finest examples of mature ghost cinema to exist in the annals of cinehistory. Both are deadly serious and mature visions, both reveal inner psychological turmoil and internal journeys of self discovery displayed via the external manifestations of spirits and ghosts, and both manage to scare the living hell out of the moviegoing audience. A better recipe does not exist for classic horror cinema.

Lewis Allen's *The Uninvited* is a story of relationships, some healthy and others quite twisted. The mood is set by the voiceover narration beginning the movie juxtaposed to the visual display of wildly frolicking waves crashing over the rocky Cornwall shore reinforcing this haunting narrative: we are told of "haunted shores... mists gather, sea fog, eerie stories." Once we listen to "the pound and stir of the waves, all senses are sharpened" which will prepare us for the "peculiar cold, which is the first warning," a cold which is "a draining of warmth from the vital centers of the living."

The first important relationship explored is between Rick Fitzgerald and his sister Pamela, 300 miles away from their London flat vacationing in rustic Cornwall when they happen to come upon a lonely, deserted country estate as their dog Bobby chases a squirrel through the house. The house, unoccupied for almost 20 years, becomes to Pamela "the loveliest thing I ever saw" and she soon declares she has "one of her feelings" that they will buy the house, if they put all the money they both have together. Brother Rick is less enthusiastic claiming his job as music critic in London is just too far to travel if they live in Cornwall. But the-devil-may-care sister tells Rick to "chuck" his critic's job and live here writing music which is his real heart's passion. Rick, who is also impressed by the house's serenity, scenic views and vast size, smiles at the prospect of writing music full-time. Rick's negative question—"suppose the house is not for sale"—is immediately addressed by Pamela's eternal optimism: "Life is not that cruel!" Both Rick and Pamela

are happy-go-lucky people with Rick s head slightly more rooted in reality and common sense Yet Pamela is much more open-minded to the existence of non-explainable things Finding out from a Mrs. Brown that the house is indeed for sale from a Commander Beech, Rick warns Pamela, "We're mildly interested, remember, not keenly interested," as they prepare to speak to the owner about buying the house.

Journeying to Commander Beech's house, the second important set of relationships is illustrated. Stella Meredith, the 20-year-old brooding, sad-eyed and hauntingly beautiful granddaughter of the Commander, greets Rick and Pamela and tells them the house is not for sale, that they will waste their time waiting for her grandfather. However, the Commander's abrupt return home results in his announcing the house is indeed for sale. Taking his granddaughter aside, Beech announces there's no point in keeping a house that Stella hasn't lived in since she was three (the home was given to his daughter Mary when Stella was born and Mary died there three years later) and a piece of property too expensive to maintain. For Stella, that house represents her only memories of her mother, and though she has not entered the house since she was three, she doesn't wish to allow her grandfather to sell her former home. The Commander is quietly abrupt, formally polite and a secret harborer of deep family secrets which he wishes to not reveal

to either Stella or to the strangers. When Rick announces 1200 pounds is all they have to buy the house, the Commander quickly accepts the price if they are making a firm offer (noting that even though the house is worth much more, with a young granddaughter as his ward, he feels more secure knowing that money will be in the bank for her). Warning the Fitzgeralds that the former tenants complained of "disturbances," and since he would rather not go into the matter, he simply terminated their lease. But he cautions, with a firm sale he cannot terminate the deal. In overwhelming sadness, Stella declares, "It was my mother's house!"

Soon, the eerie, naive Stella apologizes to Rick stating, "My mother made me apologize!" Rick, remembering that Stella's mother Mary is dead, is told that her mother's portrait, painted by her father, hangs in her room and that Stella came to the conclusion that her mother would have approved of Rick and his sister living in the home. "She lived there for three years, my years... I love that house. It's not right to hate it because somebody died there." Rick notes the repression of Stella's life, living alone with her reclusive grandfather, her social life consisting of reading Dickens from the local lending library aloud with her grandfather for fun, tells the morbidly fascinating young girl that he will show her some real excitement and he takes her sailing on a rented boat. There, letting her hair down, she laughs and loosens up and for the first time allows herself to begin to fall in love. Thus, here we have the next important relationship which the movie explores. Stella tells Rick she never knew any one who laughed so much. Rick later tells Pamela that Stella has something of a Sleeping Beauty charm about her, that he has done something toward breaking the spell, but that he is a Prince Charmless. However, even the intuitive Pam realizes that Rick who at first simply felt sorry for the young girl now "likes" her, which he readily admits. However,

the Commander, instead of being glad at the bond forming between the Fitzgeralds and his granddaughter, refuses to allow Stella to accept any invitations to visit Windward House, telling Rick that Stella "suffers with a general delicacy; she is not strong enough to make new friends:' The Commander puts his cards on the table: "Stella is not going back inside that home." To which Rick responds, "Great Scott, you believe the place is haunted!" Trying to change the motivation for not allowing Stella to visit Windward House, the Commander reminds Rick that just because he purchased the house from him does not mean that they move within the same social circles. Rick, polite yet vehement, tells the Commander that the invitations will continue.

The core relationship binding all parties together revolves around Stella's mother, Mary Meredith (represented by paintings of actress Elizabeth Russell throughout the movie and a ghostly, misty vision by movie's end), and how she came to die. Mary's best friend was a Miss Holloway, Stella's childhood nurse, who now runs a private hospital for the insane called The Mary Meredith Retreat ("Health Through Harmony"). According to Holloway, Mary's husband, simply referred to as Meredith throughout the movie, a bad sort, had an affair with a Spanish Gypsy, Carmel. When Mary first became pregnant with Stella, she moved to Europe for some time with Meredith and Carmel. Returning with Meredith and the baby alone, Mary is at peace until the Gypsy woman returned three years later still wishing to win the love of Meredith. Ordered by Mary to leave Windward, Carmel sought revenge so she took the baby from the nursery and ran outside to the seaside cliffs, near the dead tree. There the two women struggled and Carmel struck Mary down pushing her over the cliff to her death. Meredith then ordered Carmel to leave Windward forever ("the only decent thing he ever did," according to Holloway), but being out in the storm, Carmel contracted double pneumonia and died shortly thereafter in the care of Miss Holloway. This is the version accepted by all as being correct. Unfortunately, the truth of Windward House is yet to be revealed and all the hauntings are directly related to the house's seeming desire to scream out what really occurred during that three year period of disrupted tranquillity. Totally trusting in Miss Holloway's "cure" for Stella's peace of mind (and to get her out of the clutches of Rick and Windward House forever), the Commander near the end of the movie commits his granddaughter to the institution. Earlier in the movie, less sure of her virtues, Beech telephones Holloway and asks her if he can consult her about Stella. "Isn't it a bit late to consult me," Holloway responds. The Commander begs her to help him: "You're the only human being in the world to whom I can turn. The only person who wouldn't think me demented because

I believe a house could be filled with malignity, a malignity directed against a certain child."

Thus all the relationships have now clearly been established. Brother and sister Rick and Pamela are friendly, charming and adventurous. Rick at first feels sympathy, then love, for the reclusive and repressed Stella who is shackled to her all-controlling, protective grandfather, Commander Beech, who is deadly afraid that malignant spiritual forces that lurk in Windward House are out to destroy Stella, thus his over-possessiveness. Stella loves her mother and the house which she shared with her for three years, first not wishing for her mother's home to be sold, then relenting when she realizes how kind and caring the Fitzgeralds are. Soon, the stiff-upper-lipped yet playfully childish Rick (his greatest desire is to slide down the banister at Windward) falls in love with the morbidly beautiful child/woman and refuses to back off when her grandfather makes his intentions known. Miss Holloway, Stella's nurse and best friend to Mary Meredith, whose entire professional life is devoted to serving Mary's memory, convinces the Commander that only she can cure the demons raging both within Stella and within the Woodward home. The Commander trusts her. And finally, we have the triangle between Mary Meredith, her husband, and her husband's Gypsy lover Carmel with Miss Holloway claiming, out of spite, the jealous and now rejected Carmel took baby Stella from the nursery and rushed to the seaside cliffs where Mary and Carmel struggled over the child with the mother being pushed to her death.

We now come to the horror and hauntings at Windward House, where all malevolent forces are usually directed toward the vulnerable Stella. These insidious forces are first revealed after Rick and Pamela purchase Windward and for the first time unlock the door to the studio. Pamela immediately reacts by stating, "It's the one ugly room in the house!" Other reactions refer to the room being "damp" and that "it needs airing.., funny how it should strike so cold in here!" From the film's opening narration, this is the first warning—the draining cold! Rick responds by stating, "I feel completely flattened." Trying to overcome the ominous feelings they both feel, Rick decides to make this his studio by "placing the piano over there," pointing. Then having doubts himself, he inquires, "Do you think I will ever be able to write here?" Unbeknownst to the siblings, a bunch of roses brought into the room by Pamela suddenly shrivel and die.

Later, when Stella arrives by Rick's invite to Windward for her first visit, she is brought to her former nursery. "How glad this house must be to be among the living again!" she beams. Even though the nursery fills Stella with fond memories, she does remember a recurring dream: "...dark, frightening cold, then a flame would come, and all would be light, warm, peaceful. Then some one would put the flame out—I'd be terrified!" Soon her tour of the house brings her to Rick's music studio, the former art studio of her father. Stella reveals this is where my father painted my mother's portrait (referring to the numerous paintings of her mother which appear throughout the movie). "Strange to think of them here," Stella reflects. And sometimes he painted the model, a foreign girl, but people get hush-hush when I mention her (obviously Carmel). Quietly realizing the affair of which her father indulged, Stella shows her calm acceptance when she says, "If father had been as good as mother, look what I may have been!" Soon Rick is performing an original piano composition for Stella called, appropriately, "Stella by Starlight," which Stella responds to by saying, "It's the most exciting thing that ever happened to me." Rick alludes to the former use of this studio by stating, "This is the only way I can paint you— black keys and white—fingers much too clumsy." But Rick's romantic interlude suddenly is transformed most subtly: the candles dim so slightly, the melody grows strangely sad ("Why did you change it," Stella nervously asks), and soon Stella is trembling and afraid. Rick responds, "It just came out that way!" Remembering her mother's fate, Stella questions how she could ever laugh in her house. Rick comforts her, it's my house now. But Stella remembers, "She died so cruelly!" and in deep turmoil runs outside the studio, outside the house heading toward the dangerous cliffs, the exact location where her mother fell to her death. Fortunately, Rick catches up to her and grips her before she tumbles. "I had no sense of danger... this is where my mother fell, by the dead tree," Stella says.

Rick and Pamela, hoping to return the mood to a happier one, start to sing a silly song as, arm-in-arm, they prance back toward the house. However, the happiness is interrupted by a

loud scream from housekeeper Lizzy. Rick entering the house with a candle finds Lizzy in total darkness standing in the middle of the staircase, her body paralyzed with fear. "The studio door, something's there. I saw it—a crawling mist. It stood at the studio door looking down at me... the ghost of a woman!" Stella at first stands transfixed but soon runs upstairs into the studio where she passes out. Rick finds her there unconscious stating, "Pam, this room's like an ice box!" Village physician Dr. Scott calls this a nasty case of shock. Reawakening, Stella only remembers "the cold coming, the room went cold, and I was frightened."

Five-thirty a.m. the next morning—dawn—Rick sees a bright light emanating from Stella's room (the nursery) where Dr. Scott advised her to stay overnight. The overwhelming scent of mimosa permeates throughout the house as the concerned Rick and Pamela enter the nursery to investigate. The bed is empty, Stella is gone, and the window is wide open. Standing partially hidden in the window curtains, smiling, looking outside the window toward dawn, Stella stands, declaring, "I wanted to see the dawn... with her (referring to her mother)... Don't you know who is in your home—my mother. I awoke with the knowledge that someone loves me. My mother would never harm me!" But the silent look of puzzlement upon Rick's face registers the question: who or what almost lured Stella to her death only last night? Rick, who truly loves Stella, asks guilt-riddenly, "Wonder what I did to her bringing her here. That look in her eyes... that terrible happiness."

The truth will soon be known: two spirits haunt Windward House; the first makes its presence known with a deadly cold chill, the second makes its presence known with the permeating scent of mimosa.

Pamela, the optimist, feels "if a spirit comes back it's for one particular purpose," and since apparently Stella has been reunited with the spirit of her mother Mary Meredith, perhaps the hauntings will end. "Perhaps we don't have a ghost anymore! Only warmth and fragrance." But the real test will be entering the studio, the site of the more unsettling hauntings. Pamela reluctantly admits when she and Rick enter, "It may not be quite so cold, really." Rick cuts through to the truth: "It's clammy and rotten!" Demonic sobbing begins again. Pam disappointedly utters, "Mary Meredith, we're sorry you had to suffer."

This pivotal haunting sequence directly parallels the similar sequence earlier in the film when Rick and Pam first come to realize that Windward House is truly possessed. Pamela, seemingly upset with something on her mind, goes to Rick's bedroom as he happily reads in bed proclaiming "I've never been so happy in all my life!" Not wishing to spoil the mood, she retires allowing her conversation to wait until tomorrow. However, in the middle of the night, Rick is awakened by echoey female sobbing, amplified moans that radiate through out the whole of the house. Rick dons his robe and grabs a candle to investigate. Pam states, "I've searched. There's never anything there. You hear it too. I wasn't sure... I thought I was going crazy!" Rick, who had been away in London settling his affairs, asks whether the sobbing appears every night. Pam says no, "Just when you think you dreamt it, it comes again... Be calm, it will stop now." With the first flutter of the dawn breeze, the moans dissipate. Rick, truly afraid, puts on the stiff British "this business can be scientifically explained" routine adding, "I'm here now and I'm not rattled" act for Pamela before retiring to his room; the door loudly slamming shut, Rick pulls the covers up over his head. Comic relief perhaps, but it reflects the humanity inherent in Rick Fitzgerald's character.

Rick now realizes that Windward House holds inherent danger for Stella, and thinking of what's best for her, tells Stella that they will journey to London to live and then this house can be torn down. "You must get away from Windward forever!" he demands. Stella still feels an attachment for the home, cries, "You'll be tearing me apart. I hate you for that. You shan't make me forget her! You shan't!" Rick, upset, asks about "us." Stella replies, "This hasn't anything to do with you. I can't think about you when she's here!" Rick, working with Pamela, hopes to stage a bogus seance to set forth the message that the spirits of the house are now at peace, but just as Stella's state of mind is volatile, so are the spirits of the house. During the seance it appears that Rick cannot control the upturned drinking glass on which all fingers rest and press. The spirit reveals it is here to protect Stella from danger, at which point the glass flies up and smashes itself in the fireplace. Stella then sinks into a deep trance and begins speaking Spanish, which no one present can translate. Suddenly the mimosa scent returns as does the terrible cold ("It's never been cold in here," Pamela declares). Then the candles go out and a ghostly mist appears near the door. Only when the Commander breaks a glass pane to enter the house (his knocking is ignored) does the ghostly apparition disappear. Rick at this point realizes the general truth: "Stella will never be well until this house is cured."

The Commander, bursting into Windward House at the tail end of the ghostly seance, finding his granddaughter unconscious, quickly calls Miss Holloway to his home letting Dr. Scott first know he has been relieved of his medical duties. The Commander's fears about Rick's "searching into its [the house's] past" prompts him to ask Holloway to assume "Mary's place" by committing Stella to her hospital, the Mary Meredith Retreat. According to Holloway, people there are not patients but "guests" even though the high ceilings and gothic gargoyles which line the upper walls reek of Bedlam. The immense portrait of Mary Meredith which oppressively beams down in Miss Holloway's office prompts Holloway to reveal, "She's the finest human being I ever knew." Stella calmly inquires, "Does grandfather know what this place is like.., why do you hate me???" To which Holloway craftily answers, "You do feel prosecuted!" To Stella, the Windward House is oppressive and evil to all but her; here, at the Retreat, the oppressiveness of the hospital is quite apparent to Stella as her grandfather foolishly believes this is the only way to cure his ward.

Doing some detective work of their own, Rick, Pamela and Dr. Scott turn to the personal journals of the doctor who preceded Scott (who himself has only been here for 13 years) and discover that after Mary Meredith's death, when Miss Holloway treated Carmel for double pneumonia, the Gypsy's death had been caused by "criminal negligence," finding evidence of open windows and snow on the bedroom floor. Thus, in "a quiet, ladylike way," Miss Holloway murdered Carmel. Of course, Holloway was best of friends with Mary. Further journal reading is put off until later.

Dr. Scott soon discovers that Stella is being held at Holloway's Retreat, informing Rick and Pamela of the news. They plan to rescue her immediately. In the heat of such planning and concern is the returning, permeating scent of mimosa as the former doctor's medical journal flips open and pages turn. As Lizzy prepares to leave, she announces, "All the wickedness of this house is gathered around!" But no one notices the journal pages flapping, an attempt at ghostly communication from the other side for the benefit of the living.

As the rescue team travels two hours by car to free Stella Meredith, Miss Holloway has plans of her own: she calls Stella into her office and decides to set her free to return to Windward House. "What she wants (looking up at Mary's painting), I want," the sinister Miss Holloway utters. She can catch a train in 40 minutes, Holloway informs her; go straight to Windward!

Rick and company arrive some time later; Holloway greets "the rescue party" with: "I've done what she wanted at last, is that right Mary? It's all straight now, all smooth, no frayed edges!" Miss Holloway admits, almost raving—certainly out of her mind—that she freed Stella to go "to the cliffs and the rocks below." Exiting in a flash, Dr. Scott tells an attendant to look after Holloway.

Fortunately, a phone call is made to Commander Beech informing him of his granddaughter's imminent return to Windward, and though he has suffered a serious "spell" recently, he journeys on foot to protect his granddaughter. When she arrives and enters the house, she hears deep breathing, but it is only the Commander who warns her, "Please leave, get out of this house... The danger's for you... Be afraid, for heaven's sake! When you were a child the evils of this house searched out for you. Stella, go!" With that last effort, the Commander passes out as a ghostly mist appears. "I won't be afraid, mother," but then in tight close-up, Stella screams as the camera cuts away. Once again Stella is running at full speed outside the house toward the seaside cliffs and rocks below. Pausing at the very edge, the ground gives way but Rick grabs her wrist as she falls, Dr. Scott quickly lending assistance.

Rushing back inside the house to attend to the Commander, Scott and Rick glumly return, Stella already realizing her grandfather's fate. "She killed him just as she tried to kill me!"

Stella cries, thinking of the evil her mother's spirit committed. Suddenly, the doors fly open and the scent of mimosa returns, but Stella is no longer afraid. "This is what I felt in the nursery that night!" The flipping pages of the medical journal proceed to turn and this time Dr. Scott cannot ignore the warning. As he reads, Stella discovers the truth to the mystery. It seems that Mary Meredith "feared and refused motherhood," but when Meredith gets Carmel pregnant and they journey aboard, a deal is struck for Mary to adopt Stella and thus the child would inherit all the wealth and privilege. The only proviso is that the true Gypsy mother Carmel must promise never to return to Windward. For three years she is able to keep the promise, but her maternal urges grow too strong and she does return. After Carmel's return, Mary, trying to force Carmel to leave, threatens the life of baby Stella. As they struggle near the seaside cliffs, it is Carmel who rescues the baby and saves Stella's life.

"I am Carmel's child," Stella says. Stella's father said mimosa was her mother's scent, and he was correct: Stella's mother was Carmel and not Mary. At once a radiant calm overtakes Stella, who now knows the truth: "Something fighting in me, something that couldn't be calm and cold like Mary... I can be myself now!"

"She waited all these years to tell you," Pamela responds.

"She won't cry anymore," Stella declares. "Oh, mother, now I know!" Suddenly, the overwhelming mimosa fragrance vanishes as the sound of distant laughter echoes and then fades.

As they all leave the room, Rick leading the way, Rick's face records sudden horror as he walks through the double-doors. "Get back, all of you!" Rick alone goes outside into the hallway, onto the staircase, a candelabra in hand, and confronts the angered spirit of Mary Meredith (portrayed by actress Elizabeth Russell). "Mary Meredith, where are you. Time someone faced the icy rage of yours!" The ghostly mist congeals into semi-human form. "Too late, we are on to you now. You tried to kill their child, but you fell over the cliff. We're not frightened of you any more. From now on, this house is for the living!" With that pronouncement, Rick throws the candles at the fleeting spirit which disappears, seemingly forever. Lizzy's cat, always too afraid to journey up the staircase, now nonchalantly bounces up the stairs. Rick, maintaining his composure, states, "I had a narrow escape... She might have been my mother-in-law!"

Returning to the premise of this chapter, it is apparent to see the complex scripting and detailed character relationships which exist in *The Uninvited*.

Mary Meredith, mistakenly considered to be the benign mother of reclusive daughter Stella, turns out to be the vile, cold and insidious malignant spirit which invades Windward House. Just as the oppressiveness of the Mary Meredith Retreat, a thinly disguised insane asylum, subtly mirrors Mary's personality with its claustrophobic high walls, gothic aloofness and prison-like regimentation, the hospital's motto—"Health Through Harmony"—reflects the ultimate solution to Stella's internal struggles and the return of harmony to Windward House. Two dominant female spirits running amok, both with secrets to hide or reveal, butt cosmic energies in a single household. As Rick declares, as long as the house is sick, Stella will be sick. And literally, the truth has set her free, free to be her own person as she admits at movie's end. As Rick has constantly accused Stella of living someone else's life throughout the entire movie, at the end Stella can finally be Stella and find peace in the fact that Mary was not the kind, protective mother so many believed her to be and that Carmel's spirit would not find peace until daughter Stella came to know the truth about her real mother. As Commander Beech demands of Miss Holloway when he commits Stella to her asylum, "assume Mary's place," which Holloway does quite literally, displaying her insanity in the transformation.

Holloway becomes the cold, calculating murderess when she plots to release Stella so she can go immediately to the seaside cliffs and the rocks below, in other words, go to her death. Commander Beech, at first regimented and aloof, but ultimately self-sacrificing and protective, tries to maintain peace of mind for granddaughter Stella by cocooning her away in his protective bubble. This works fine for her childhood years, but now a 20-year-old woman, Stella firmly demands, "I'm on strike" and has a mind to do what she feels is best. Even her "first-love" experience with Rick is not the ultimate solution, for in rage she states that "this hasn't anything to do with you... I can't think about you when she's here!" Thus, in more ways than one, the interference of Mary Meredith prevents Stella psychologically from bonding with any other living human being. Truly, her life is stuck in this netherworld between the living and the dead, and until the dead (and living) release their hold on her, she might as well be as ectoplasmic as Carmel or Mary.

And this introduces our second premise: revealing the internal (character motivations) via the external (the hauntings). In Stella's psyche she cannot live, she cannot prosper, she cannot evolve or move ahead until the demons have been exorcised from her mind. Her life is truly that of another, the restlessness in Windward House reflects the restlessness of her psychological state. She cannot commit herself to Rick or anyone else unless all this ghostly baggage has been cleared from her mind, just as the house must be purged of its wandering spirits before the Fitzgeralds can get a decent night's sleep. These conflicting spirits invading Windward are the conflicting forces which exist inside her. She feels guilt over being the cause of her mother's death and she feels guilt over her grandfather's

all-consuming sadness, which resulted with daughter Mary's death or murder. Once the truth is revealed, that Mary was inherently evil and that Carmel, even if the "other woman," is still a protective, caring mother and that Stella is neither guilty or tainted in any way, only then can Stella let go of the past and forge a new future ahead, in London, or at Windward, with Rick. Unfortunately, her grandfather, a force of both good and of evil (he did withhold knowledge, he was selfish about Stella's burgeoning relationship with Rick, and he sought to prevent his young ward from bonding with others), had to die for her to be totally free to forge her own life. Even though he was alive, the influence the grandfather held over his granddaughter was as oppressive and binding as the influence that Mary and Carmel held over her.

The Uninvited is a marvelous exercise in bone-chilling horror and an archetypal example of the sophistication of the Hollywood horror film. The film cleverly disguises the physical, external hauntings under a veil of internal, psychological tension. The heart of any classic ghost story focuses upon the ambivalence between whether the ghosts are real or merely figments of the imagination. Once the viewer comes to understand that the haunted house is almost always the symbolic representation of the diseased psyche of one pivotal individual, the movie then takes on a richness that transcends the horror film genre becoming instead a drama of complex human interaction. *The Uninvited*'s script, cinematography, direction, music and acting congeal to produce a multi-layered tapestry of exquisite cinematic horror whose adult orientation makes the uneasiness and fear all the more real. Achieving an artistic pinnacle for the horror film genre, this film is a cornerstone by which all other ghost movies may be judged. What better compliment is there?

CREDITS: Producer: Charles Brackett; Director: Lewis Allen; Screenplay: Dodie Smith and Frank Partos; Based upon the Novel by Dorothy Macardle; Director of Photography: Charles Lang, Jr.; Musical Score: Victor Young; Editor: Doane Harrison; Art Designer: Hans Dreier and Ernst Fegte; Special Effects: Farciot Edouart; Set Designer: Stephen Seymour; 98 minutes; Released by Paramount, 1944

CAST: Ray Milland...Roderick/Rick Fitzgerald, Ruth Hussey.. Pamela Fitzgerald, Gail Russell... Stella Meredith, Donald Crisp…Commander Beech, Alan Napier…Dr. Scott, Cornelia Otis Skinner...Miss Holloway, Barbara Everest... Lizzie Flynn, Dorothy Stickney...Miss Hird, Jessica Newcombe...Miss Ellis, John Kieran...Foreword Narrator, Rita Page... Annie, David Clyde...Boot Owner, Norman Ainsley…Chauffeur, Evan Thomas...Col. Carlton, Ottola Nesmith…Mrs. Carlton, Portrait of Mary Meredith...Elizabeth Russell, Betty Farrington...Voice of Mary Meredith

AUTHORS

Robert Alan Crick, a graduate of Murray State University in Murray, KY., holds a Master's Degree in English and currently teaches high school English and journalism in Russeliville, KY. His previous writing efforts have appeared in *Epi-log Journal*, *Scarlet Street*, *Midnight Marquee*, and *English Journal* as well as *Guilty Pleasures of the Horror* Film from Midnight Marquee Press.

Dennis Fischer is the author of the book *Horror Film Directors* (McFarland, 1991) and is currently working on a follow-up on science fiction directors. His wife is busy creating life in her womb with a view on a project which should be completed around Halloween 1996. Their previous joint creation, Jared Fischer, is just learning to read at the age of three.

Jeff Hillegass has had work published in *Cinemacabre*, *Little Shoppe of Horrors*, and *Gruesome Twosome*. Despite an aversion to professional sports, he works as an editor for NFL Films, but justifies it with the fact that the company s early films served as an inspiration for director Sam Peckinpah's slow-motion bloodbaths in *The Wild Bunch*. Jeff lives in New Jersey with his wife Kathryn, his cat Aston, and his dog Griffin. The dog would have been named Martin, after James Bond's Aston Martin DB5 in *Goldfinger*, but Kathryn nixed the idea.

Tom Johnson, well known Hammer fan, has co-authored *Peter Cushing*: *The Gentle Man of Horror and Hammer Film: An Exhaustive Filmography* both from McFarland. He has also contributed to many film magazines including *Midnight Marquee*, *Filmfax*, and *Monsters from the Vault*.

Randy Palmer became a monster movie fan at age five with a theatrical viewing of *The Fly*; began writing professionally in 1971 for *Famous Monsters*, eventually became an editor at Warren Publishing; also a writer for *Fangoria*, *Gorezone*, *Cinefantastique*, *Imagi-Movies*, Britain's Hammer-oriented *Halls of Horror*, and other publications of the cinemagination. He also writes video game reviews and articles for *PC Entertainment*, *Sega Guide* (incorporated into *Game Players* mag), and is a writer-editor for one of the earliest video game publications, *Videogamning Illustrated* (later changed to *Video & Computer Gaming Illustrated*). His book on Paul Blaisdell is scheduled for a 1996 release from McFarland.

John E. Parnum is an author, editor, archivist, and magician extraordinaire who worked for 31 years in the advertising department of Merck Pharmaceuticals before retiring to devote full time to writing, collecting horror memorabilia, and prestidigitation. He was Editor-in-Chief of *Cinemacabre* and has written articles and stories for such publications as *Midnight Marquee*, *Photon*, *The Monster Times*, *Bits and Pieces*, *Gateways*, and others. Inspired by his pet python Monty, he is currently working on a book on snakes in horror, fantasy, and science-fiction films called *The Slithering Cinema*, based on an article that originally appeared in the 25th anniversary issue of *MidMar* and which will be updated in an upcoming issue of *The Scream Factory*. He resides in Wayne, PA.

Gary Don Rhodes is the author of *Lugosi: A Portrait of His Life and Career*, the 1996 McFarland reference book. He contributes to film journals ranging from *Classic Images* to *Cult Movies*. Rhodes currently teaches at the University of Oklahoma. His numerous documentary films cover such topics as jazz and cultural history, being offered on videocassette through companies such as V.I.E.W. after their initial PBS broadcasts. He is currently working on a hook-length analysis of *White Zombie* for Midnight Marquee Press.

Bryan Senn is the author of *Golden Horrors: A Critical Filmography of 46 Works of Terror Cinema, 1931-1939* (McFarland, 1996) and co-author of *Fantastic Cinema Subject Guide* (McFarland, 1992), as well as contributing chapters to the previous Midnight Marquee Press volumes *Bela Lugosi* and *Guilty Pleasure of the Horror Cinema*. He's looking forward to one day showing *The Haunting* to his infant son Dominic and sharing the chills (and potential night mares) that this film classic still induces.

Kevin G. Shinnick has contributed articles and interviews to *Videooze*, *Chiller Theatre*, *Dark Muse*, and *Scarlet Street*. A struggling actor, Kevin had a run in with ghosts portraying Antonio Salieri in a recent production of Amadeus. He would like to thank Patty Phillips for the typing, his daughter Katie for being his daughter Katie, and Mr. Robert Quarry for being 'Uncle Bob."

David H. Smith works for a great metropolitan newspaper in South Florida, and just recently celebrated a crystal wedding anniversary with his indulgent wife Lynn; their young son Cohn enables him to justify watching English-dubbed movies starring men in rubber suits again and again. David plans to become a fixture on the Midnight Marquee Press author roster, has contributed to several genre magazines and fanzines, hopes to someday complete his Skywald magazine collection, and thinks the mellotron is the most awesome musical instrument ever developed.

Don G. Smith is an associate professor in history and philosophy of education at Eastern Illinois University. He has published in *Midnight Marquee*, *Scarlet Street*, *Filmfax*, *Movie Collector's World*, etc. He is the author of *Lon Chancy, Jr.* (McFarland and Company, 1995). and is currently writing *The Cinema of Edgar Allan Poe*, also for McFarland and Company.

John Soister, a sixties' fanzine editor (one-shot *House of Horrors*), co-editor (*Photon*, briefly). and all-around LoC curmudgeon, has contributed to *Midnight Marquee Actors Series: Bela Lugosi*. He teaches high school modern and classical languages and is currently working on a book on Universal for Mid Mar Press. John lives in Orwigsburg, PA with his wife Nancy and children: Jake, Katelyn, and Jeremy.

Gary J. Svehla created his first publishing venture at the ripe old age of 13, *Gore Creatures*. 43 years later he is still publishing the magazine, now called *Midnight Marquee*, as well as overseeing Midnight Marquee Press, a full time job for the two person team of Gary and Susan. Gary still teaches high school English. He has contributed to *Monsterland, Amazing Cinema, Movie Club, Monsters from the Vault, Bits & Pieces*, and *Monster Times* as well as numerous MidMar titles.

Steve Vertlieb is a longtime journalist and writer on vintage films and film music, and member of the International Film Music Critics Association. Steve Vertlieb met science fiction icon Forry Ackerman when he was 19, and since that time he has written reviews and articles for dozens of publications, on such diverse topics as Star Trek, King Kong, the music of Bernard Herrmann, the films of Boris Karloff, Bela Lugosi and Orson Welles, and interviewed several.

*If you enjoyed this book
please call, write or e-mail for a free catalog.
Midnight Marquee Press, Inc.
9721 Britinay Lane
Baltimore, MD 21234
410-665-1198
www.midmar.com*

www.ingramcontent.com/pod-product-compliance
Lightning Source LLC
Chambersburg PA
CBHW081722100526

44591CB00016B/2467